BLACK HAMMER™

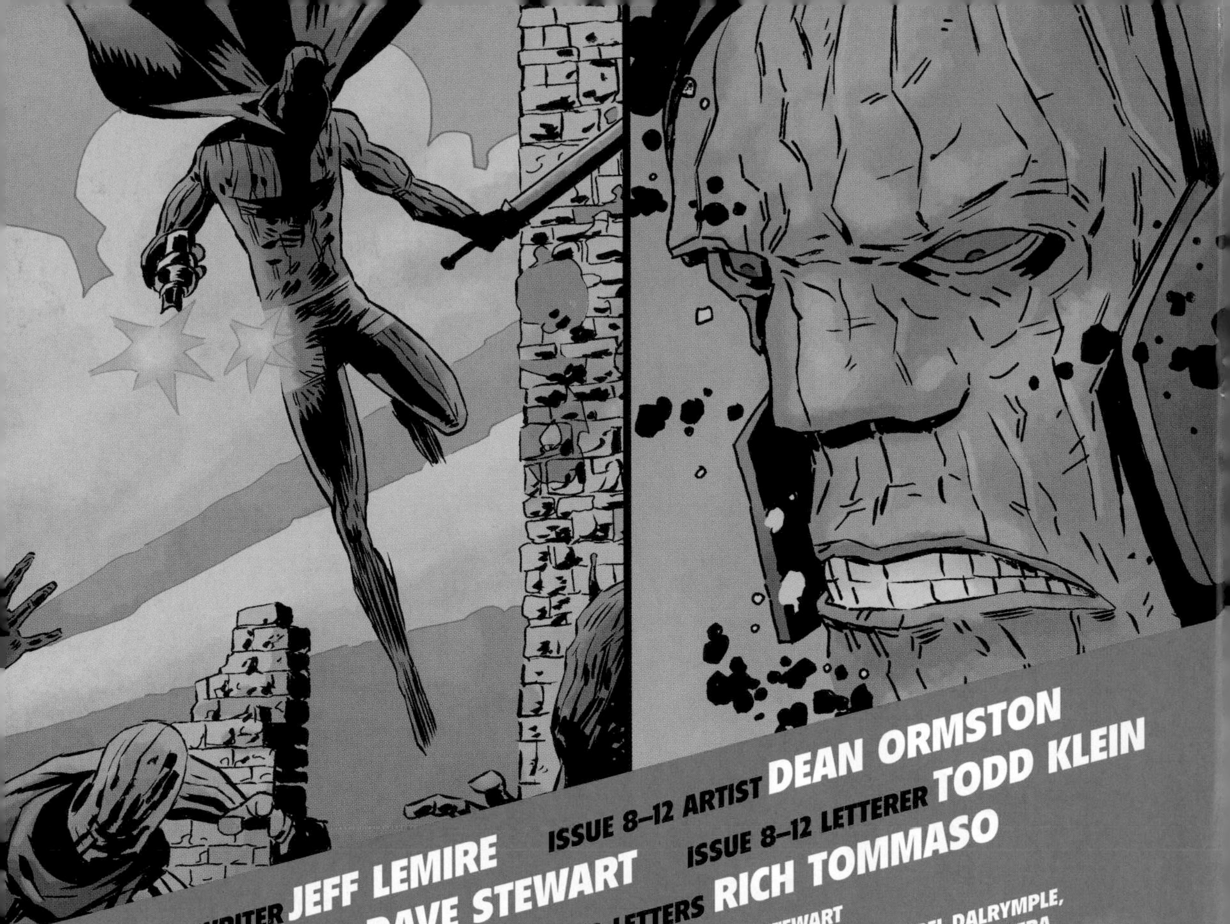

WRITER **JEFF LEMIRE**

ISSUE 8–12 ARTIST **DEAN ORMSTON**

ISSUE 8–12 COLORIST **DAVE STEWART**

ISSUE 8–12 LETTERER **TODD KLEIN**

ISSUE 6–7 ART, COLORS, AND LETTERS **RICH TOMMASO**

COVER BY DEAN ORMSTON AND DAVE STEWART

CHAPTER BREAKS BY DEAN ORMSTON WITH DAVE STEWART, RICH TOMMASO, FAREL DALRYMPLE, CHRISTIAN WARD, BILL SIENKIEWICZ, SANFORD GREENE, MICHEL FIFFE, PAOLO AND JOE RIVERA, AND PAUL POPE WITH DAVE STEWART

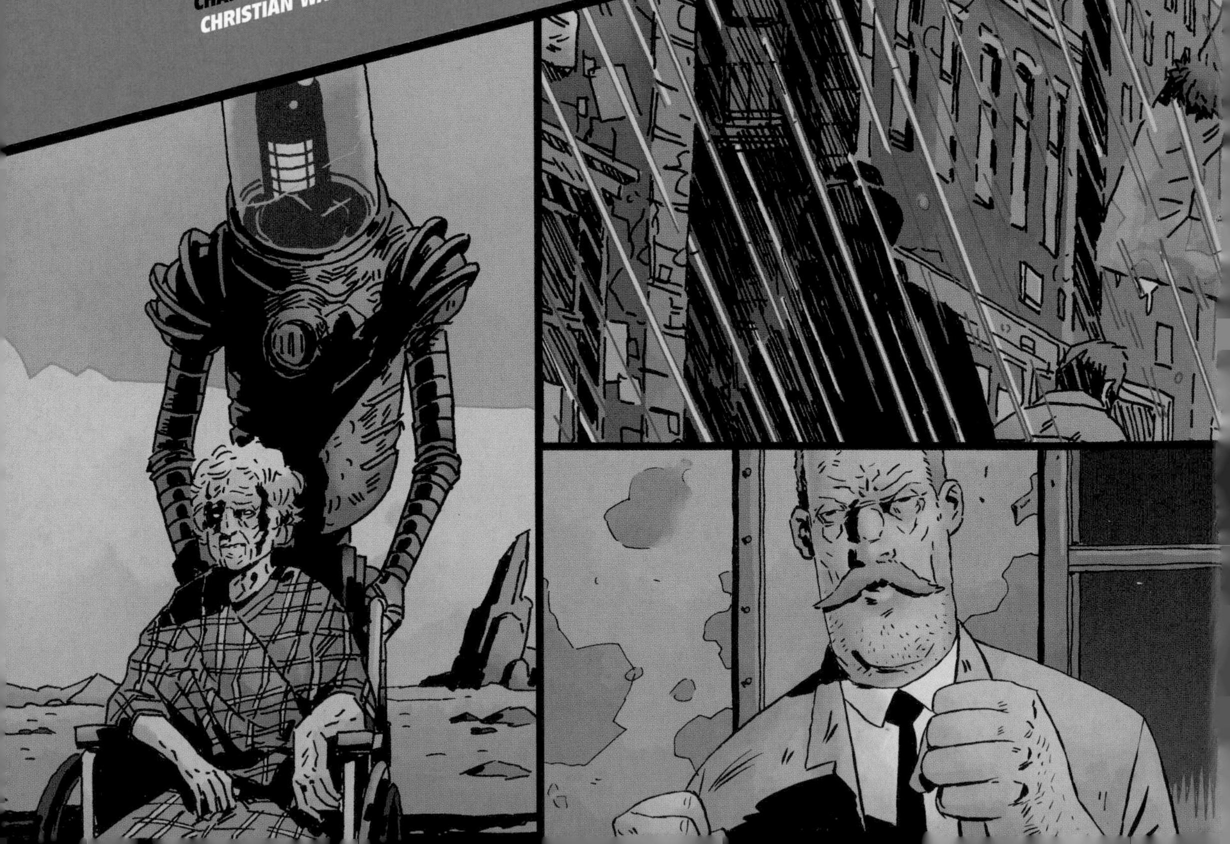

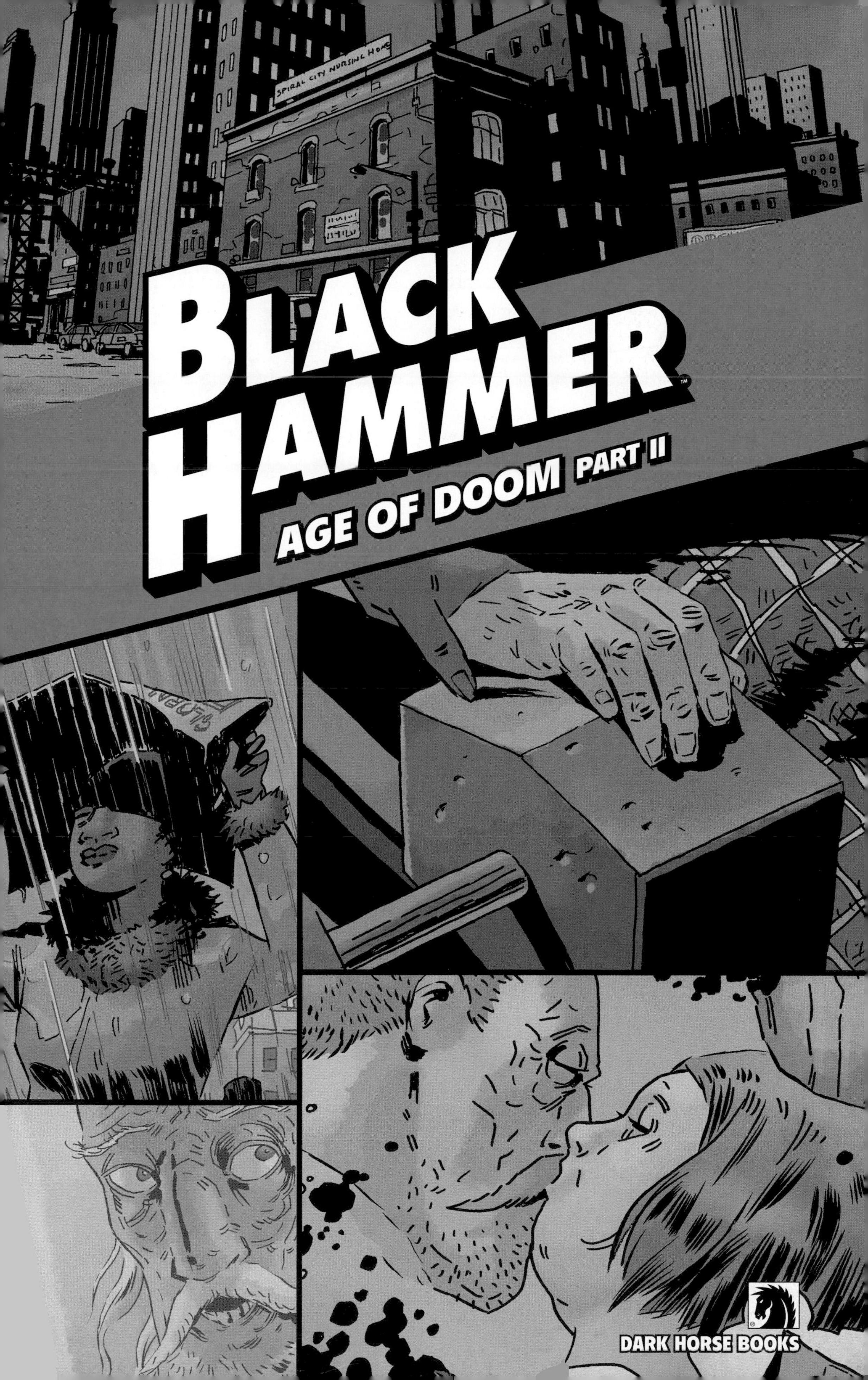
SPIRAL CITY NURSING HOME
BLACK HAMMER™
AGE OF DOOM PART II
DARK HORSE BOOKS

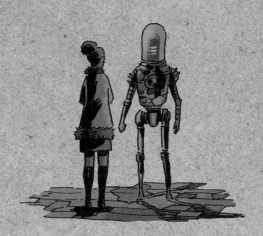

PRESIDENT & PUBLISHER
MIKE RICHARDSON

EDITOR
DANIEL CHABON

ASSISTANT EDITORS
CHUCK HOWITT
AND BRETT ISRAEL

DESIGNER
ETHAN KIMBERLING

DIGITAL ART TECHNICIAN
JOSIE CHRISTENSEN

BLACK HAMMER CREATED BY JEFF LEMIRE AND DEAN ORMSTON

BLACK HAMMER: AGE OF DOOM PART II

Black Hammer: Age of Doom™ © 2018, 2019 171 Studios, Inc., and Dean Ormston. Dark Horse Books® and the Dark Horse logo are registered trademarks of Dark Horse Comics LLC. All rights reserved. No portion of this publication may be reproduced or transmitted, in any form or by any means, without the express written permission of Dark Horse Comics LLC. Names, characters, places, and incidents featured in this publication either are the product of the author's imagination or are used fictitiously. Any resemblance to actual persons (living or dead), events, institutions, or locales, without satiric intent, is coincidental.

Collects issues #6–#12 of the Dark Horse Comics series *Black Hammer: Age of Doom.*

Library of Congress Cataloging-in-Publication Data

Names: Lemire, Jeff, writer. | Ormston, Dean, artist. | Stewart, Dave,
  colourist, cover artist. | Klein, Todd, letterer.
Title: Age of doom. Part II / writer, Jeff Lemire ; artist, Dean Ormston ;
  colorist, Dave Stewart ; letterer, Todd Klein ; cover by Dean Ormston and
  Dave Stewart.
Description: First edition. | Milwaukie, OR : Dark Horse Books, 2019. |
  Series: Black Hammer ; 4 | "Collects issues #6–#12 of the Dark Horse
  Comics series Black Hammer: Age of Doom."
Identifiers: LCCN 2019015199 | ISBN 9781506708164 (paperback)
Subjects: LCSH: Comic books, strips, etc.
Classification: LCC PN6728.B51926 L365 2019 | DDC 741.5/973--dc23
LC record available at https://lccn.loc.gov/2019015199

Published by
Dark Horse Books
A division of Dark Horse Comics LLC
10956 SE Main Street
Milwaukie, OR 97222

DarkHorse.com

To find a comics shop in your area, visit comicshoplocator.com

First edition: December 2019
ISBN 978-1-50670-816-4
Digital ISBN 978-1-50670-856-0

10 9 8 7 6 5 4 3 2 1
Printed in China

NEIL HANKERSON Executive Vice President TOM WEDDLE Chief Financial Officer RANDY STRADLEY Vice President of Publishing NICK McWHORTER Chief Business Development Officer DALE LaFOUNTAIN Chief Information Officer MATT PARKINSON Vice President of Marketing CARA NIECE Vice President of Production and Scheduling MARK BERNARDI Vice President of Book Trade and Digital Sales KEN LIZZI General Counsel DAVE MARSHALL Editor in Chief DAVEY ESTRADA Editorial Director CHRIS WARNER Senior Books Editor CARY GRAZZINI Director of Specialty Projects LIA RIBACCHI Art Director VANESSA TODD-HOLMES Director of Print Purchasing MATT DRYER Director of Digital Art and Prepress MICHAEL GOMBOS Senior Director of Licensed Publications KARI YADRO Director of Custom Programs KARI TORSON Director of International Licensing SEAN BRICE Director of Trade Sales

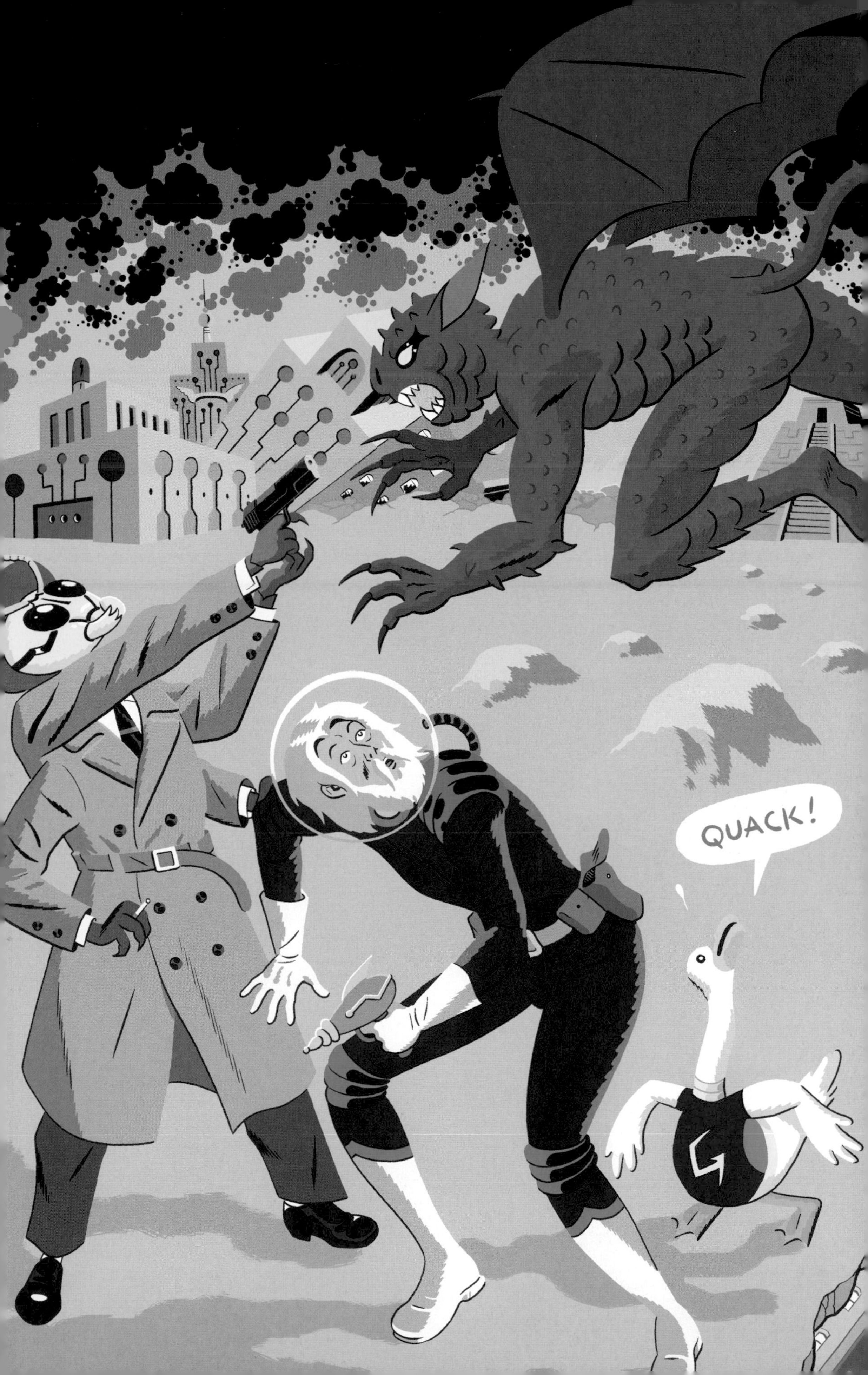
QUACK!

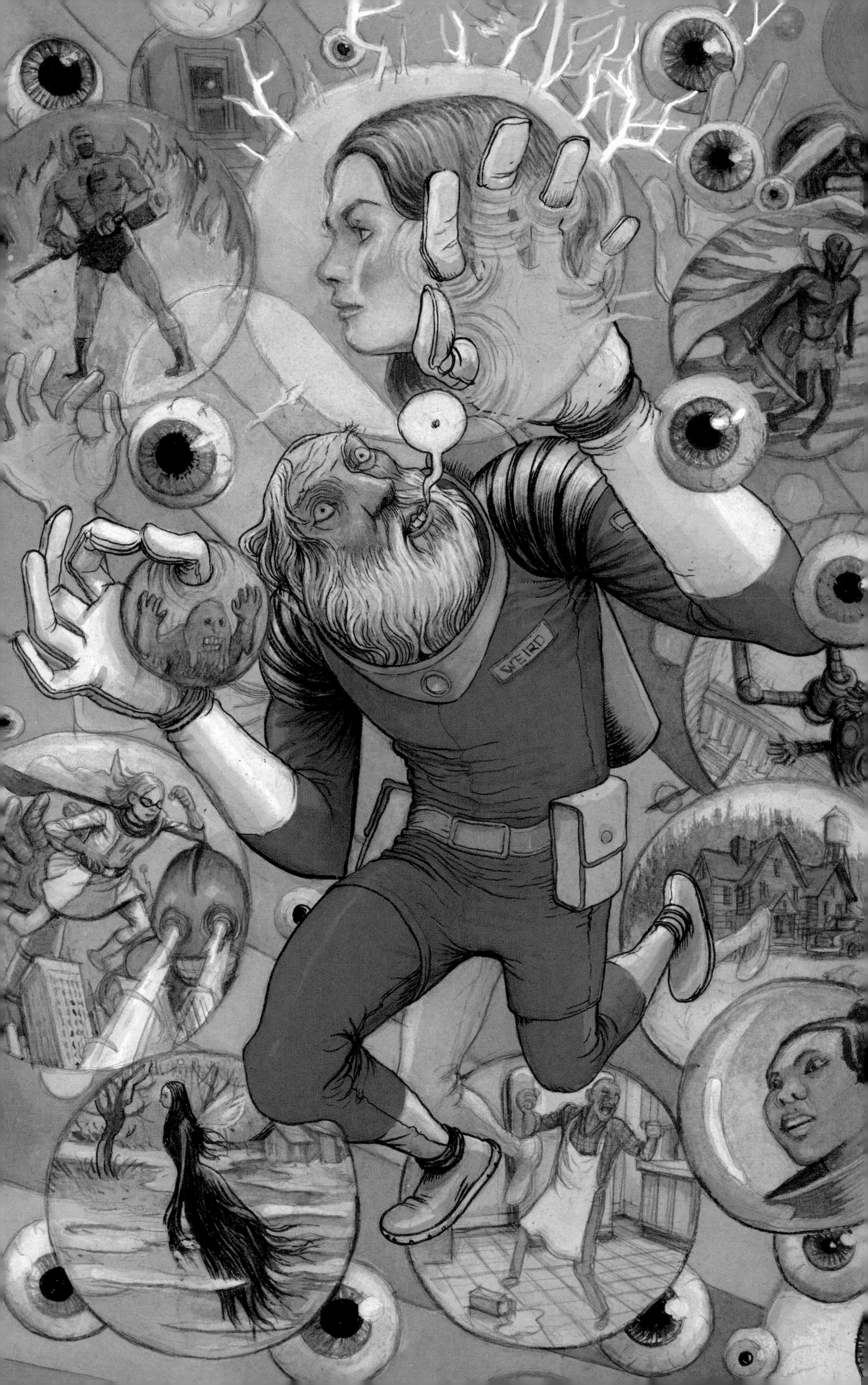
WEIRD

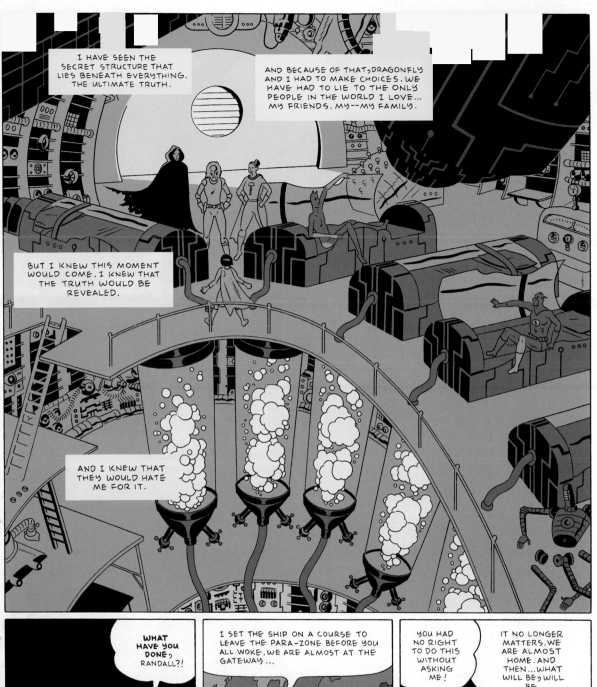

I HAVE SEEN THE SECRET STRUCTURE THAT LIES BENEATH EVERYTHING. THE ULTIMATE TRUTH.

AND BECAUSE OF THAT, DRAGONFLY AND I HAD TO MAKE CHOICES. WE HAVE HAD TO LIE TO THE ONLY PEOPLE IN THE WORLD I LOVE... MY FRIENDS. MY--MY FAMILY.

BUT I KNEW THIS MOMENT WOULD COME. I KNEW THAT THE TRUTH WOULD BE REVEALED.

AND I KNEW THAT THEY WOULD HATE ME FOR IT.

WHAT HAVE YOU DONE, RANDALL?!

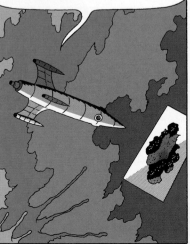

I SET THE SHIP ON A COURSE TO LEAVE THE PARA-ZONE BEFORE YOU ALL WOKE. WE ARE ALMOST AT THE GATEWAY...

YOU HAD NO RIGHT TO DO THIS WITHOUT ASKING ME!

IT NO LONGER MATTERS. WE ARE ALMOST HOME. AND THEN...WHAT WILL BE, WILL BE...

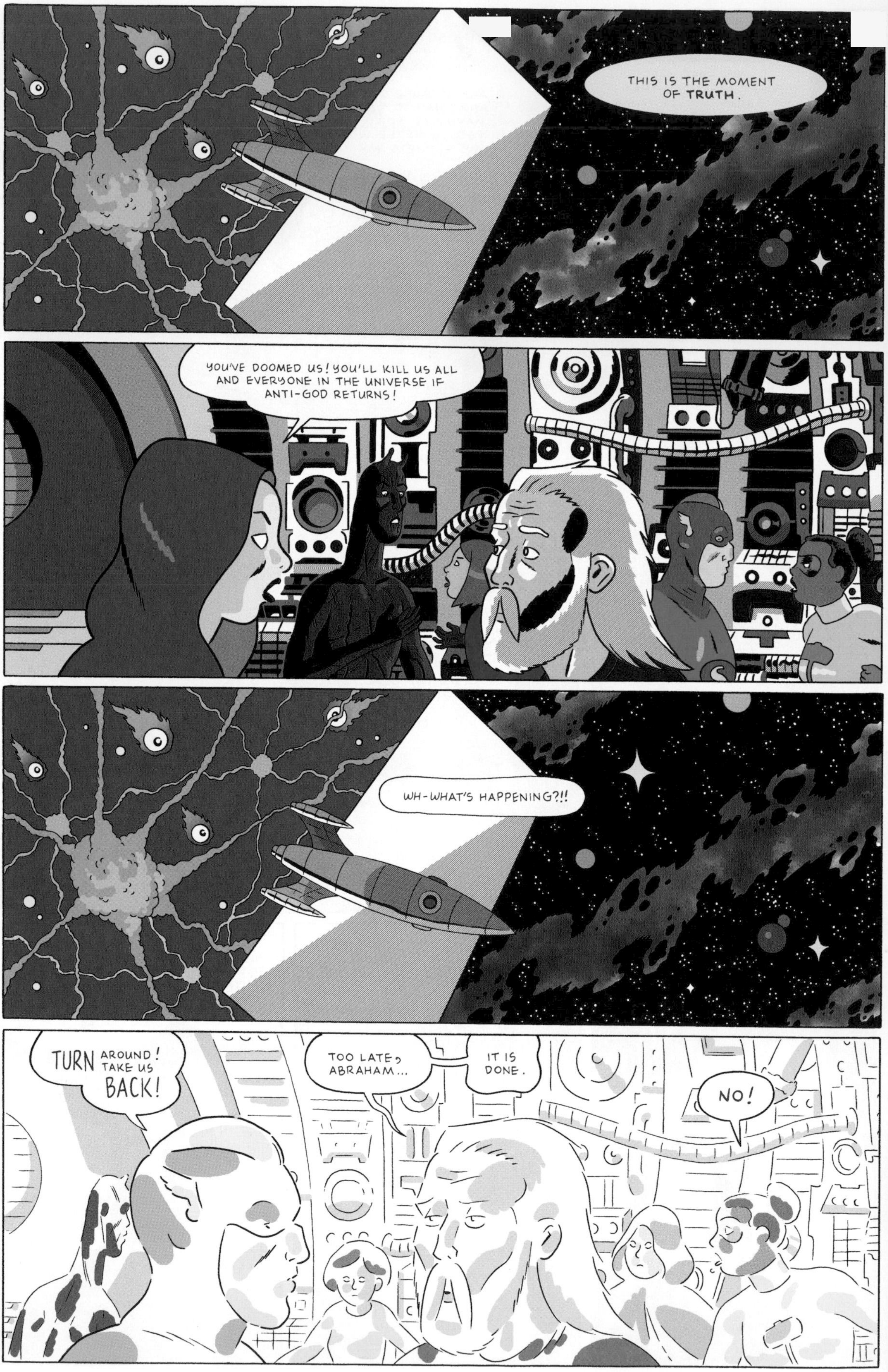
THIS IS THE MOMENT OF TRUTH.
YOU'VE DOOMED US! YOU'LL KILL US ALL AND EVERYONE IN THE UNIVERSE IF ANTI-GOD RETURNS!
WH-WHAT'S HAPPENING?!!
TURN AROUND! TAKE US BACK!
TOO LATE, ABRAHAM...
IT IS DONE.
NO!

I HAVE SEEN THE PATTERN OF REALITY. I HAVE SEEN EVERYTHING. BUT THIS...

THIS I DID NOT SEE COMING.
HELLO?

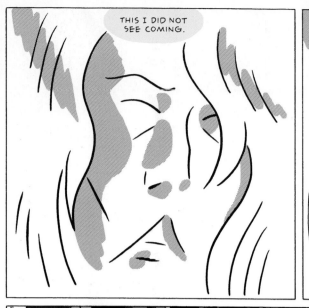

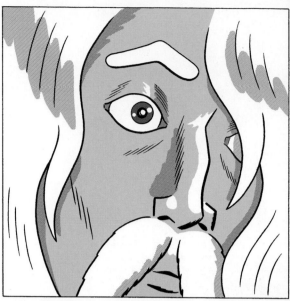

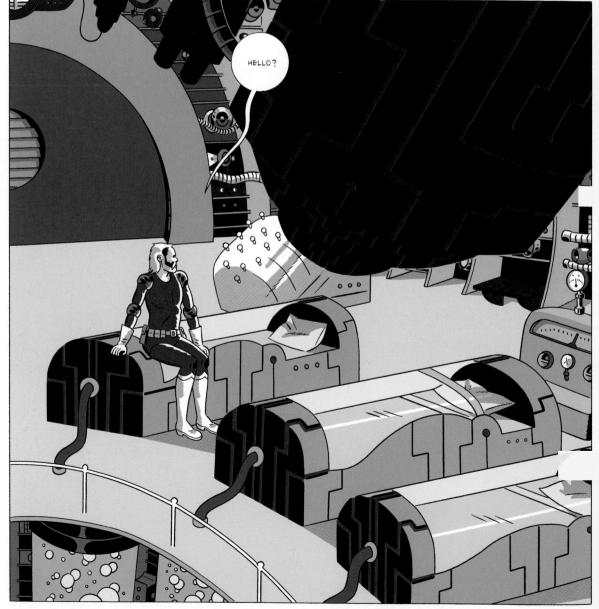

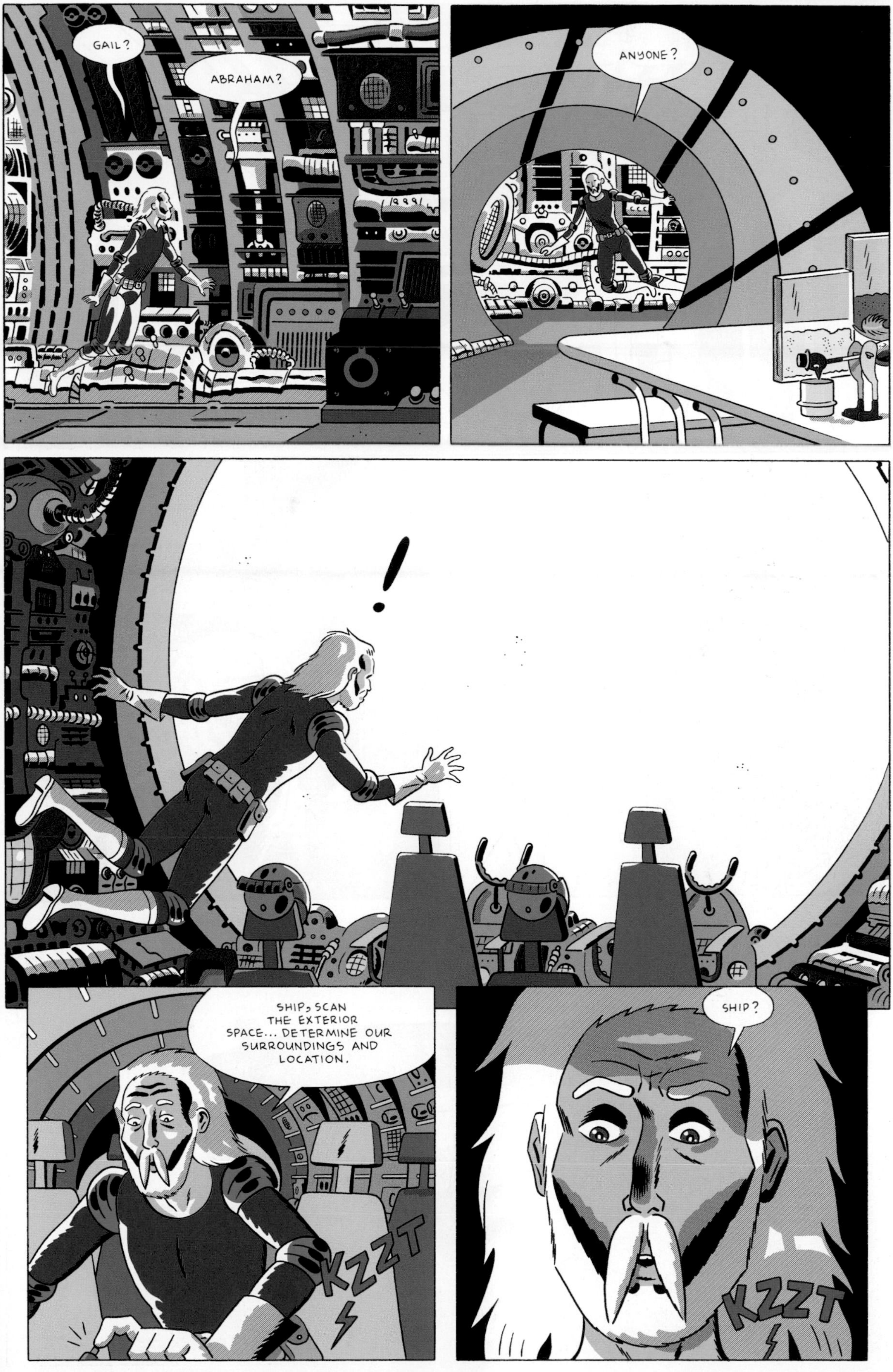
GAIL?
ABRAHAM?
ANYONE?
!
SHIP, SCAN THE EXTERIOR SPACE... DETERMINE OUR SURROUNDINGS AND LOCATION.
KZZT
SHIP?
KZZT

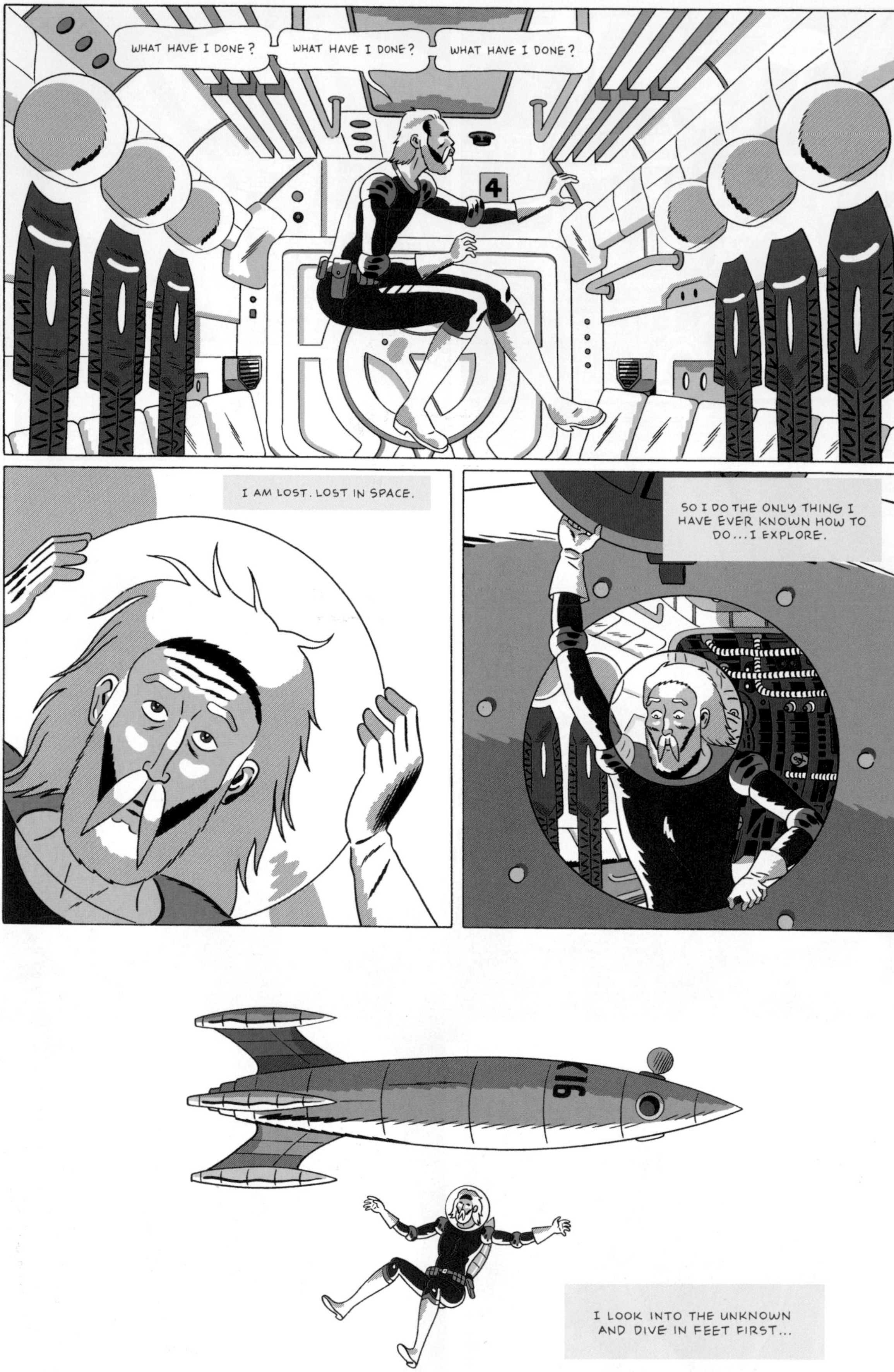
WHAT HAVE I DONE?
WHAT HAVE I DONE?
WHAT HAVE I DONE?
4
I AM LOST. LOST IN SPACE.
SO I DO THE ONLY THING I HAVE EVER KNOWN HOW TO DO... I EXPLORE.
I LOOK INTO THE UNKNOWN AND DIVE IN FEET FIRST...

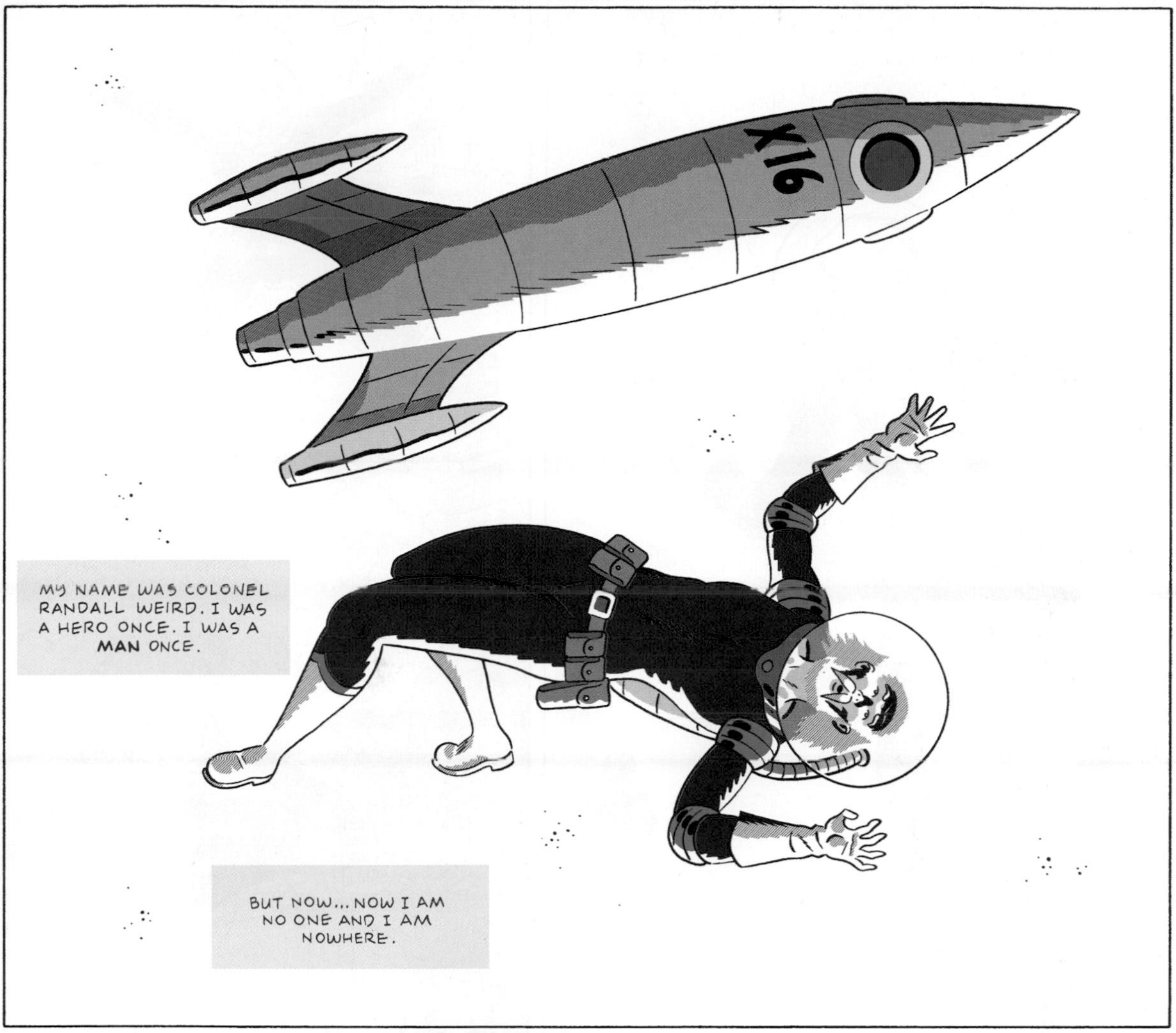
X16
MY NAME WAS COLONEL RANDALL WEIRD. I WAS A HERO ONCE. I WAS A **MAN** ONCE.
BUT NOW... NOW I AM NO ONE AND I AM NOWHERE.

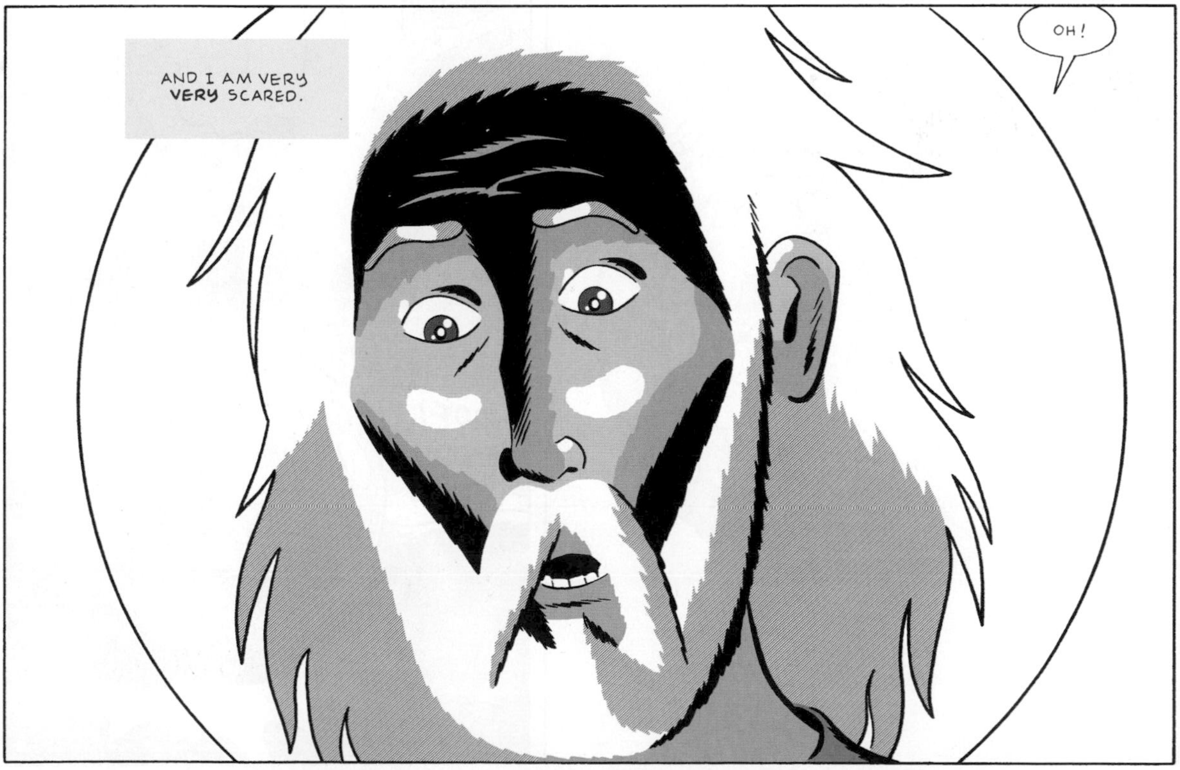
AND I AM VERY **VERY** SCARED.
OH!

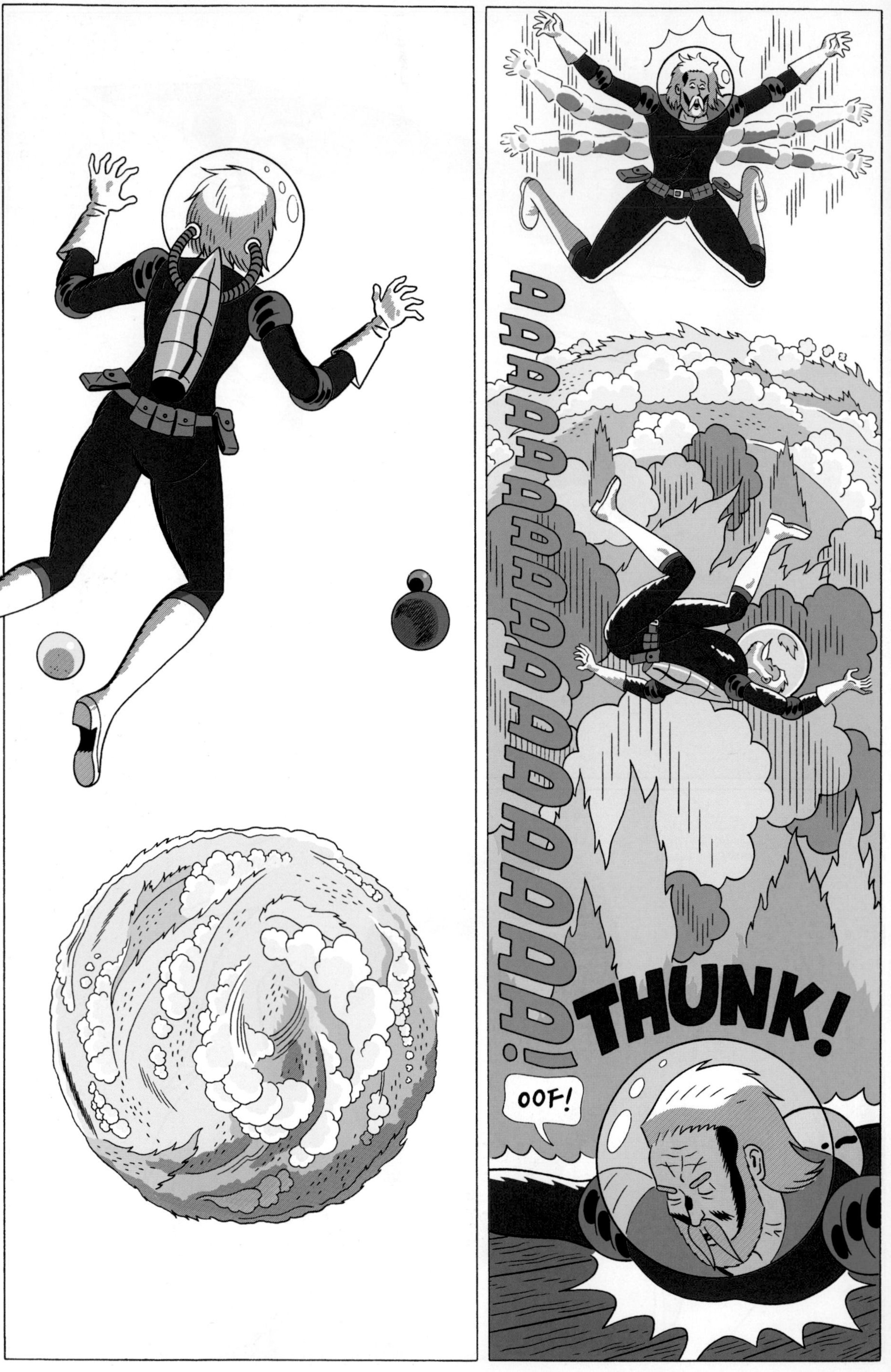
AAAAAAAAAAAAAAA!
THUNK!
OOF!

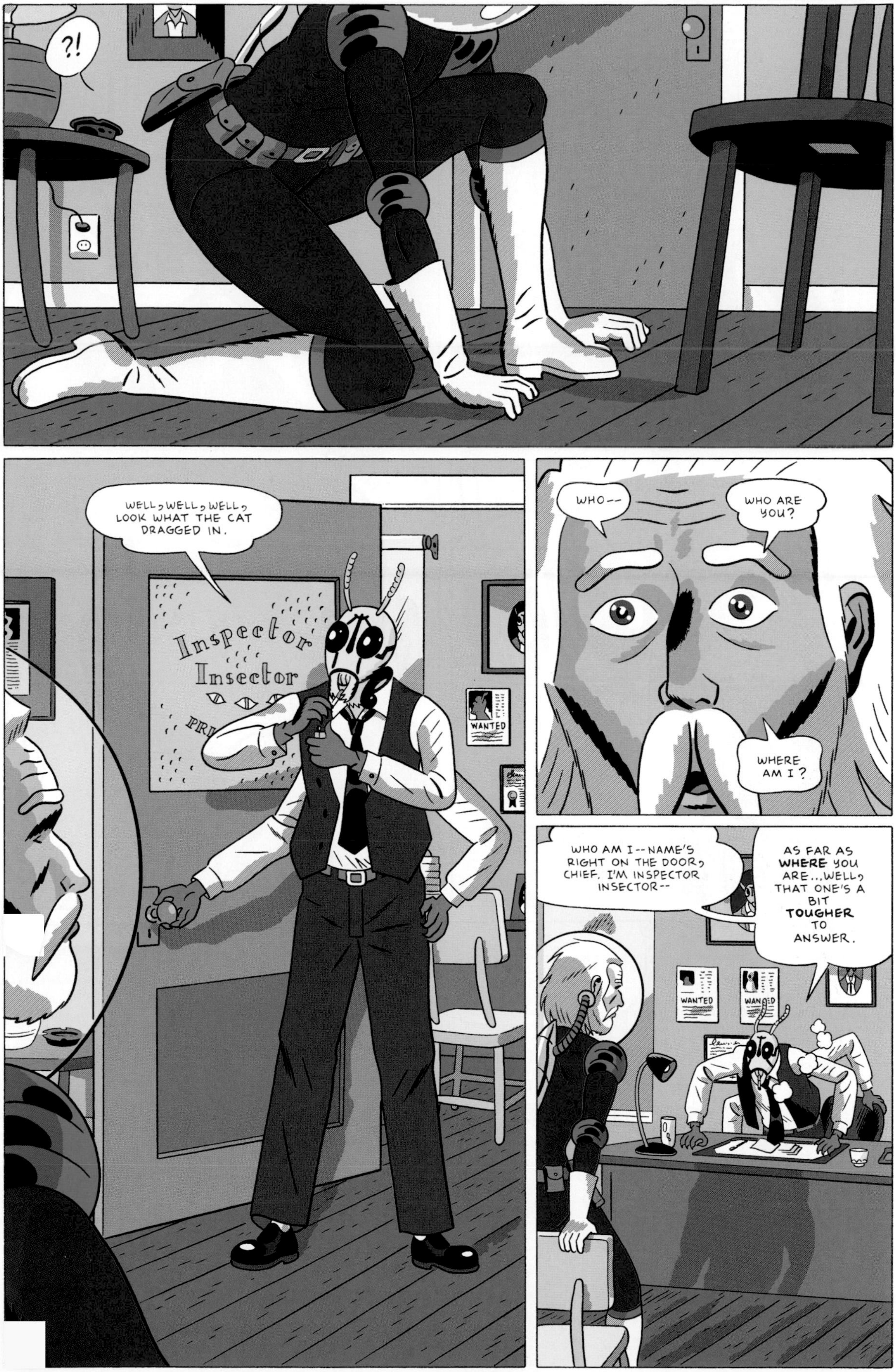
?!
WELL, WELL, WELL, LOOK WHAT THE CAT DRAGGED IN.
Inspector Insector
WANTED
WHO--
WHO ARE YOU?
WHERE AM I?
WHO AM I--NAME'S RIGHT ON THE DOOR, CHIEF. I'M INSPECTOR INSECTOR--
AS FAR AS WHERE YOU ARE...WELL, THAT ONE'S A BIT TOUGHER TO ANSWER.
WANTED
WANTED

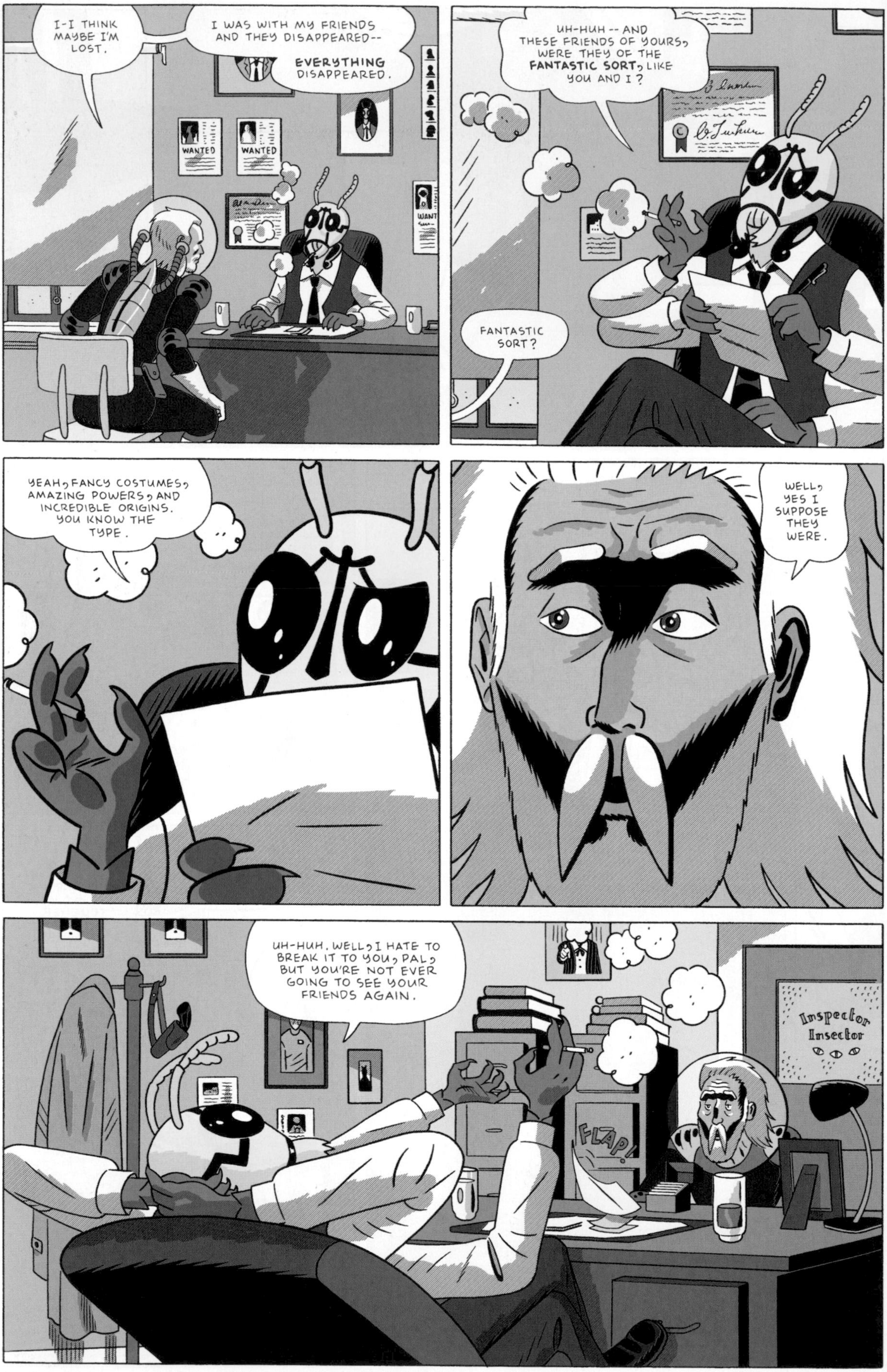
I-I THINK MAYBE I'M LOST.
I WAS WITH MY FRIENDS AND THEY DISAPPEARED-- EVERYTHING DISAPPEARED.
WANTED
WANTED
UH-HUH -- AND THESE FRIENDS OF YOURS, WERE THEY OF THE FANTASTIC SORT, LIKE YOU AND I?
FANTASTIC SORT?
YEAH, FANCY COSTUMES, AMAZING POWERS, AND INCREDIBLE ORIGINS. YOU KNOW THE TYPE.
WELL, YES I SUPPOSE THEY WERE.
UH-HUH. WELL, I HATE TO BREAK IT TO YOU, PAL, BUT YOU'RE NOT EVER GOING TO SEE YOUR FRIENDS AGAIN.
FLAP!
Inspector Insector

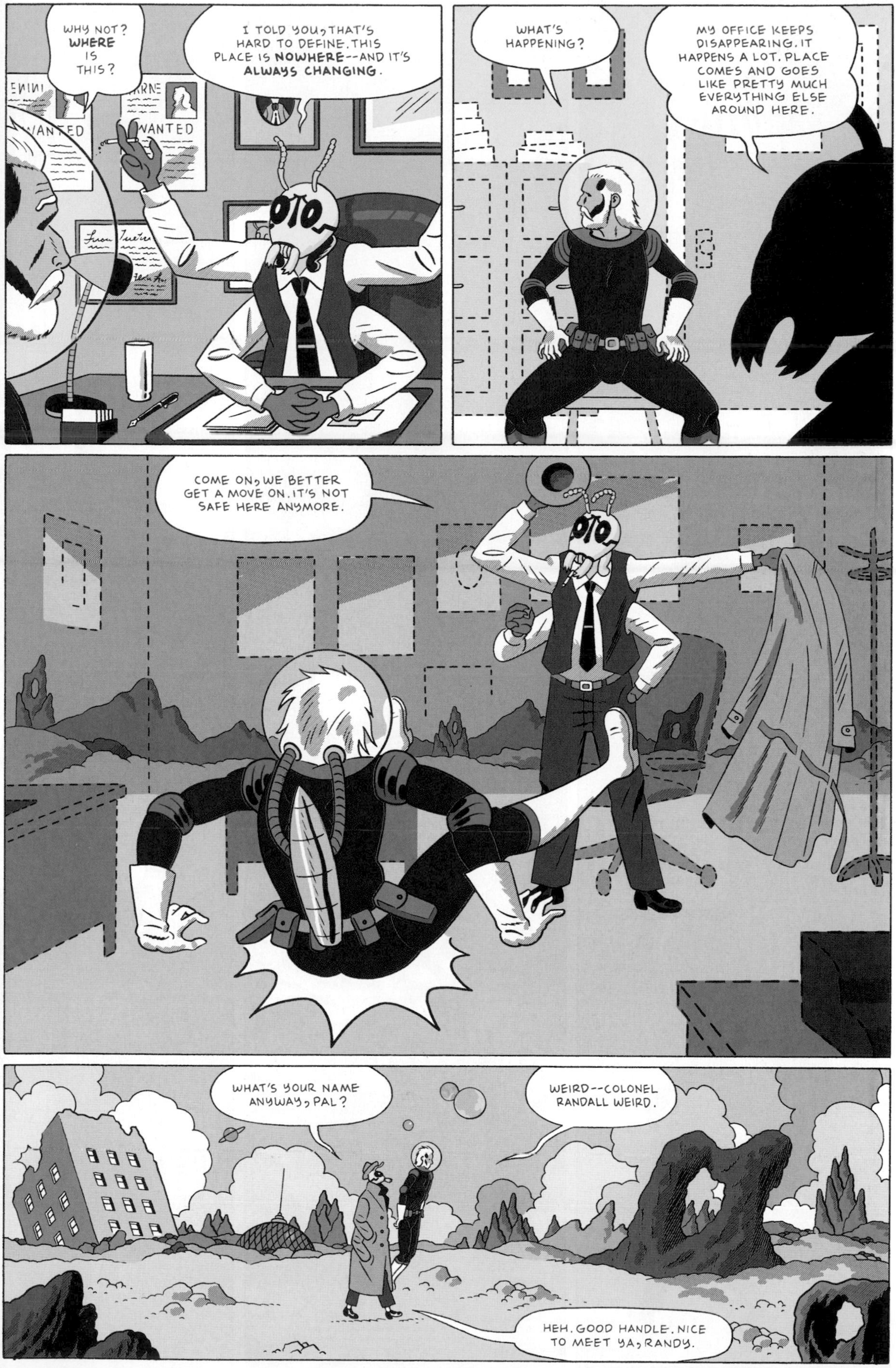
WHY NOT? WHERE IS THIS?
I TOLD YOU, THAT'S HARD TO DEFINE. THIS PLACE IS NOWHERE--AND IT'S ALWAYS CHANGING.
WANTED
WANTED
WHAT'S HAPPENING?
MY OFFICE KEEPS DISAPPEARING. IT HAPPENS A LOT. PLACE COMES AND GOES LIKE PRETTY MUCH EVERYTHING ELSE AROUND HERE.
COME ON, WE BETTER GET A MOVE ON. IT'S NOT SAFE HERE ANYMORE.
WHAT'S YOUR NAME ANYWAY, PAL?
WEIRD--COLONEL RANDALL WEIRD.
HEH. GOOD HANDLE. NICE TO MEET YA, RANDY.

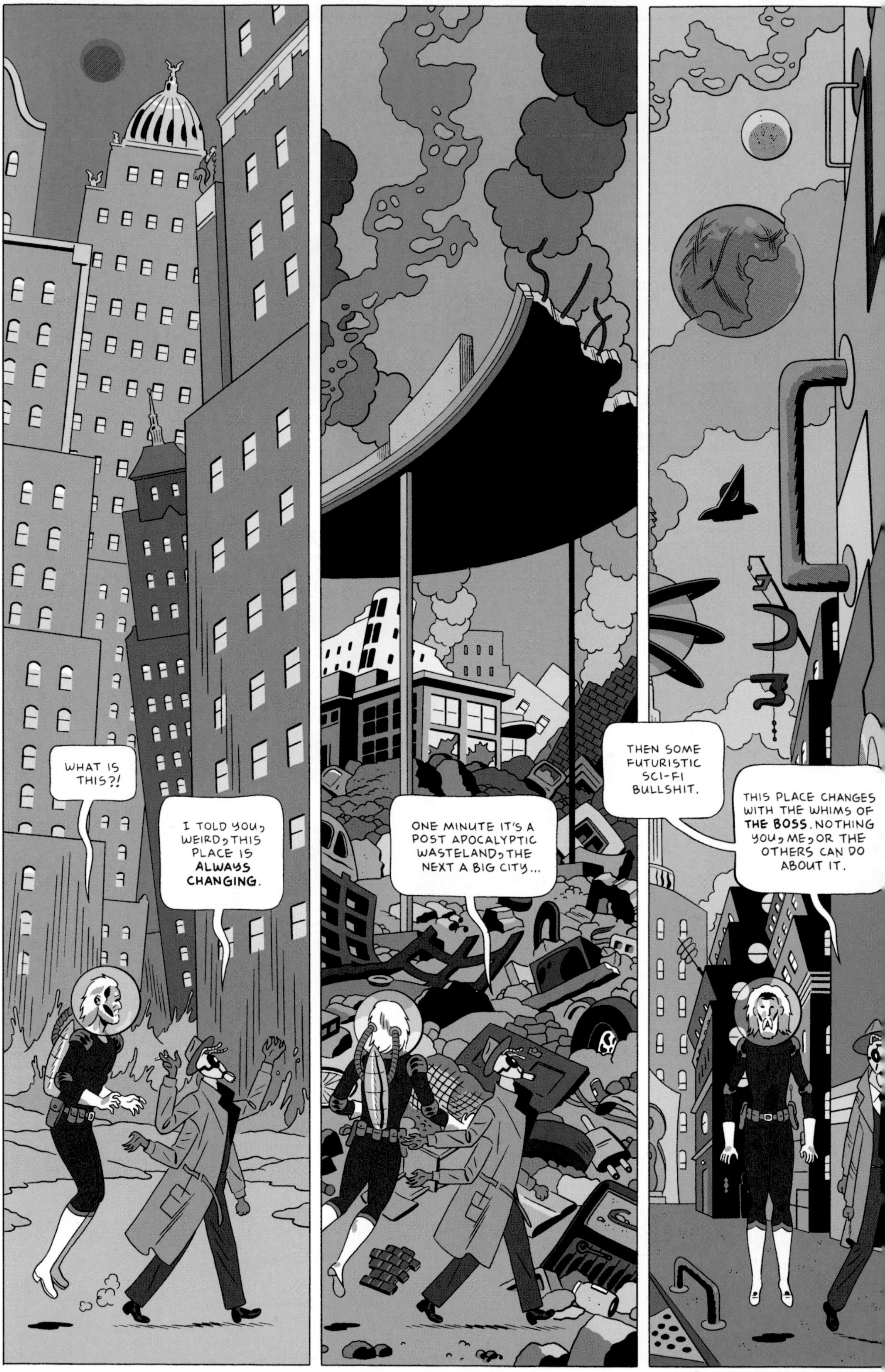
WHAT IS THIS?!
I TOLD YOU, WEIRD, THIS PLACE IS ALWAYS CHANGING.
ONE MINUTE IT'S A POST APOCALYPTIC WASTELAND, THE NEXT A BIG CITY...
THEN SOME FUTURISTIC SCI-FI BULLSHIT.
THIS PLACE CHANGES WITH THE WHIMS OF THE BOSS. NOTHING YOU, ME, OR THE OTHERS CAN DO ABOUT IT.

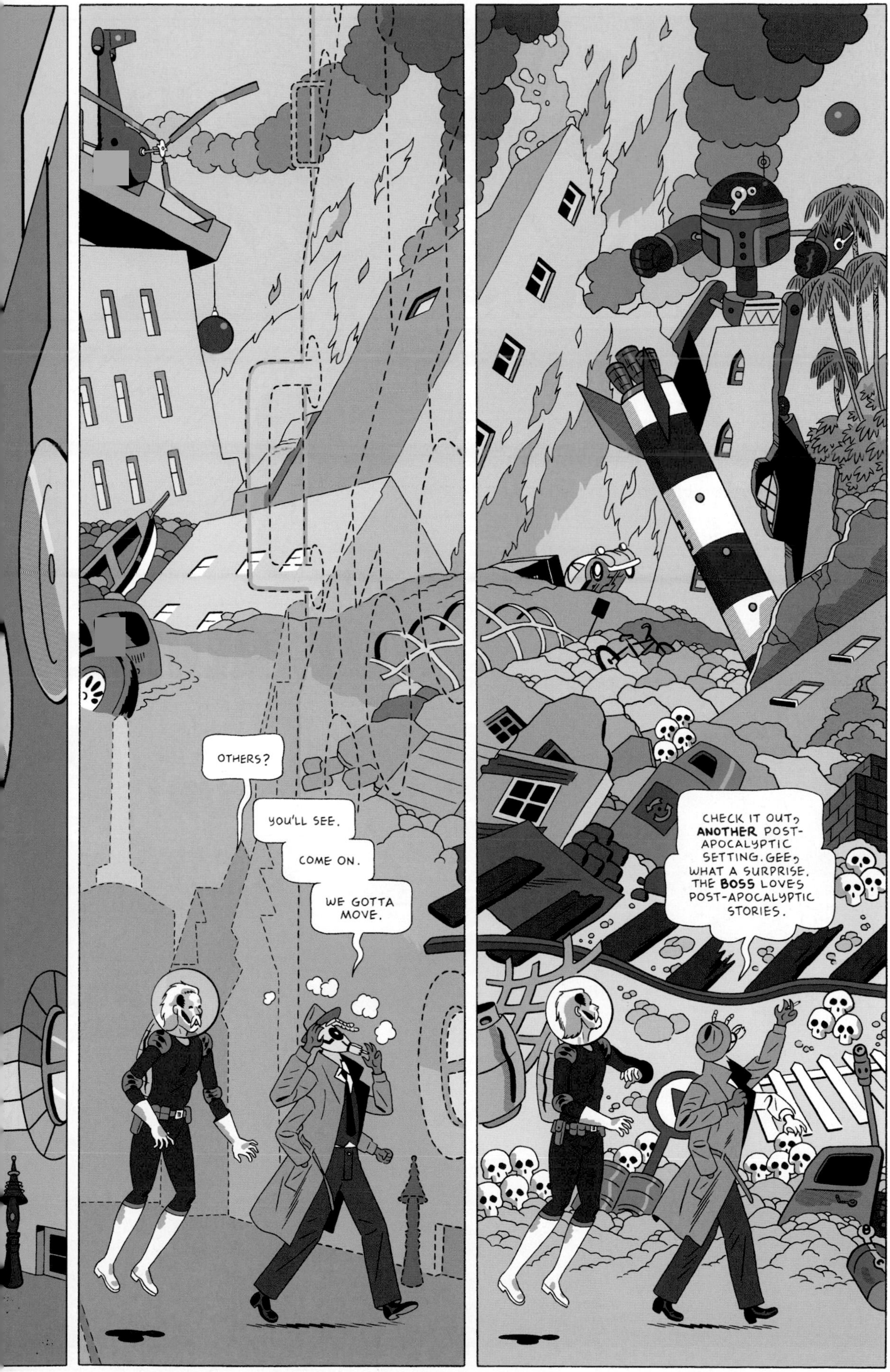
OTHERS?
YOU'LL SEE.
COME ON.
WE GOTTA MOVE.
CHECK IT OUT, ANOTHER POST-APOCALYPTIC SETTING. GEE, WHAT A SURPRISE. THE BOSS LOVES POST-APOCALYPTIC STORIES.

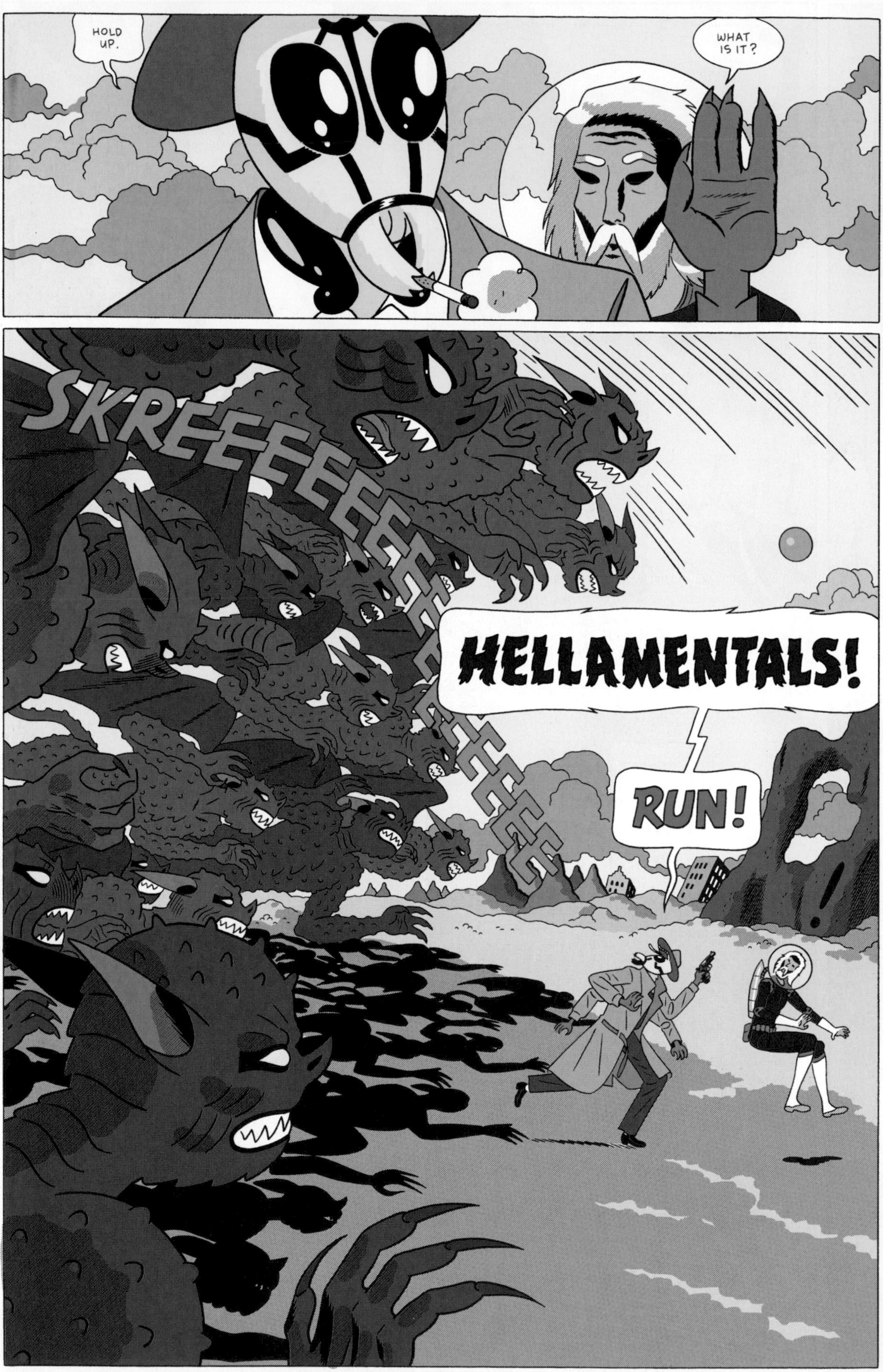
HOLD UP.
WHAT IS IT?
SKREEEEEEEEEEEEEEEEEEEE
HELLAMENTALS!
RUN!

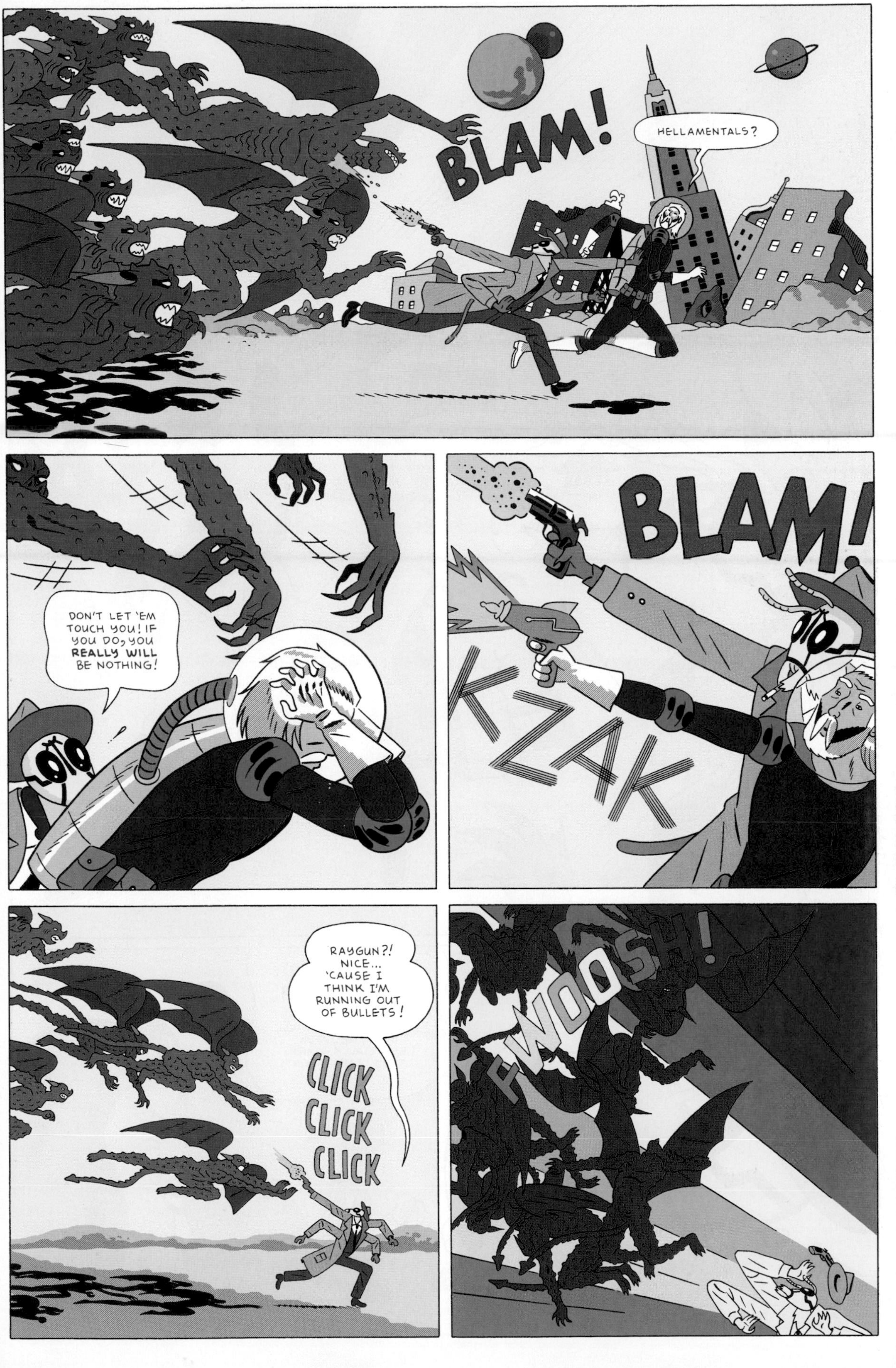
BLAM!
HELLAMENTALS?
DON'T LET 'EM TOUCH YOU! IF YOU DO, YOU **REALLY WILL** BE NOTHING!
BLAM!
KZAK
RAYGUN?! NICE... 'CAUSE I THINK I'M RUNNING OUT OF BULLETS!
CLICK
CLICK
CLICK
FWOOSH!

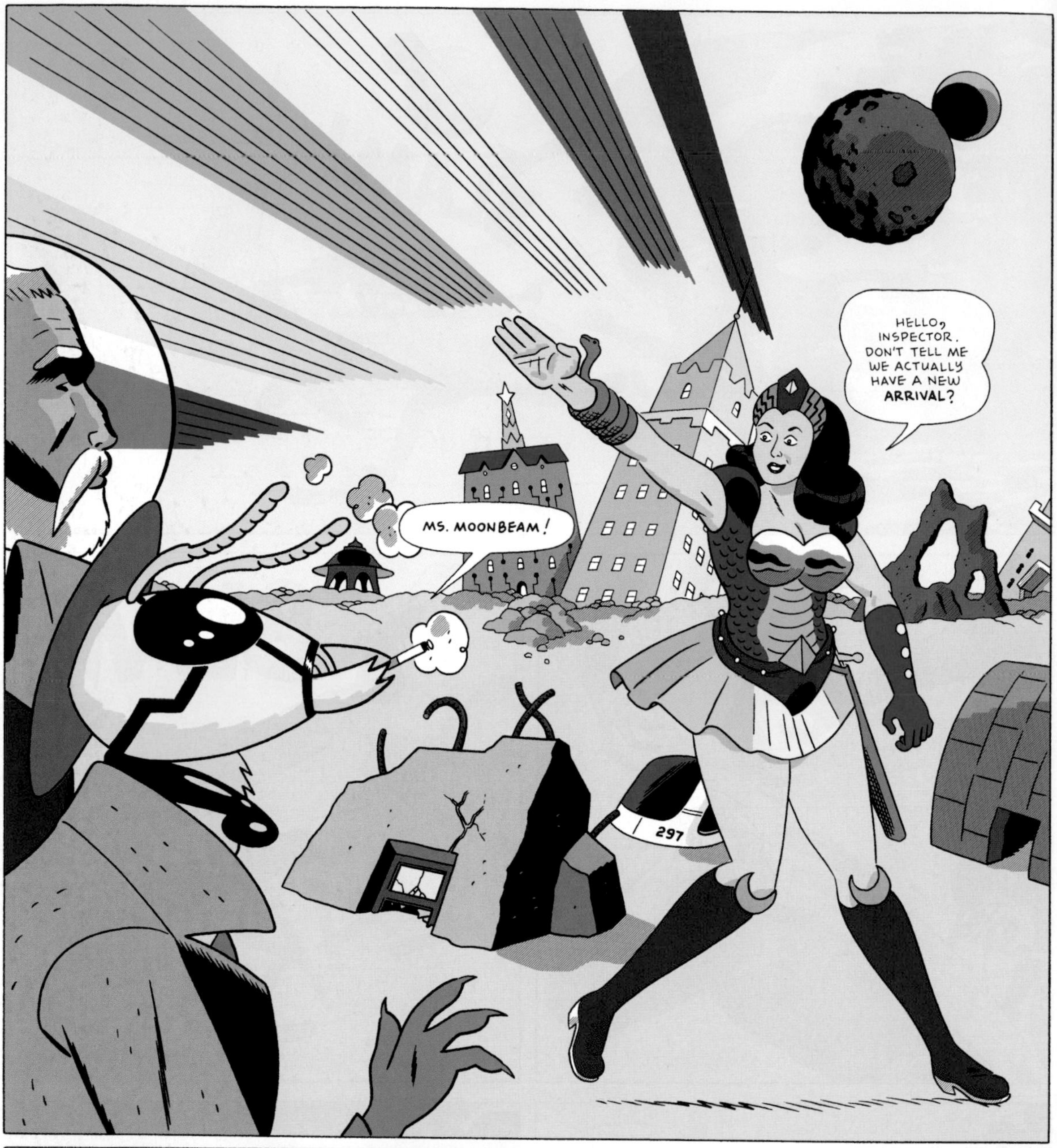
HELLO, INSPECTOR. DON'T TELL ME WE ACTUALLY HAVE A NEW **ARRIVAL**?
MS. MOONBEAM!
297

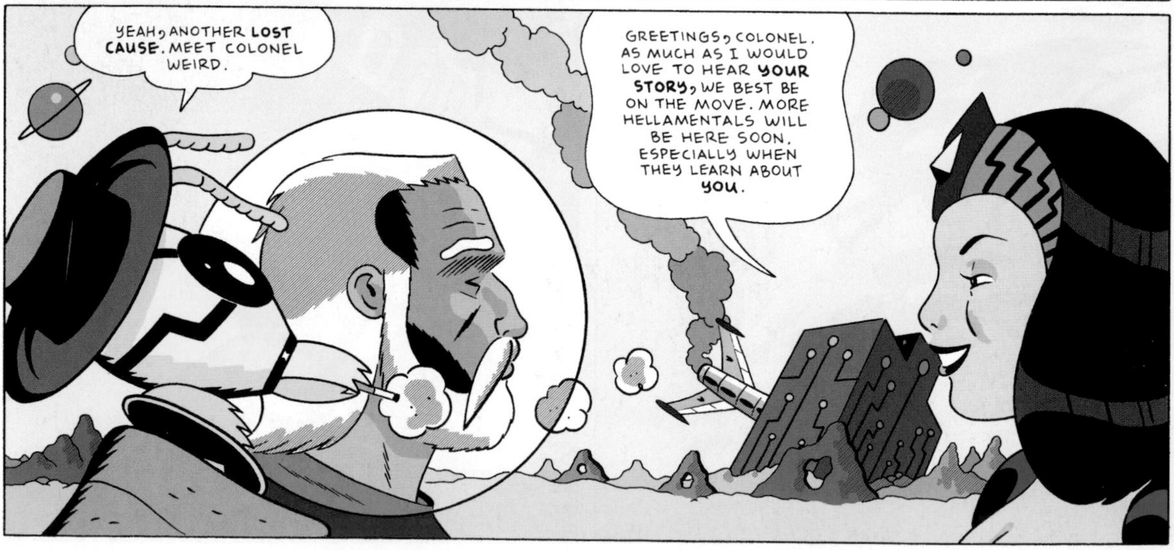
YEAH, ANOTHER **LOST CAUSE**. MEET COLONEL WEIRD.
GREETINGS, COLONEL. AS MUCH AS I WOULD LOVE TO HEAR **YOUR STORY**, WE BEST BE ON THE MOVE. MORE HELLAMENTALS WILL BE HERE SOON. ESPECIALLY WHEN THEY LEARN ABOUT **YOU**.

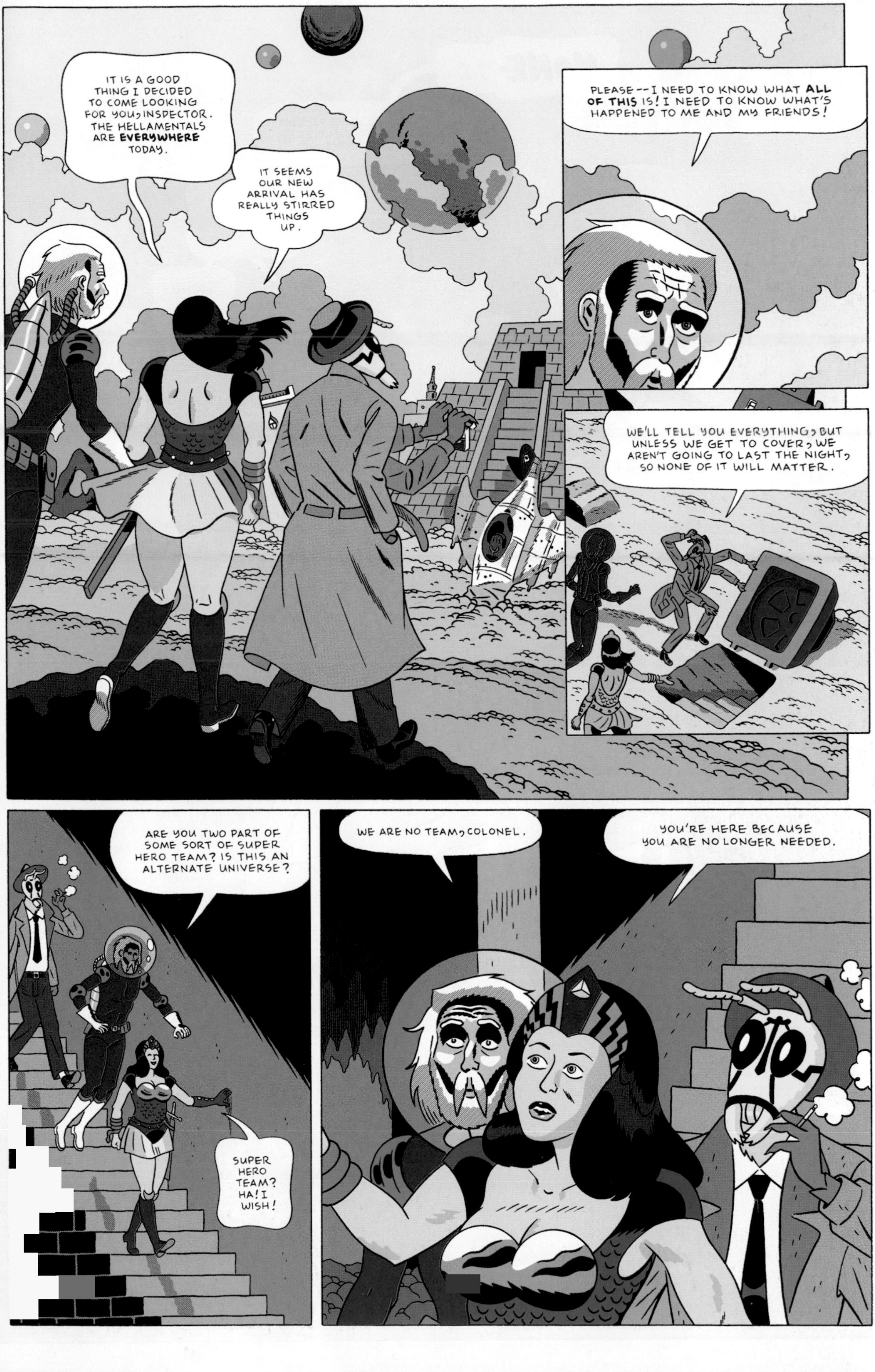
IT IS A GOOD THING I DECIDED TO COME LOOKING FOR YOU, INSPECTOR. THE HELLAMENTALS ARE **EVERYWHERE** TODAY.
IT SEEMS OUR NEW ARRIVAL HAS REALLY STIRRED THINGS UP.
PLEASE--I NEED TO KNOW WHAT **ALL OF THIS** IS! I NEED TO KNOW WHAT'S HAPPENED TO ME AND MY FRIENDS!
WE'LL TELL YOU EVERYTHING, BUT UNLESS WE GET TO COVER, WE AREN'T GOING TO LAST THE NIGHT, SO NONE OF IT WILL MATTER.
ARE YOU TWO PART OF SOME SORT OF SUPER HERO TEAM? IS THIS AN ALTERNATE UNIVERSE?
SUPER HERO TEAM? HA! I WISH!
WE ARE NO TEAM, COLONEL.
YOU'RE HERE BECAUSE YOU ARE NO LONGER NEEDED.

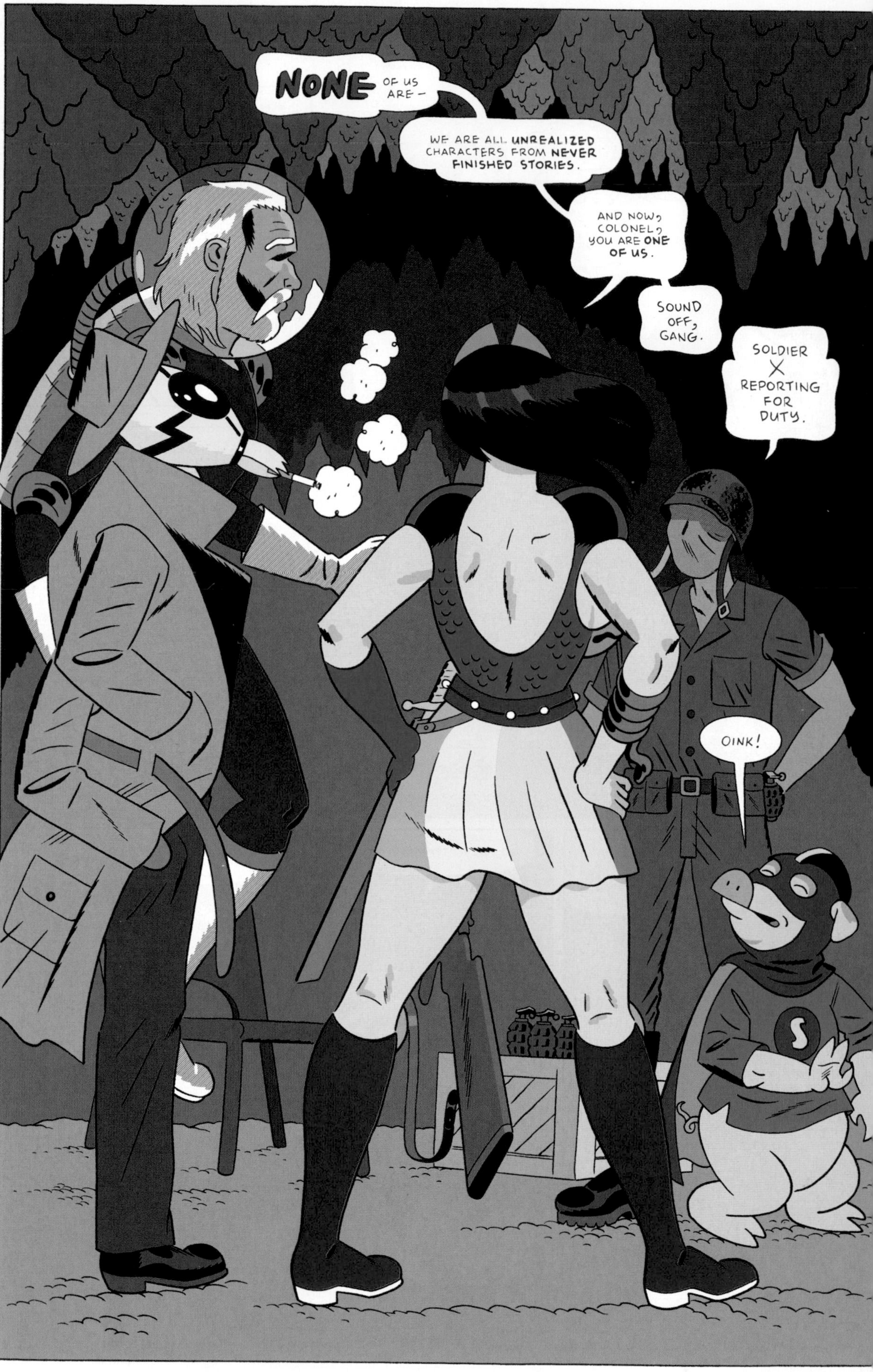
NONE OF US ARE–
WE ARE ALL UNREALIZED CHARACTERS FROM NEVER FINISHED STORIES.
AND NOW, COLONEL, YOU ARE ONE OF US.
SOUND OFF, GANG.
SOLDIER X REPORTING FOR DUTY.
OINK!

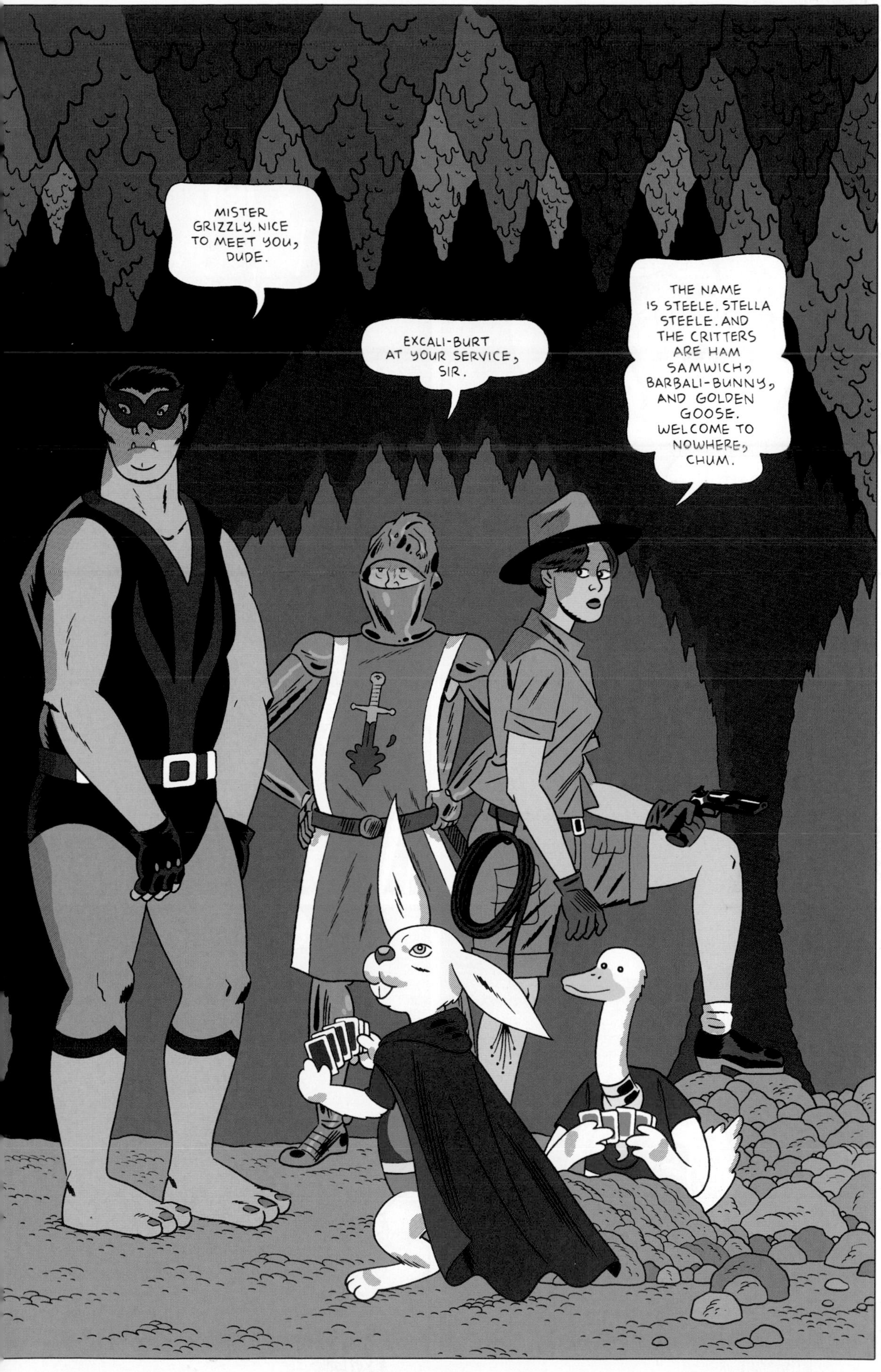
MISTER GRIZZLY. NICE TO MEET YOU, DUDE.
EXCALI-BURT AT YOUR SERVICE, SIR.
THE NAME IS STEELE. STELLA STEELE. AND THE CRITTERS ARE HAM SAMWICH, BARBALI-BUNNY, AND GOLDEN GOOSE. WELCOME TO NOWHERE, CHUM.

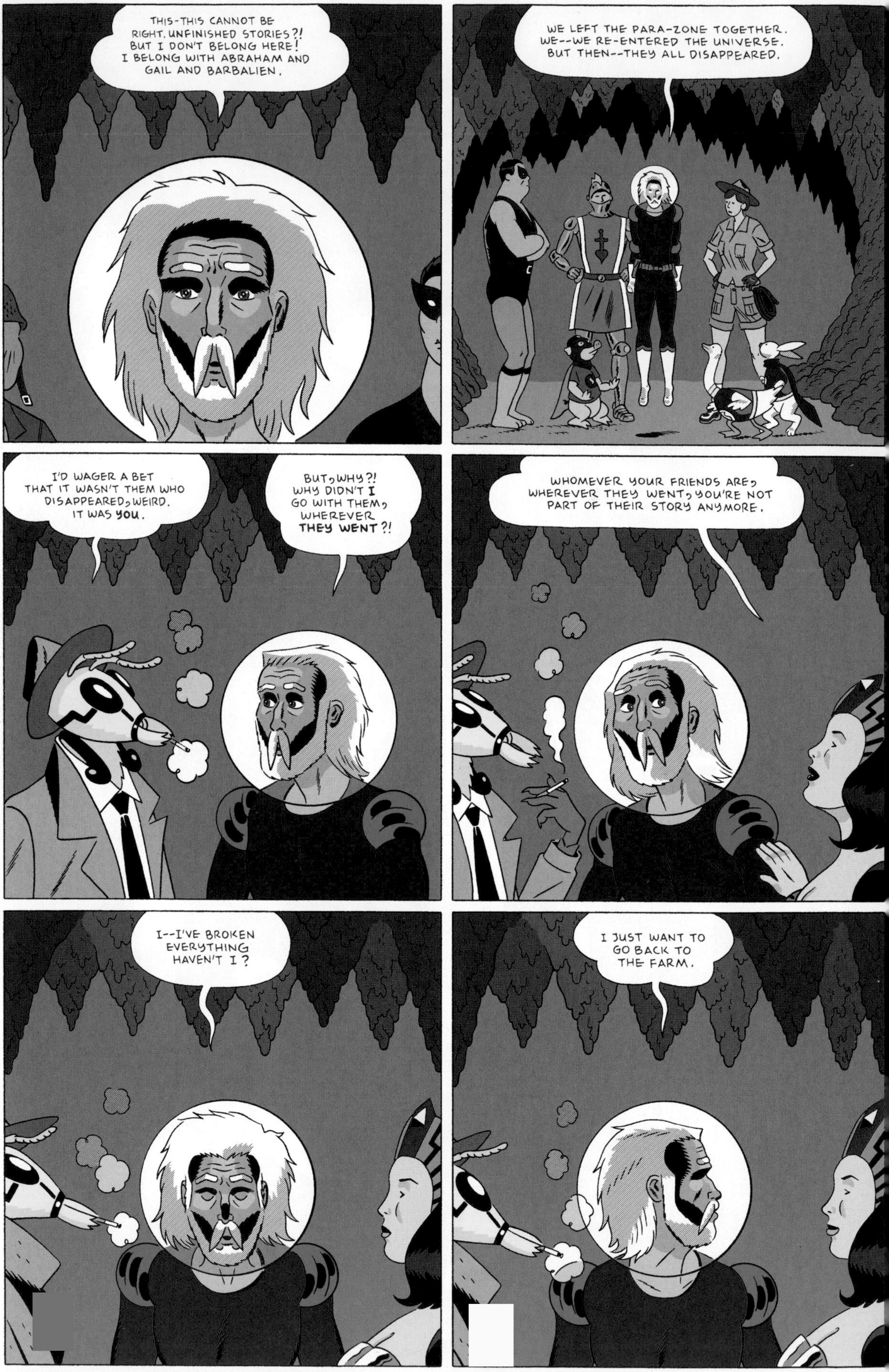
THIS-THIS CANNOT BE RIGHT. UNFINISHED STORIES?! BUT I DON'T BELONG HERE! I BELONG WITH ABRAHAM AND GAIL AND BARBALIEN.
WE LEFT THE PARA-ZONE TOGETHER. WE--WE RE-ENTERED THE UNIVERSE. BUT THEN--THEY ALL DISAPPEARED.
I'D WAGER A BET THAT IT WASN'T THEM WHO DISAPPEARED, WEIRD. IT WAS YOU.
BUT, WHY?! WHY DIDN'T I GO WITH THEM, WHEREVER THEY WENT?!
WHOMEVER YOUR FRIENDS ARE, WHEREVER THEY WENT, YOU'RE NOT PART OF THEIR STORY ANYMORE.
I--I'VE BROKEN EVERYTHING HAVEN'T I?
I JUST WANT TO GO BACK TO THE FARM.

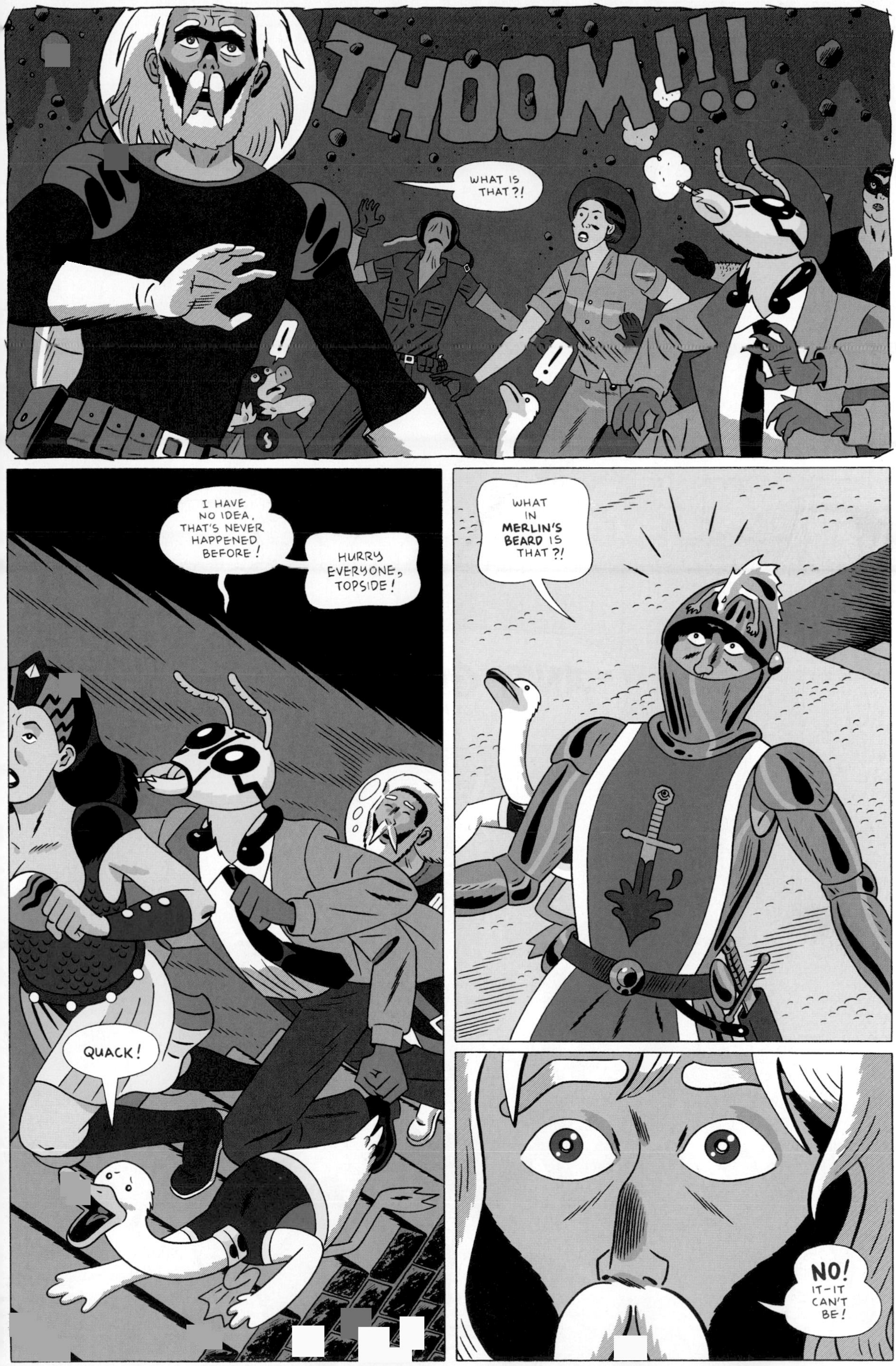
THOOM!!!
WHAT IS THAT?!
I HAVE NO IDEA. THAT'S NEVER HAPPENED BEFORE!
HURRY EVERYONE, TOPSIDE!
QUACK!
WHAT IN MERLIN'S BEARD IS THAT?!
NO! IT-IT CAN'T BE!

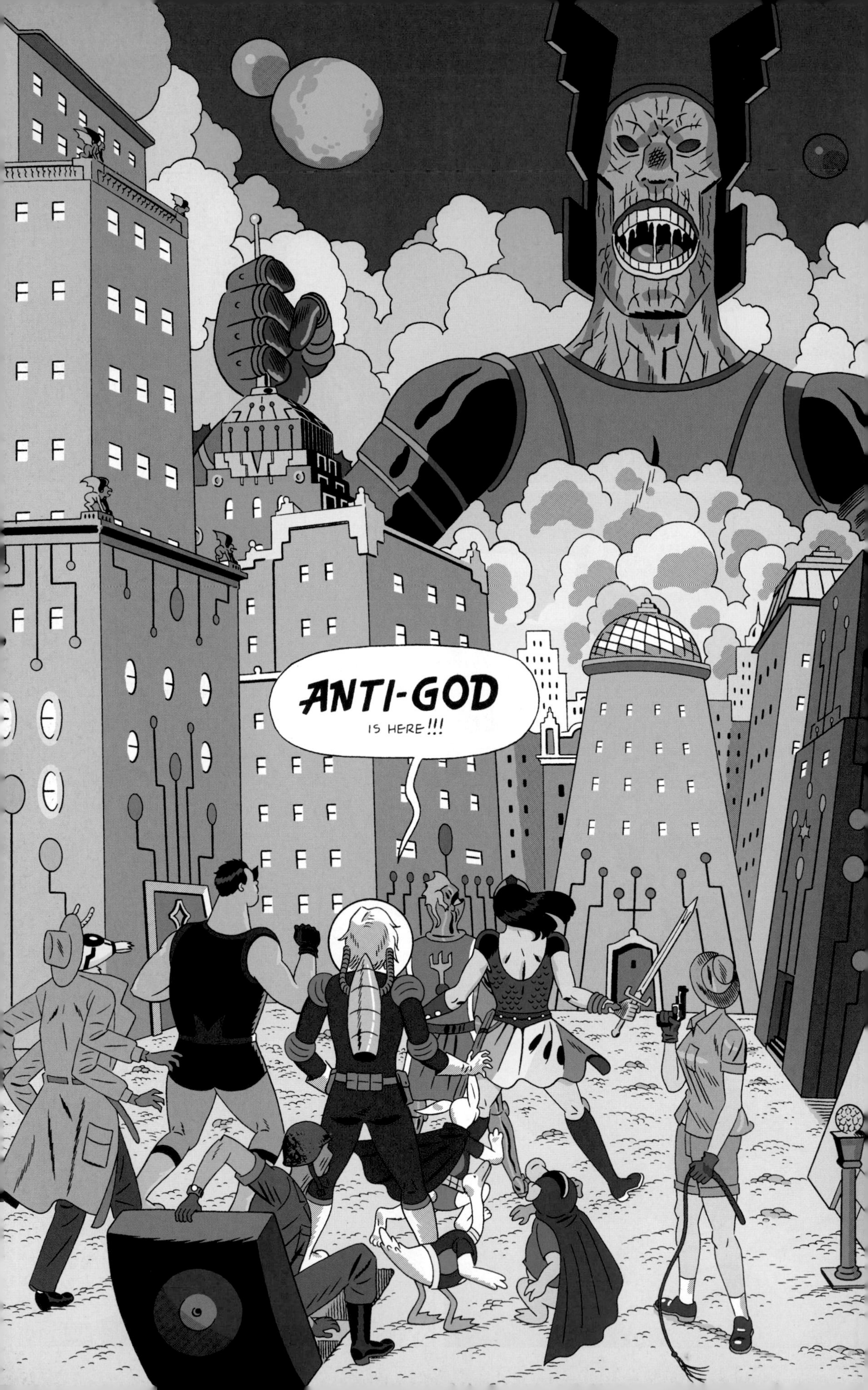
ANTI-GOD
IS HERE!!!

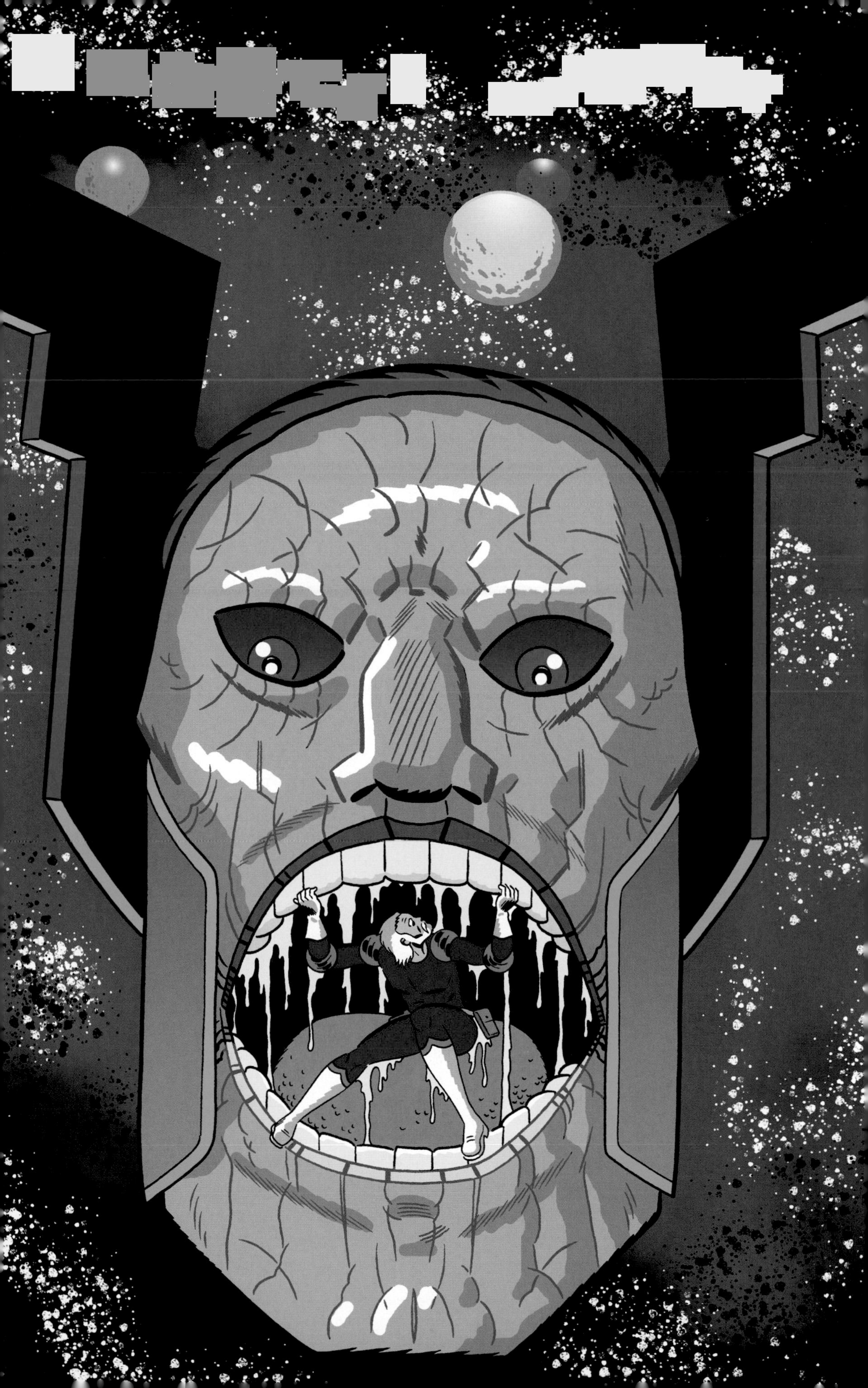

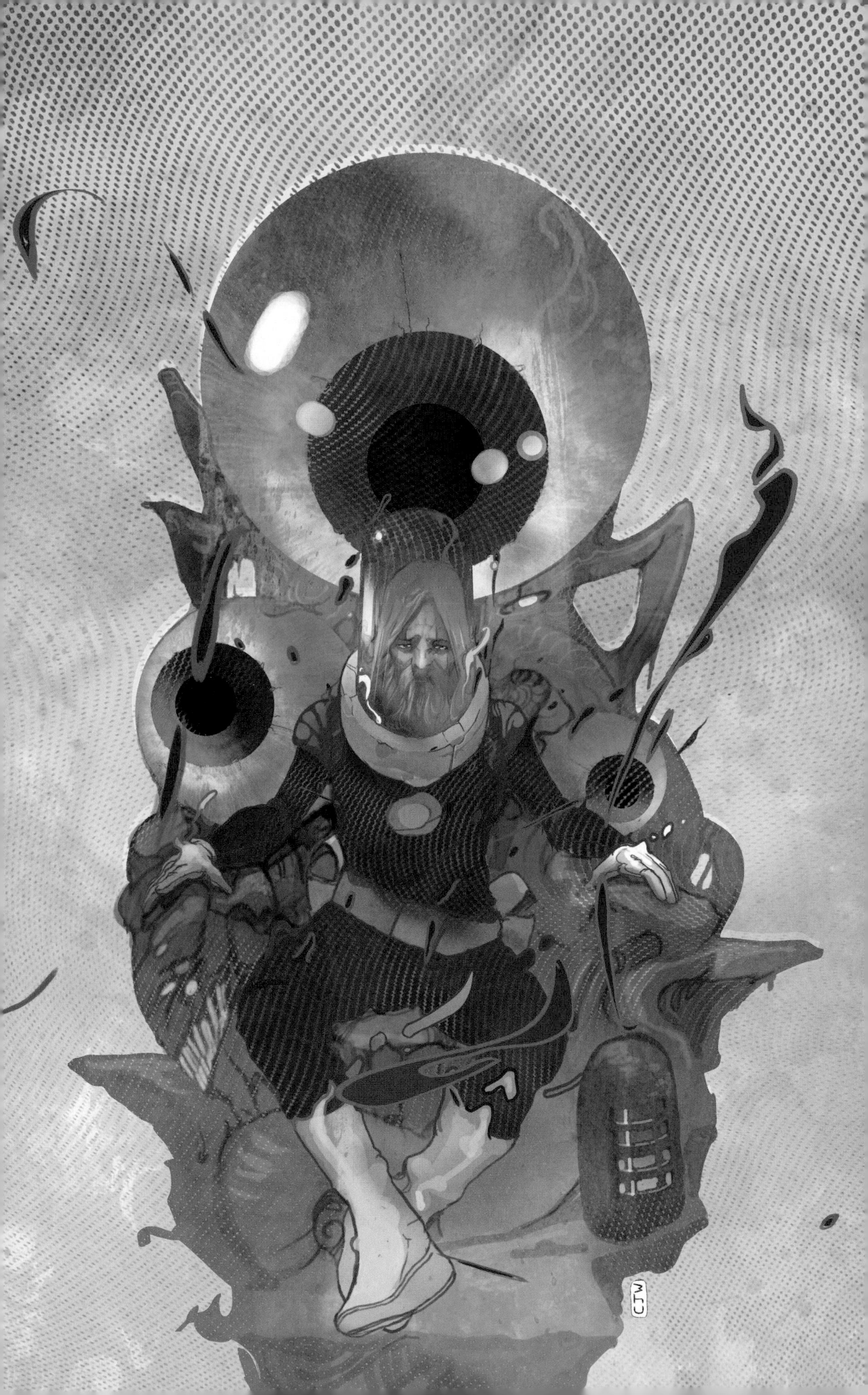
CJW

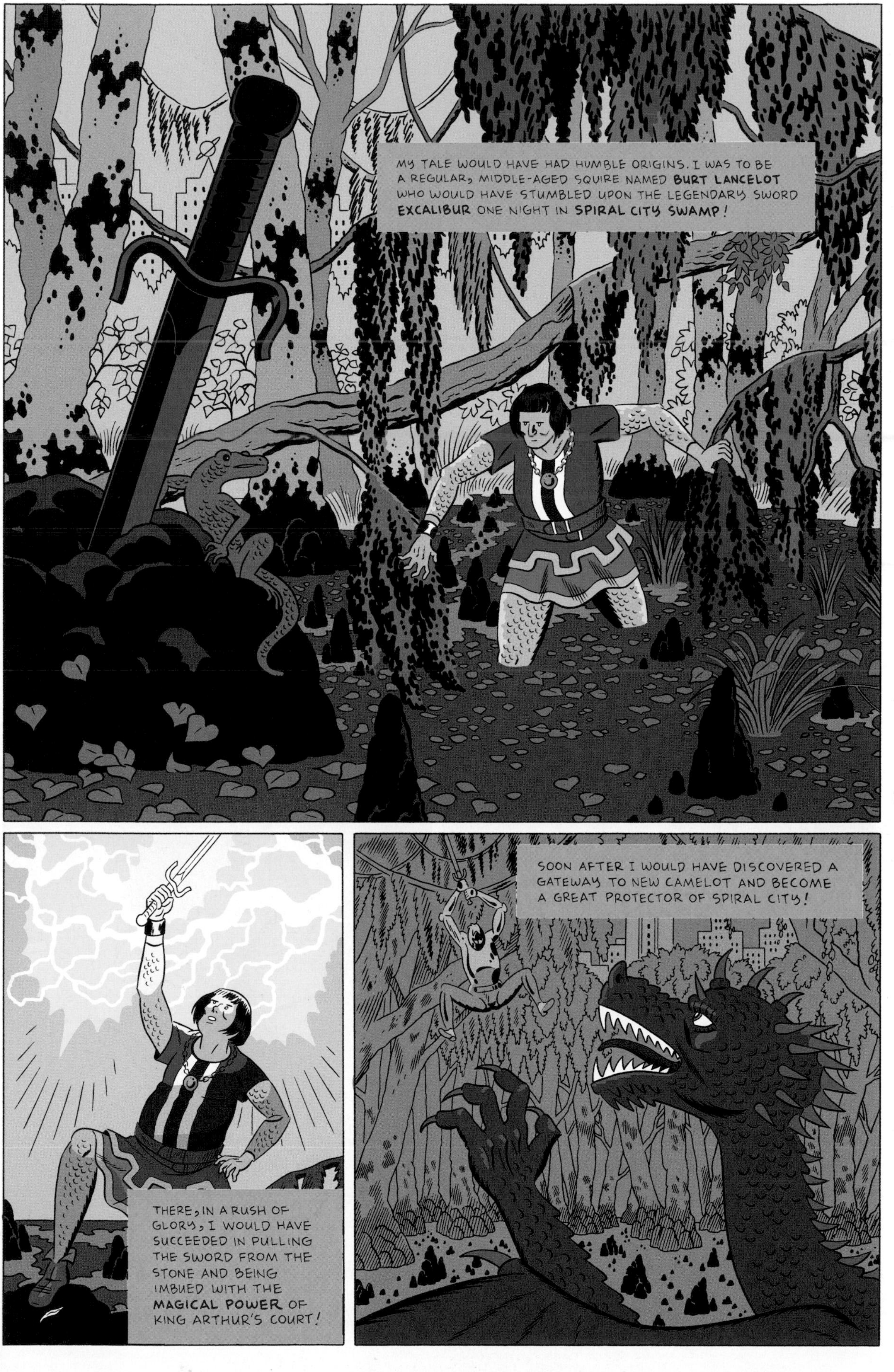
MY TALE WOULD HAVE HAD HUMBLE ORIGINS. I WAS TO BE A REGULAR, MIDDLE-AGED SQUIRE NAMED **BURT LANCELOT** WHO WOULD HAVE STUMBLED UPON THE LEGENDARY SWORD **EXCALIBUR** ONE NIGHT IN **SPIRAL CITY SWAMP**!
THERE, IN A RUSH OF GLORY, I WOULD HAVE SUCCEEDED IN PULLING THE SWORD FROM THE STONE AND BEING IMBUED WITH THE **MAGICAL POWER** OF KING ARTHUR'S COURT!
SOON AFTER I WOULD HAVE DISCOVERED A GATEWAY TO NEW CAMELOT AND BECOME A GREAT PROTECTOR OF SPIRAL CITY!

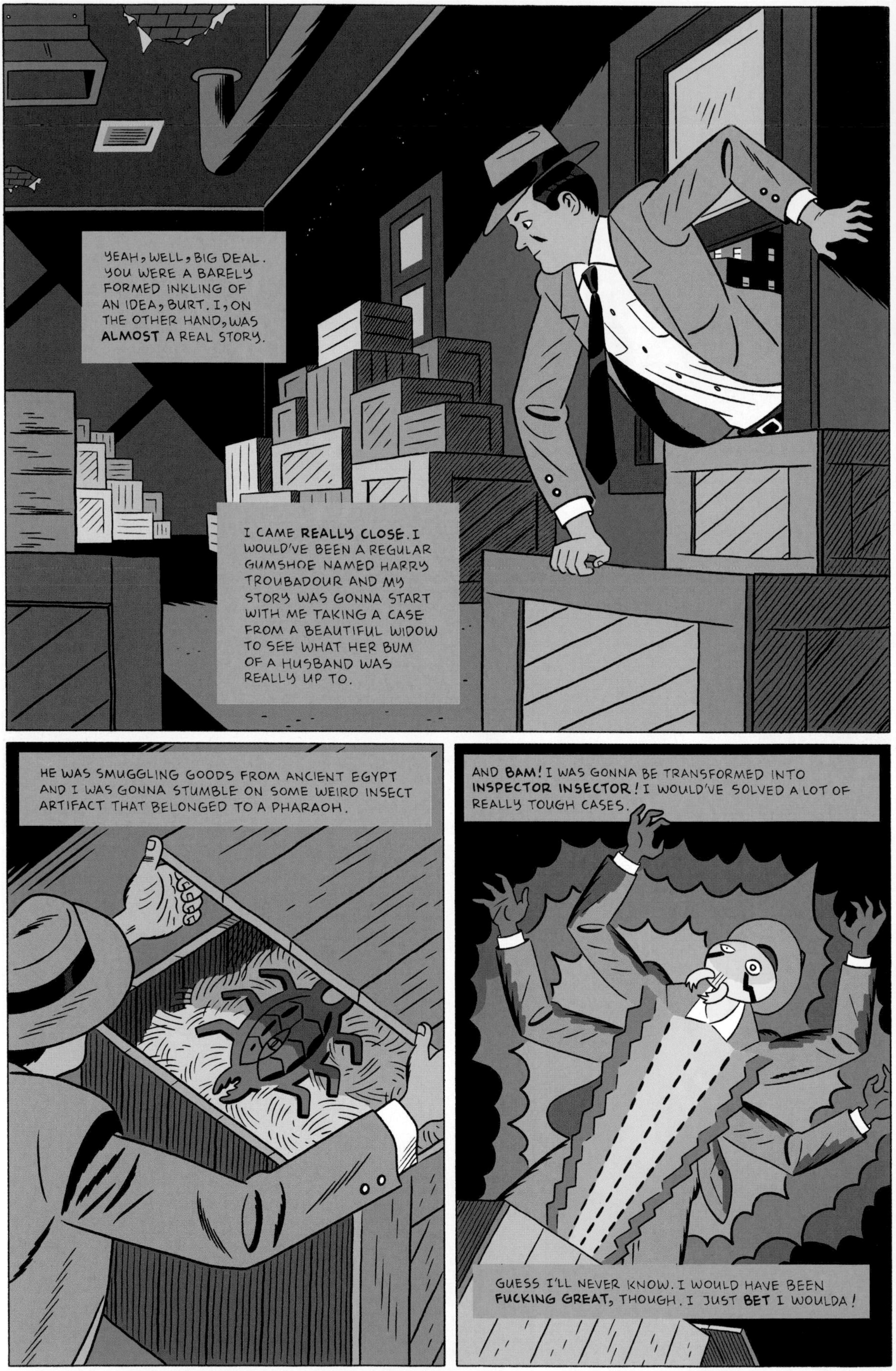
YEAH, WELL, BIG DEAL. YOU WERE A BARELY FORMED INKLING OF AN IDEA, BURT. I, ON THE OTHER HAND, WAS **ALMOST** A REAL STORY.
I CAME **REALLY CLOSE**. I WOULD'VE BEEN A REGULAR GUMSHOE NAMED HARRY TROUBADOUR AND MY STORY WAS GONNA START WITH ME TAKING A CASE FROM A BEAUTIFUL WIDOW TO SEE WHAT HER BUM OF A HUSBAND WAS REALLY UP TO.
HE WAS SMUGGLING GOODS FROM ANCIENT EGYPT AND I WAS GONNA STUMBLE ON SOME WEIRD INSECT ARTIFACT THAT BELONGED TO A PHARAOH.
AND **BAM**! I WAS GONNA BE TRANSFORMED INTO **INSPECTOR INSECTOR**! I WOULD'VE SOLVED A LOT OF REALLY TOUGH CASES.
GUESS I'LL NEVER KNOW. I WOULD HAVE BEEN **FUCKING GREAT**, THOUGH. I JUST **BET** I WOULDA!

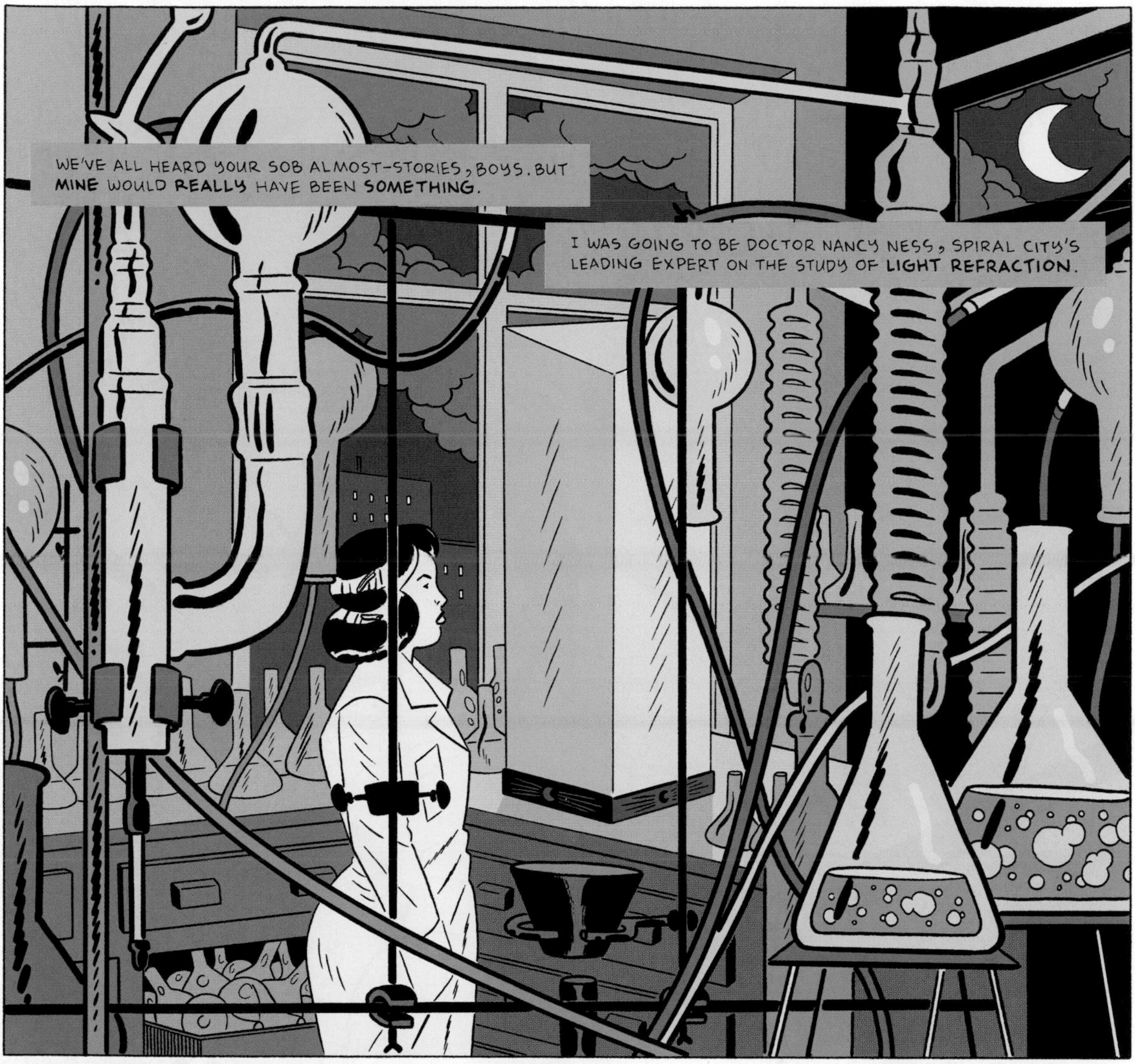
WE'VE ALL HEARD YOUR SOB ALMOST-STORIES, BOYS. BUT MINE WOULD REALLY HAVE BEEN SOMETHING.
I WAS GOING TO BE DOCTOR NANCY NESS, SPIRAL CITY'S LEADING EXPERT ON THE STUDY OF LIGHT REFRACTION.

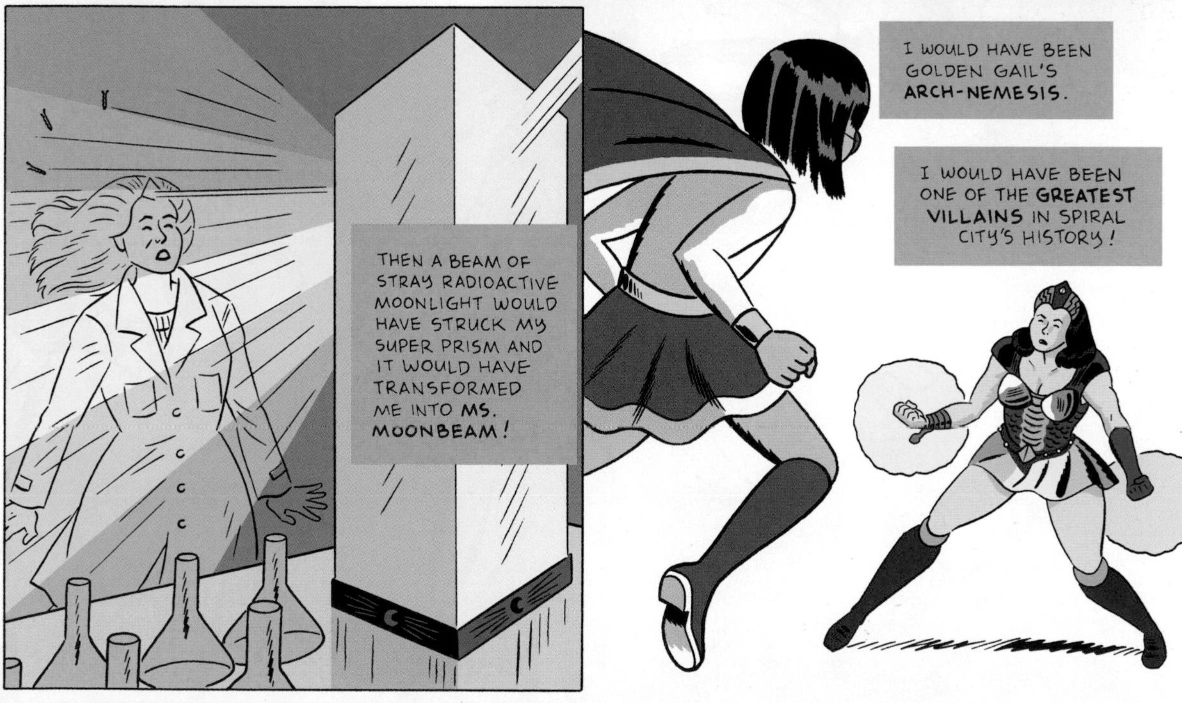
THEN A BEAM OF STRAY RADIOACTIVE MOONLIGHT WOULD HAVE STRUCK MY SUPER PRISM AND IT WOULD HAVE TRANSFORMED ME INTO MS. MOONBEAM!
I WOULD HAVE BEEN GOLDEN GAIL'S ARCH-NEMESIS.
I WOULD HAVE BEEN ONE OF THE GREATEST VILLAINS IN SPIRAL CITY'S HISTORY!

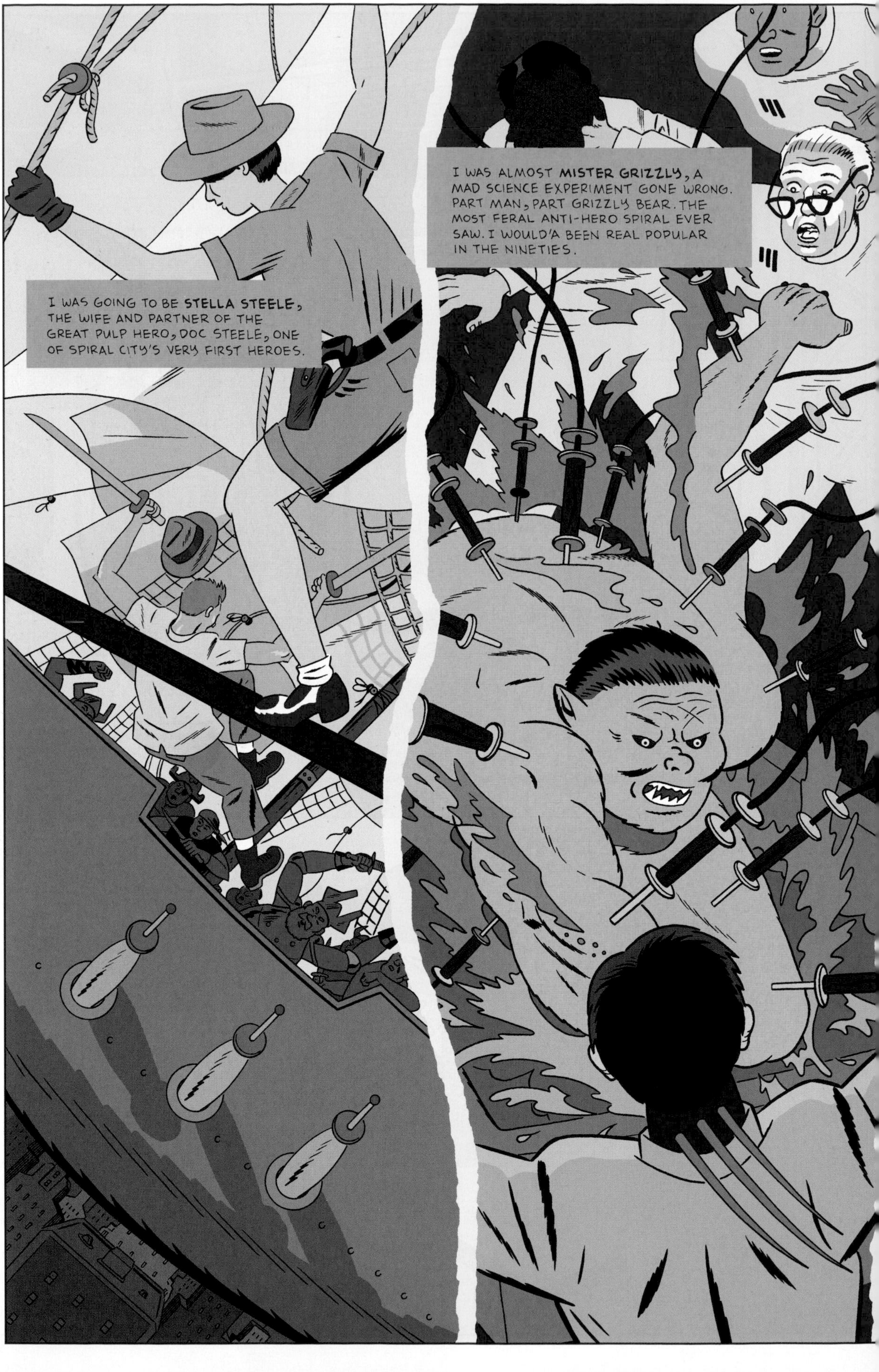
I WAS GOING TO BE STELLA STEELE, THE WIFE AND PARTNER OF THE GREAT PULP HERO, DOC STEELE, ONE OF SPIRAL CITY'S VERY FIRST HEROES.
I WAS ALMOST MISTER GRIZZLY, A MAD SCIENCE EXPERIMENT GONE WRONG. PART MAN, PART GRIZZLY BEAR. THE MOST FERAL ANTI-HERO SPIRAL EVER SAW. I WOULD'A BEEN REAL POPULAR IN THE NINETIES.

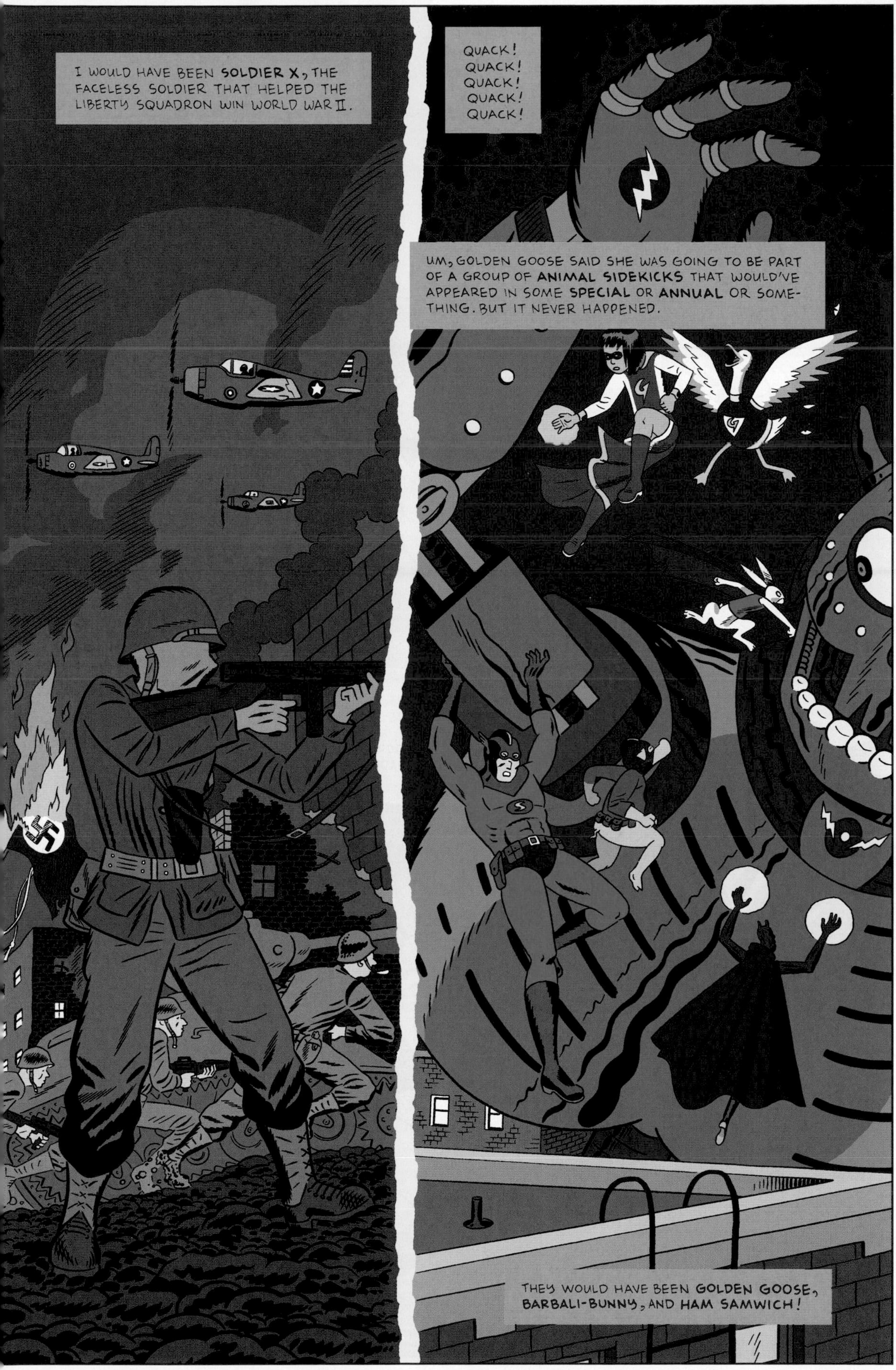
I WOULD HAVE BEEN SOLDIER X, THE FACELESS SOLDIER THAT HELPED THE LIBERTY SQUADRON WIN WORLD WAR II.
QUACK! QUACK! QUACK! QUACK! QUACK!
UM, GOLDEN GOOSE SAID SHE WAS GOING TO BE PART OF A GROUP OF ANIMAL SIDEKICKS THAT WOULD'VE APPEARED IN SOME SPECIAL OR ANNUAL OR SOMETHING. BUT IT NEVER HAPPENED.
THEY WOULD HAVE BEEN GOLDEN GOOSE, BARBALI-BUNNY, AND HAM SAMWICH!

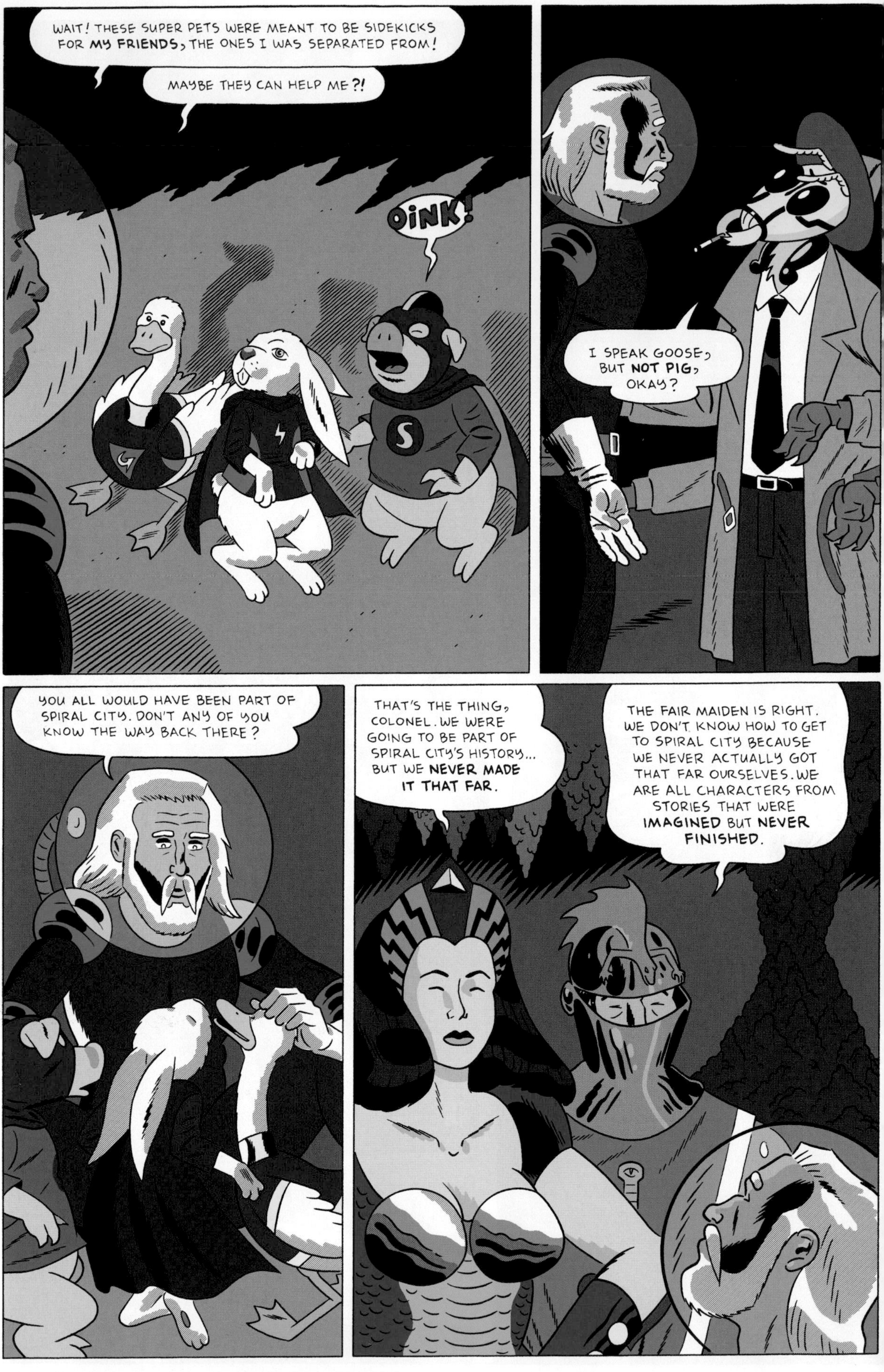
WAIT! THESE SUPER PETS WERE MEANT TO BE SIDEKICKS FOR **MY FRIENDS**, THE ONES I WAS SEPARATED FROM!
MAYBE THEY CAN HELP ME?!
OINK!
I SPEAK GOOSE, BUT **NOT PIG**, OKAY?
YOU ALL WOULD HAVE BEEN PART OF SPIRAL CITY. DON'T ANY OF YOU KNOW THE WAY BACK THERE?
THAT'S THE THING, COLONEL. WE WERE GOING TO BE PART OF SPIRAL CITY'S HISTORY... BUT WE **NEVER MADE IT THAT FAR**.
THE FAIR MAIDEN IS RIGHT. WE DON'T KNOW HOW TO GET TO SPIRAL CITY BECAUSE WE NEVER ACTUALLY GOT THAT FAR OURSELVES. WE ARE ALL CHARACTERS FROM STORIES THAT WERE **IMAGINED** BUT **NEVER FINISHED**.

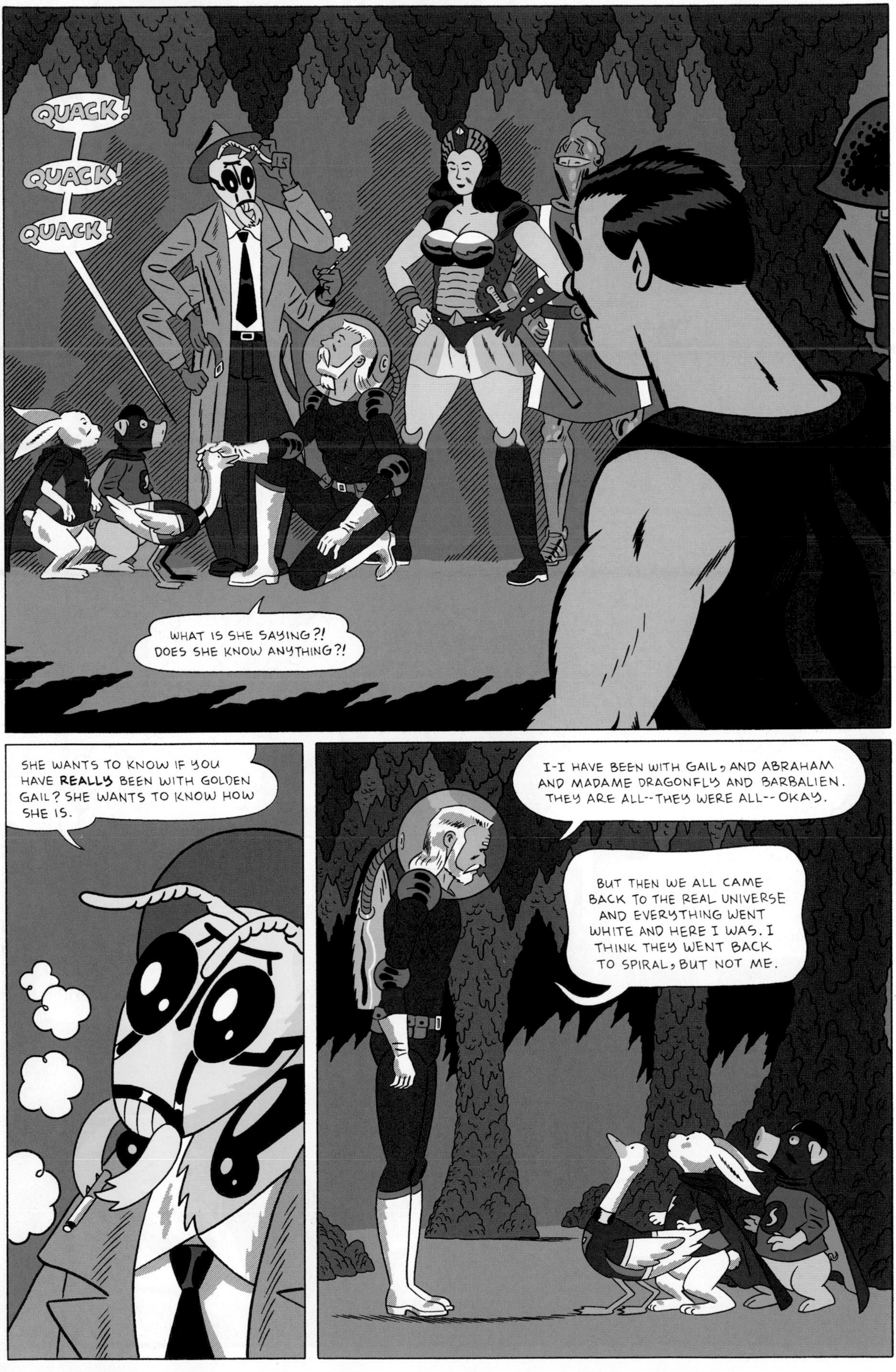
QUACK!
QUACK!
QUACK!
WHAT IS SHE SAYING?! DOES SHE KNOW ANYTHING?!
SHE WANTS TO KNOW IF YOU HAVE **REALLY** BEEN WITH GOLDEN GAIL? SHE WANTS TO KNOW HOW SHE IS.
I-I HAVE BEEN WITH GAIL, AND ABRAHAM AND MADAME DRAGONFLY AND BARBALIEN. THEY ARE ALL--THEY WERE ALL--OKAY.
BUT THEN WE ALL CAME BACK TO THE REAL UNIVERSE AND EVERYTHING WENT WHITE AND HERE I WAS. I THINK THEY WENT BACK TO SPIRAL, BUT NOT ME.

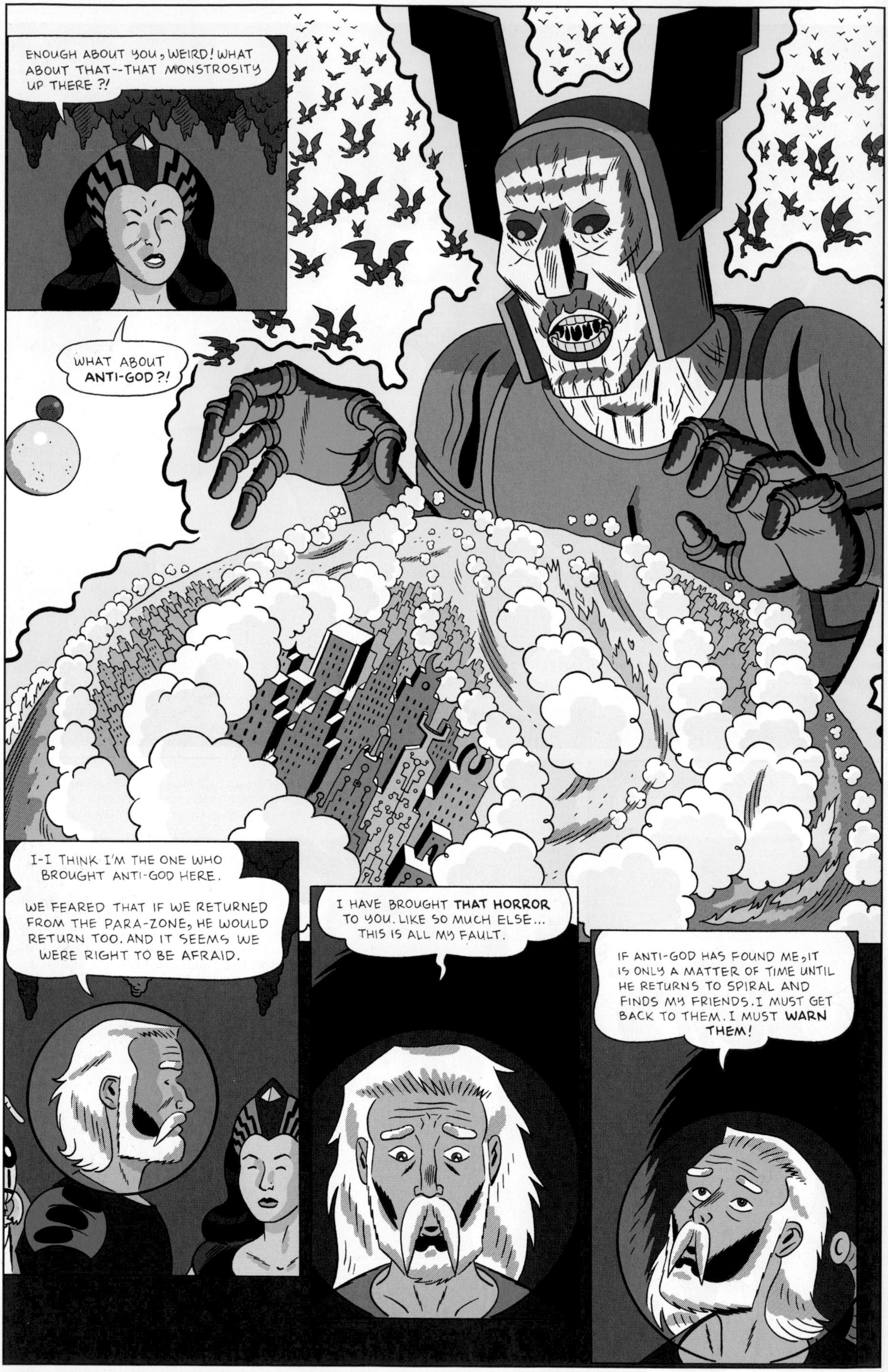
ENOUGH ABOUT YOU, WEIRD! WHAT ABOUT THAT--THAT MONSTROSITY UP THERE?!
WHAT ABOUT ANTI-GOD?!
I-I THINK I'M THE ONE WHO BROUGHT ANTI-GOD HERE.
WE FEARED THAT IF WE RETURNED FROM THE PARA-ZONE, HE WOULD RETURN TOO. AND IT SEEMS WE WERE RIGHT TO BE AFRAID.
I HAVE BROUGHT THAT HORROR TO YOU. LIKE SO MUCH ELSE... THIS IS ALL MY FAULT.
IF ANTI-GOD HAS FOUND ME, IT IS ONLY A MATTER OF TIME UNTIL HE RETURNS TO SPIRAL AND FINDS MY FRIENDS. I MUST GET BACK TO THEM. I MUST WARN THEM!

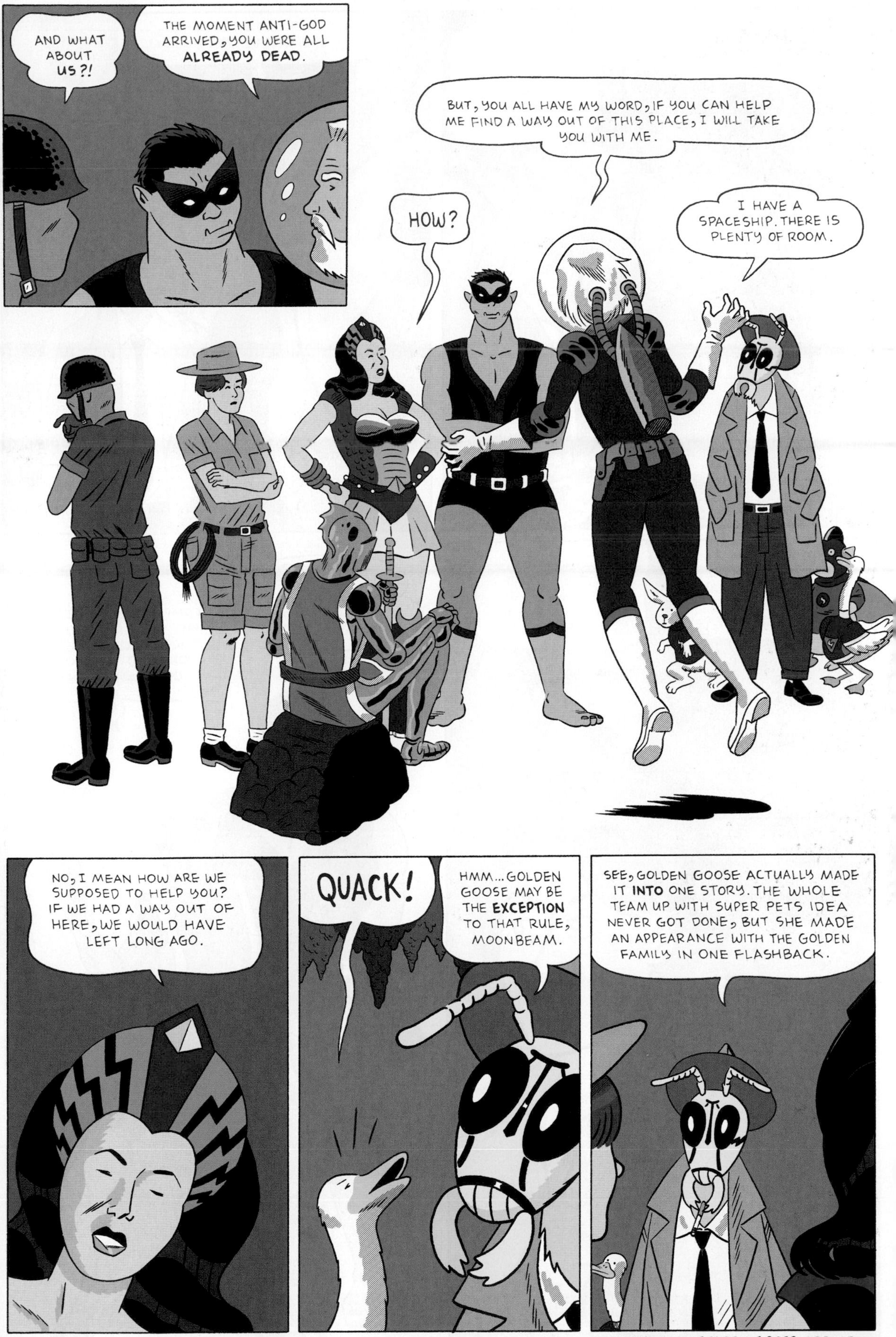
AND WHAT ABOUT US?!
THE MOMENT ANTI-GOD ARRIVED, YOU WERE ALL ALREADY DEAD.
BUT, YOU ALL HAVE MY WORD, IF YOU CAN HELP ME FIND A WAY OUT OF THIS PLACE, I WILL TAKE YOU WITH ME.
HOW?
I HAVE A SPACESHIP. THERE IS PLENTY OF ROOM.
NO, I MEAN HOW ARE WE SUPPOSED TO HELP YOU? IF WE HAD A WAY OUT OF HERE, WE WOULD HAVE LEFT LONG AGO.
QUACK!
HMM... GOLDEN GOOSE MAY BE THE EXCEPTION TO THAT RULE, MOONBEAM.
SEE, GOLDEN GOOSE ACTUALLY MADE IT INTO ONE STORY. THE WHOLE TEAM UP WITH SUPER PETS IDEA NEVER GOT DONE, BUT SHE MADE AN APPEARANCE WITH THE GOLDEN FAMILY IN ONE FLASHBACK.

*EDITOR'S NOTE: GOLDEN GOOSE APPEARED IN *BLACK HAMMER SERIES 1* #8!

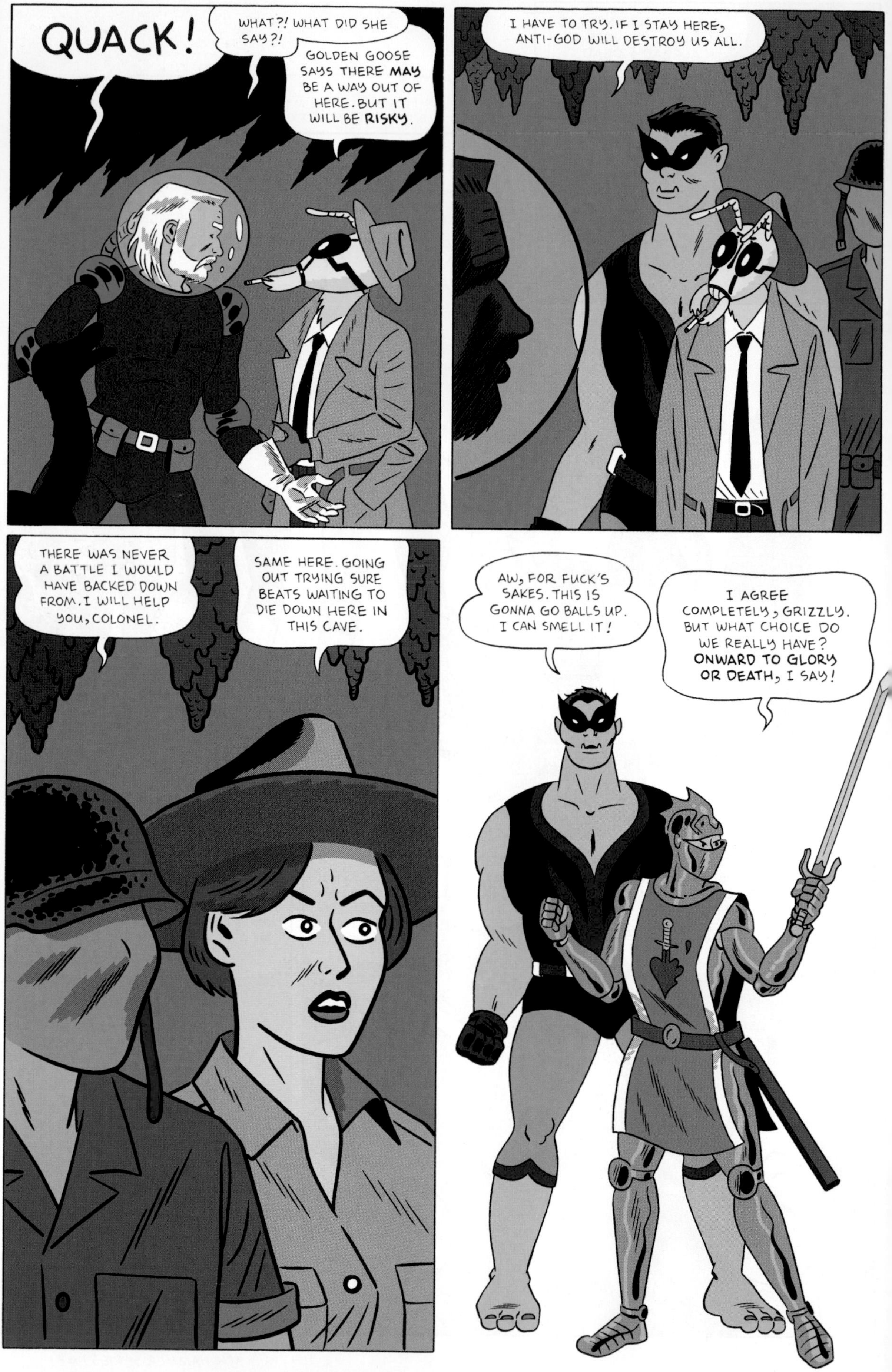
QUACK!
WHAT?! WHAT DID SHE SAY?!
GOLDEN GOOSE SAYS THERE **MAY** BE A WAY OUT OF HERE. BUT IT WILL BE **RISKY**.
I HAVE TO TRY. IF I STAY HERE, ANTI-GOD WILL DESTROY US ALL.
THERE WAS NEVER A BATTLE I WOULD HAVE BACKED DOWN FROM. I WILL HELP YOU, COLONEL.
SAME HERE. GOING OUT TRYING SURE BEATS WAITING TO DIE DOWN HERE IN THIS CAVE.
AW, FOR FUCK'S SAKES. THIS IS GONNA GO BALLS UP. I CAN SMELL IT!
I AGREE COMPLETELY, GRIZZLY. BUT WHAT CHOICE DO WE REALLY HAVE? **ONWARD TO GLORY OR DEATH**, I SAY!

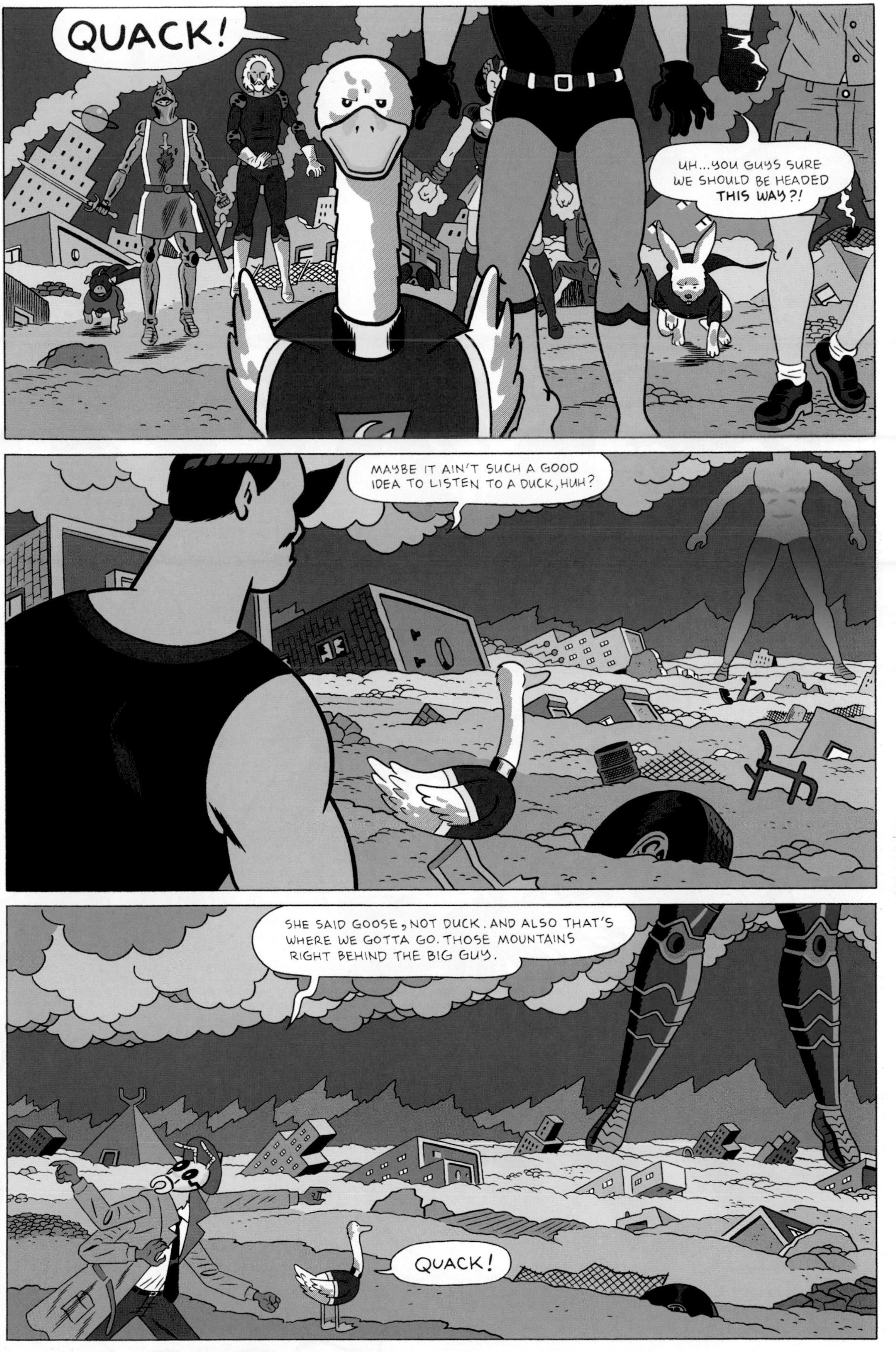
QUACK!
UH...YOU GUYS SURE WE SHOULD BE HEADED THIS WAY?!
MAYBE IT AIN'T SUCH A GOOD IDEA TO LISTEN TO A DUCK, HUH?
SHE SAID GOOSE, NOT DUCK. AND ALSO THAT'S WHERE WE GOTTA GO. THOSE MOUNTAINS RIGHT BEHIND THE BIG GUY.
QUACK!

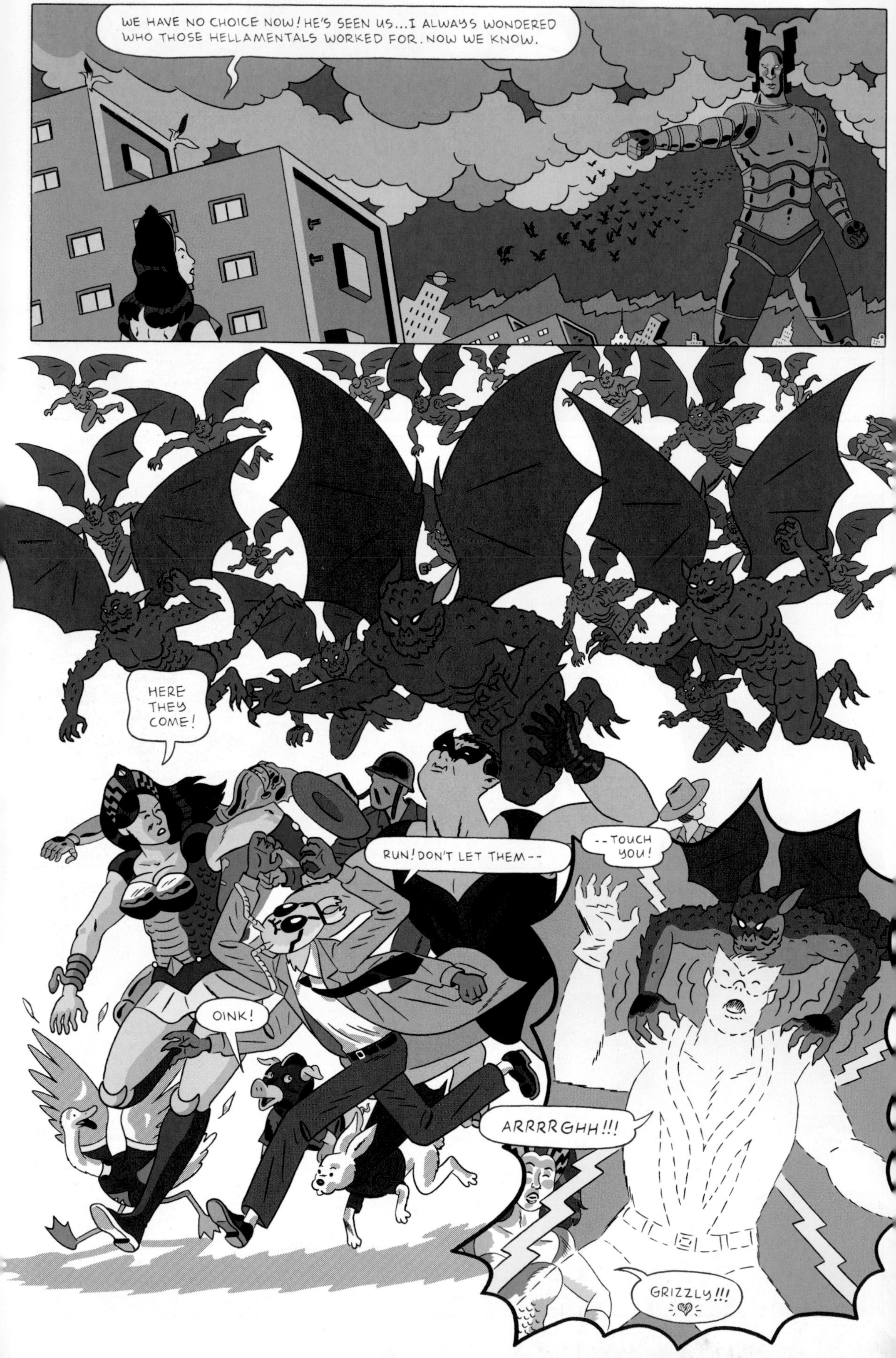
WE HAVE NO CHOICE NOW! HE'S SEEN US...I ALWAYS WONDERED WHO THOSE HELLAMENTALS WORKED FOR. NOW WE KNOW.
HERE THEY COME!
RUN! DON'T LET THEM--
--TOUCH YOU!
OINK!
ARRRRGHH!!!
GRIZZLY!!!

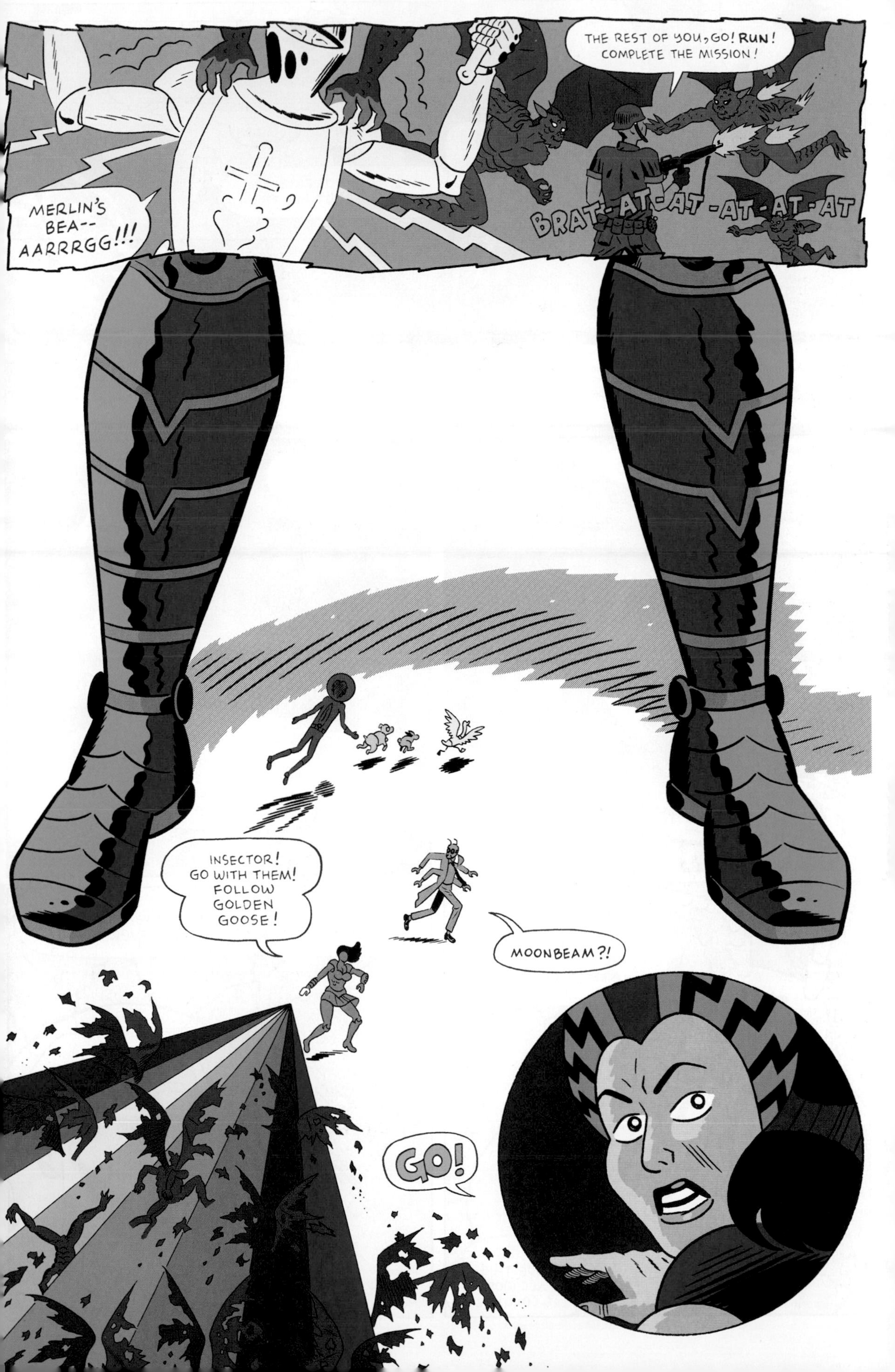
THE REST OF YOU, GO! RUN! COMPLETE THE MISSION!
MERLIN'S BEA--AARRRGG!!!
BRAT-AT-AT-AT-AT-AT
INSECTOR! GO WITH THEM! FOLLOW GOLDEN GOOSE!
MOONBEAM?!
GO!

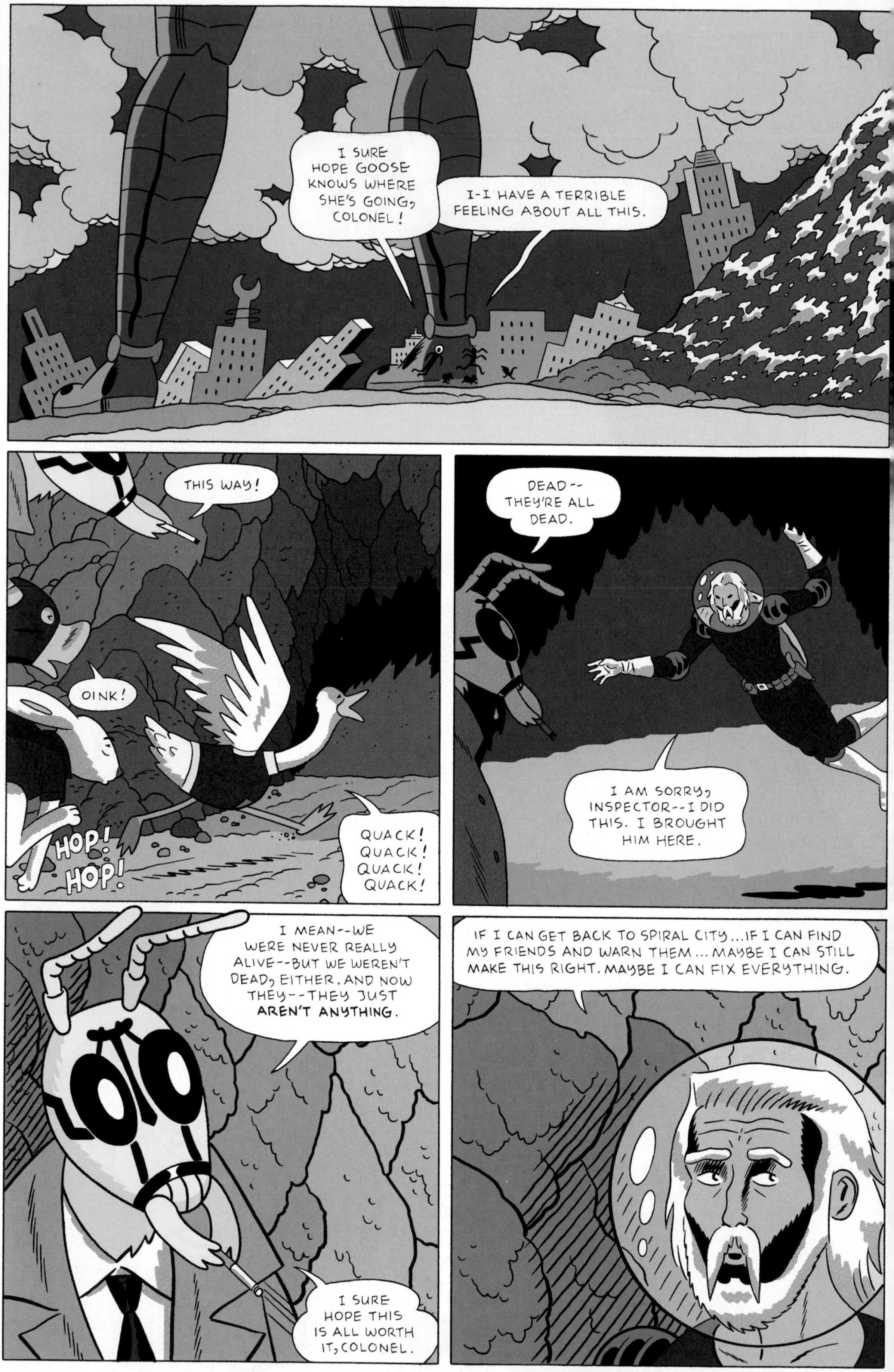

I SURE HOPE GOOSE KNOWS WHERE SHE'S GOING, COLONEL!
I-I HAVE A TERRIBLE FEELING ABOUT ALL THIS.
THIS WAY!
OINK!
HOP! HOP!
QUACK! QUACK! QUACK! QUACK!
DEAD-- THEY'RE ALL DEAD.
I AM SORRY, INSPECTOR--I DID THIS. I BROUGHT HIM HERE.
I MEAN--WE WERE NEVER REALLY ALIVE--BUT WE WEREN'T DEAD, EITHER. AND NOW THEY--THEY JUST **AREN'T ANYTHING**.
I SURE HOPE THIS IS ALL WORTH IT, COLONEL.
IF I CAN GET BACK TO SPIRAL CITY... IF I CAN FIND MY FRIENDS AND WARN THEM... MAYBE I CAN STILL MAKE THIS RIGHT. MAYBE I CAN FIX EVERYTHING.

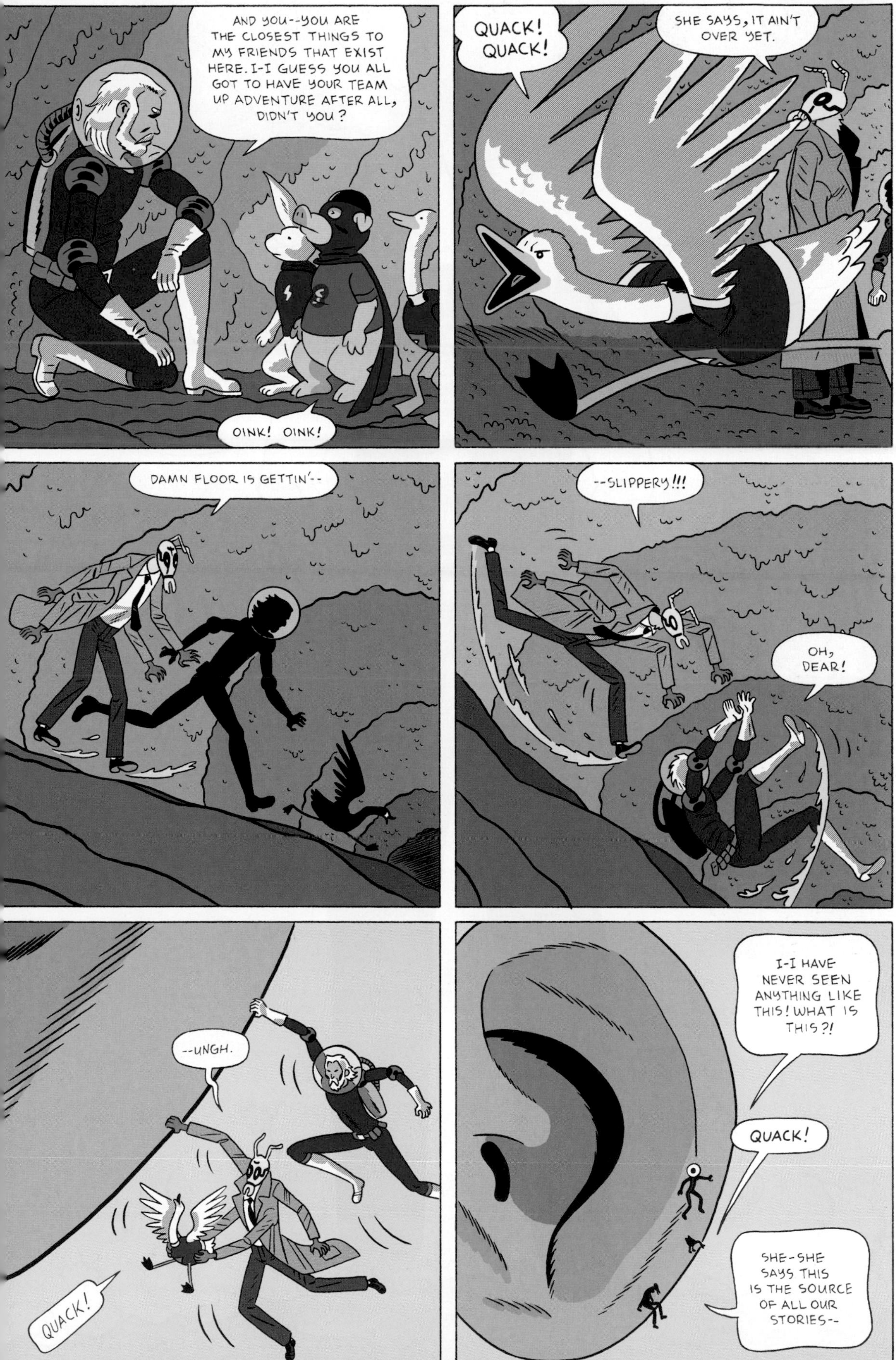
AND YOU--YOU ARE THE CLOSEST THINGS TO MY FRIENDS THAT EXIST HERE. I-I GUESS YOU ALL GOT TO HAVE YOUR TEAM UP ADVENTURE AFTER ALL, DIDN'T YOU?
OINK! OINK!
QUACK! QUACK!
SHE SAYS, IT AIN'T OVER YET.
DAMN FLOOR IS GETTIN'--
--SLIPPERY!!!
OH, DEAR!
--UNGH.
QUACK!
I-I HAVE NEVER SEEN ANYTHING LIKE THIS! WHAT IS THIS?!
QUACK!
SHE-SHE SAYS THIS IS THE SOURCE OF ALL OUR STORIES--

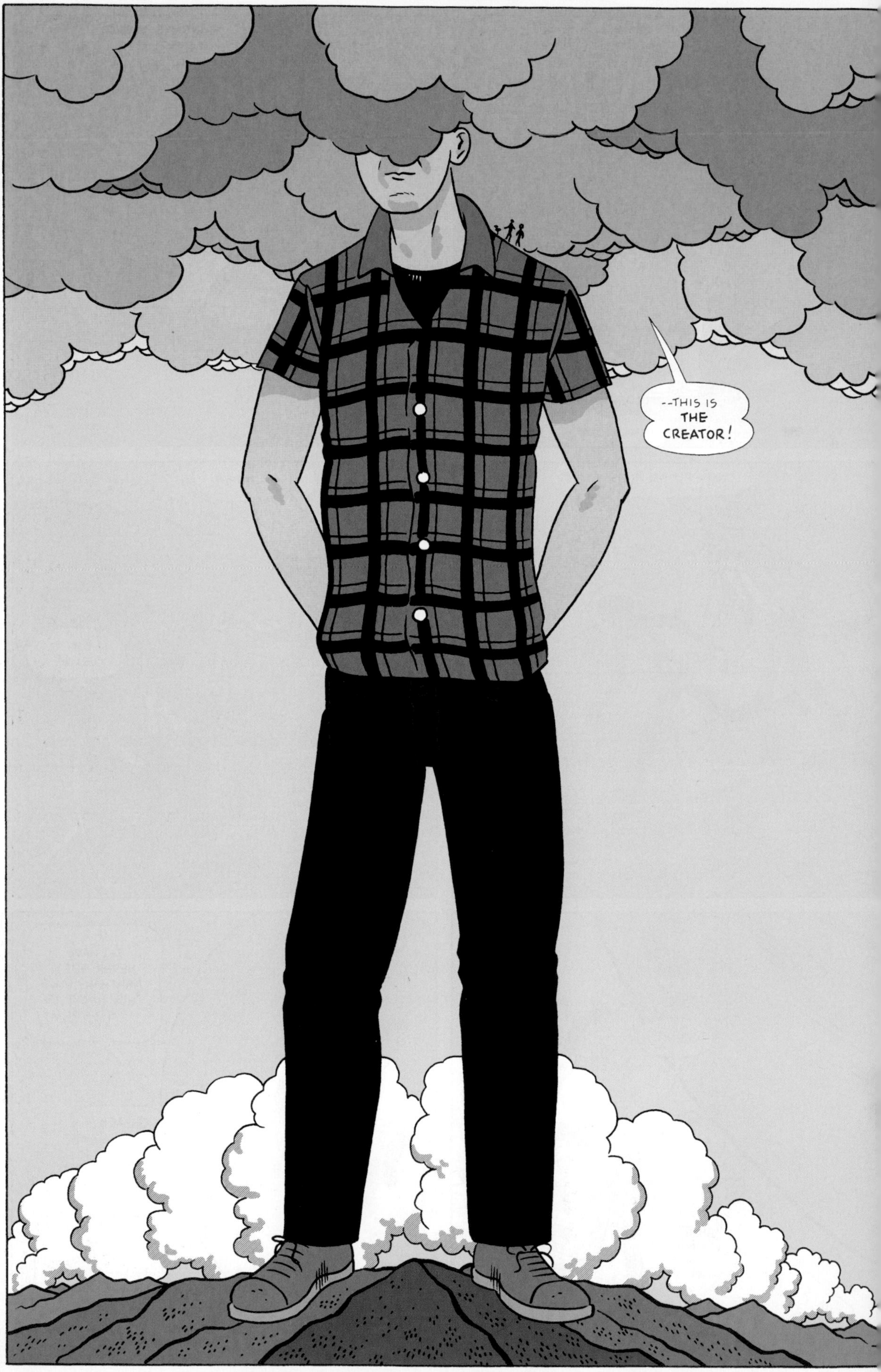
--THIS IS THE CREATOR!

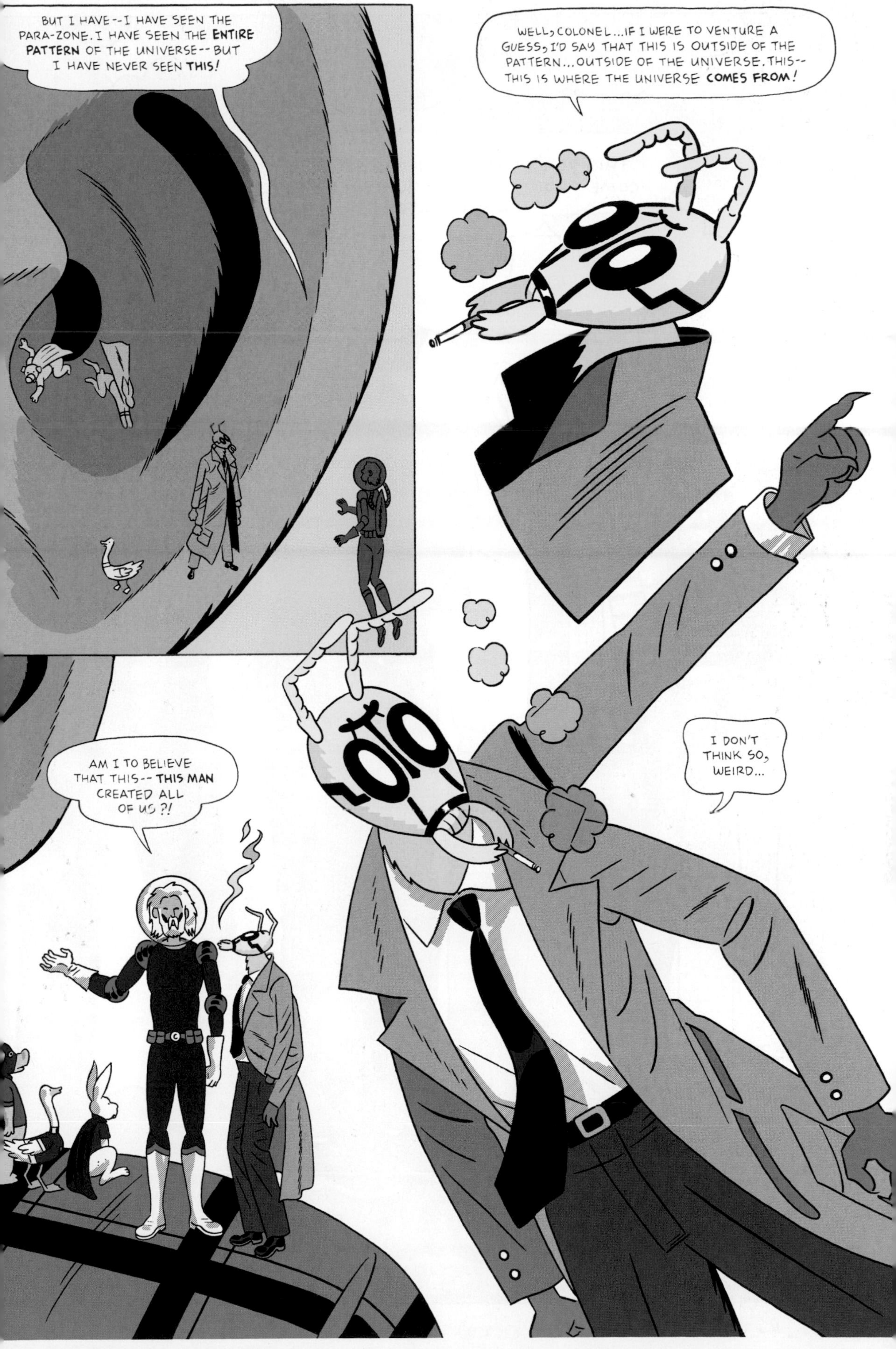
BUT I HAVE--I HAVE SEEN THE PARA-ZONE. I HAVE SEEN THE **ENTIRE PATTERN** OF THE UNIVERSE--BUT I HAVE NEVER SEEN **THIS**!
WELL, COLONEL...IF I WERE TO VENTURE A GUESS, I'D SAY THAT THIS IS OUTSIDE OF THE PATTERN...OUTSIDE OF THE UNIVERSE. THIS--THIS IS WHERE THE UNIVERSE **COMES FROM**!
AM I TO BELIEVE THAT THIS--**THIS MAN** CREATED ALL OF US?!
I DON'T THINK SO, WEIRD...

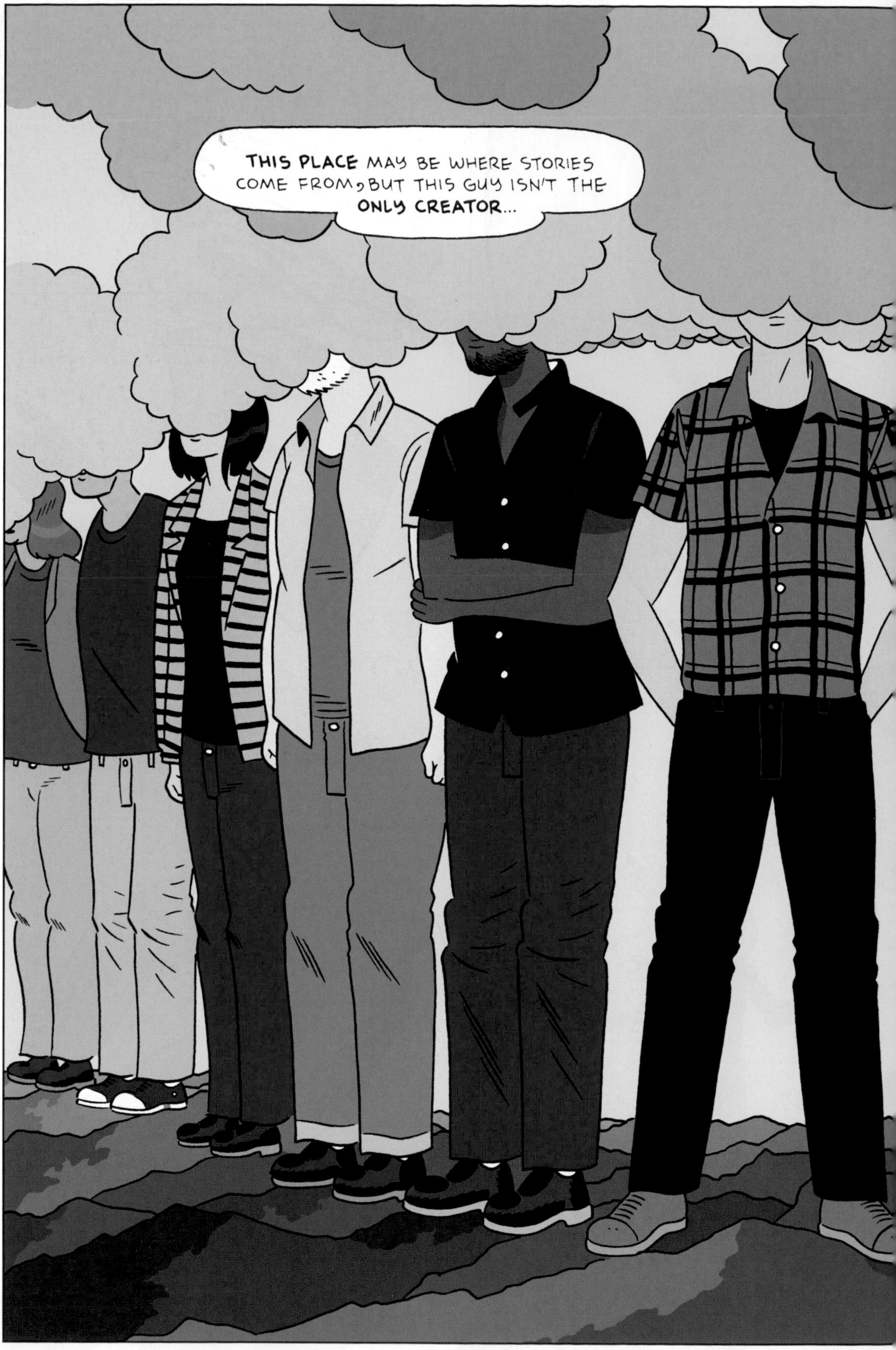
THIS PLACE MAY BE WHERE STORIES COME FROM, BUT THIS GUY ISN'T THE ONLY CREATOR...

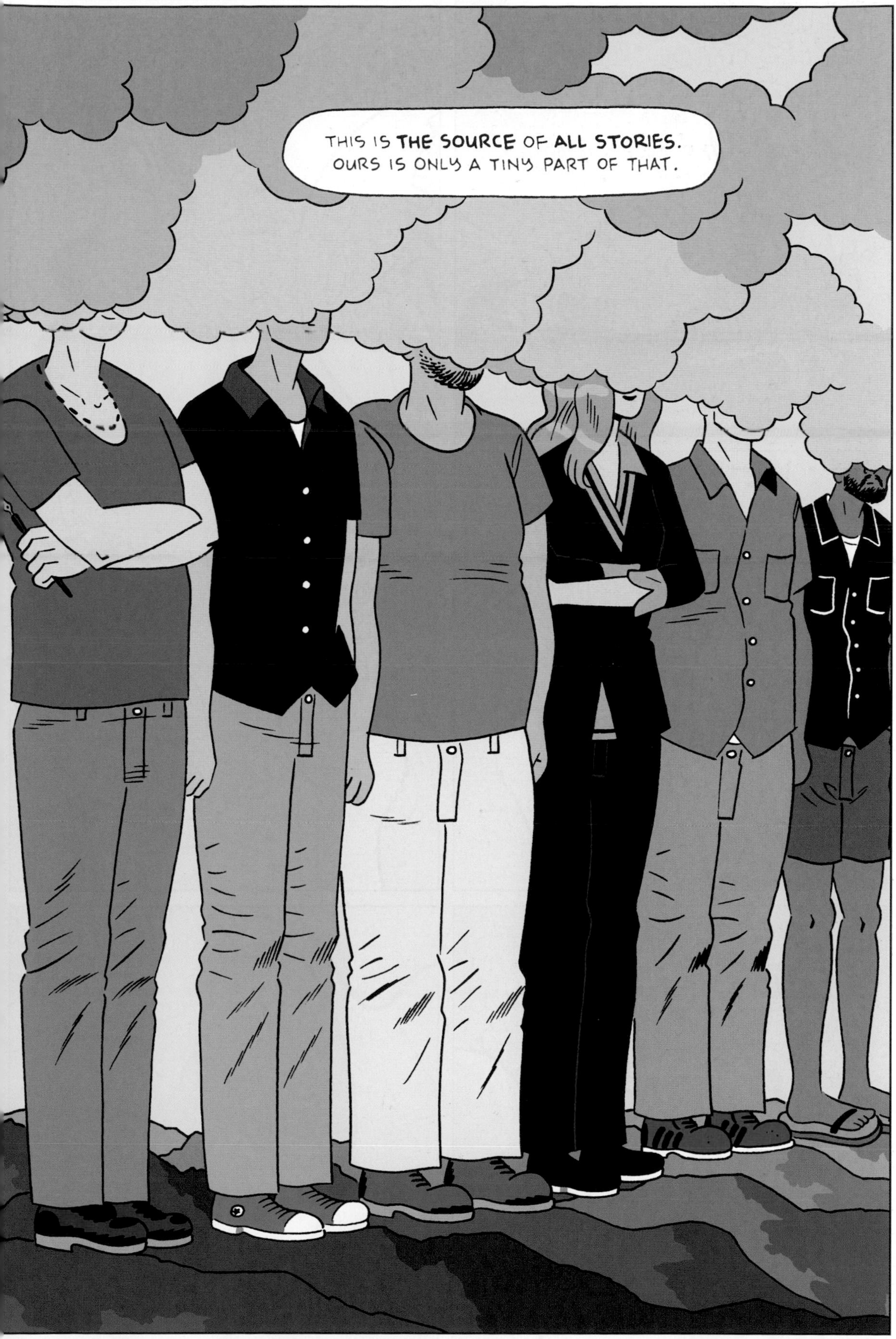
THIS IS **THE SOURCE** OF **ALL STORIES.** OURS IS ONLY A TINY PART OF THAT.

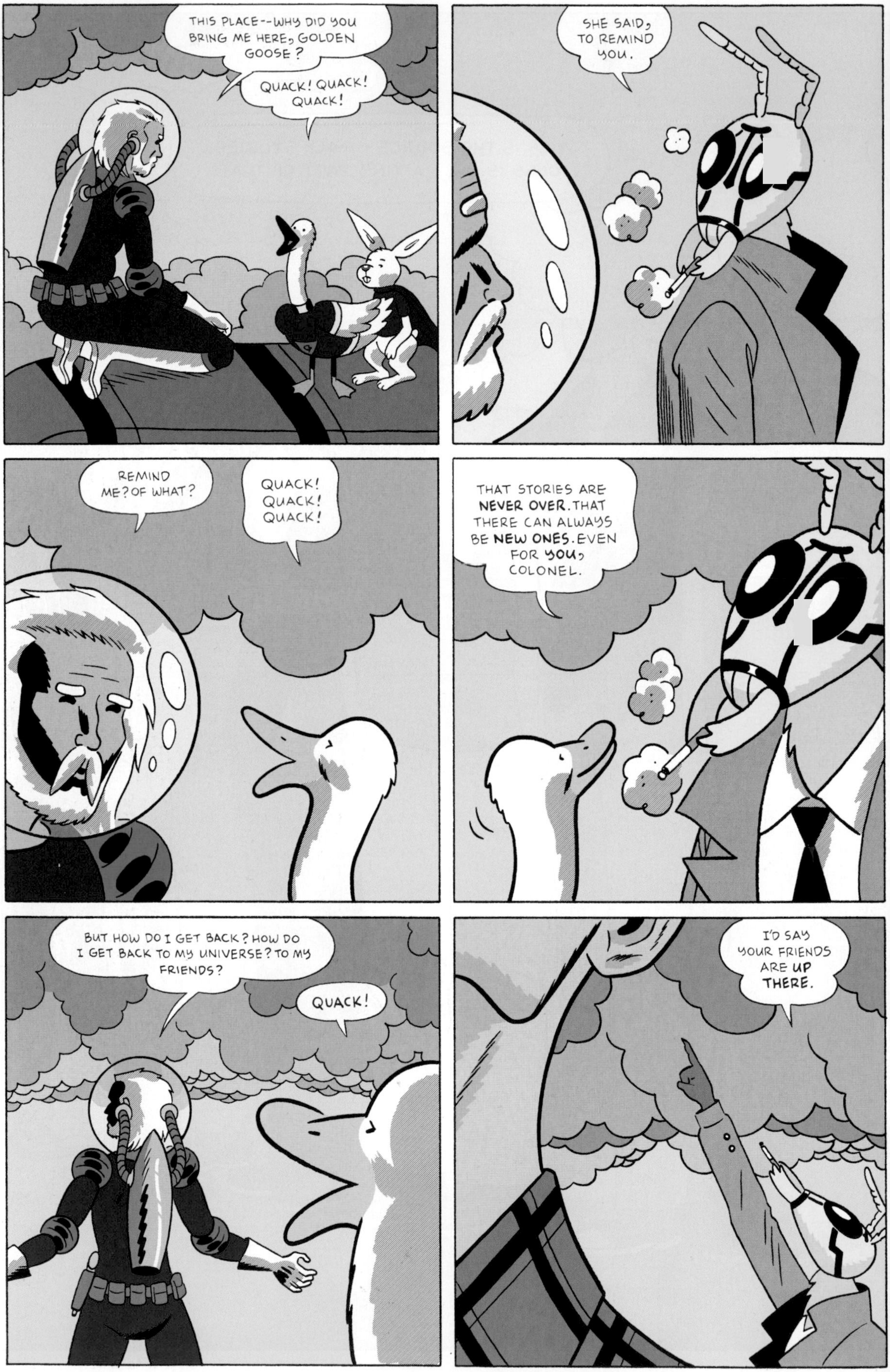
THIS PLACE--WHY DID YOU BRING ME HERE, GOLDEN GOOSE?
QUACK! QUACK! QUACK!
SHE SAID, TO REMIND YOU.
REMIND ME? OF WHAT?
QUACK! QUACK! QUACK!
THAT STORIES ARE NEVER OVER. THAT THERE CAN ALWAYS BE NEW ONES. EVEN FOR YOU, COLONEL.
BUT HOW DO I GET BACK? HOW DO I GET BACK TO MY UNIVERSE? TO MY FRIENDS?
QUACK!
I'D SAY YOUR FRIENDS ARE UP THERE.

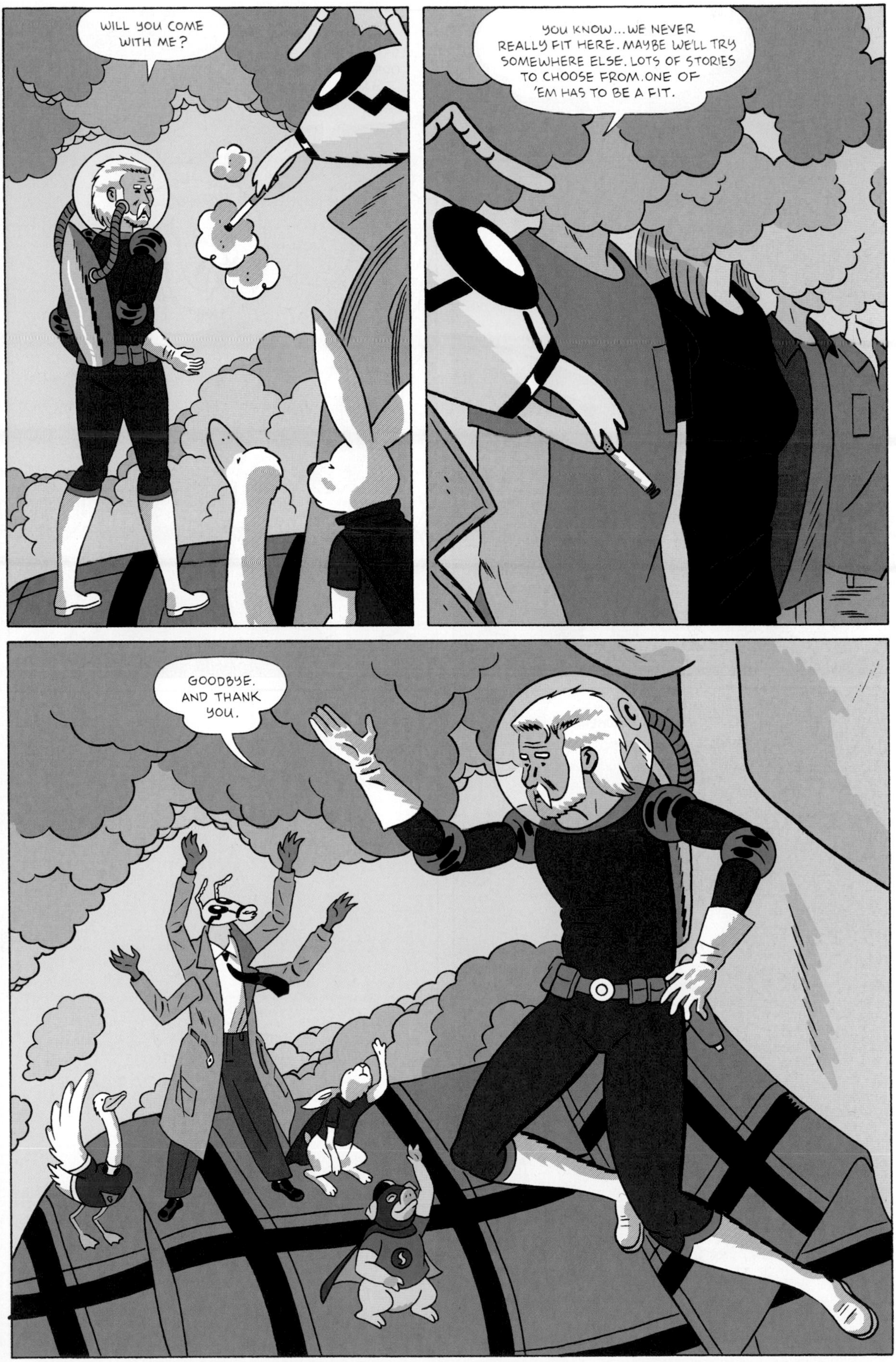
WILL YOU COME WITH ME?
YOU KNOW... WE NEVER REALLY FIT HERE. MAYBE WE'LL TRY SOMEWHERE ELSE. LOTS OF STORIES TO CHOOSE FROM. ONE OF 'EM HAS TO BE A FIT.
GOODBYE. AND THANK YOU.

OINK!

GOOD LUCK, COLONEL. I HOPE YOU FIND YOUR FRIENDS. I HOPE YOU FIND YOUR WAY BACK TO SPIRAL CITY.

SO DO I, INSPECTOR. GOLDEN GOOSE WAS RIGHT. OUR STORY MAY HAVE **CHANGED**, BUT IS NOT FINISHED YET...

I KNOW THEY ARE OUT THERE **SOMEWHERE**.

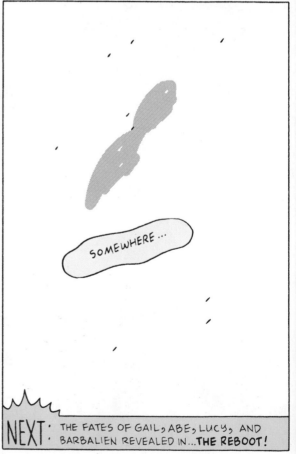

SOMEWHERE...

NEXT: THE FATES OF GAIL, ABE, LUCY, AND BARBALIEN REVEALED IN...**THE REBOOT!**

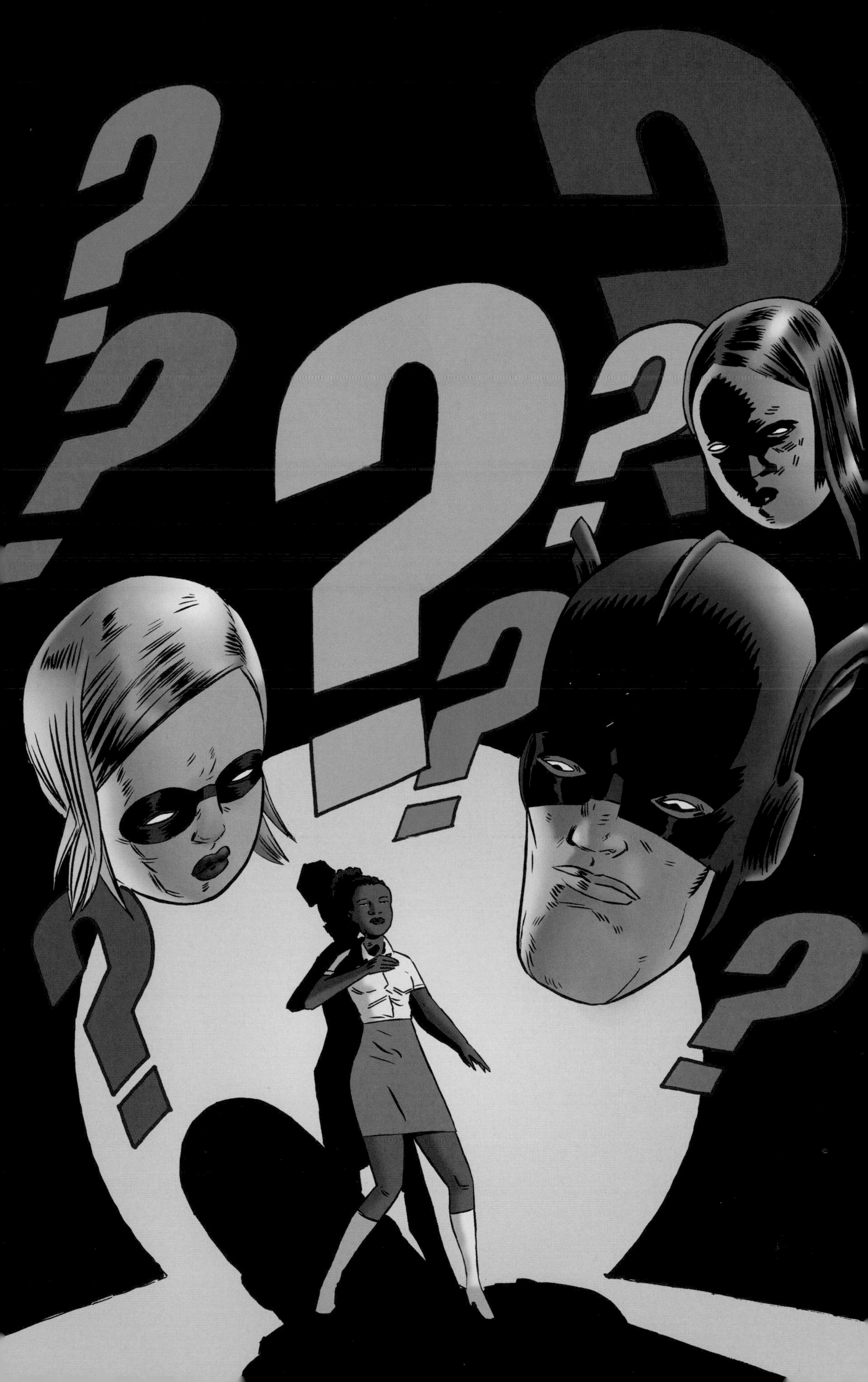

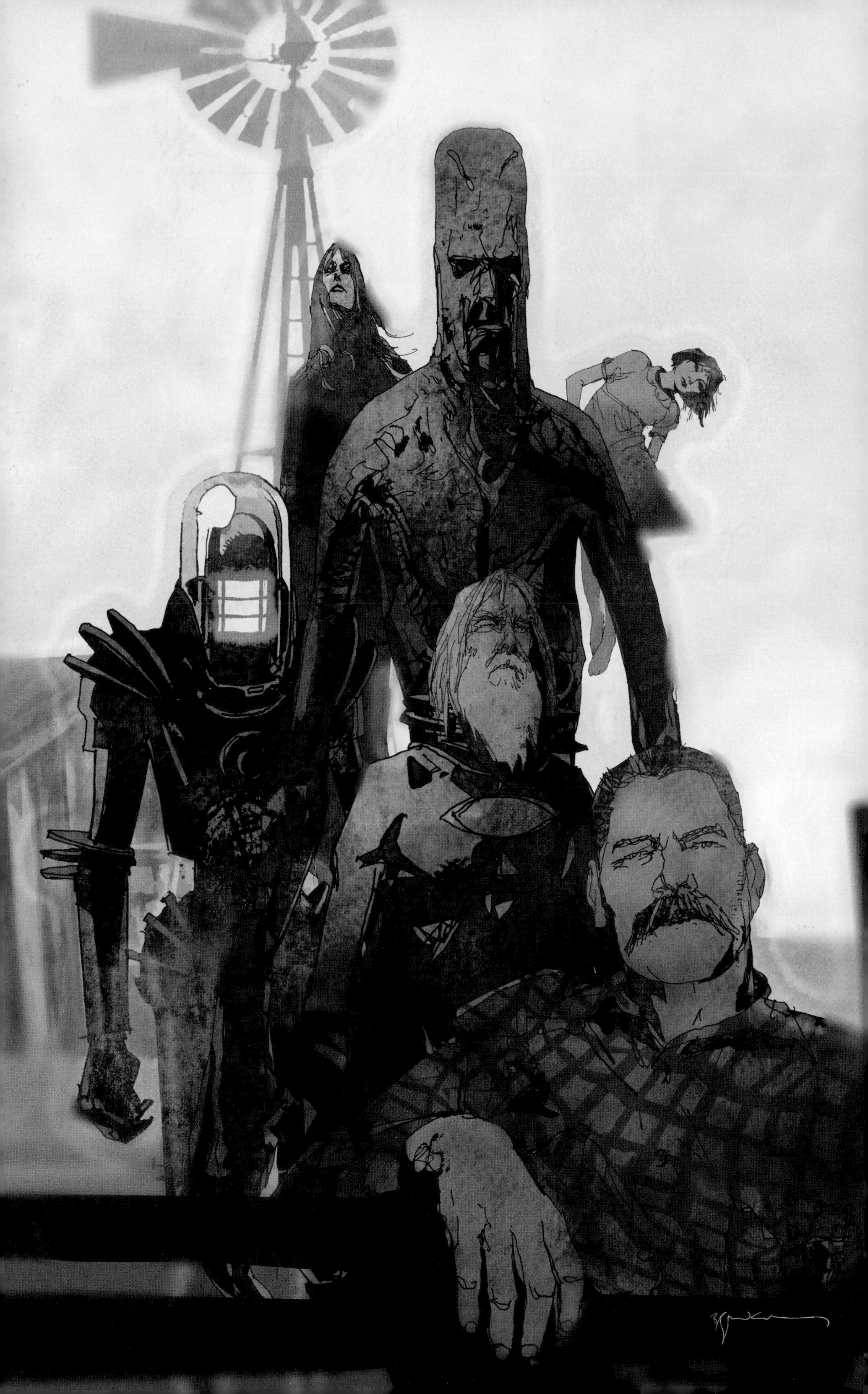

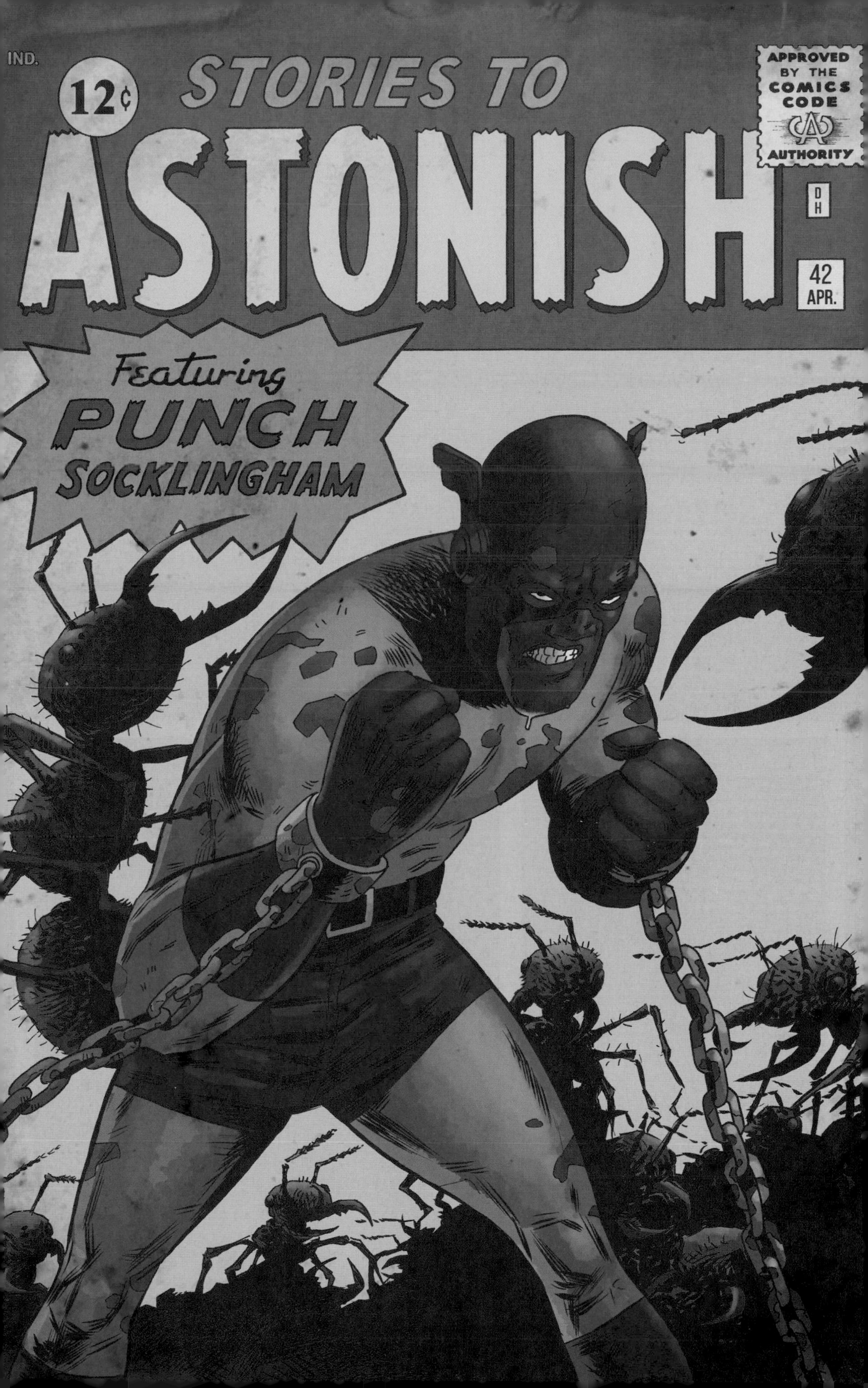

IND.
12¢
STORIES TO
ASTONISH
APPROVED BY THE COMICS CODE AUTHORITY
DH
42
APR.
Featuring
PUNCH
SOCKLINGHAM

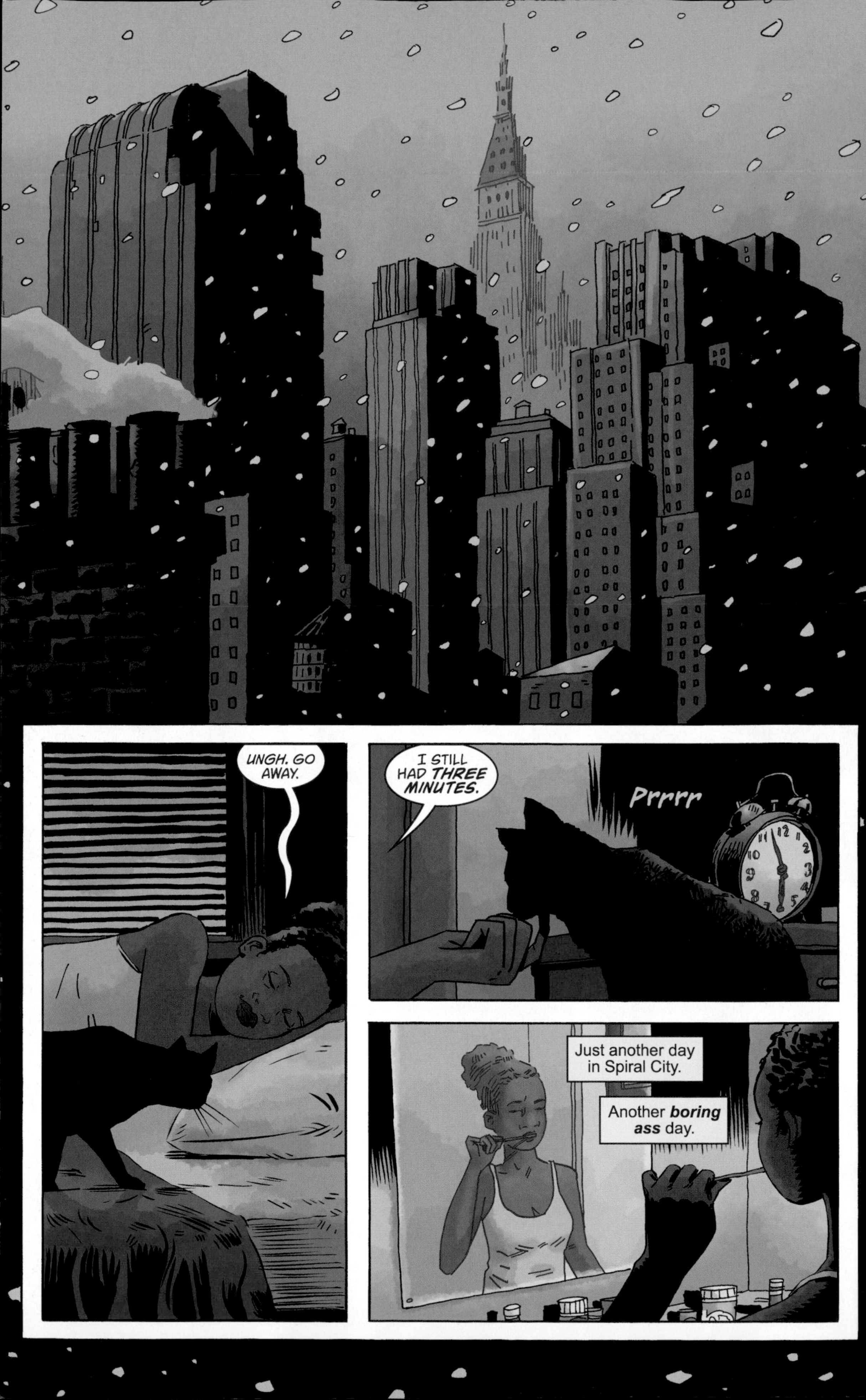
UNGH. GO AWAY.
I STILL HAD THREE MINUTES.
Prrrr
Just another day in Spiral City.
Another boring ass day.

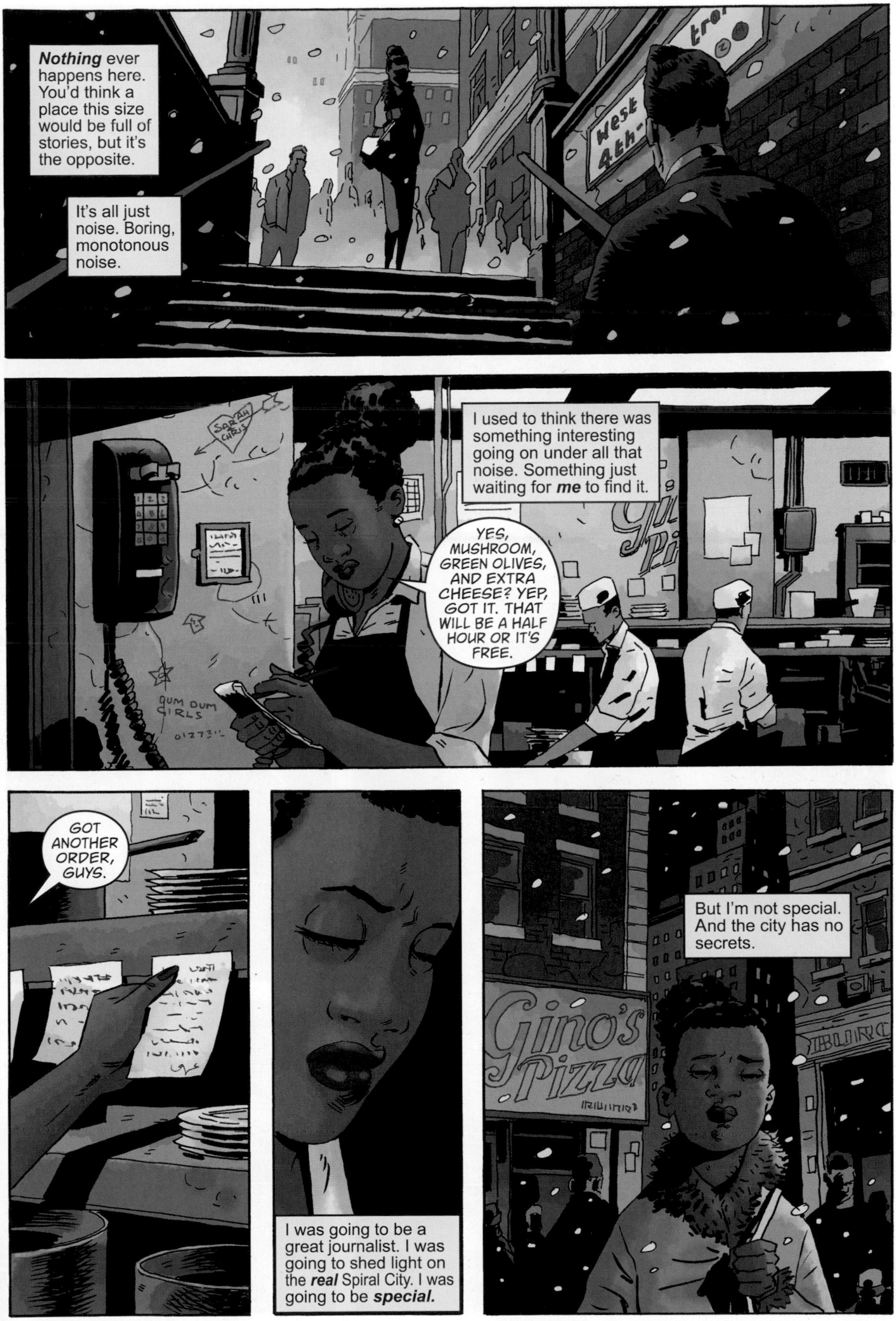

Nothing ever happens here. You'd think a place this size would be full of stories, but it's the opposite.
It's all just noise. Boring, monotonous noise.
West 4th-
I used to think there was something interesting going on under all that noise. Something just waiting for **me** to find it.
YES, MUSHROOM, GREEN OLIVES, AND EXTRA CHEESE? YEP, GOT IT. THAT WILL BE A HALF HOUR OR IT'S FREE.
DUM DUM GIRLS
GOT ANOTHER ORDER, GUYS.
I was going to be a great journalist. I was going to shed light on the ***real*** Spiral City. I was going to be ***special.***
But I'm not special. And the city has no secrets.
Gino's Pizza

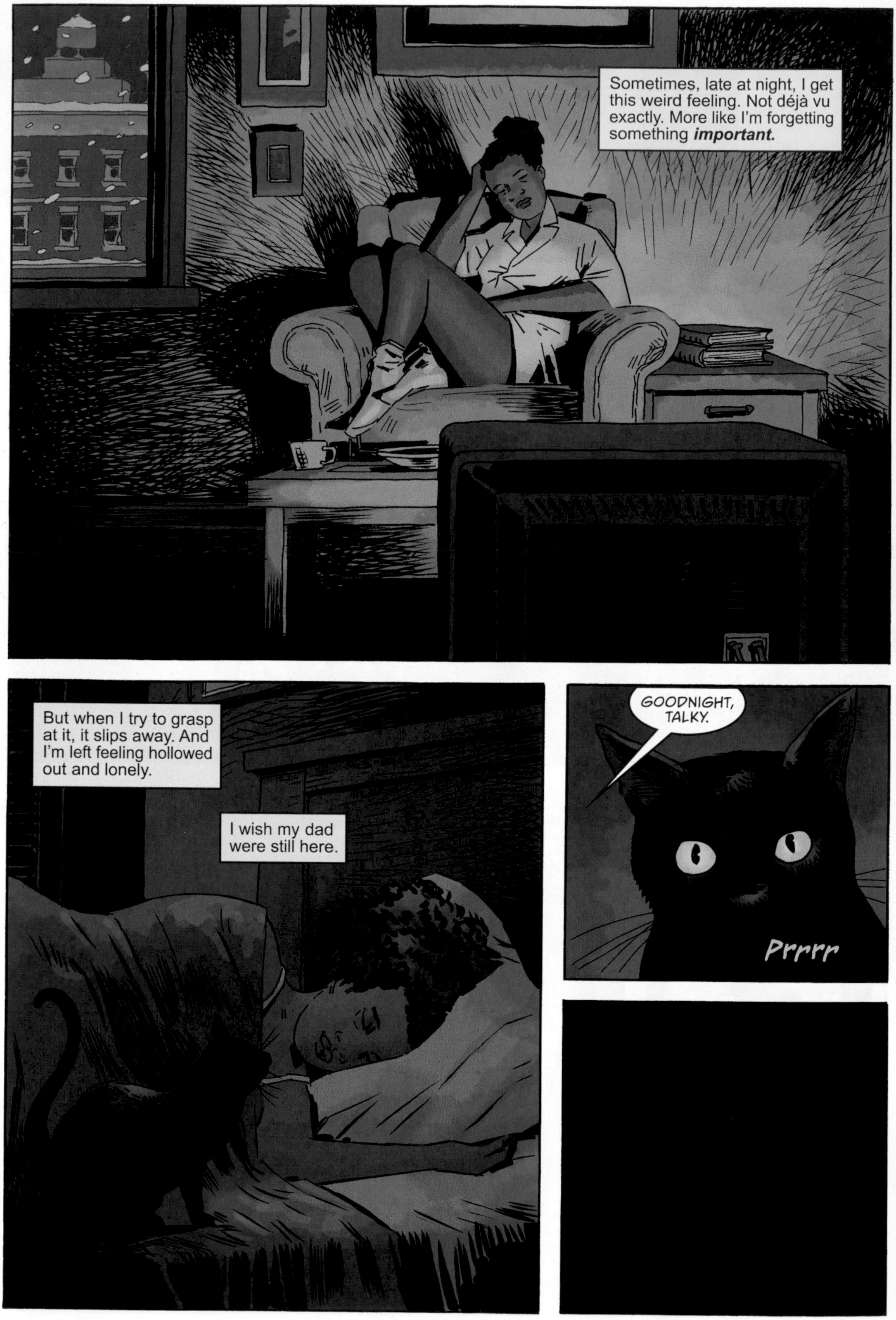
Sometimes, late at night, I get this weird feeling. Not déjà vu exactly. More like I'm forgetting something ***important.***
But when I try to grasp at it, it slips away. And I'm left feeling hollowed out and lonely.
I wish my dad were still here.
GOODNIGHT, TALKY.
Prrrr

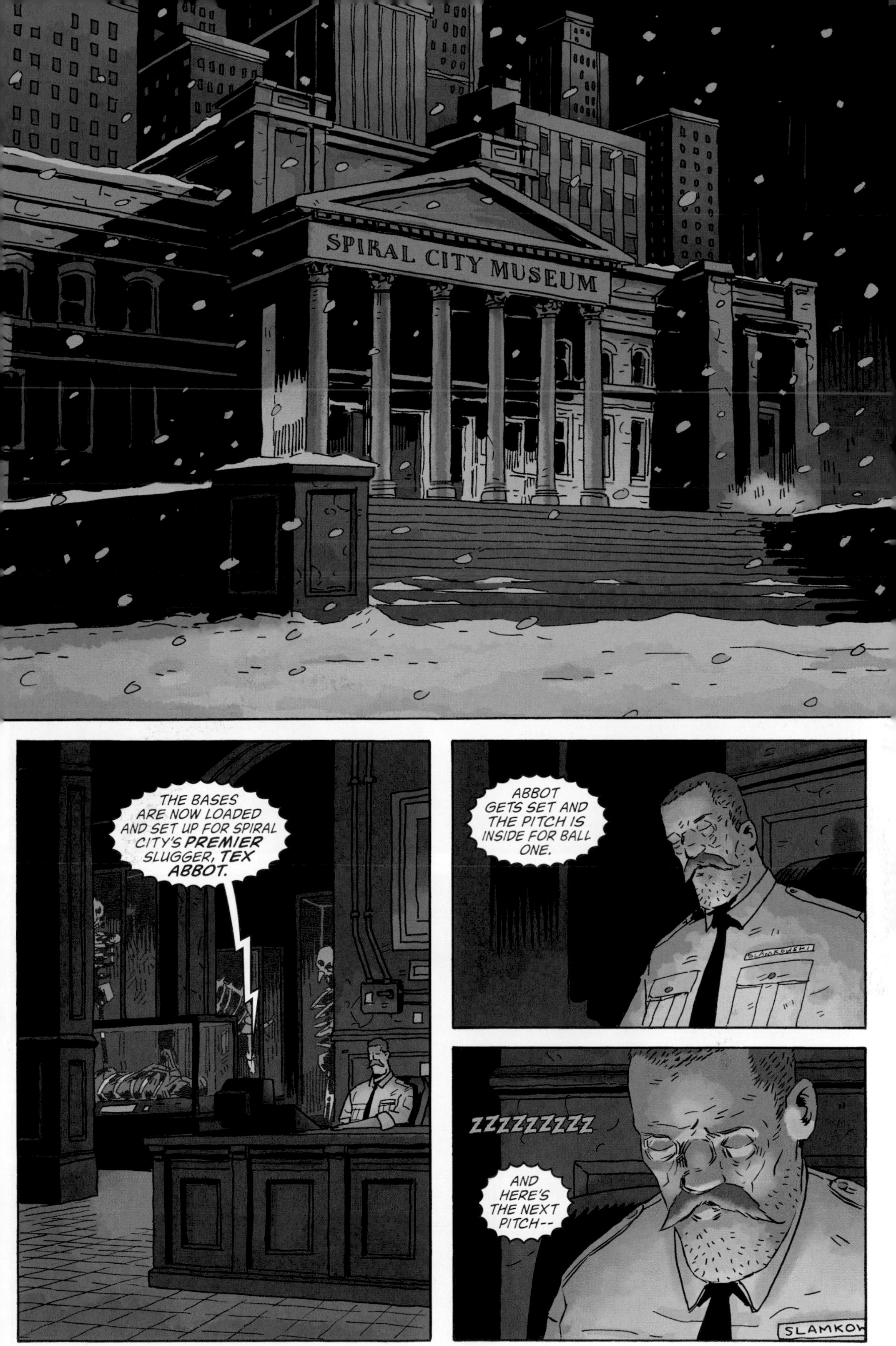
SPIRAL CITY MUSEUM
THE BASES ARE NOW LOADED AND SET UP FOR SPIRAL CITY'S **PREMIER** SLUGGER, **TEX ABBOT**.
ABBOT GETS SET AND THE PITCH IS INSIDE FOR BALL ONE.
ZZZZZZZZ
AND HERE'S THE NEXT PITCH--
SLAMKOW

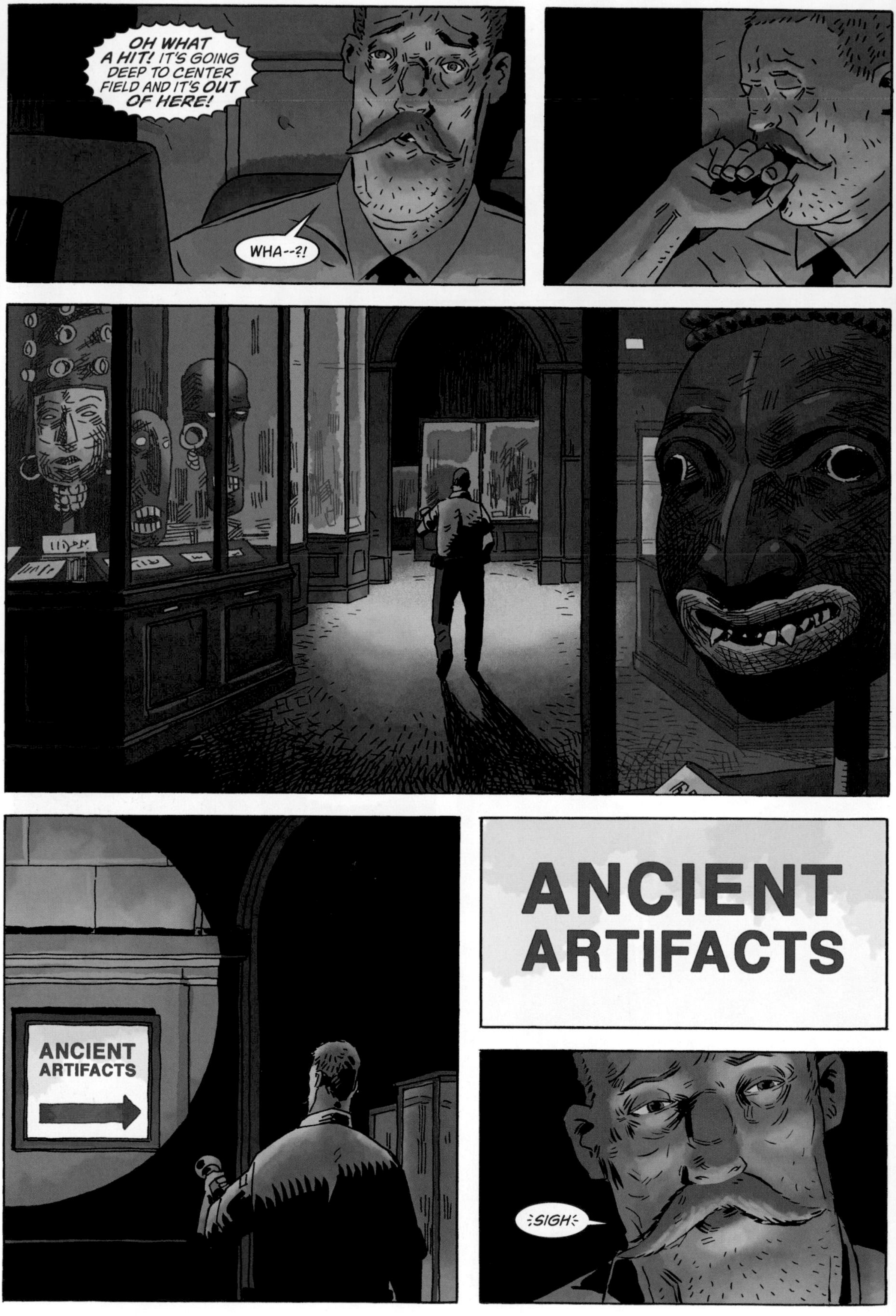
OH WHAT A HIT! IT'S GOING DEEP TO CENTER FIELD AND IT'S OUT OF HERE!
WHA--?!
ANCIENT ARTIFACTS
ANCIENT ARTIFACTS
SIGH

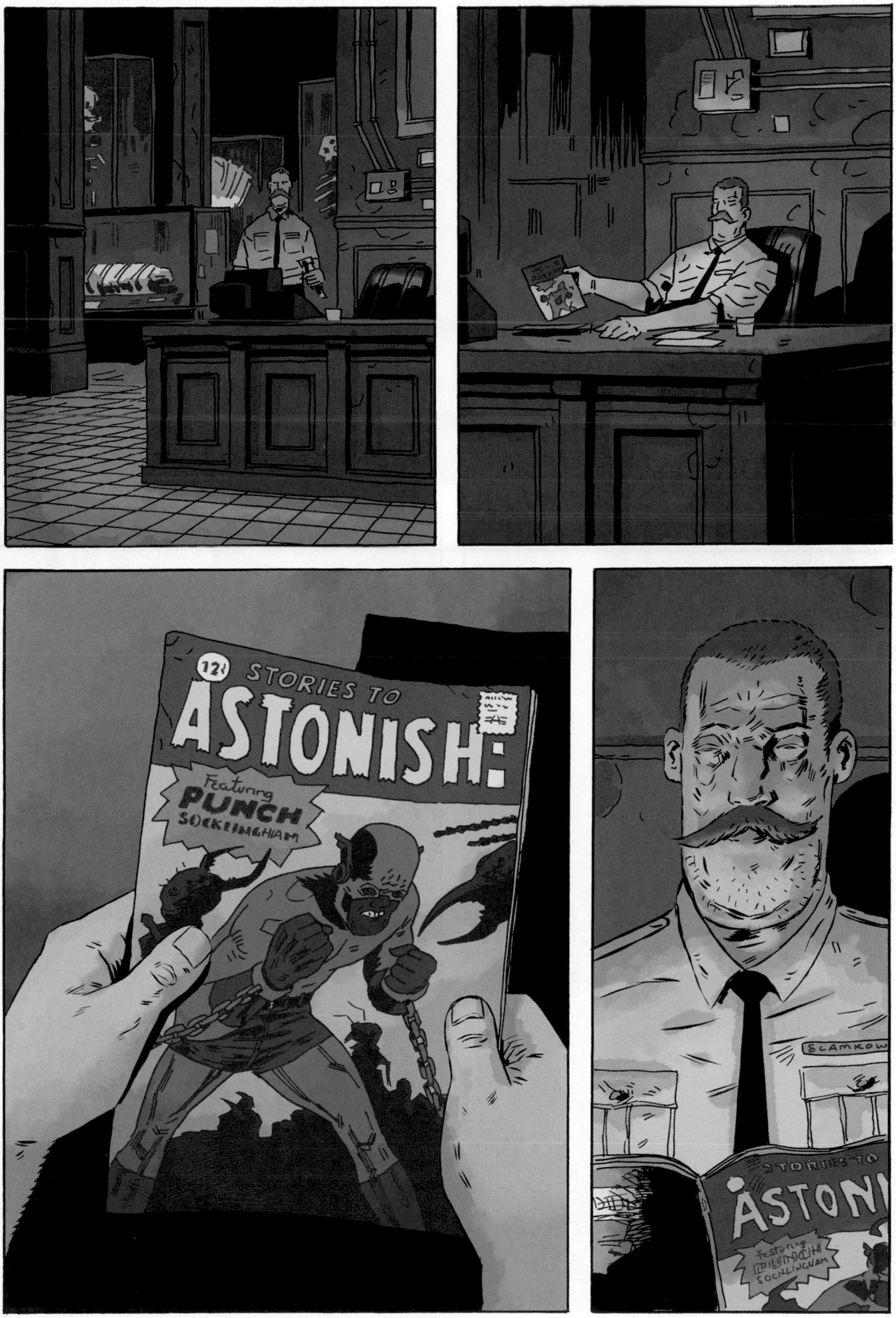
12¢
STORIES TO
ASTONISH:
Featuring
PUNCH
SOCKLINGHAM
SLAMKOW
STORIES TO
ASTONI
Featuring
SOCKLINGHAM

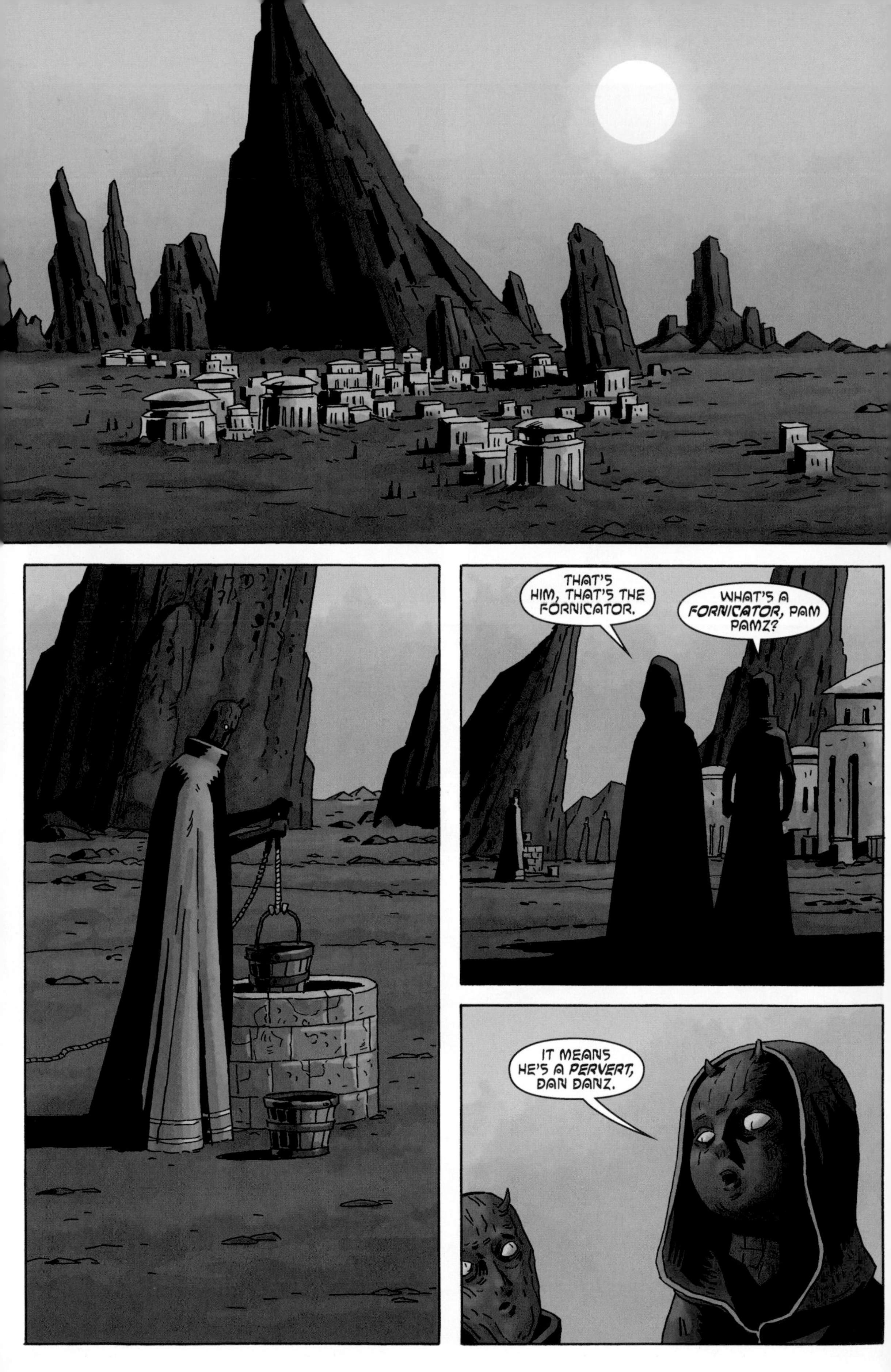
THAT'S HIM, THAT'S THE FORNICATOR.
WHAT'S A *FORNICATOR*, PAM PAMZ?
IT MEANS HE'S A *PERVERT*, DAN DANZ.

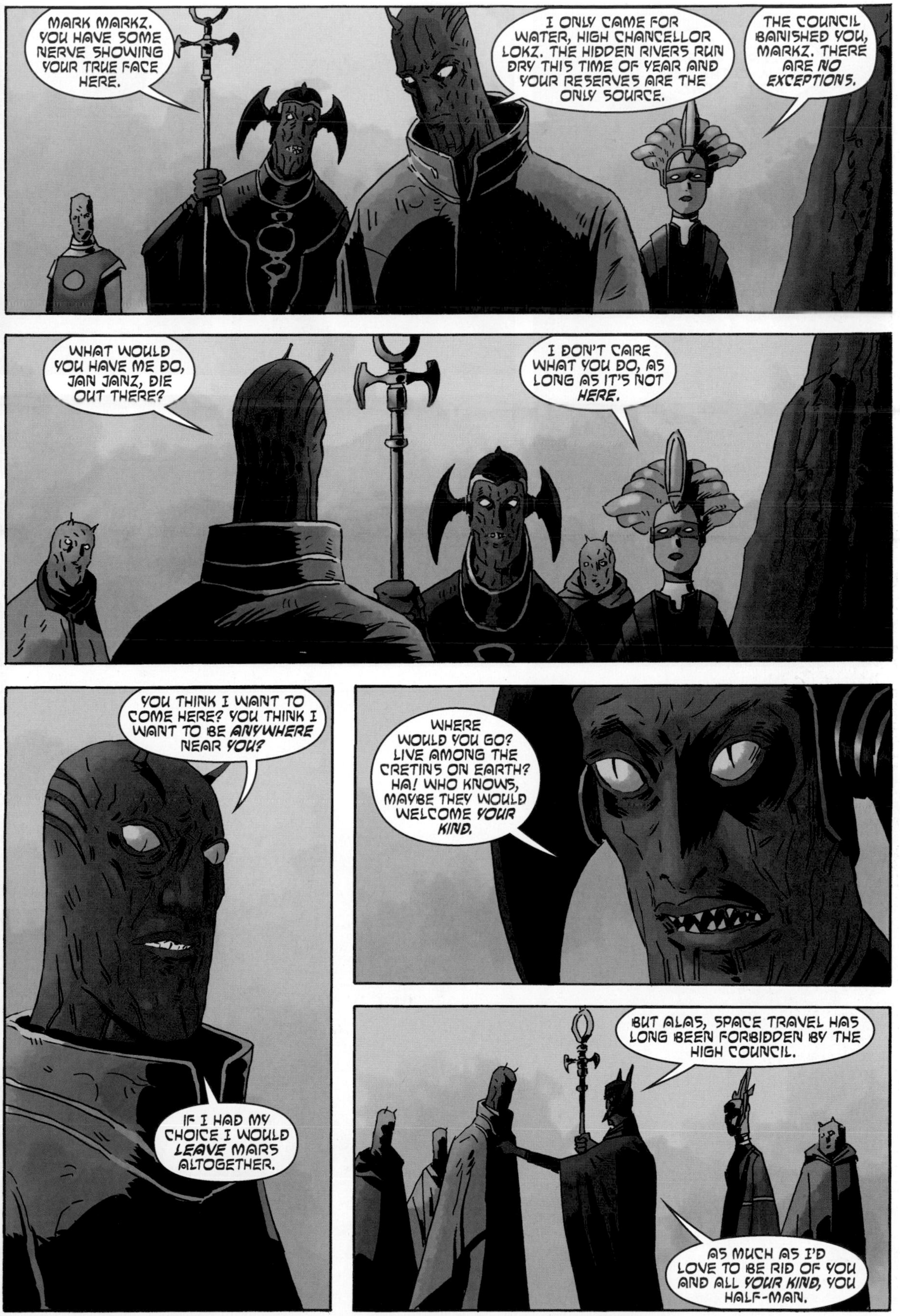
MARK MARKZ. YOU HAVE SOME NERVE SHOWING YOUR TRUE FACE HERE.
I ONLY CAME FOR WATER, HIGH CHANCELLOR LOKZ. THE HIDDEN RIVERS RUN DRY THIS TIME OF YEAR AND YOUR RESERVES ARE THE ONLY SOURCE.
THE COUNCIL BANISHED YOU, MARKZ. THERE ARE *NO EXCEPTIONS.*
WHAT WOULD YOU HAVE ME DO, JAN JANZ, DIE OUT THERE?
I DON'T CARE WHAT YOU DO, AS LONG AS IT'S NOT *HERE.*
YOU THINK I WANT TO COME HERE? YOU THINK I WANT TO BE *ANYWHERE* NEAR *YOU?*
IF I HAD MY CHOICE I WOULD *LEAVE* MARS ALTOGETHER.
WHERE WOULD YOU GO? LIVE AMONG THE CRETINS ON EARTH? HA! WHO KNOWS, MAYBE THEY WOULD WELCOME *YOUR KIND.*
BUT ALAS, SPACE TRAVEL HAS LONG BEEN FORBIDDEN BY THE HIGH COUNCIL.
AS MUCH AS I'D LOVE TO BE RID OF YOU AND ALL *YOUR KIND,* YOU HALF-MAN.

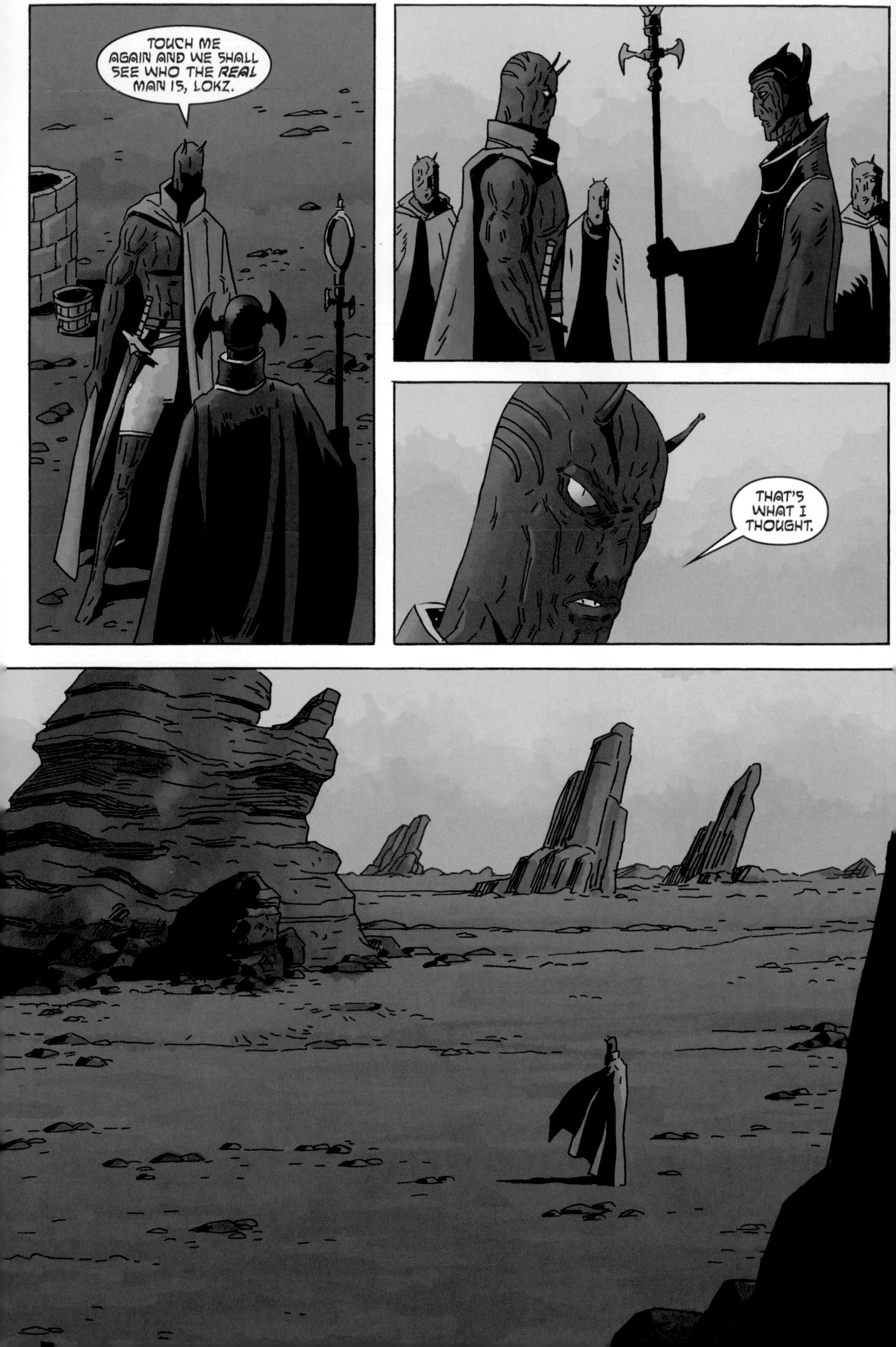
TOUCH ME AGAIN AND WE SHALL SEE WHO THE *REAL* MAN IS, LOKZ.
THAT'S WHAT I THOUGHT.

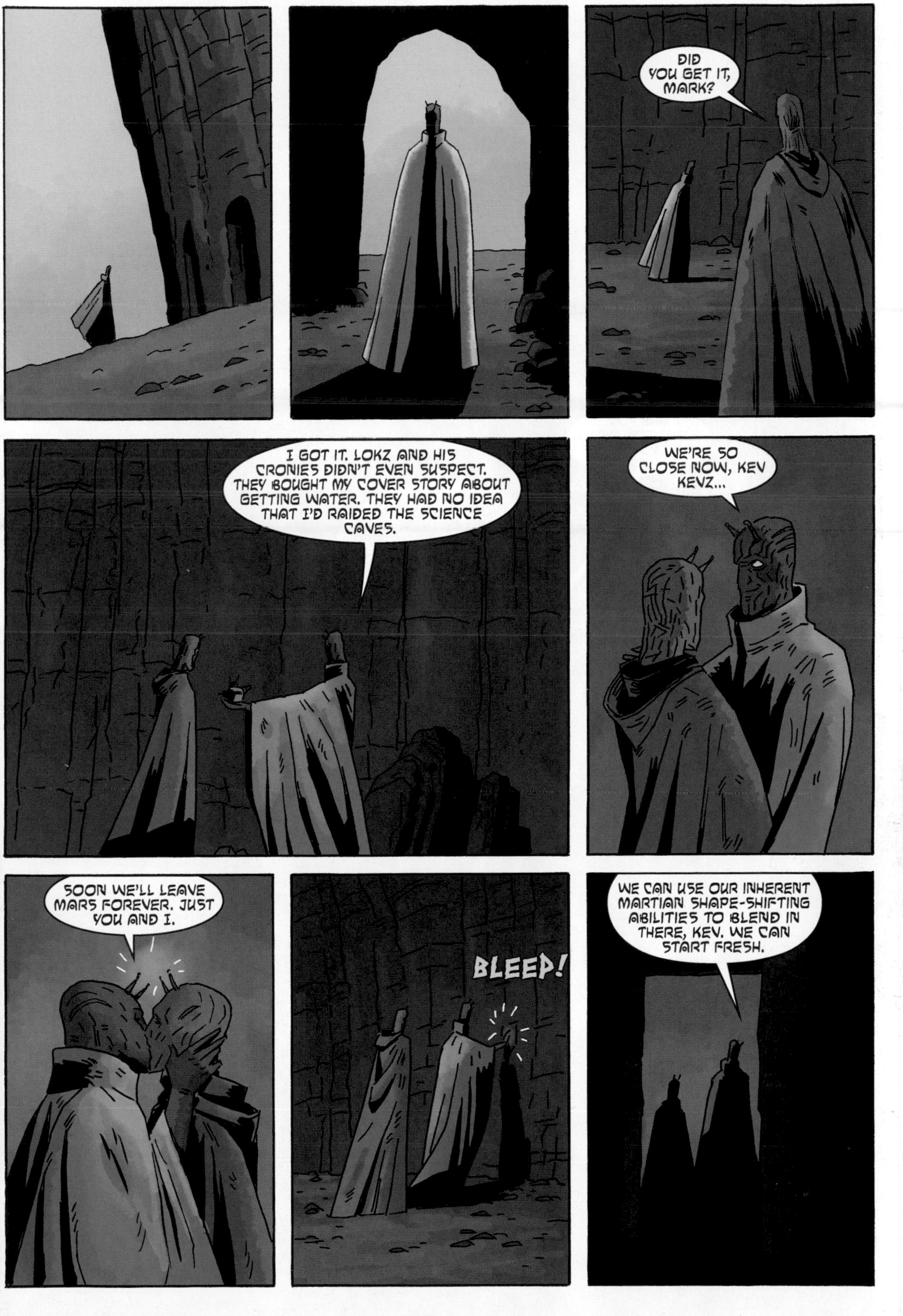
DID YOU GET IT, MARK?
I GOT IT. LOKZ AND HIS CRONIES DIDN'T EVEN SUSPECT. THEY BOUGHT MY COVER STORY ABOUT GETTING WATER. THEY HAD NO IDEA THAT I'D RAIDED THE SCIENCE CAVES.
WE'RE SO CLOSE NOW, KEV KEVZ...
SOON WE'LL LEAVE MARS FOREVER. JUST YOU AND I.
BLEEP!
WE CAN USE OUR INHERENT MARTIAN SHAPE-SHIFTING ABILITIES TO BLEND IN THERE, KEV. WE CAN START FRESH.

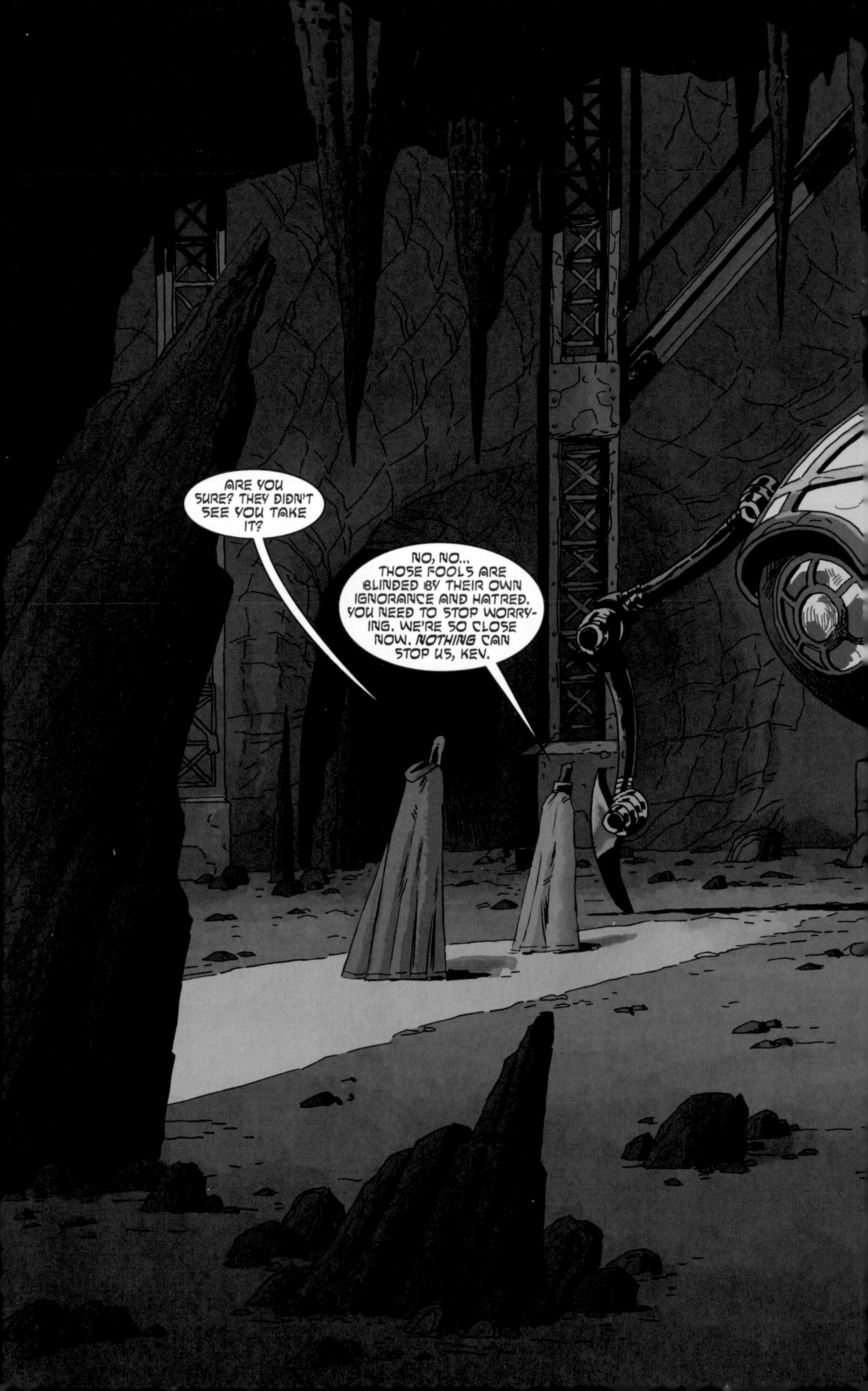
ARE YOU SURE? THEY DIDN'T SEE YOU TAKE IT?
NO, NO... THOSE FOOLS ARE BLINDED BY THEIR OWN IGNORANCE AND HATRED. YOU NEED TO STOP WORRYING. WE'RE SO CLOSE NOW. *NOTHING* CAN STOP US, KEV.

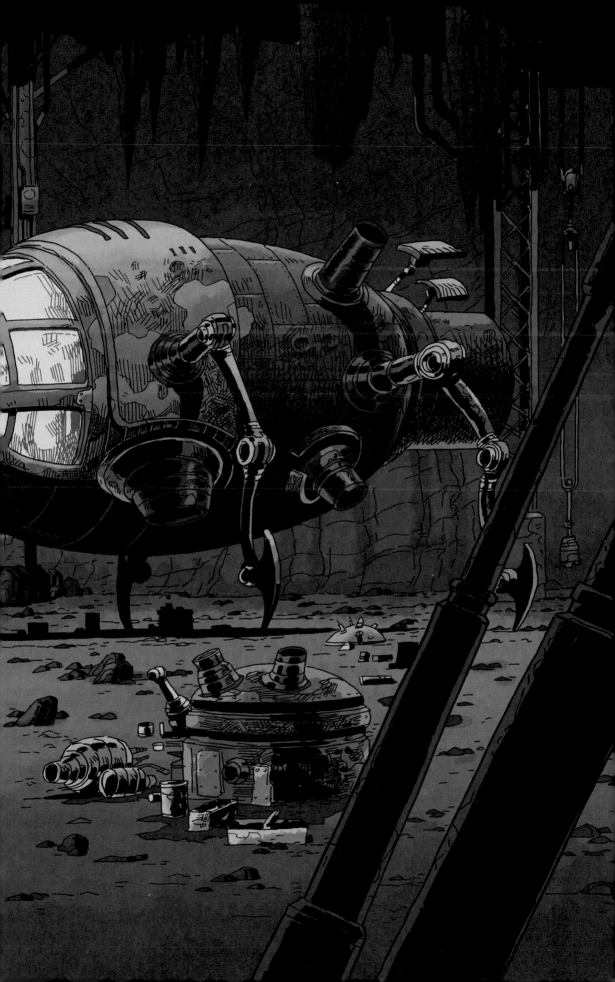

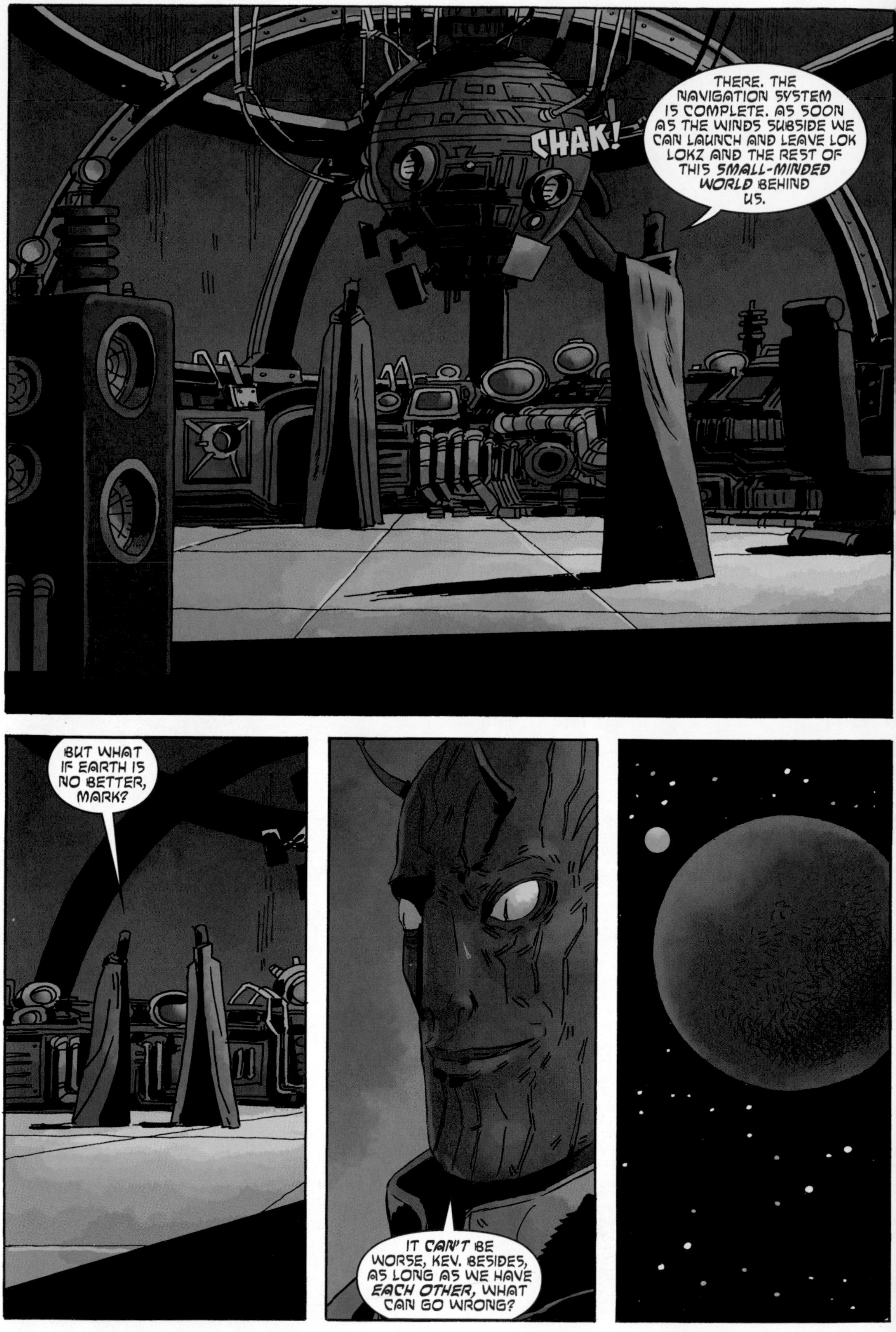
CHAK!
THERE. THE NAVIGATION SYSTEM IS COMPLETE. AS SOON AS THE WINDS SUBSIDE WE CAN LAUNCH AND LEAVE LOK LOKZ AND THE REST OF THIS SMALL-MINDED WORLD BEHIND US.
BUT WHAT IF EARTH IS NO BETTER, MARK?
IT CAN'T BE WORSE, KEV. BESIDES, AS LONG AS WE HAVE EACH OTHER, WHAT CAN GO WRONG?

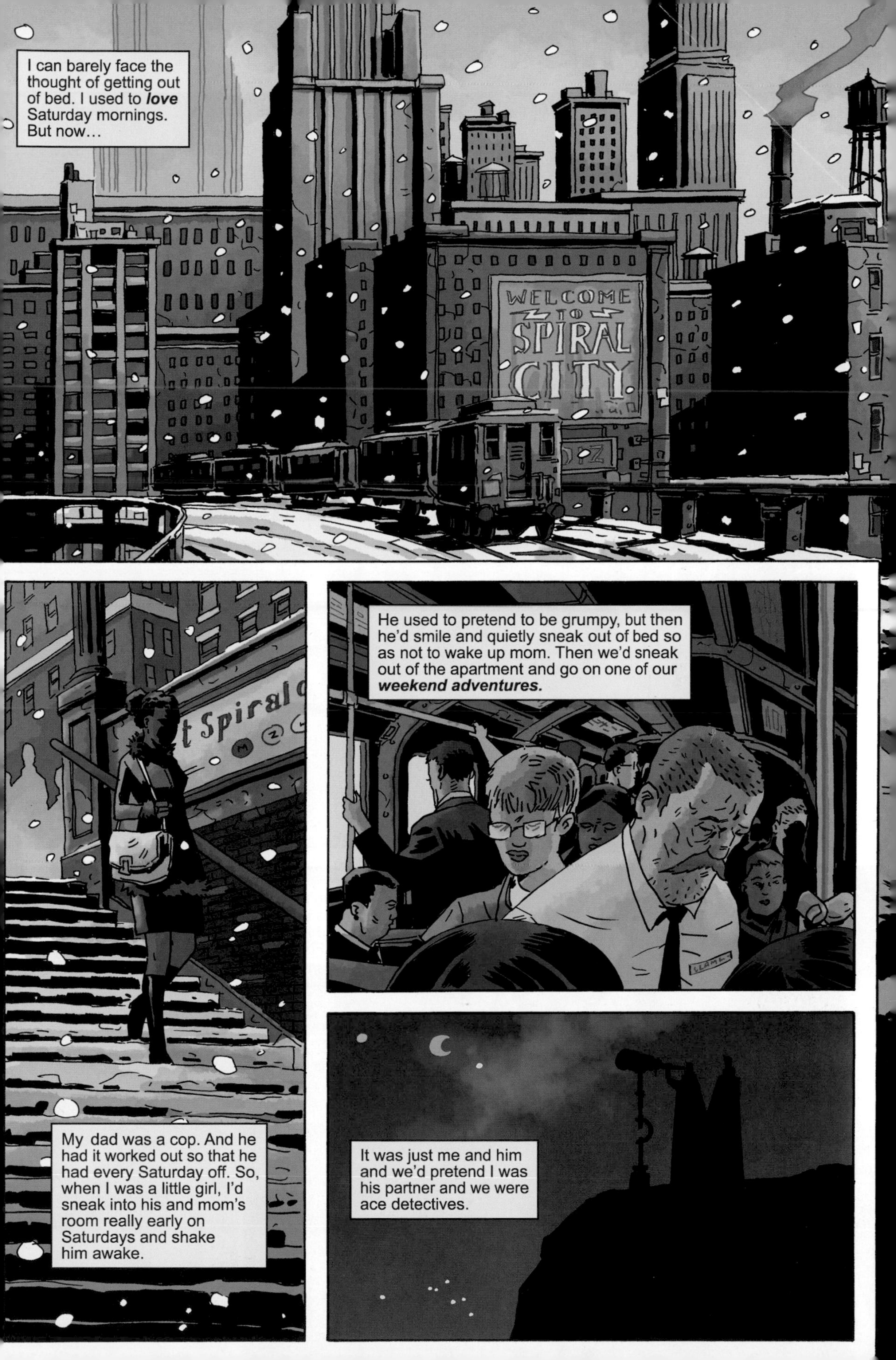
I can barely face the thought of getting out of bed. I used to ***love*** Saturday mornings. But now…
WELCOME TO SPIRAL CITY
My dad was a cop. And he had it worked out so that he had every Saturday off. So, when I was a little girl, I'd sneak into his and mom's room really early on Saturdays and shake him awake.
He used to pretend to be grumpy, but then he'd smile and quietly sneak out of bed so as not to wake up mom. Then we'd sneak out of the apartment and go on one of our ***weekend adventures.***
It was just me and him and we'd pretend I was his partner and we were ace detectives.

It was silly, really, but we'd go get a greasy breakfast and come up with an imaginary crime we could solve that day.

Then we'd spend the weekend finding "clues."

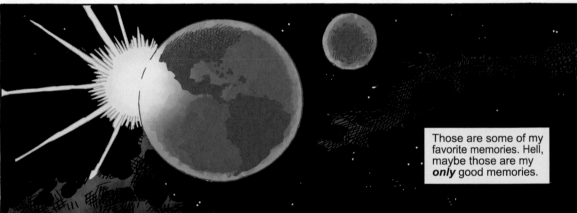

Those are some of my favorite memories. Hell, maybe those are my *only* good memories.

When I turned thirteen my dad was killed. He was a downtown cop and he responded to a domestic abuse call late one Friday night…

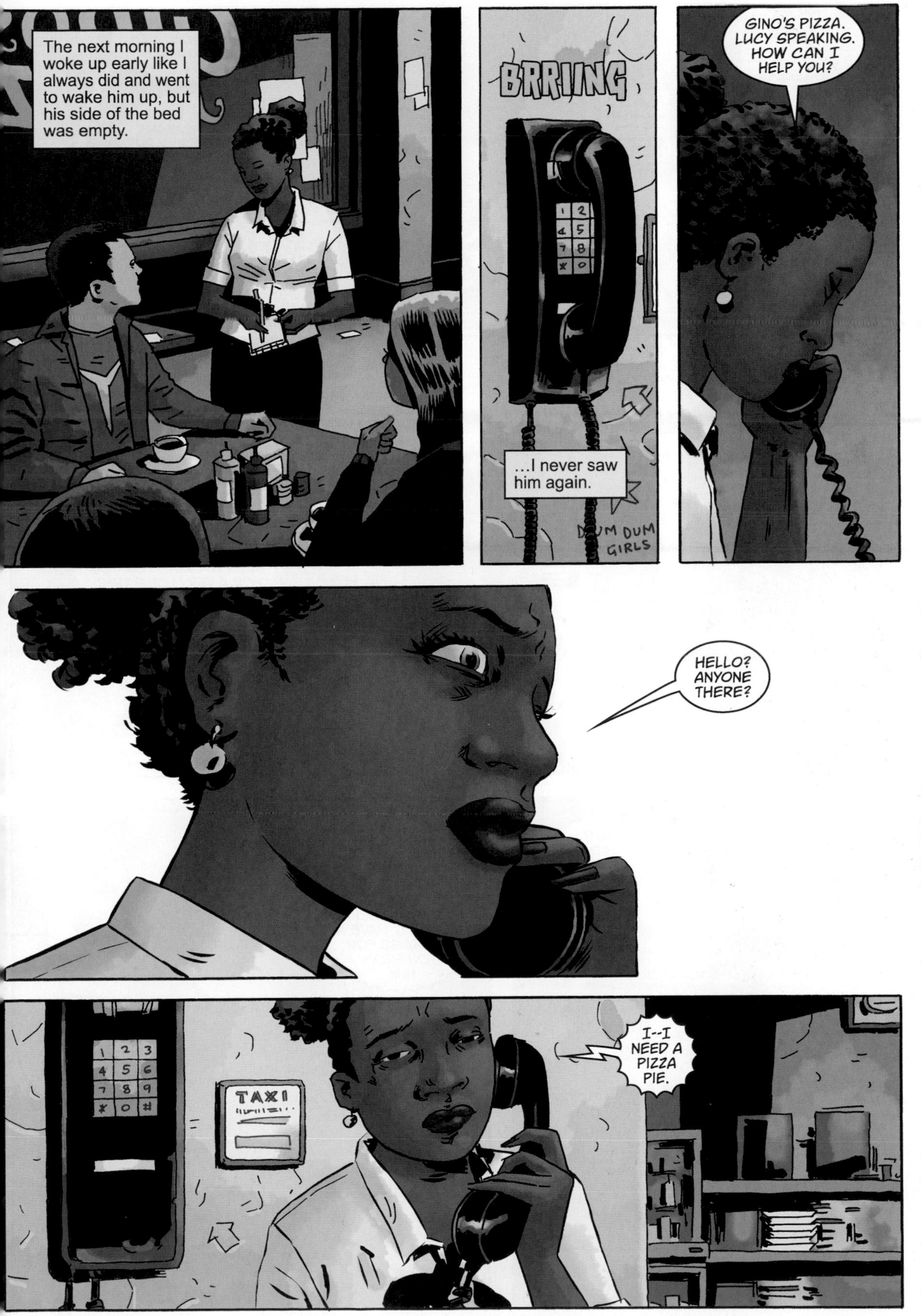
The next morning I woke up early like I always did and went to wake him up, but his side of the bed was empty.
BRRIING
...I never saw him again.
DUM DUM GIRLS
GINO'S PIZZA. LUCY SPEAKING. HOW CAN I HELP YOU?
HELLO? ANYONE THERE?
TAXI
I--I NEED A PIZZA PIE.

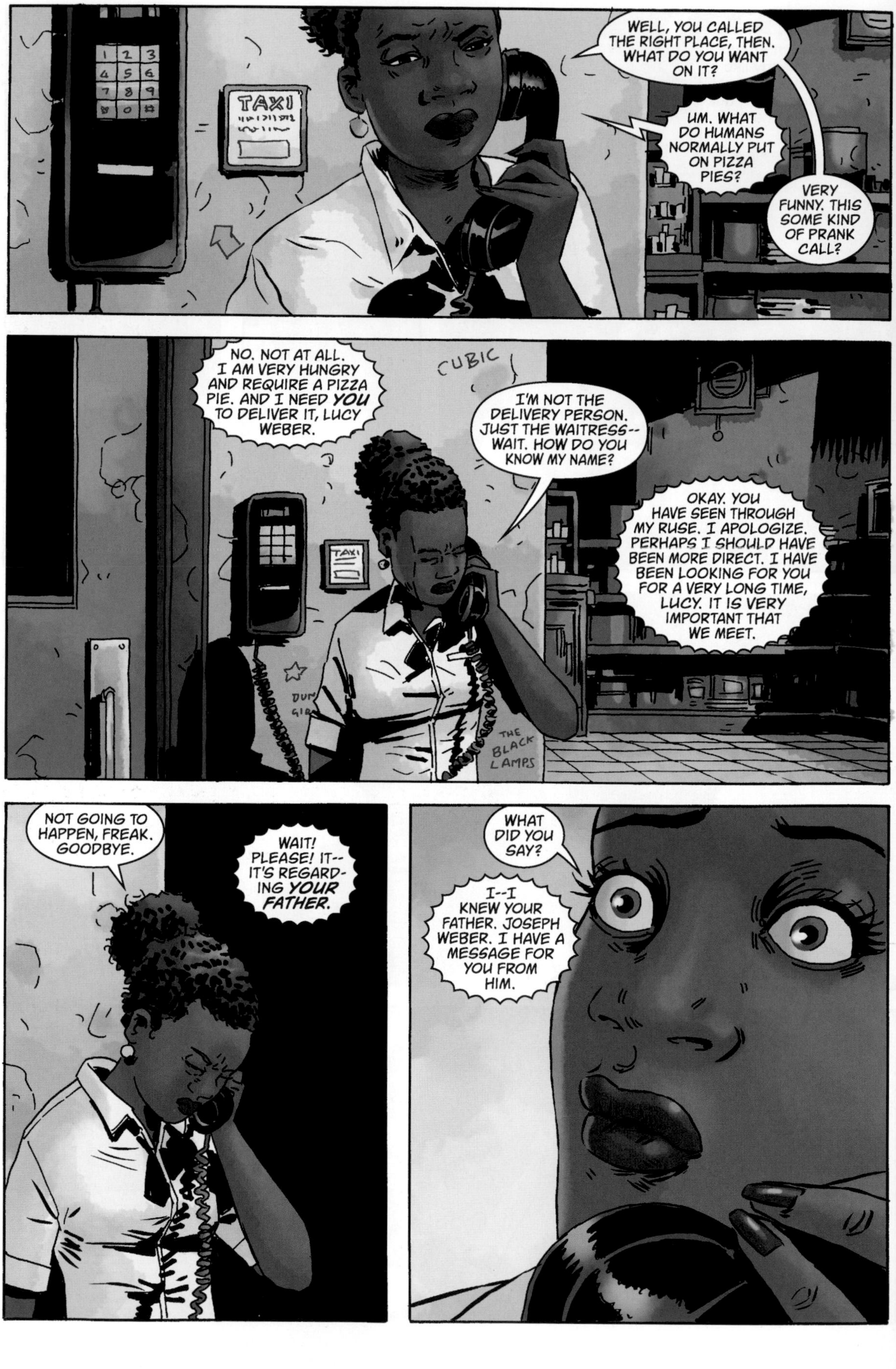
TAXI
WELL, YOU CALLED THE RIGHT PLACE, THEN. WHAT DO YOU WANT ON IT?
UM. WHAT DO HUMANS NORMALLY PUT ON PIZZA PIES?
VERY FUNNY. THIS SOME KIND OF PRANK CALL?
NO. NOT AT ALL. I AM VERY HUNGRY AND REQUIRE A PIZZA PIE. AND I NEED YOU TO DELIVER IT, LUCY WEBER.
CUBIC
I'M NOT THE DELIVERY PERSON. JUST THE WAITRESS-- WAIT. HOW DO YOU KNOW MY NAME?
OKAY. YOU HAVE SEEN THROUGH MY RUSE. I APOLOGIZE. PERHAPS I SHOULD HAVE BEEN MORE DIRECT. I HAVE BEEN LOOKING FOR YOU FOR A VERY LONG TIME, LUCY. IT IS VERY IMPORTANT THAT WE MEET.
THE BLACK LAMPS
NOT GOING TO HAPPEN, FREAK. GOODBYE.
WAIT! PLEASE! IT-- IT'S REGARDING YOUR FATHER.
WHAT DID YOU SAY?
I--I KNEW YOUR FATHER. JOSEPH WEBER. I HAVE A MESSAGE FOR YOU FROM HIM.

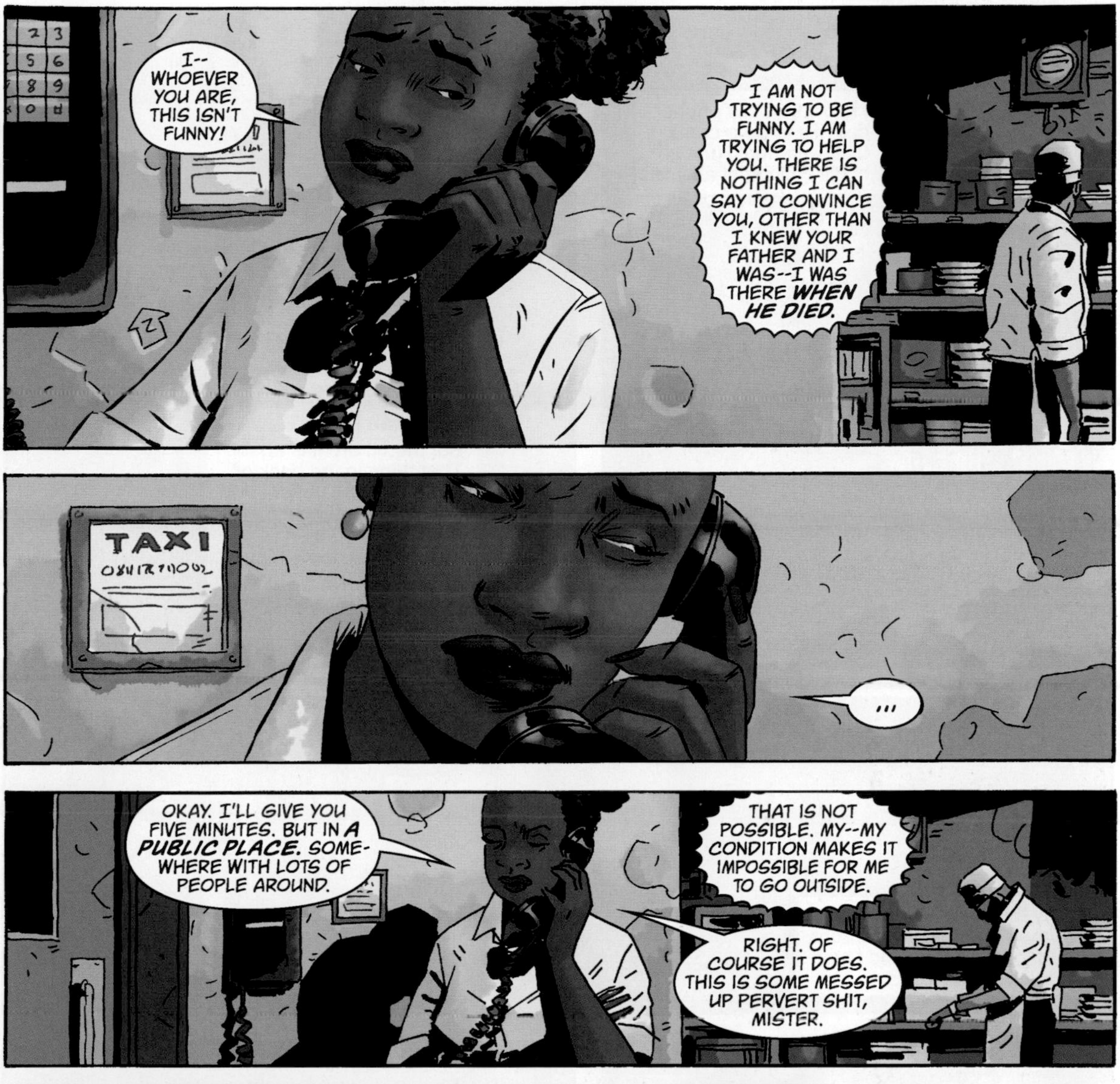
I-- WHOEVER YOU ARE, THIS ISN'T FUNNY!
I AM NOT TRYING TO BE FUNNY. I AM TRYING TO HELP YOU. THERE IS NOTHING I CAN SAY TO CONVINCE YOU, OTHER THAN I KNEW YOUR FATHER AND I WAS--I WAS THERE ***WHEN HE DIED.***
TAXI
...
OKAY. I'LL GIVE YOU FIVE MINUTES. BUT IN ***A PUBLIC PLACE.*** SOME-WHERE WITH LOTS OF PEOPLE AROUND.
THAT IS NOT POSSIBLE. MY--MY CONDITION MAKES IT IMPOSSIBLE FOR ME TO GO OUTSIDE.
RIGHT. OF COURSE IT DOES. THIS IS SOME MESSED UP PERVERT SHIT, MISTER.
I AM NO PERVERT AND I AM NO ***MISTER.*** I HAVE SAID ALL I CAN OVER THE PHONE. I AM AT 181 CARLAW AVENUE, APARTMENT 308. THE CHOICE IS YOURS. BUT I TRULY HOPE YOU DECIDE TO COME, LUCY. WHAT I HAVE TO TELL YOU WILL ***CHANGE YOUR LIFE.***
CLICK
HELLO?

What was that I said about there being ***no secrets*** in Spiral City?

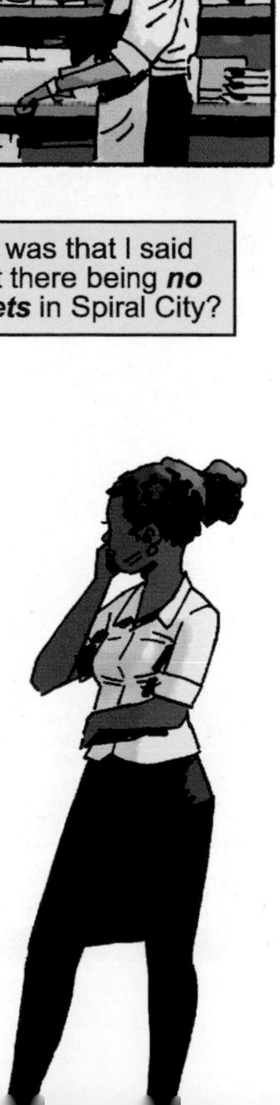

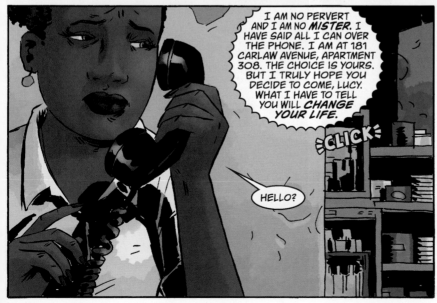

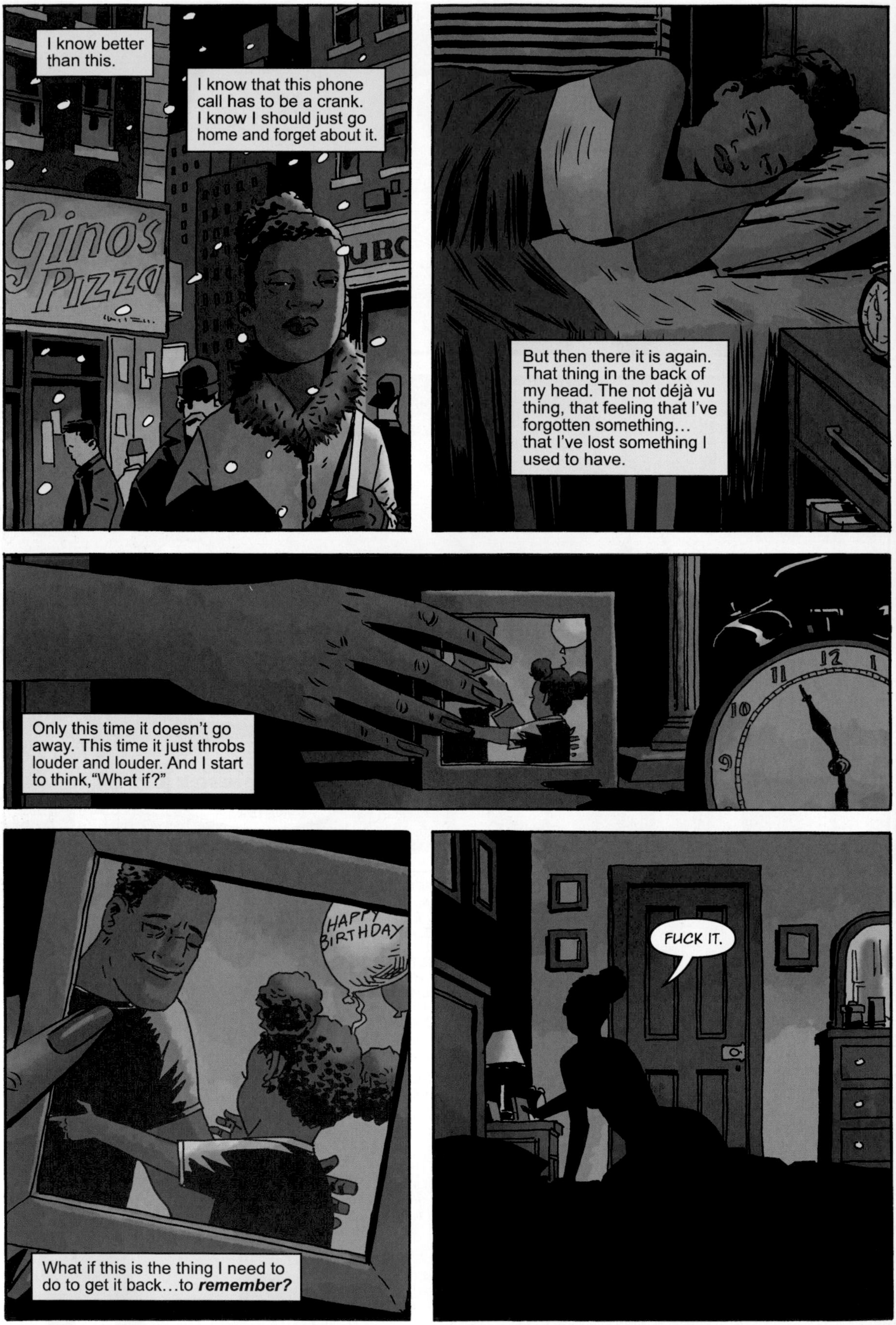
I know better than this.
I know that this phone call has to be a crank. I know I should just go home and forget about it.
GINO'S PIZZA
But then there it is again. That thing in the back of my head. The not déjà vu thing, that feeling that I've forgotten something… that I've lost something I used to have.
Only this time it doesn't go away. This time it just throbs louder and louder. And I start to think,"What if?"
HAPPY BIRTHDAY
What if this is the thing I need to do to get it back…to ***remember?***
FUCK IT.

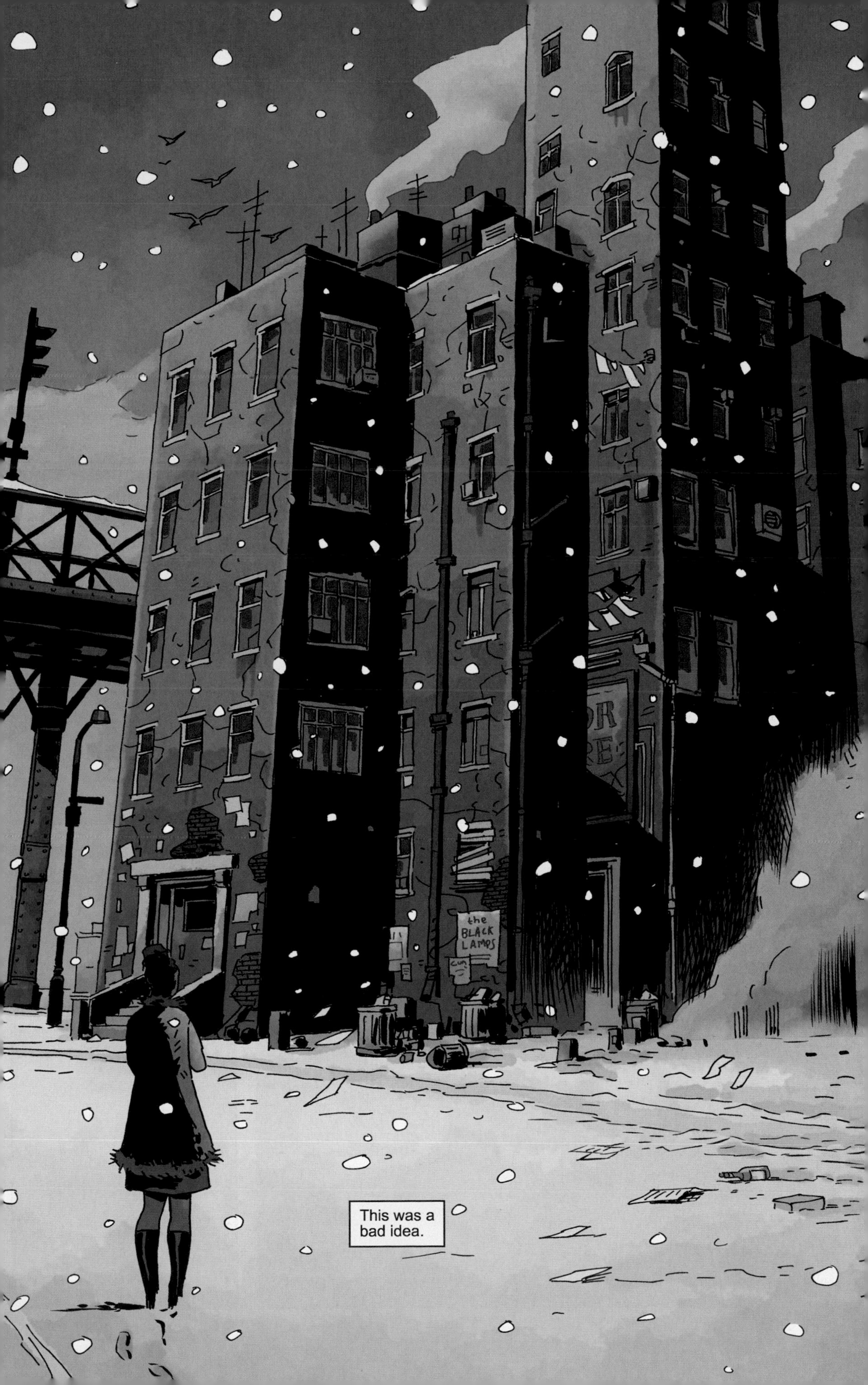
the BLACK LAMPS
This was a bad idea.

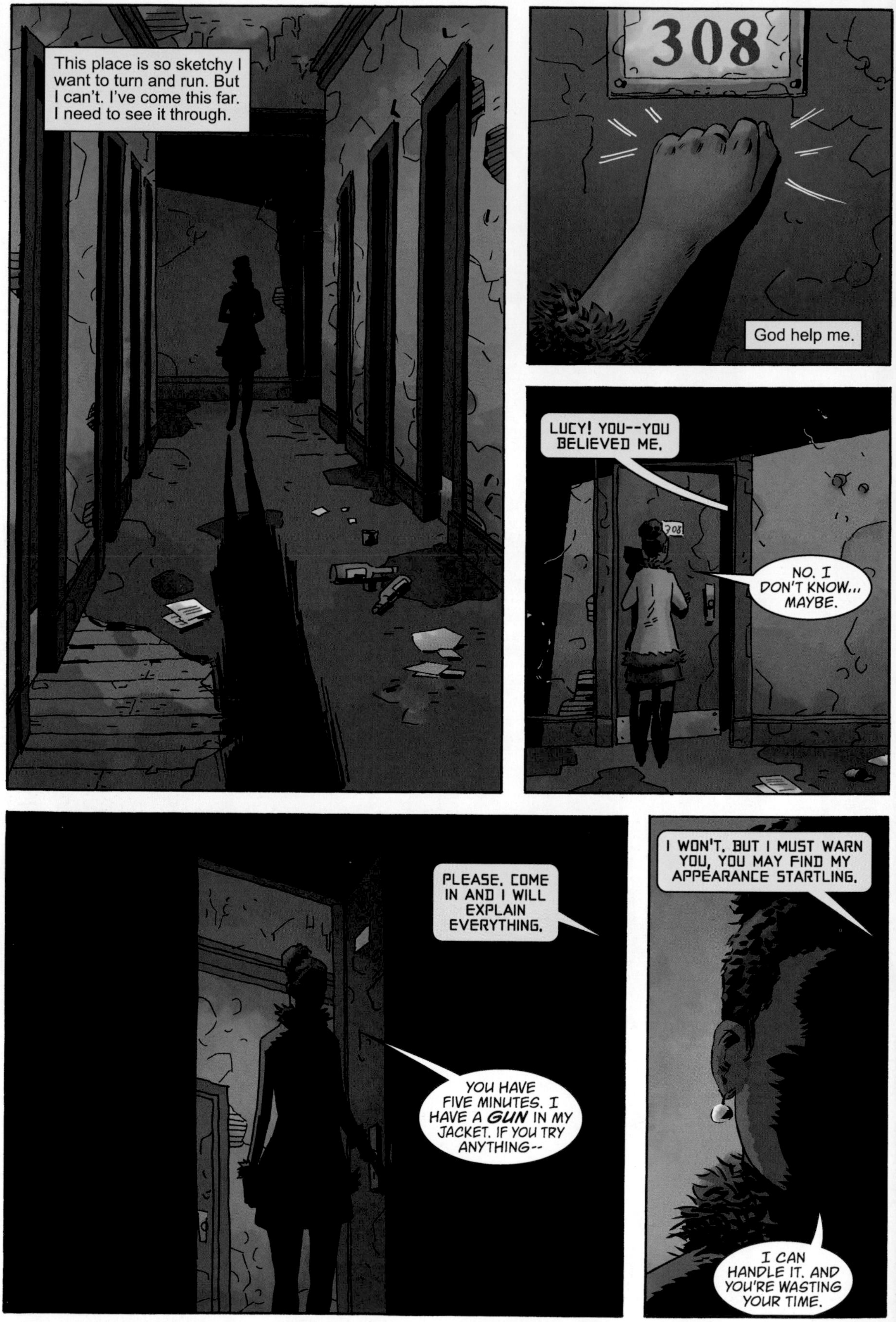

This place is so sketchy I want to turn and run. But I can't. I've come this far. I need to see it through.
308
God help me.
LUCY! YOU--YOU BELIEVED ME.
NO. I DON'T KNOW... MAYBE.
PLEASE. COME IN AND I WILL EXPLAIN EVERYTHING.
YOU HAVE FIVE MINUTES. I HAVE A GUN IN MY JACKET. IF YOU TRY ANYTHING--
I WON'T. BUT I MUST WARN YOU, YOU MAY FIND MY APPEARANCE STARTLING.
I CAN HANDLE IT. AND YOU'RE WASTING YOUR TIME.

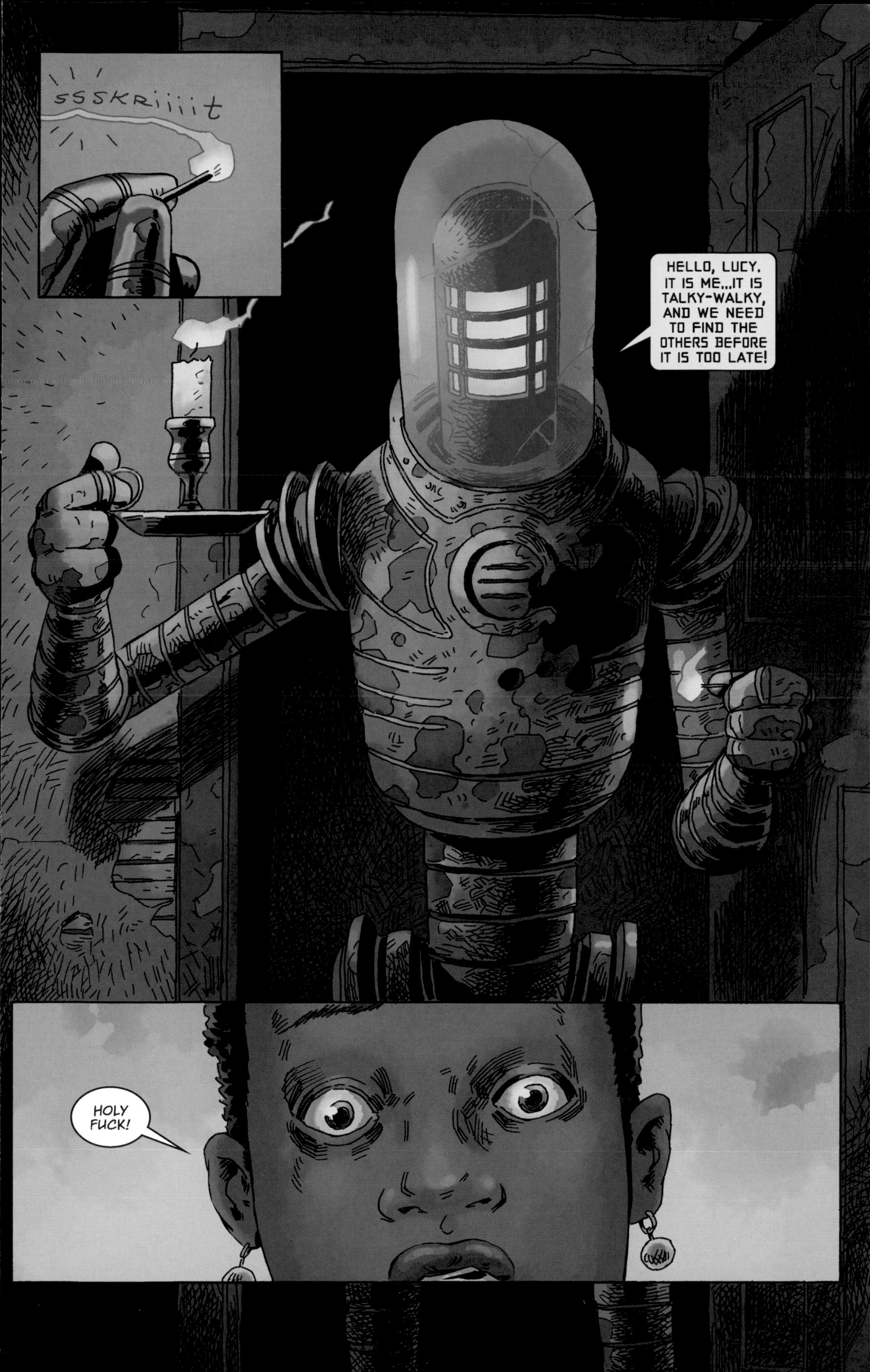
SSSKRiiiiit
HELLO, LUCY. IT IS ME...IT IS TALKY-WALKY, AND WE NEED TO FIND THE OTHERS BEFORE IT IS TOO LATE!
HOLY FUCK!

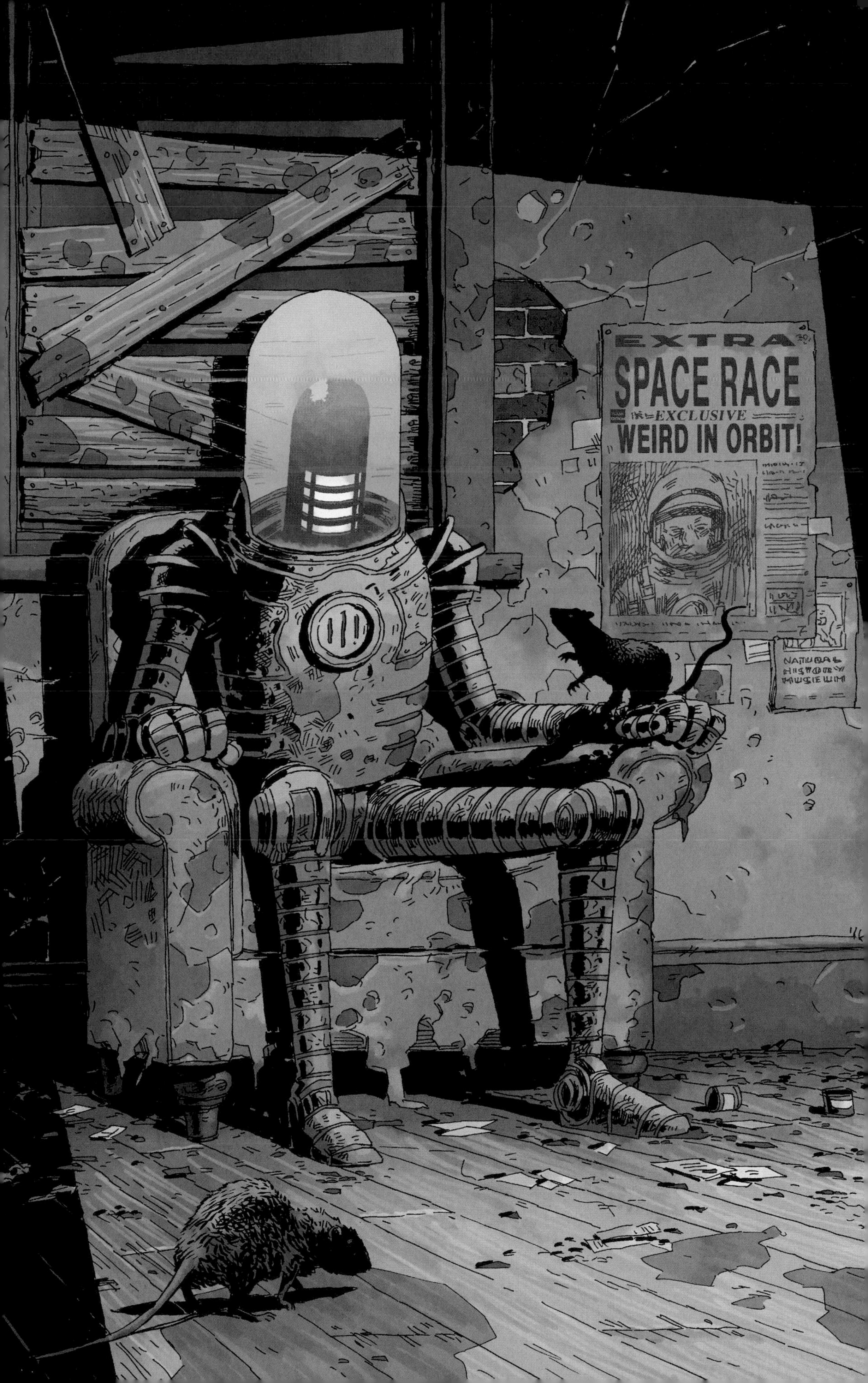
EXTRA
SPACE RACE
EXCLUSIVE
WEIRD IN ORBIT!
NATURAL
HISTORY
MUSEUM

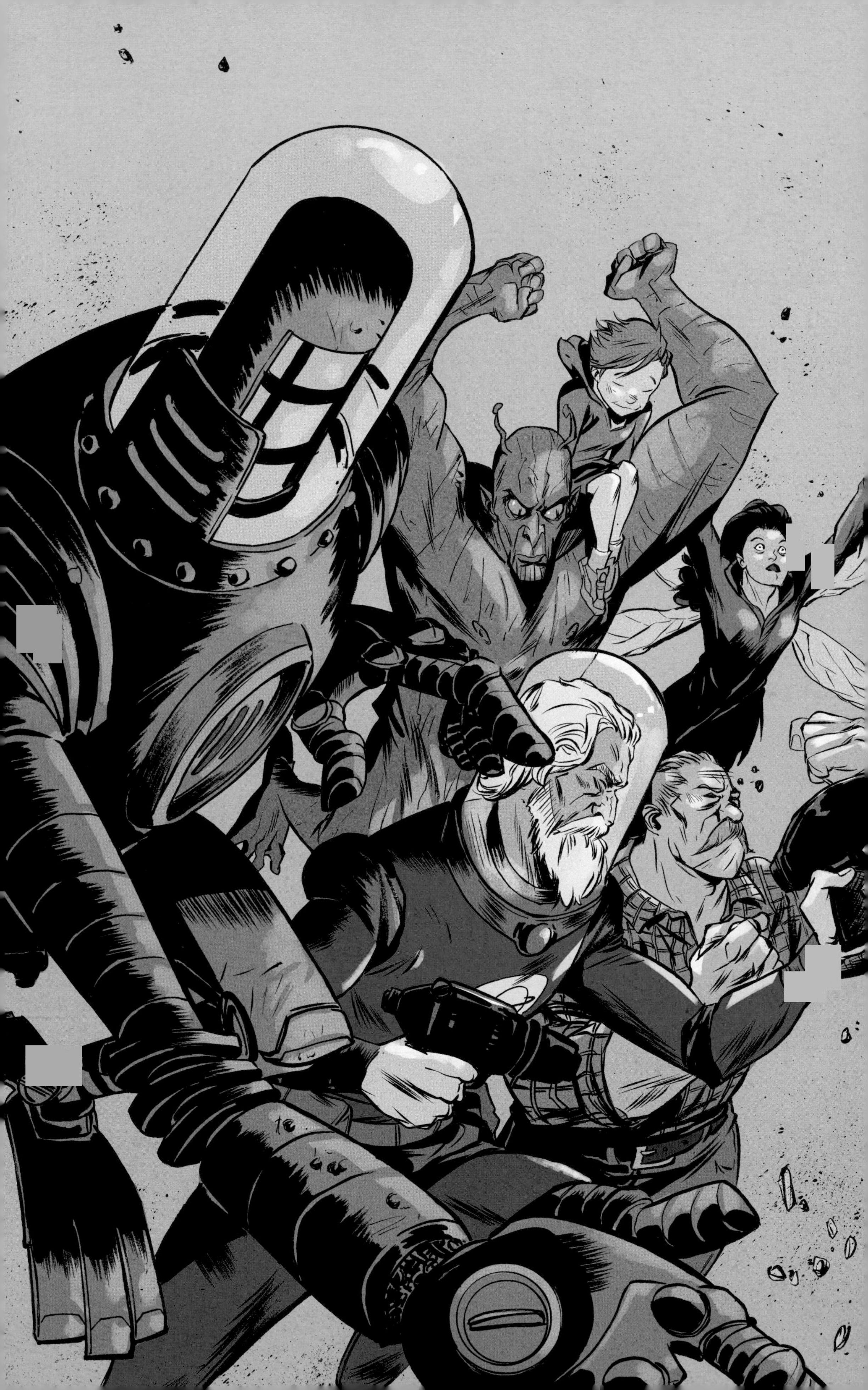

KRA-KOOM!

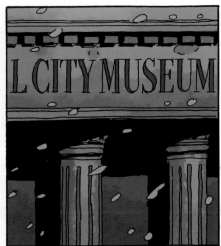

L CITY MUSEUM

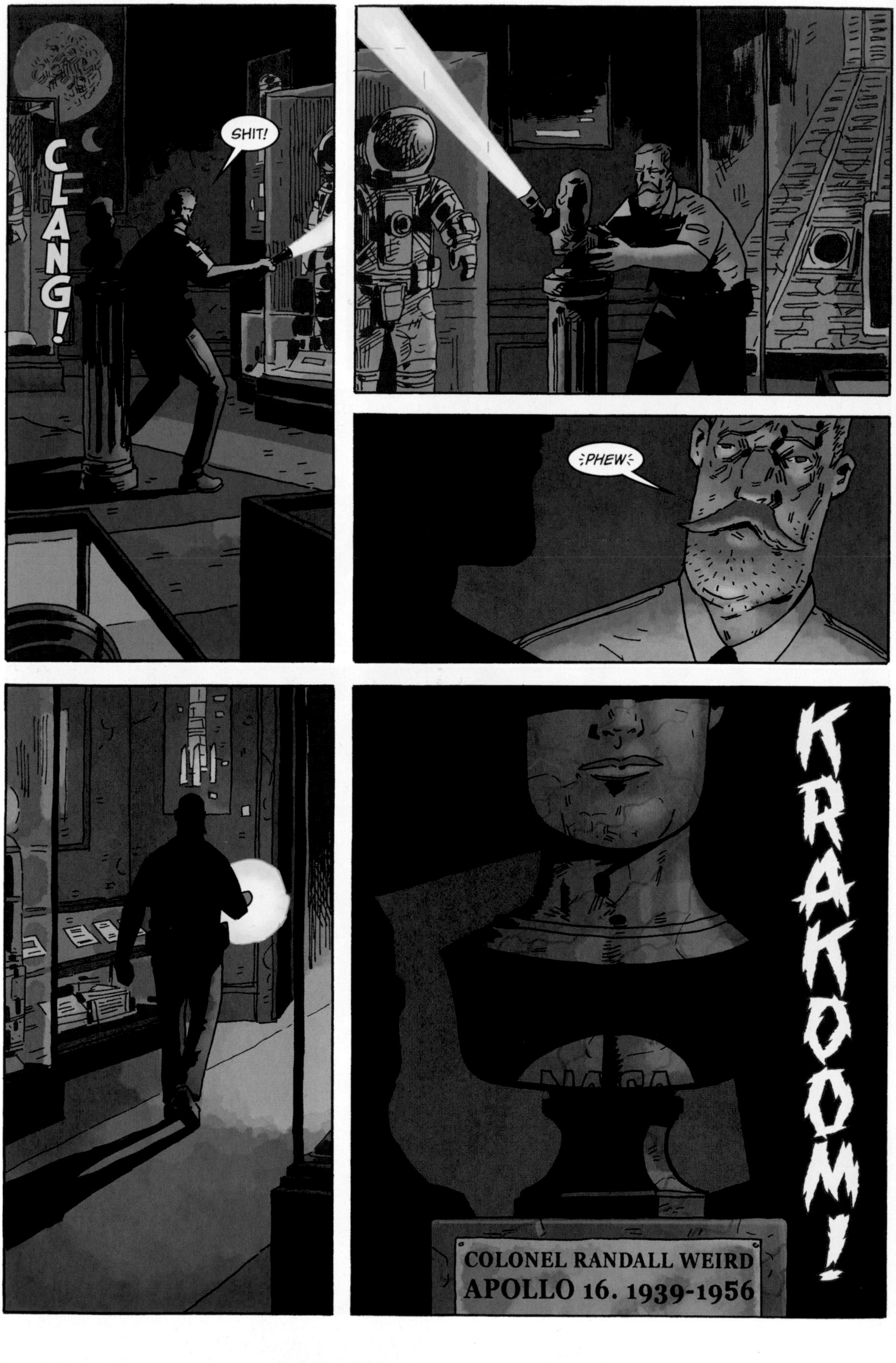
CLANG!
SHIT!
PHEW
KRAKOOM!
COLONEL RANDALL WEIRD
APOLLO 16. 1939-1956

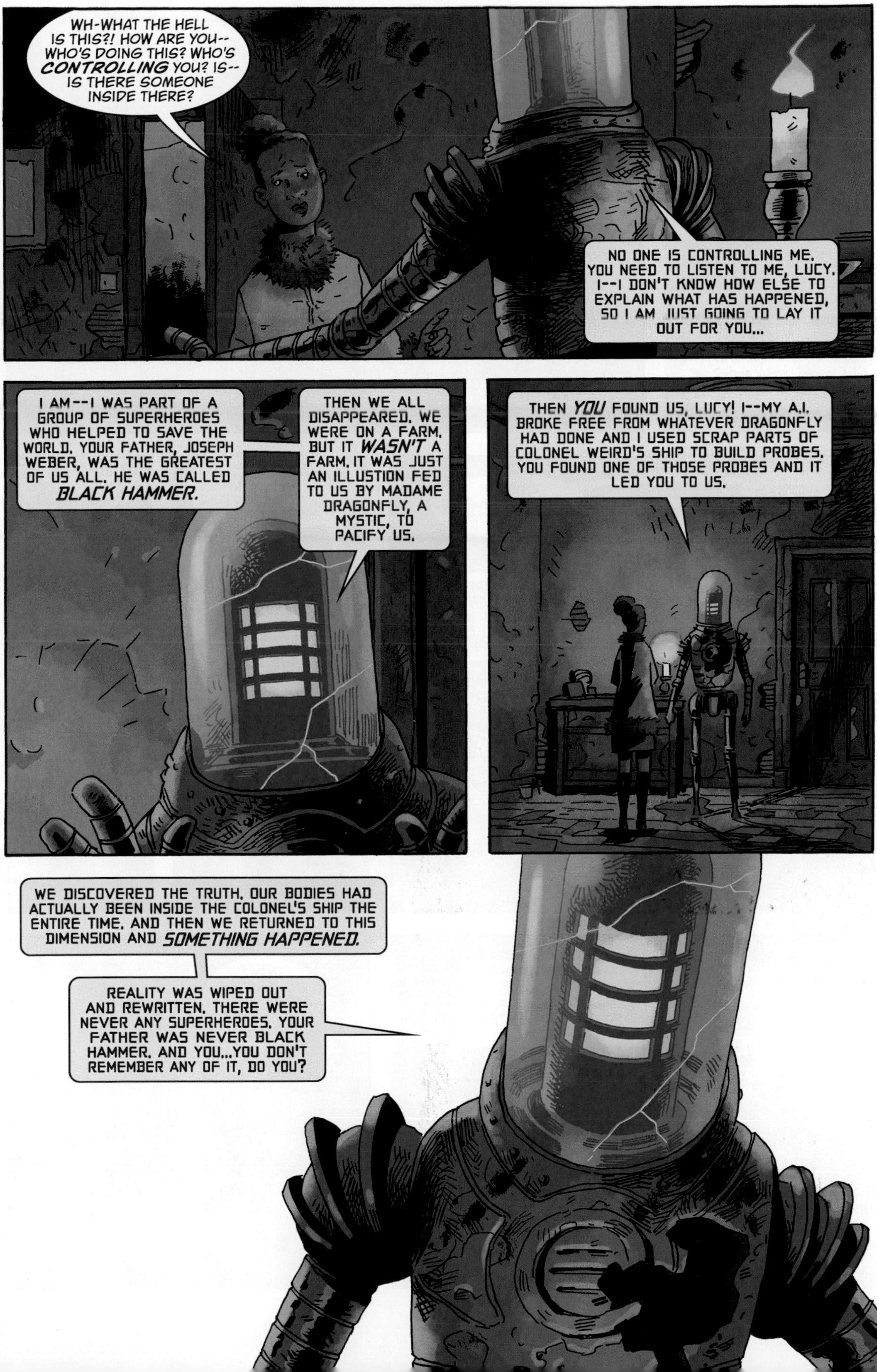
WH-WHAT THE HELL IS THIS?! HOW ARE YOU-- WHO'S DOING THIS? WHO'S CONTROLLING YOU? IS-- IS THERE SOMEONE INSIDE THERE?
NO ONE IS CONTROLLING ME. YOU NEED TO LISTEN TO ME, LUCY. I--I DON'T KNOW HOW ELSE TO EXPLAIN WHAT HAS HAPPENED, SO I AM JUST GOING TO LAY IT OUT FOR YOU...
I AM--I WAS PART OF A GROUP OF SUPERHEROES WHO HELPED TO SAVE THE WORLD. YOUR FATHER, JOSEPH WEBER, WAS THE GREATEST OF US ALL. HE WAS CALLED BLACK HAMMER.
THEN WE ALL DISAPPEARED. WE WERE ON A FARM. BUT IT WASN'T A FARM. IT WAS JUST AN ILLUSTION FED TO US BY MADAME DRAGONFLY, A MYSTIC, TO PACIFY US.
THEN YOU FOUND US, LUCY! I--MY A.I. BROKE FREE FROM WHATEVER DRAGONFLY HAD DONE AND I USED SCRAP PARTS OF COLONEL WEIRD'S SHIP TO BUILD PROBES. YOU FOUND ONE OF THOSE PROBES AND IT LED YOU TO US.
WE DISCOVERED THE TRUTH. OUR BODIES HAD ACTUALLY BEEN INSIDE THE COLONEL'S SHIP THE ENTIRE TIME. AND THEN WE RETURNED TO THIS DIMENSION AND SOMETHING HAPPENED.
REALITY WAS WIPED OUT AND REWRITTEN. THERE WERE NEVER ANY SUPERHEROES. YOUR FATHER WAS NEVER BLACK HAMMER. AND YOU...YOU DON'T REMEMBER ANY OF IT, DO YOU?

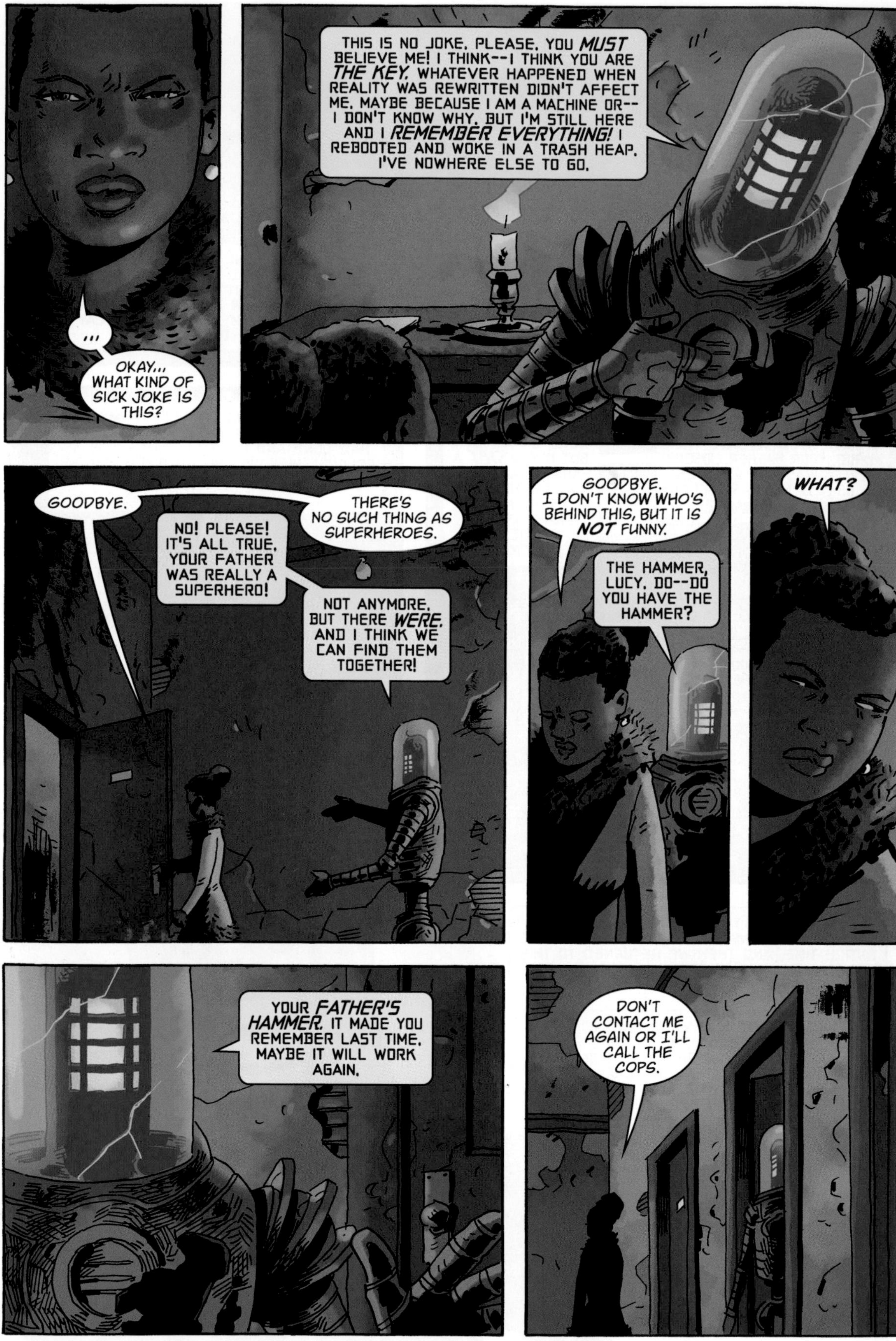
...
OKAY... WHAT KIND OF SICK JOKE IS THIS?
THIS IS NO JOKE. PLEASE, YOU MUST BELIEVE ME! I THINK--I THINK YOU ARE THE KEY. WHATEVER HAPPENED WHEN REALITY WAS REWRITTEN DIDN'T AFFECT ME, MAYBE BECAUSE I AM A MACHINE OR--I DON'T KNOW WHY. BUT I'M STILL HERE AND I REMEMBER EVERYTHING! I REBOOTED AND WOKE IN A TRASH HEAP. I'VE NOWHERE ELSE TO GO.
THERE'S NO SUCH THING AS SUPERHEROES.
NO! PLEASE! IT'S ALL TRUE, YOUR FATHER WAS REALLY A SUPERHERO!
GOODBYE.
NOT ANYMORE, BUT THERE WERE. AND I THINK WE CAN FIND THEM TOGETHER!
GOODBYE. I DON'T KNOW WHO'S BEHIND THIS, BUT IT IS NOT FUNNY.
THE HAMMER, LUCY. DO--DO YOU HAVE THE HAMMER?
WHAT?
YOUR FATHER'S HAMMER. IT MADE YOU REMEMBER LAST TIME. MAYBE IT WILL WORK AGAIN.
DON'T CONTACT ME AGAIN OR I'LL CALL THE COPS.

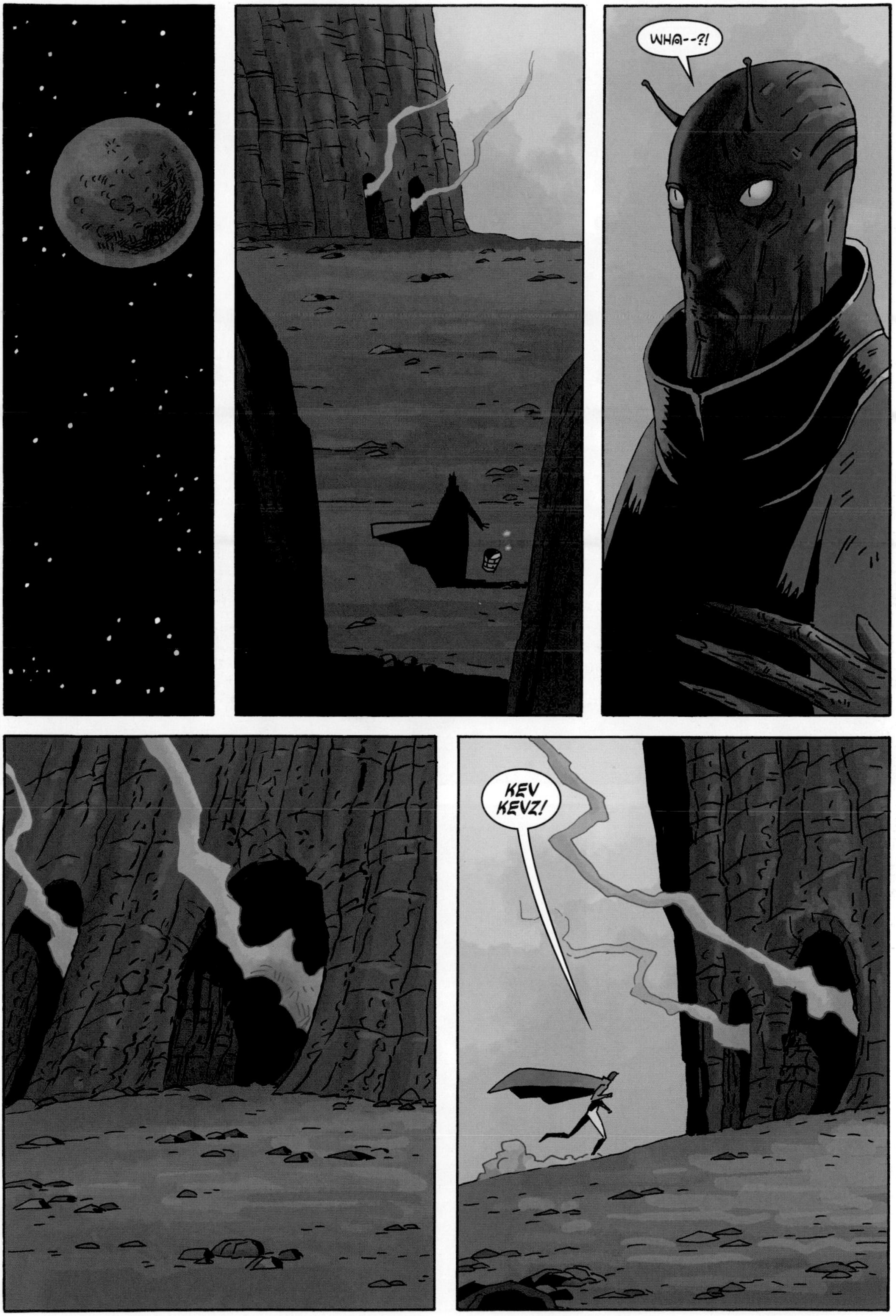
WHA--?!
KEV KEVZ!

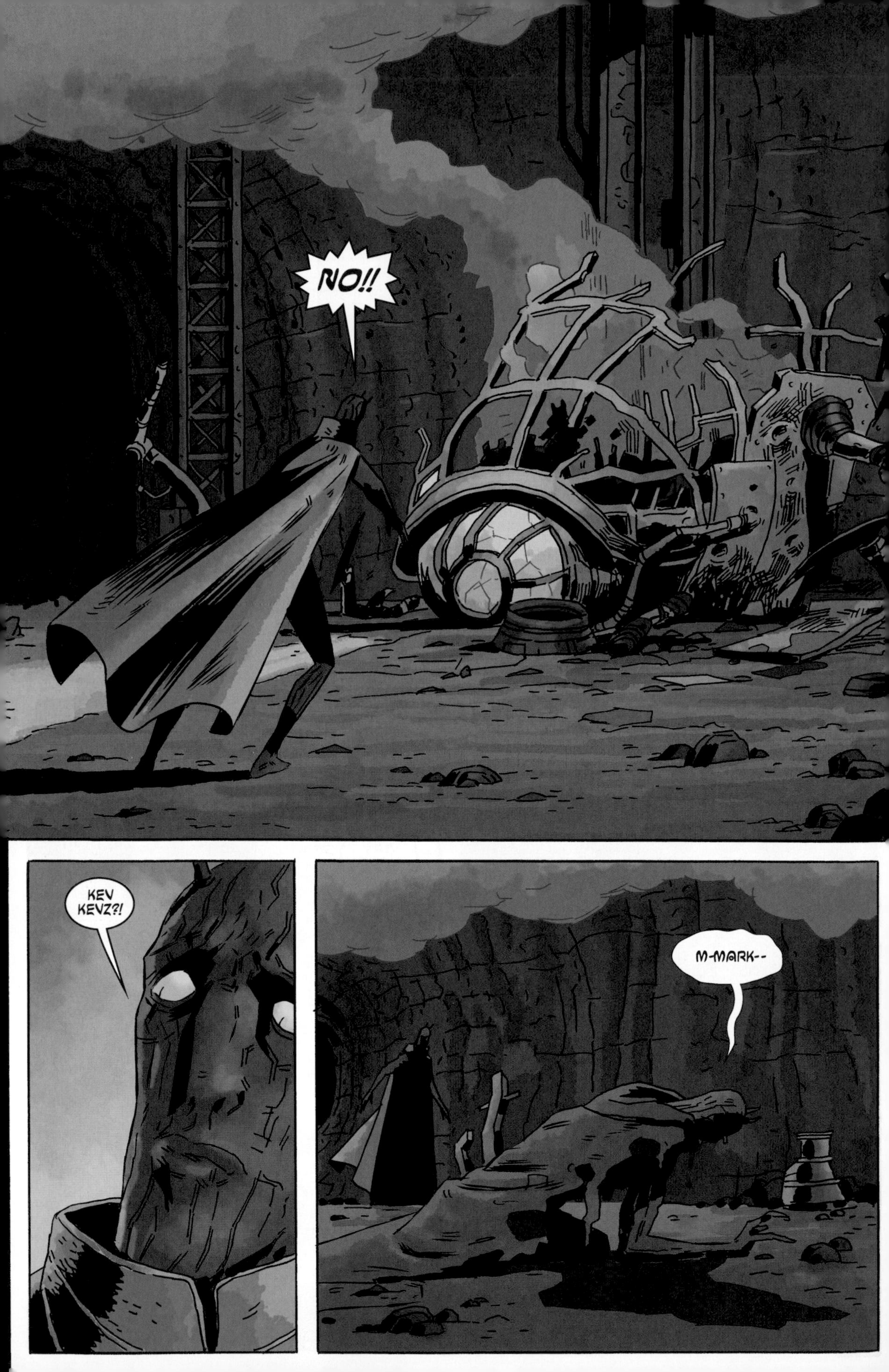
NO!!
KEV KEVZ?!
M-MARK--

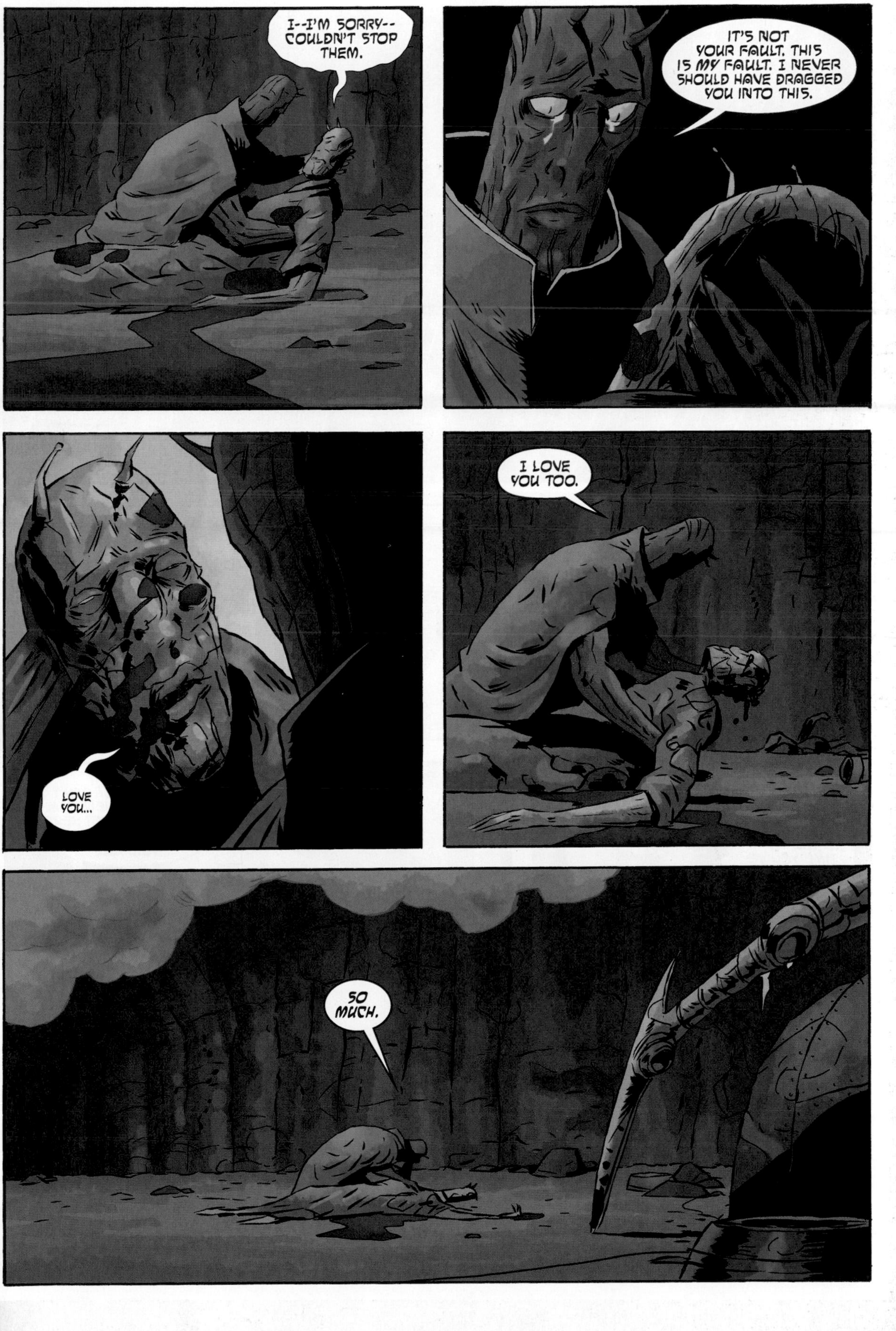
I--I'M SORRY-- COULDN'T STOP THEM.
IT'S NOT YOUR FAULT. THIS IS MY FAULT. I NEVER SHOULD HAVE DRAGGED YOU INTO THIS.
LOVE YOU...
I LOVE YOU TOO.
SO MUCH.

YOU'RE OVER A HALF HOUR LATE, LUCY!

I KNOW. I'M SORRY. THE F-BUS WAS LATE AND I HAD TO **WALK** ALL THE WAY HERE IN THE RAIN.

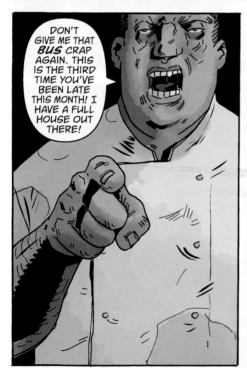

DON'T GIVE ME THAT **BUS** CRAP AGAIN. THIS IS THE THIRD TIME YOU'VE BEEN LATE THIS MONTH! I HAVE A FULL HOUSE OUT THERE!

OKAY, OKAY. NOT LIKE **YOU** CAN'T SERVE THEM THEIR DAMN PIZZA UNTIL I GET HERE. IT'S NOT ROCKET SCIENCE!

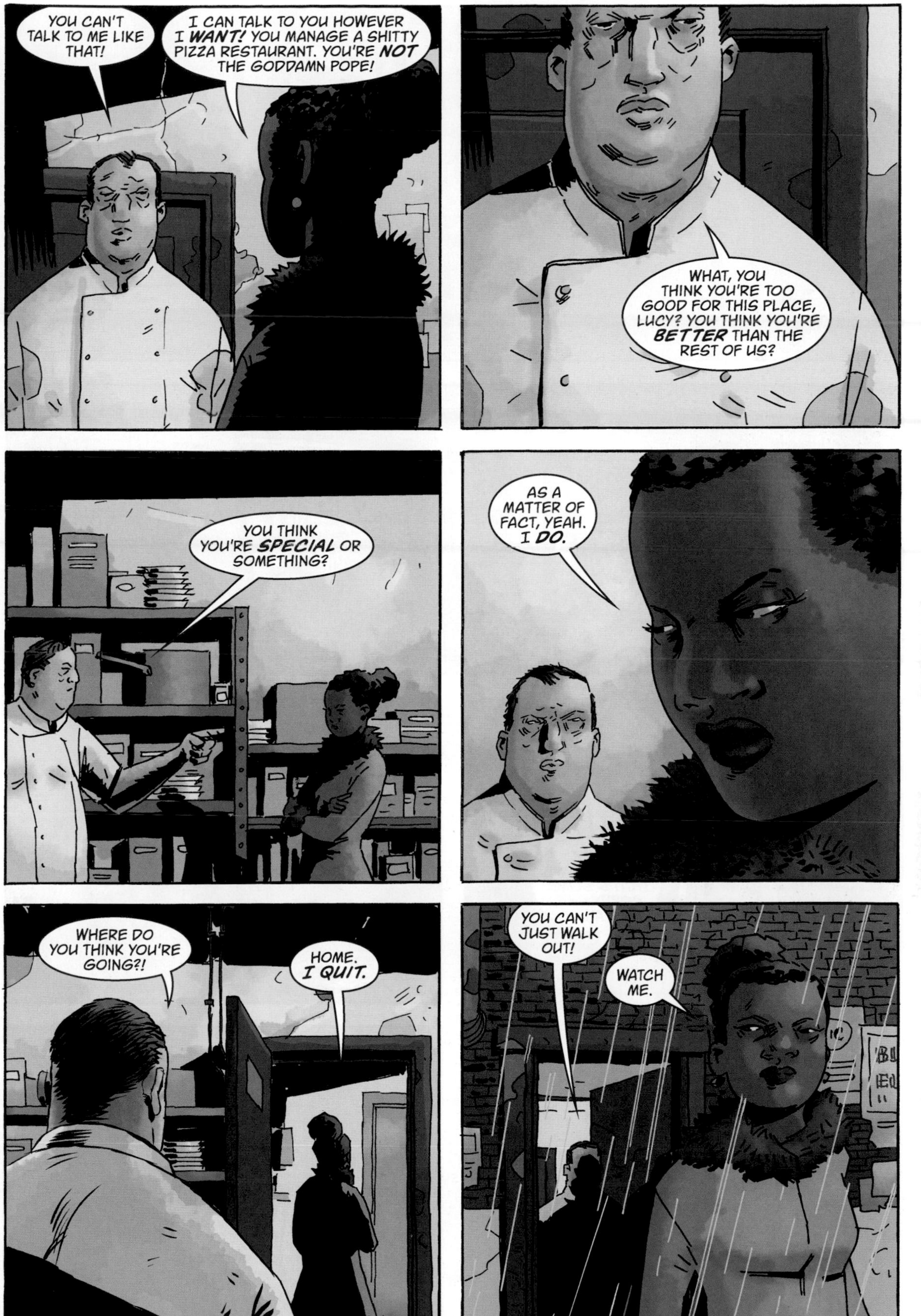
YOU CAN'T TALK TO ME LIKE THAT!
I CAN TALK TO YOU HOWEVER I WANT! YOU MANAGE A SHITTY PIZZA RESTAURANT. YOU'RE NOT THE GODDAMN POPE!
WHAT, YOU THINK YOU'RE TOO GOOD FOR THIS PLACE, LUCY? YOU THINK YOU'RE BETTER THAN THE REST OF US?
YOU THINK YOU'RE SPECIAL OR SOMETHING?
AS A MATTER OF FACT, YEAH. I DO.
WHERE DO YOU THINK YOU'RE GOING?!
HOME. I QUIT.
YOU CAN'T JUST WALK OUT!
WATCH ME.

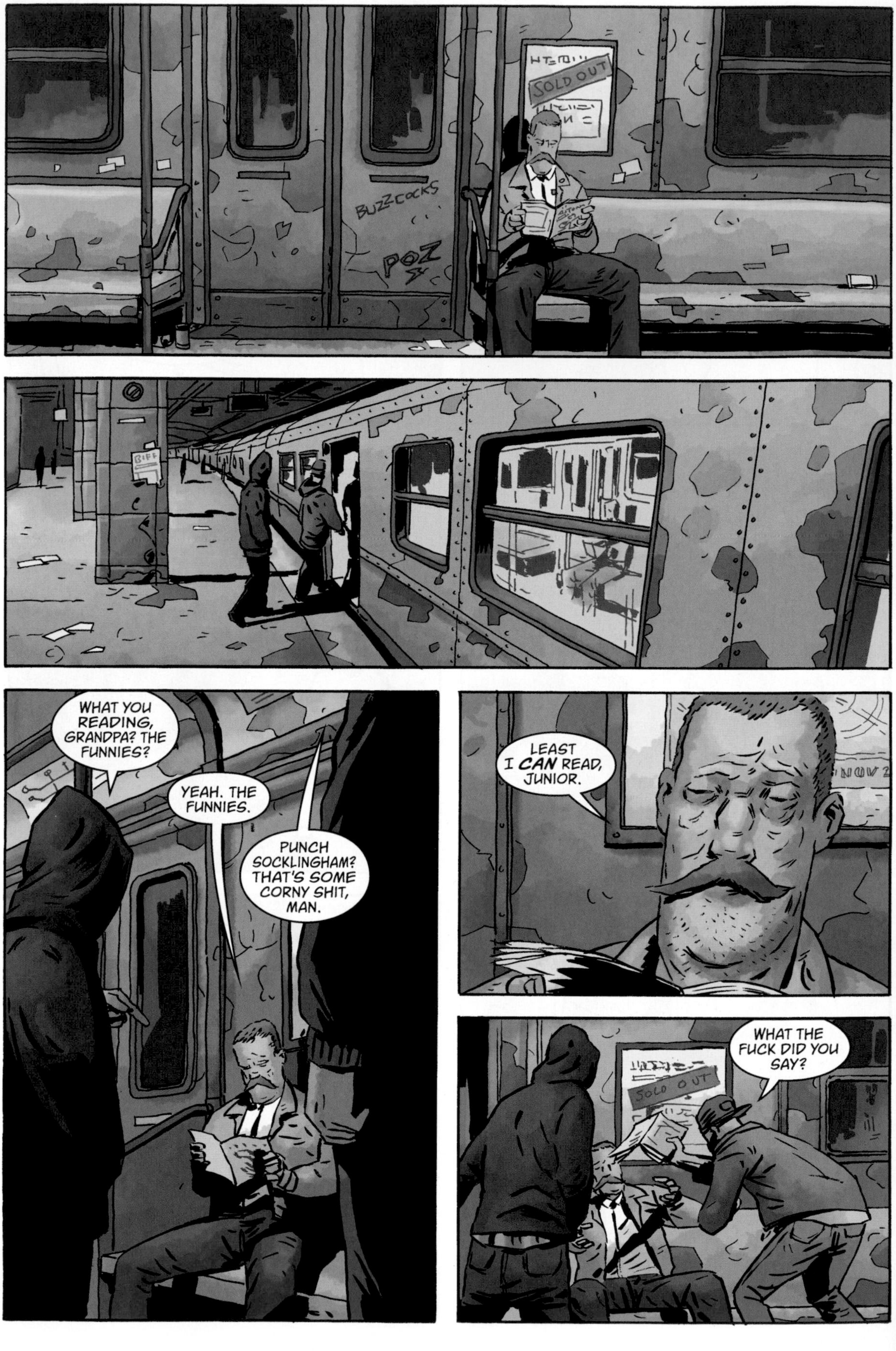

SOLD OUT
BUZZCOCKS
POZ
BIFF
WHAT YOU READING, GRANDPA? THE FUNNIES?
YEAH. THE FUNNIES.
PUNCH SOCKLINGHAM? THAT'S SOME CORNY SHIT, MAN.
LEAST I CAN READ, JUNIOR.
SOLD OUT
WHAT THE FUCK DID YOU SAY?

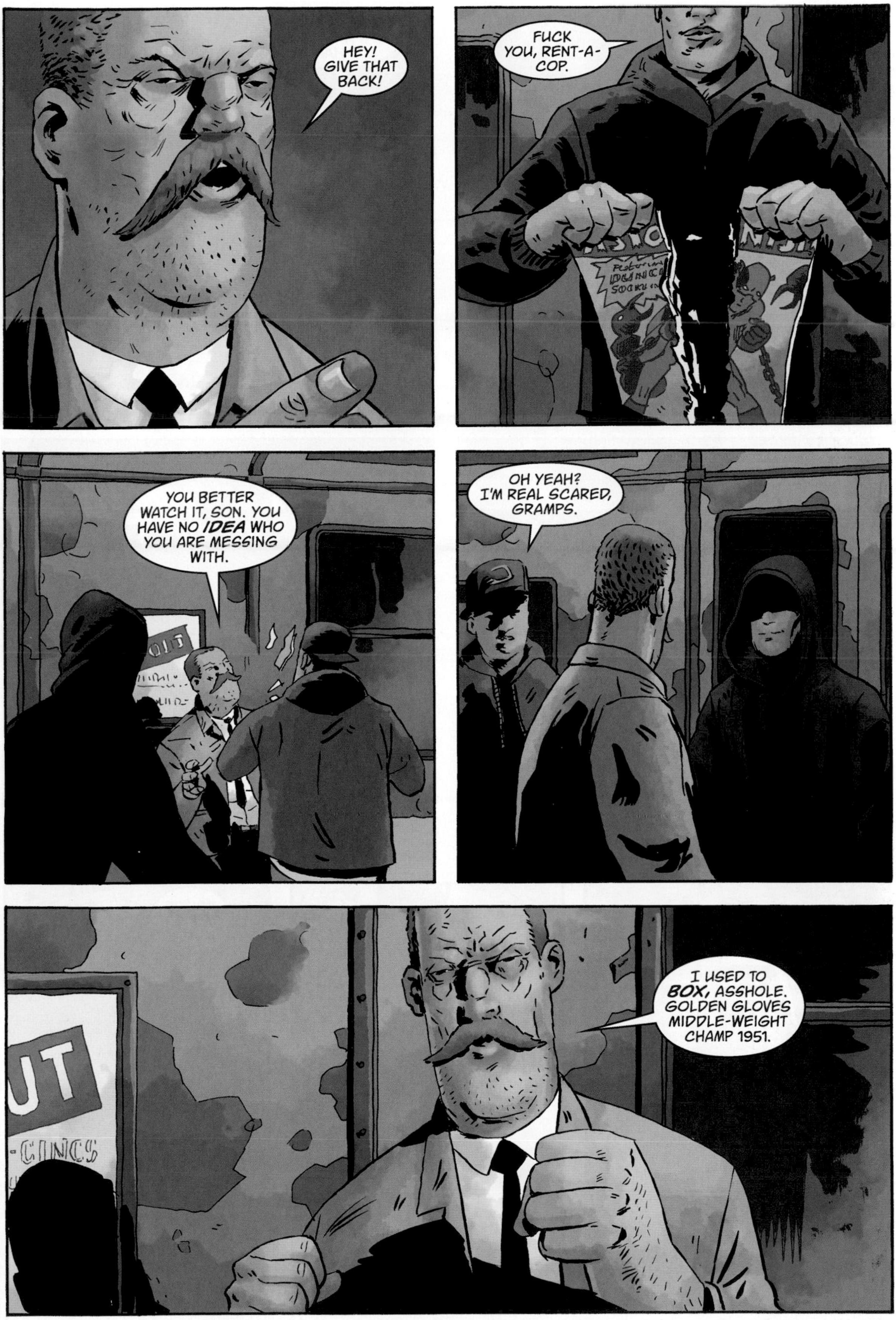
HEY! GIVE THAT BACK!
FUCK YOU, RENT-A-COP.
YOU BETTER WATCH IT, SON. YOU HAVE NO *IDEA* WHO YOU ARE MESSING WITH.
OH YEAH? I'M REAL SCARED, GRAMPS.
I USED TO **BOX,** ASSHOLE. GOLDEN GLOVES MIDDLE-WEIGHT CHAMP 1951.

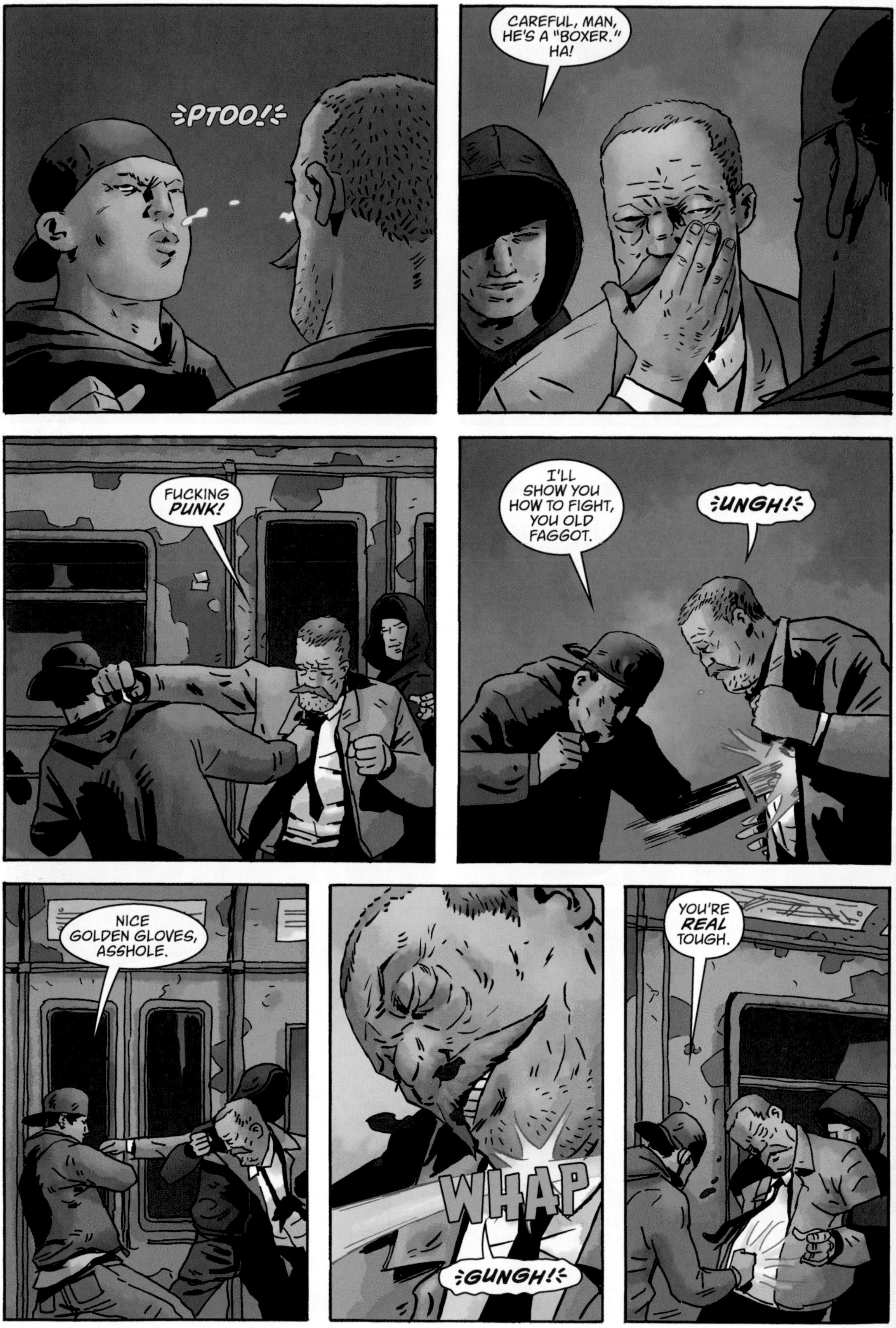
PTOO!
CAREFUL, MAN, HE'S A "BOXER." HA!
FUCKING PUNK!
I'LL SHOW YOU HOW TO FIGHT, YOU OLD FAGGOT.
UNGH!
NICE GOLDEN GLOVES, ASSHOLE.
WHAP
GUNGH!
YOU'RE REAL TOUGH.

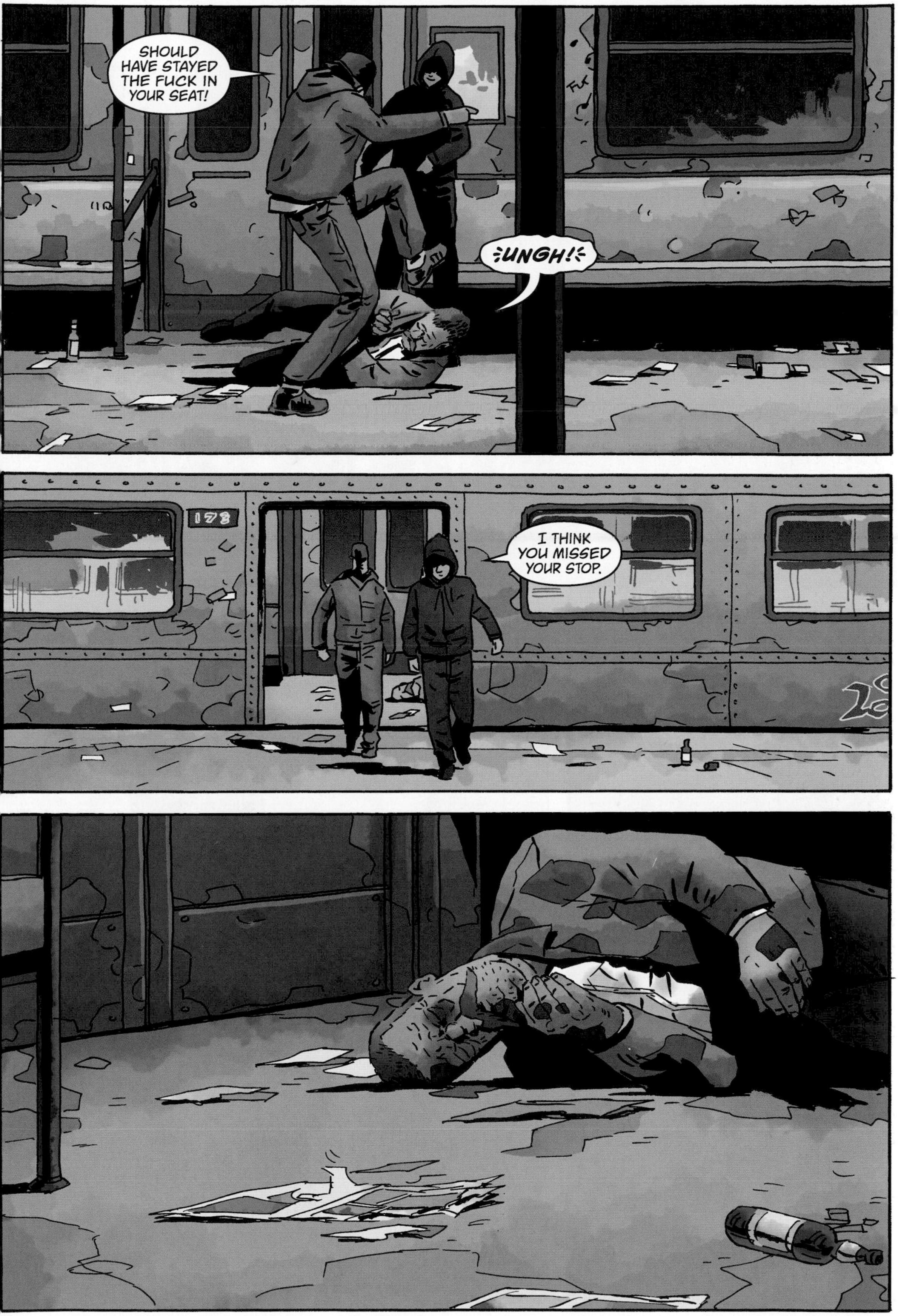
SHOULD HAVE STAYED THE FUCK IN YOUR SEAT!
UNGH!
178
I THINK YOU MISSED YOUR STOP.

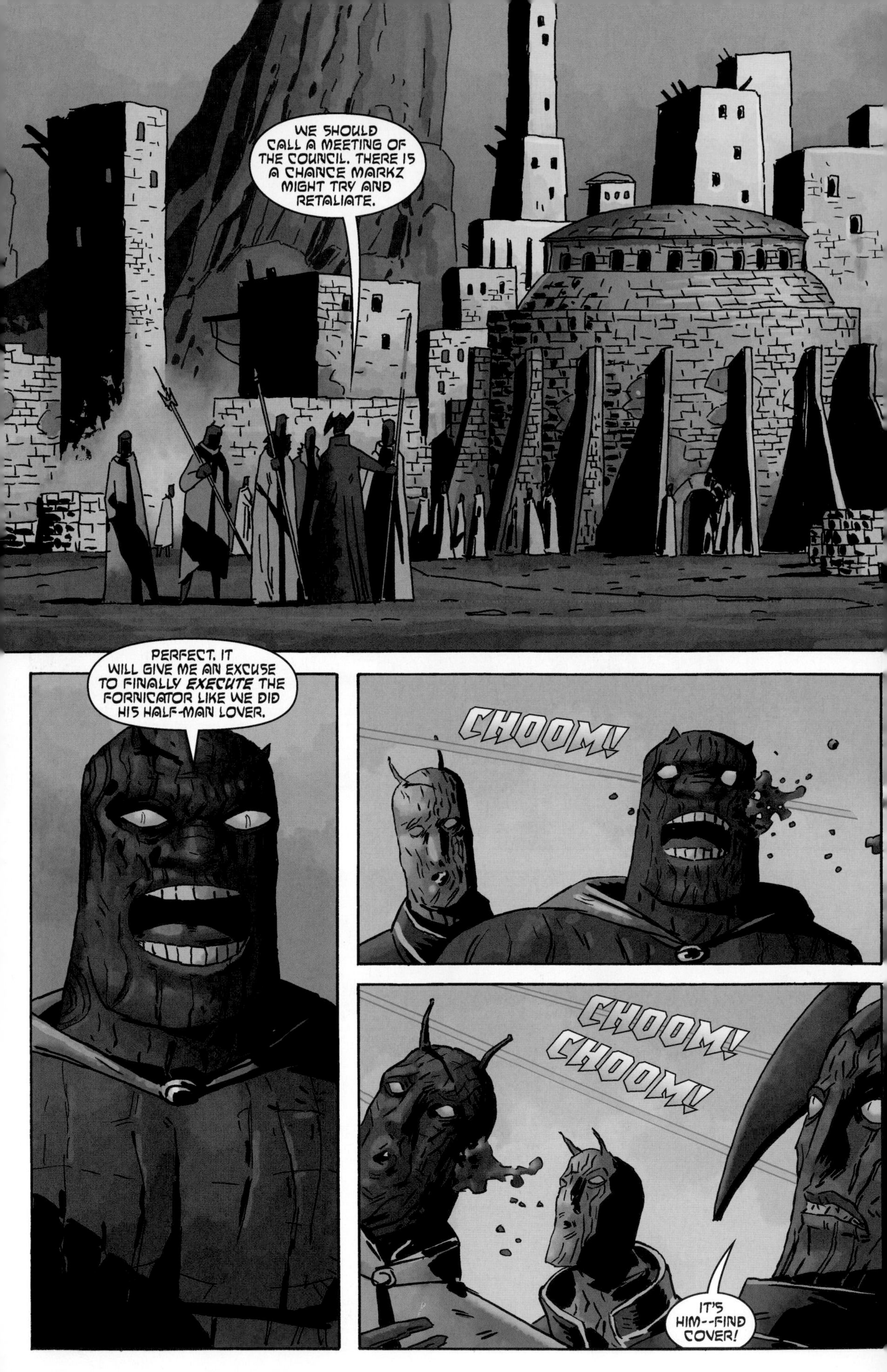
WE SHOULD CALL A MEETING OF THE COUNCIL. THERE IS A CHANCE MARKZ MIGHT TRY AND RETALIATE.
PERFECT. IT WILL GIVE ME AN EXCUSE TO FINALLY *EXECUTE* THE FORNICATOR LIKE WE DID HIS HALF-MAN LOVER.
CHOOM!
CHOOM!
CHOOM!
IT'S HIM--FIND COVER!

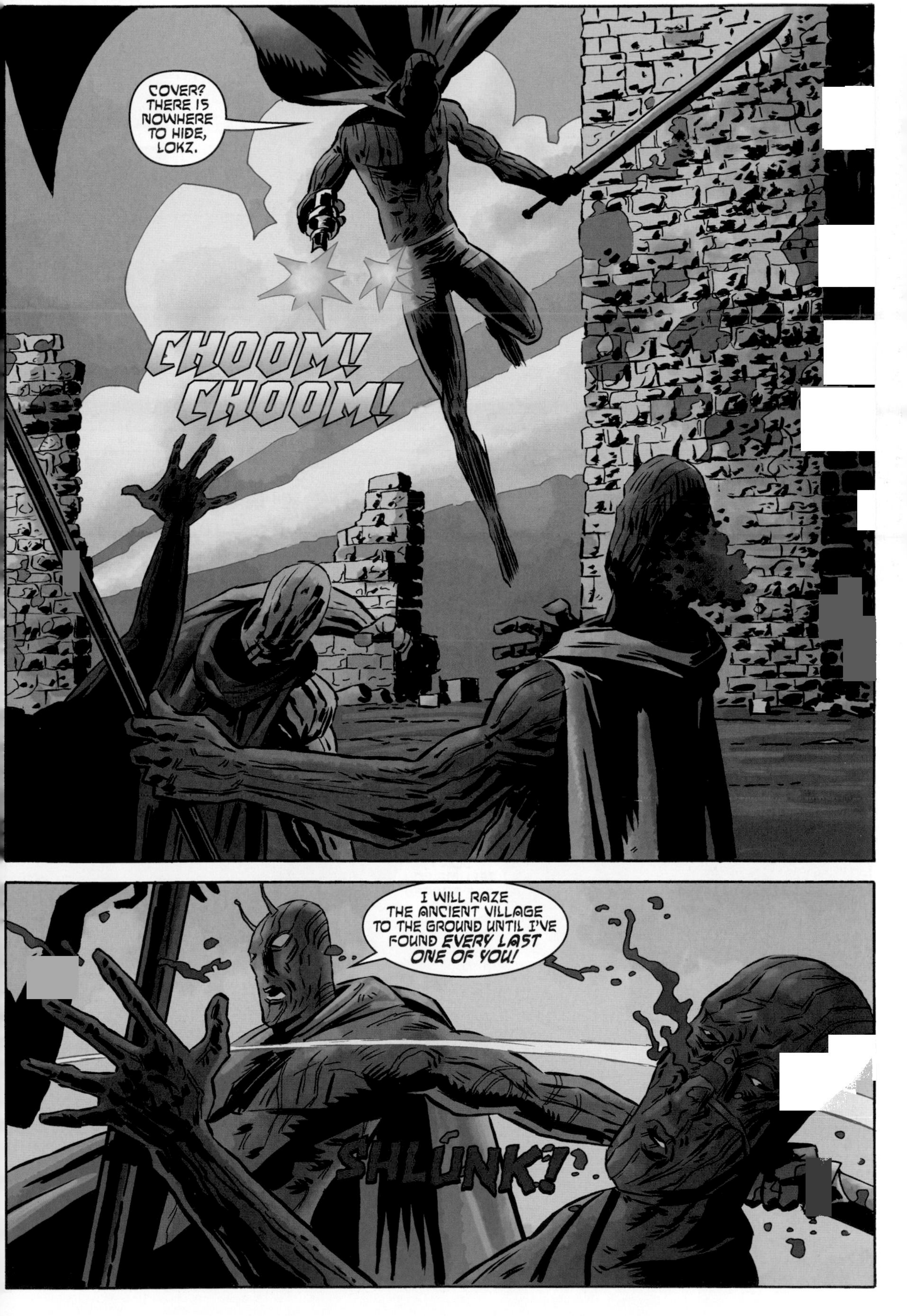
COVER? THERE IS NOWHERE TO HIDE, LOKZ.
CHOOM! CHOOM!
I WILL RAZE THE ANCIENT VILLAGE TO THE GROUND UNTIL I'VE FOUND EVERY LAST ONE OF YOU!
SHLUNK!

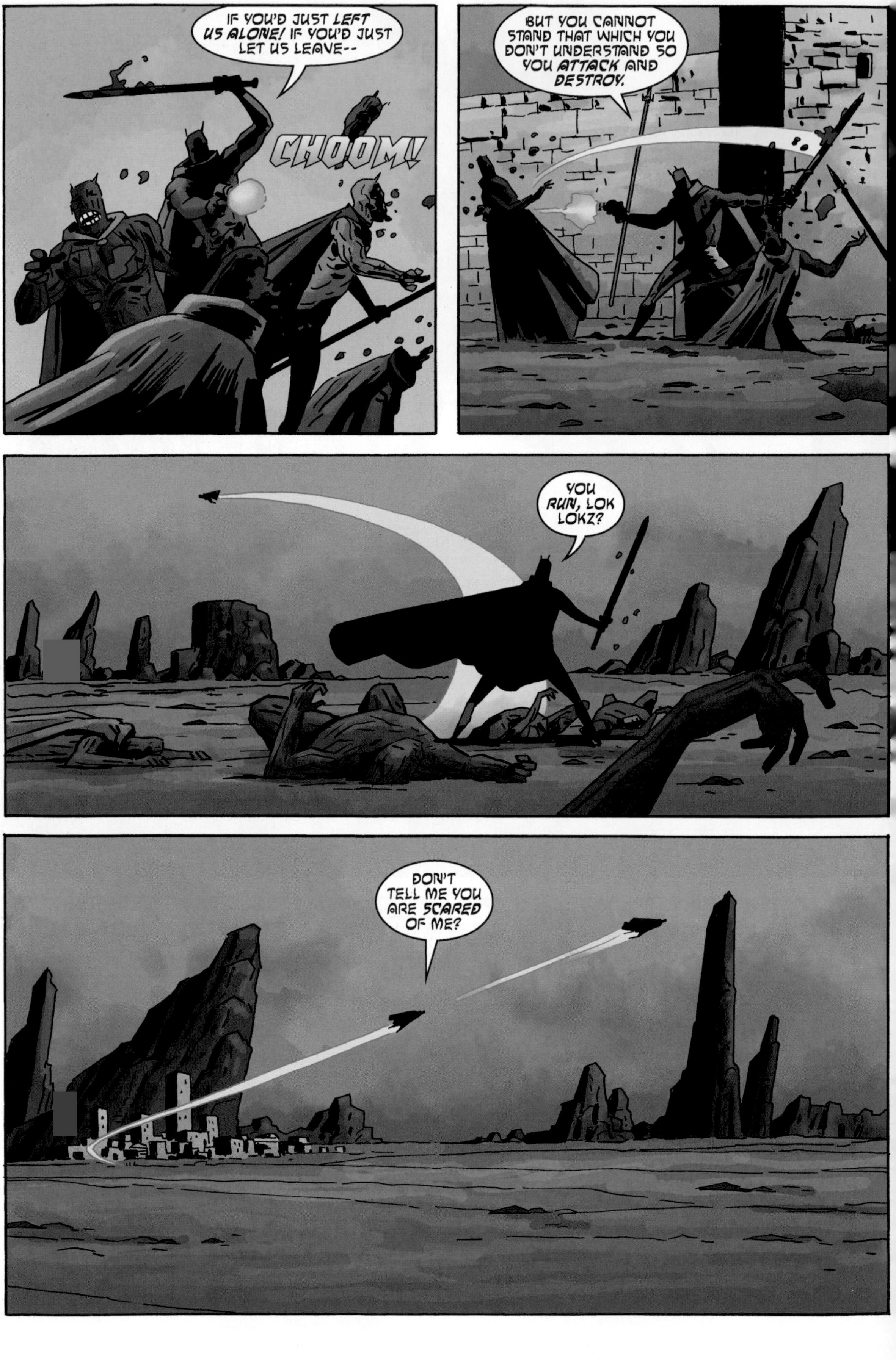
IF YOU'D JUST LEFT US ALONE! IF YOU'D JUST LET US LEAVE--
CHOOM!
BUT YOU CANNOT STAND THAT WHICH YOU DON'T UNDERSTAND SO YOU ATTACK AND DESTROY.
YOU RUN, LOK LOKZ?
DON'T TELL ME YOU ARE SCARED OF ME?

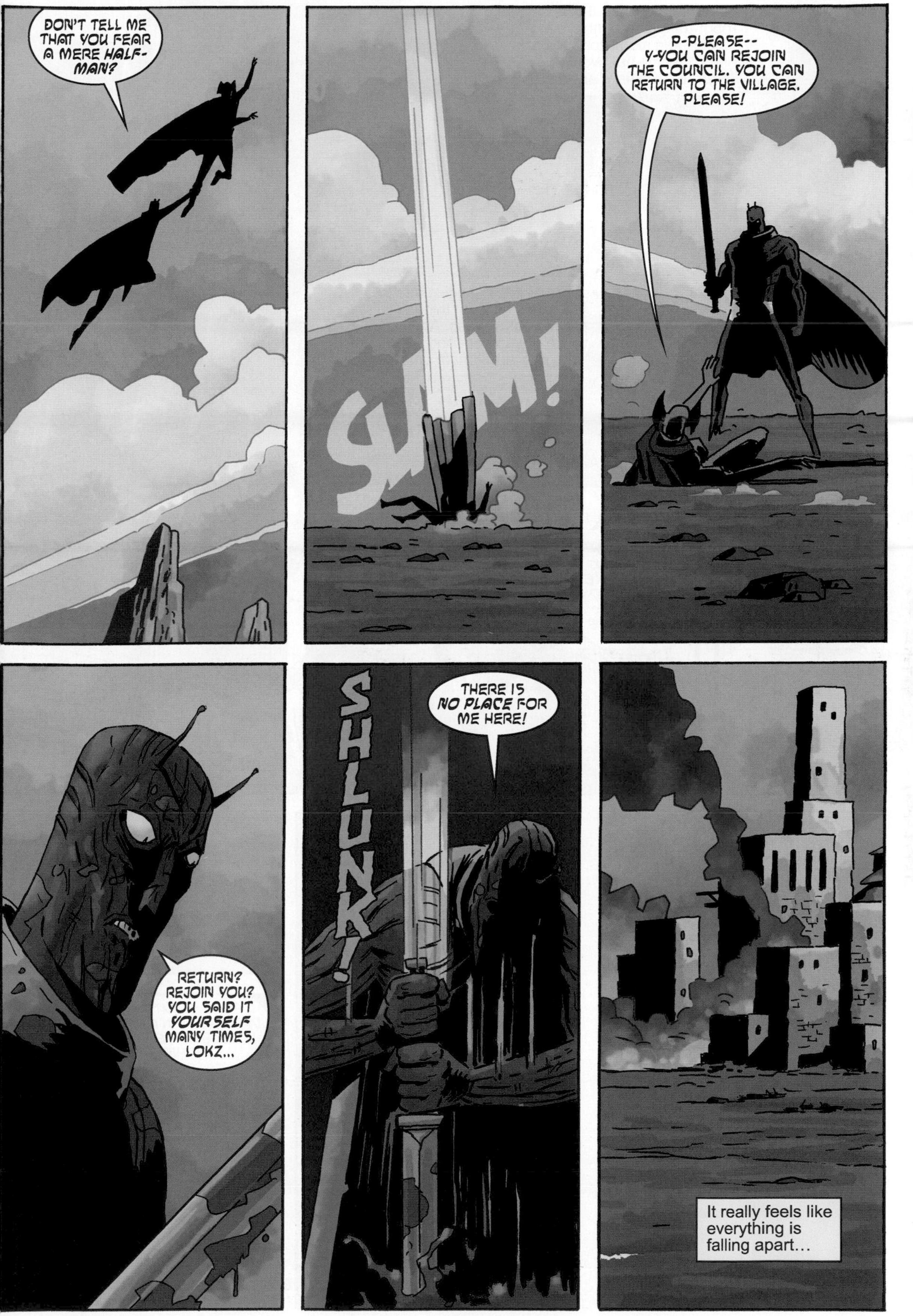
DON'T TELL ME THAT YOU FEAR A MERE HALF-MAN?
SLAM!
P-PLEASE-- Y-YOU CAN REJOIN THE COUNCIL. YOU CAN RETURN TO THE VILLAGE. PLEASE!
RETURN? REJOIN YOU? YOU SAID IT YOURSELF MANY TIMES, LOKZ...
SHLUNK!
THERE IS NO PLACE FOR ME HERE!
It really feels like everything is falling apart...

I try to forget about that weird robot-thing and all the crazy shit he told me. I don't tell anyone. How the hell would I *even begin* to explain it anyway?!

But it keeps nagging me. That thing. That thing I can't quite grasp. And two days later I find myself at my mom's.

EMPIRE C
CLOTHING E

...HERE'S THE LAST OF IT. WHY THE SUDDEN URGE TO TAKE A TRIP DOWN MEMORY LANE, LUCY?

I JUST WANTED TO CHECK IT OUT. HAVEN'T LOOKED AT ANY OF DAD'S OLD STUFF SINCE I WAS A KID.

WELL, YOU'RE WELCOME TO ANY OF IT. SHOULD PROBABLY GIVE IT TO THE SALVATION ARMY ANYWAY.

OH, COME ON, MOM. THIS IS ALL WE HAVE LEFT OF DAD. WE CAN'T GET RID OF THIS STUFF.

SPIRAL CITY SLUGGER

MOM...DOES THE NAME BLACK HAMMER MEAN ANYTHING TO YOU?

WHAT *IS* THAT? THE BRITISH POLICE SHOW ON BBC AMERICA?

NO. IT'S.... IT'S NOTHING. AND YOU'RE SURE THIS IS ALL OF IT?

YEP, ALL THE STUFF THAT'S NOT IN STORAGE.

STORAGE?

SURE. I PUT A LOT OF YOUR DAD'S STUFF IN A STORAGE LOCKER IN THE BOROUGHS. BIGGER STUFF, LIKE HIS *TOOLS* AND WHAT NOT.

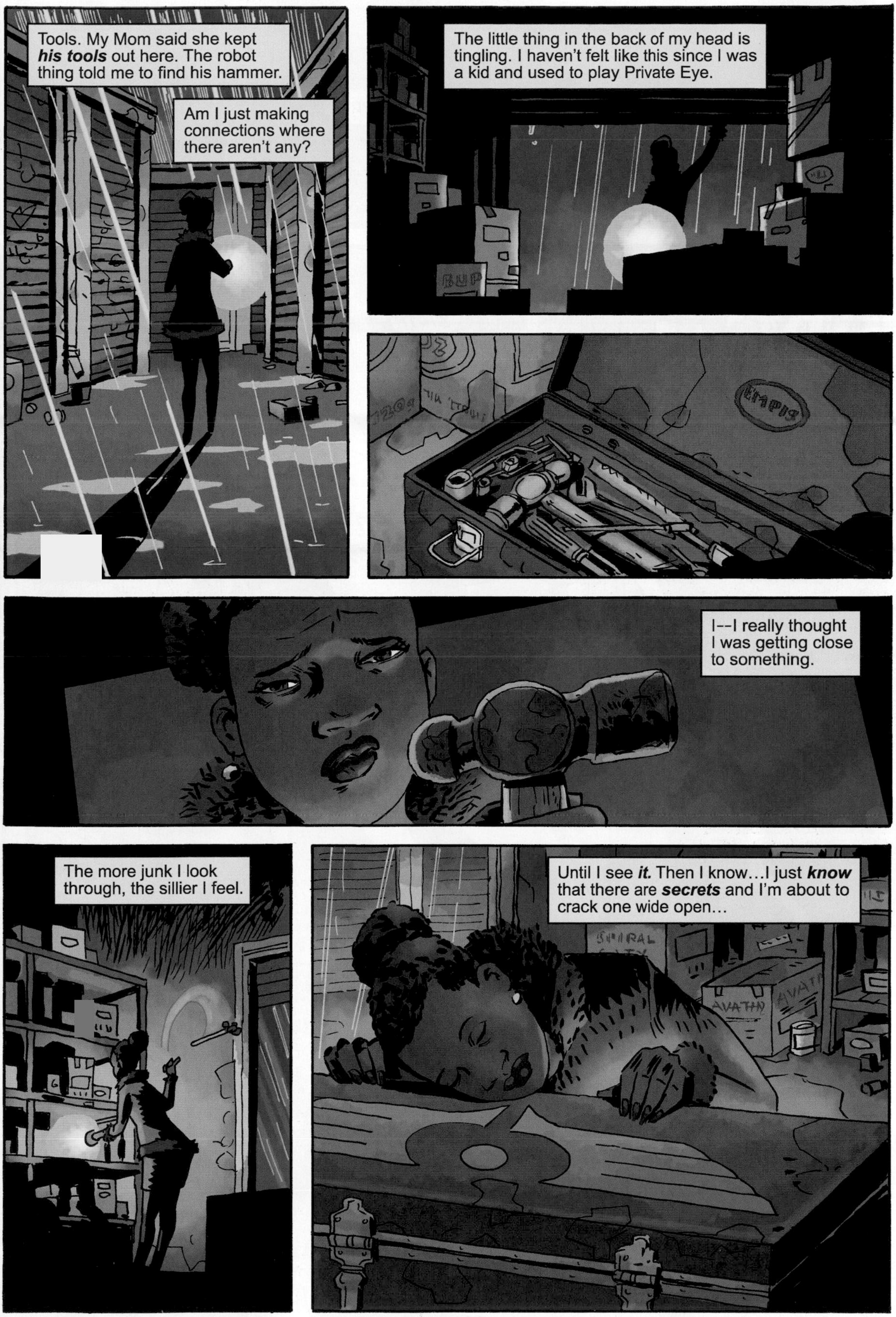

Tools. My Mom said she kept ***his tools*** out here. The robot thing told me to find his hammer.
Am I just making connections where there aren't any?
The little thing in the back of my head is tingling. I haven't felt like this since I was a kid and used to play Private Eye.
I--I really thought I was getting close to something.
The more junk I look through, the sillier I feel.
Until I see ***it.*** Then I know…I just ***know*** that there are ***secrets*** and I'm about to crack one wide open…

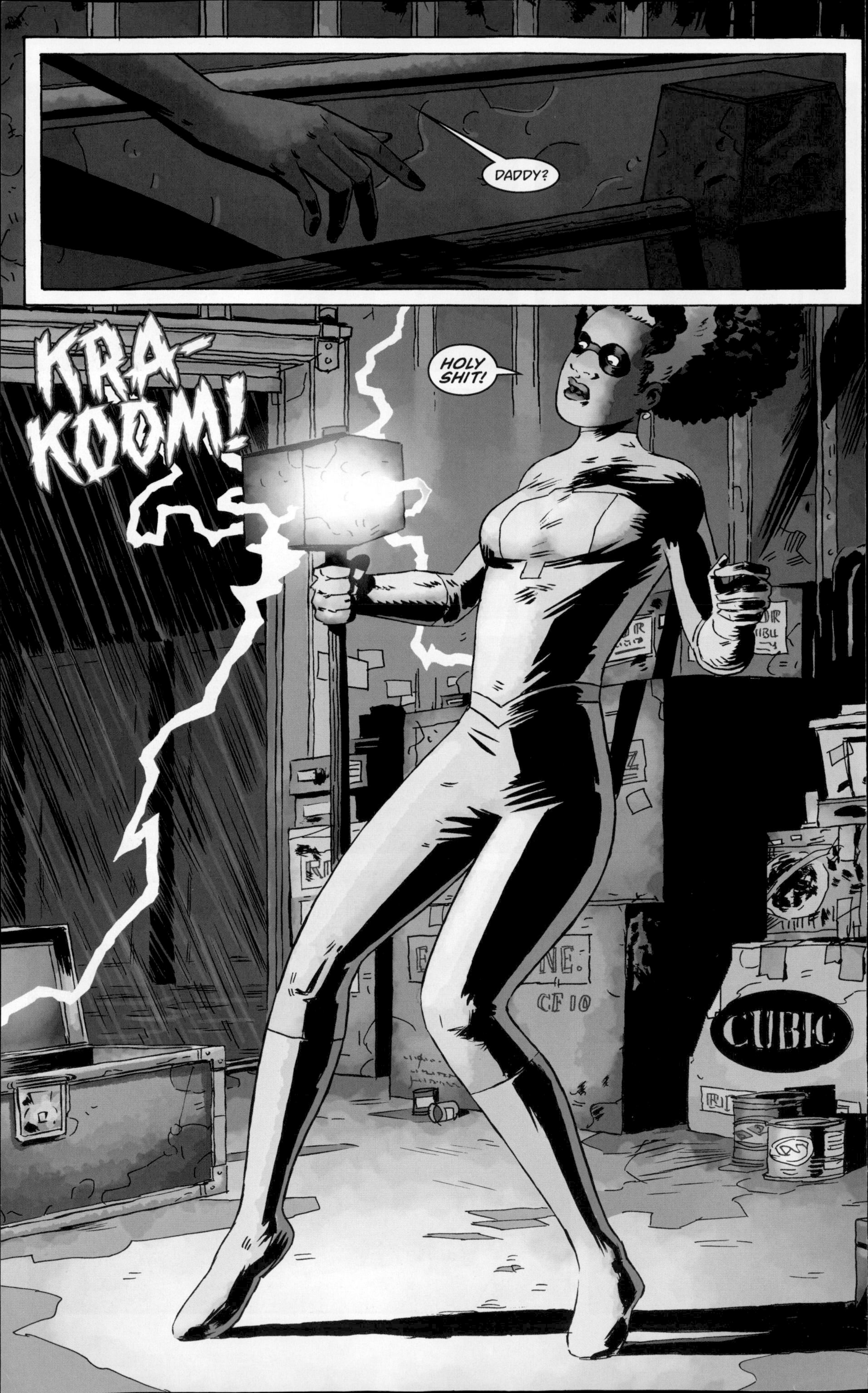
DADDY?
KRA-KOOM!
HOLY SHIT!
CUBIC

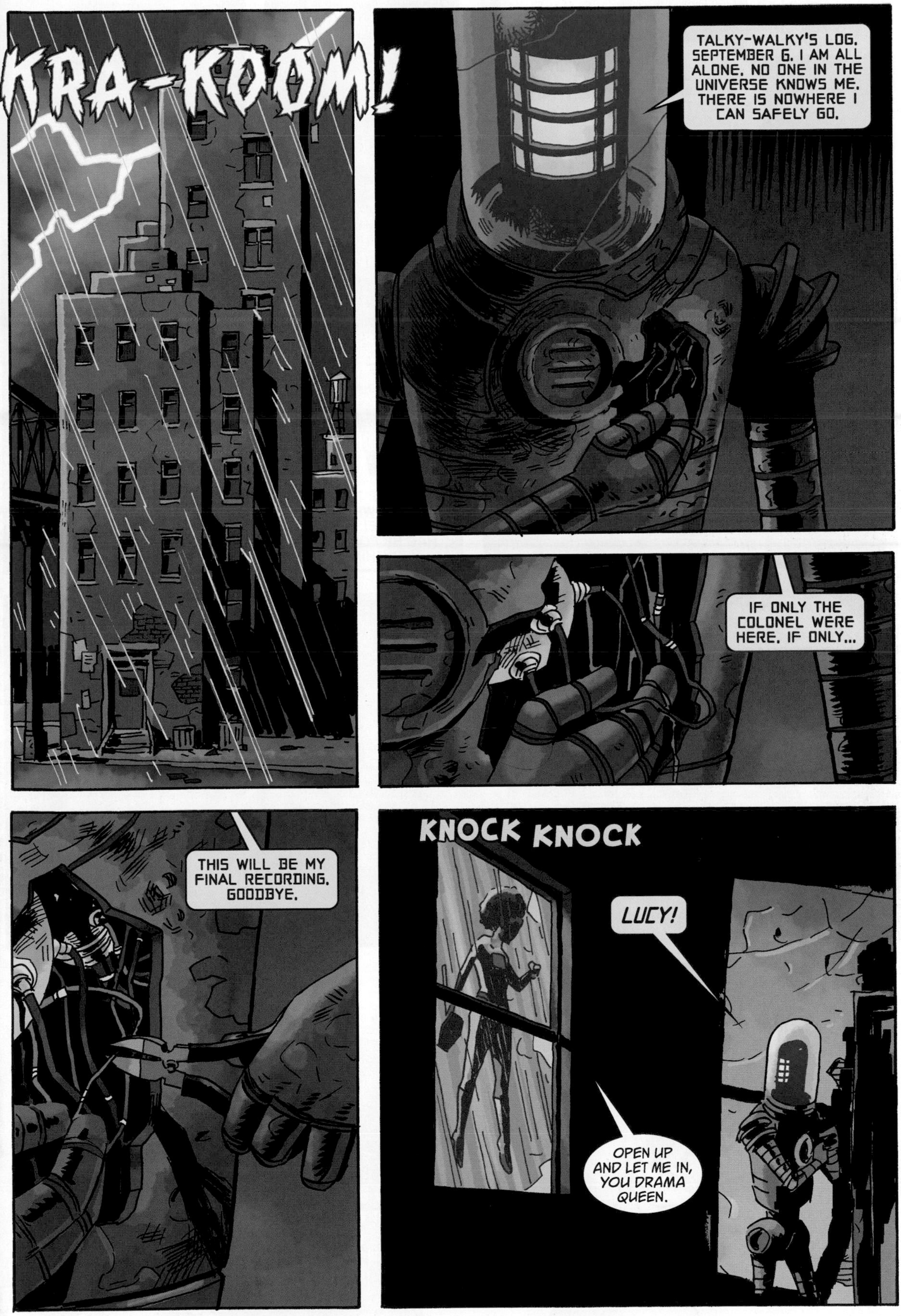
KRA-KOOM!
TALKY-WALKY'S LOG. SEPTEMBER 6. I AM ALL ALONE. NO ONE IN THE UNIVERSE KNOWS ME. THERE IS NOWHERE I CAN SAFELY GO.
IF ONLY THE COLONEL WERE HERE. IF ONLY...
THIS WILL BE MY FINAL RECORDING. GOODBYE.
KNOCK KNOCK
LUCY!
OPEN UP AND LET ME IN, YOU DRAMA QUEEN.

YOU BELIEVED ME! I--I HAD GIVEN UP HOPE!

WELL, I'M BACK. AND I REMEMBER *EVERYTHING*. I'M SORRY I DOUBTED YOU, TALKY.

PLEASE, IT WAS NOT YOUR FAULT. YOU'RE HERE, LUCY. THAT'S ALL THAT MATTERS NOW.

I HAVE TO ASK, TALKY. WHERE IS COLONEL WEIRD? HAS HE FORGOTTEN EVERYTHING TOO?

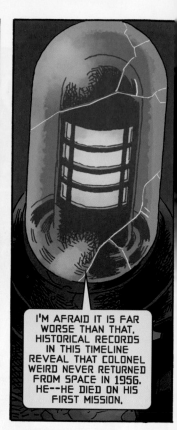

I'M AFRAID IT IS FAR WORSE THAN THAT. HISTORICAL RECORDS IN THIS TIMELINE REVEAL THAT COLONEL WEIRD NEVER RETURNED FROM SPACE IN 1956. HE--HE DIED ON HIS FIRST MISSION.

I'M SORRY. WHAT ABOUT THE *OTHERS*? GAIL, MADAME DRAGONFLY, ABE? DO YOU KNOW WHERE THEY ARE?

OF COURSE I DO. I HAVE HAD *A LOT* OF TIME ON MY HANDS TO RESEARCH. BUT IT WON'T BE EASY. NONE OF THEM HAVE ANY RECOLLECTION OF WHO THEY REALLY ARE. I--I DON'T KNOW WHAT TO DO!

I DO. WE'RE GOING TO *FIND THEM*, TALKY. AND WE'RE GOING TO GET THEM ALL *HOME*.

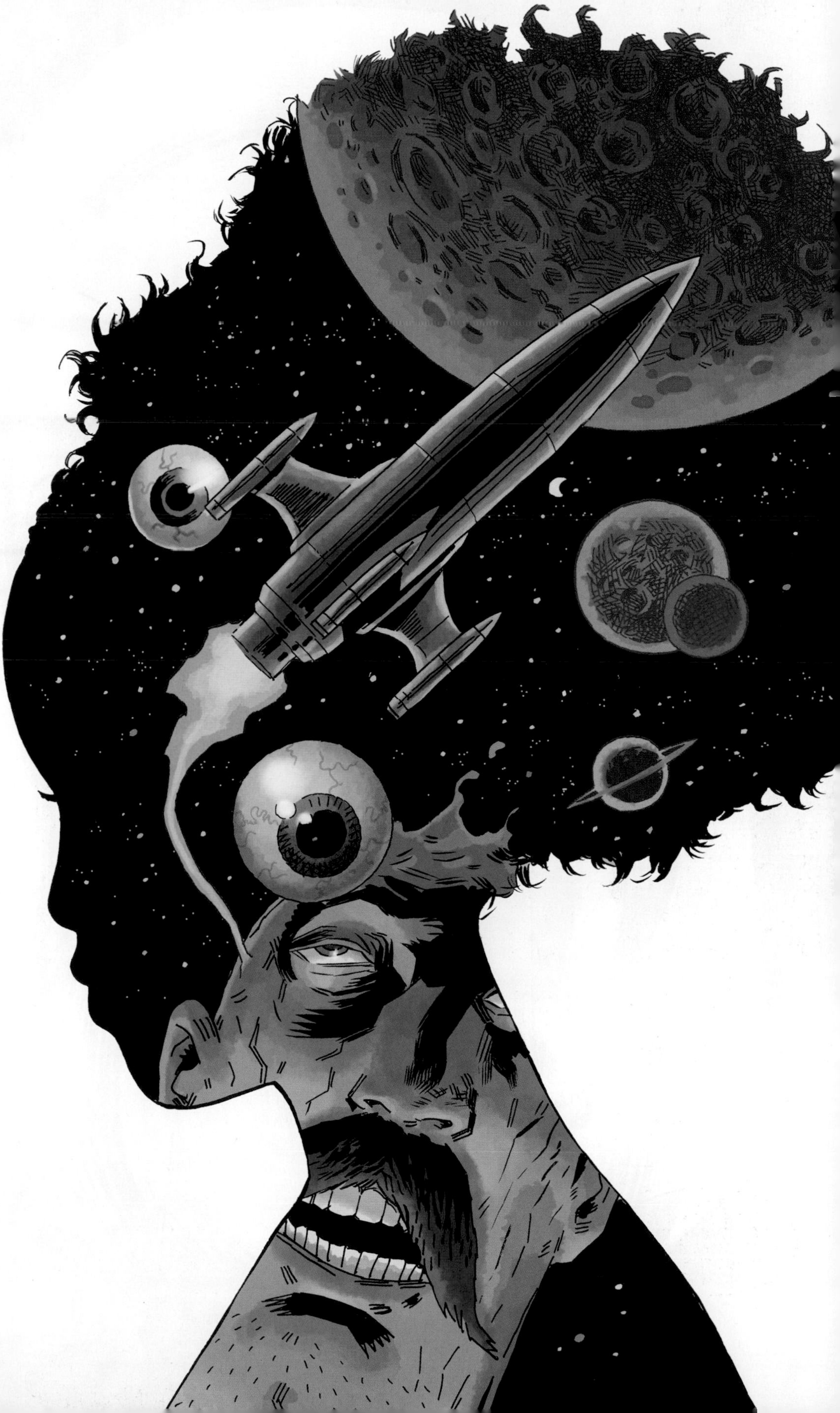

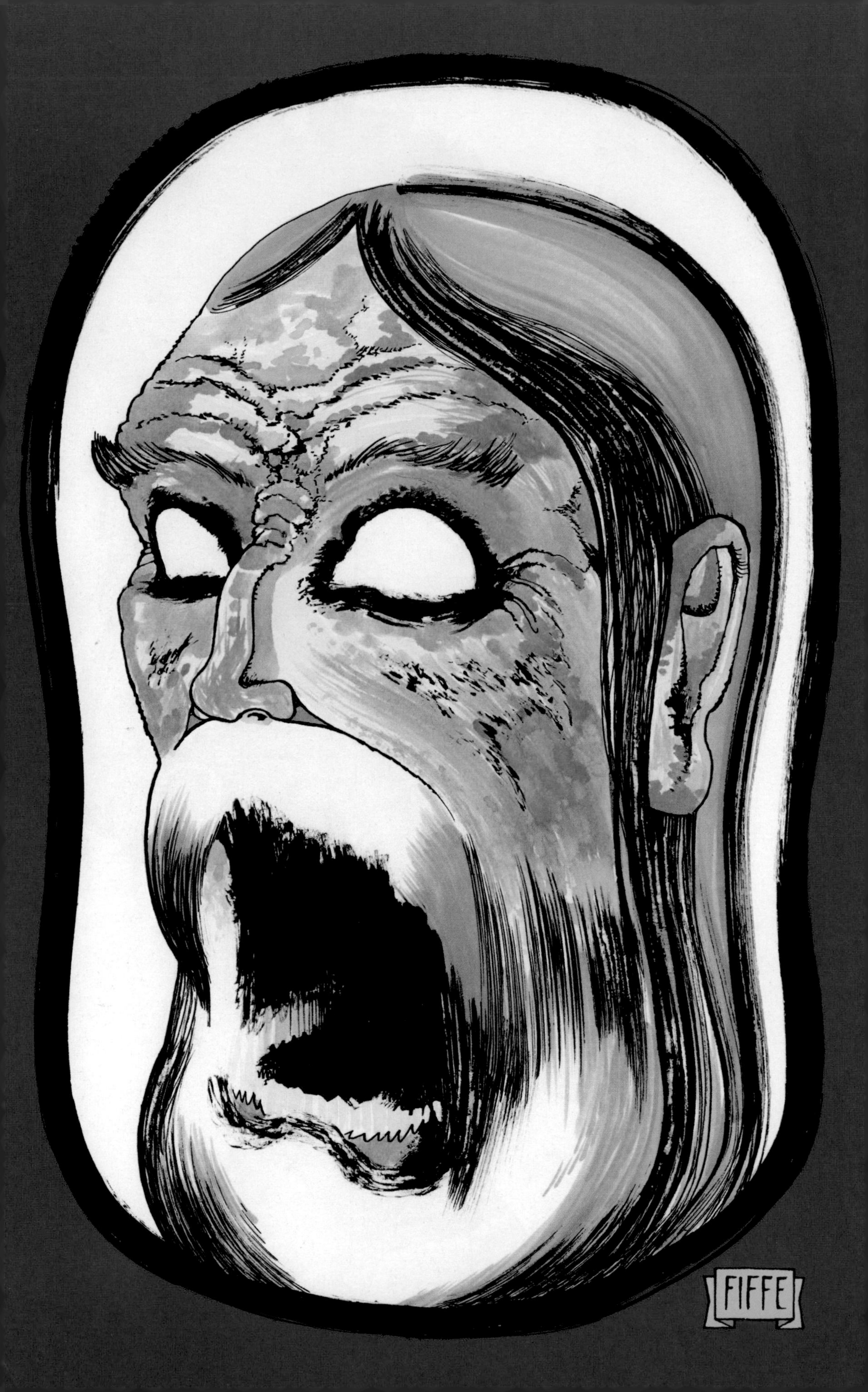
FIFFE

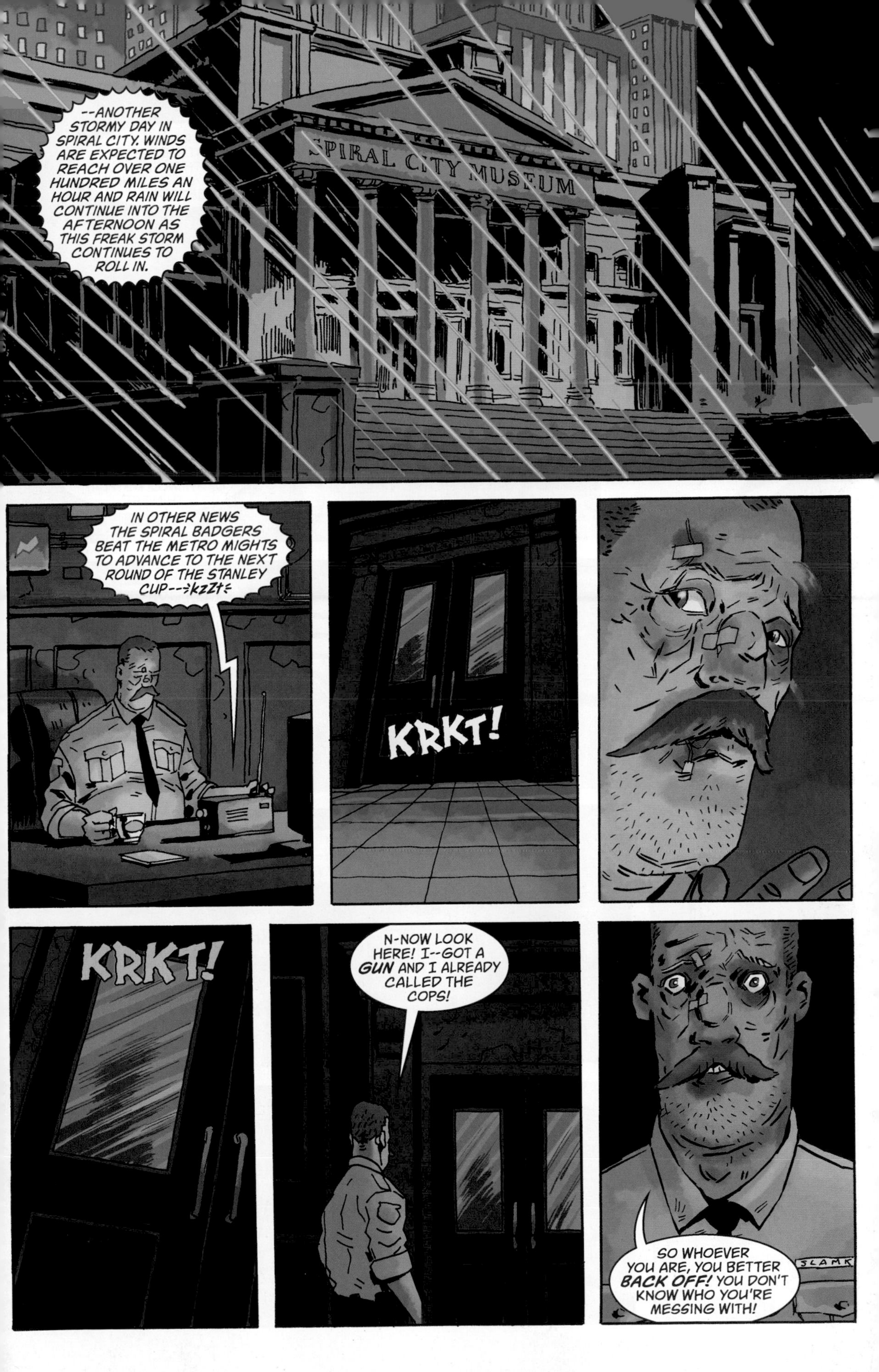
--ANOTHER STORMY DAY IN SPIRAL CITY. WINDS ARE EXPECTED TO REACH OVER ONE HUNDRED MILES AN HOUR AND RAIN WILL CONTINUE INTO THE AFTERNOON AS THIS FREAK STORM CONTINUES TO ROLL IN.
SPIRAL CITY MUSEUM
IN OTHER NEWS THE SPIRAL BADGERS BEAT THE METRO MIGHTS TO ADVANCE TO THE NEXT ROUND OF THE STANLEY CUP--≯kzZt≮
KRKT!
KRKT!
N-NOW LOOK HERE! I--GOT A GUN AND I ALREADY CALLED THE COPS!
SO WHOEVER YOU ARE, YOU BETTER BACK OFF! YOU DON'T KNOW WHO YOU'RE MESSING WITH!
SLAMK

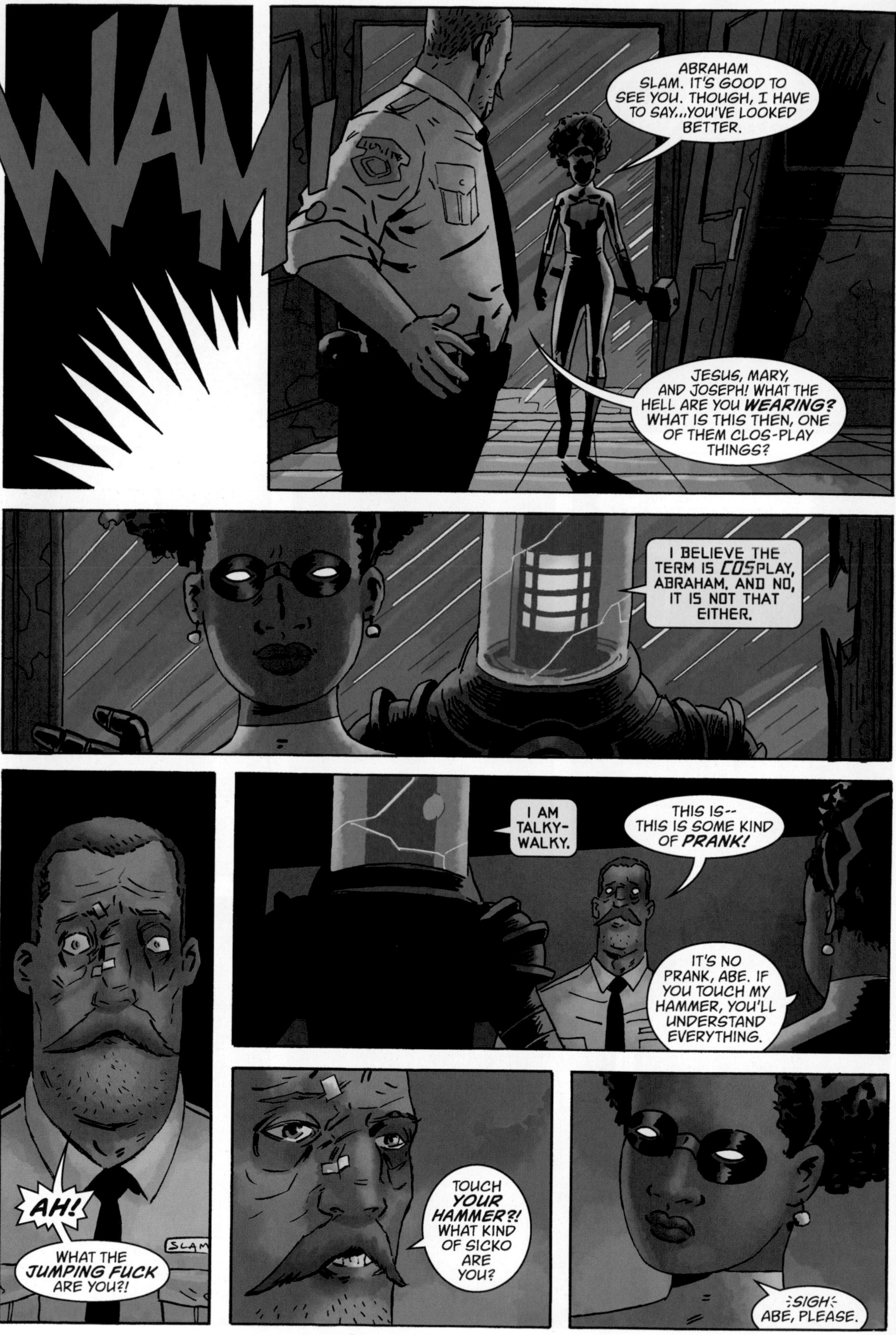
WAM!
ABRAHAM SLAM. IT'S GOOD TO SEE YOU. THOUGH, I HAVE TO SAY...YOU'VE LOOKED BETTER.
JESUS, MARY, AND JOSEPH! WHAT THE HELL ARE YOU WEARING? WHAT IS THIS THEN, ONE OF THEM CLOS-PLAY THINGS?
I BELIEVE THE TERM IS COSPLAY, ABRAHAM. AND NO, IT IS NOT THAT EITHER.
AH!
WHAT THE JUMPING FUCK ARE YOU?!
SLAM
I AM TALKY-WALKY.
THIS IS-- THIS IS SOME KIND OF PRANK!
IT'S NO PRANK, ABE. IF YOU TOUCH MY HAMMER, YOU'LL UNDERSTAND EVERYTHING.
TOUCH YOUR HAMMER?! WHAT KIND OF SICKO ARE YOU?
SIGH ABE, PLEASE.

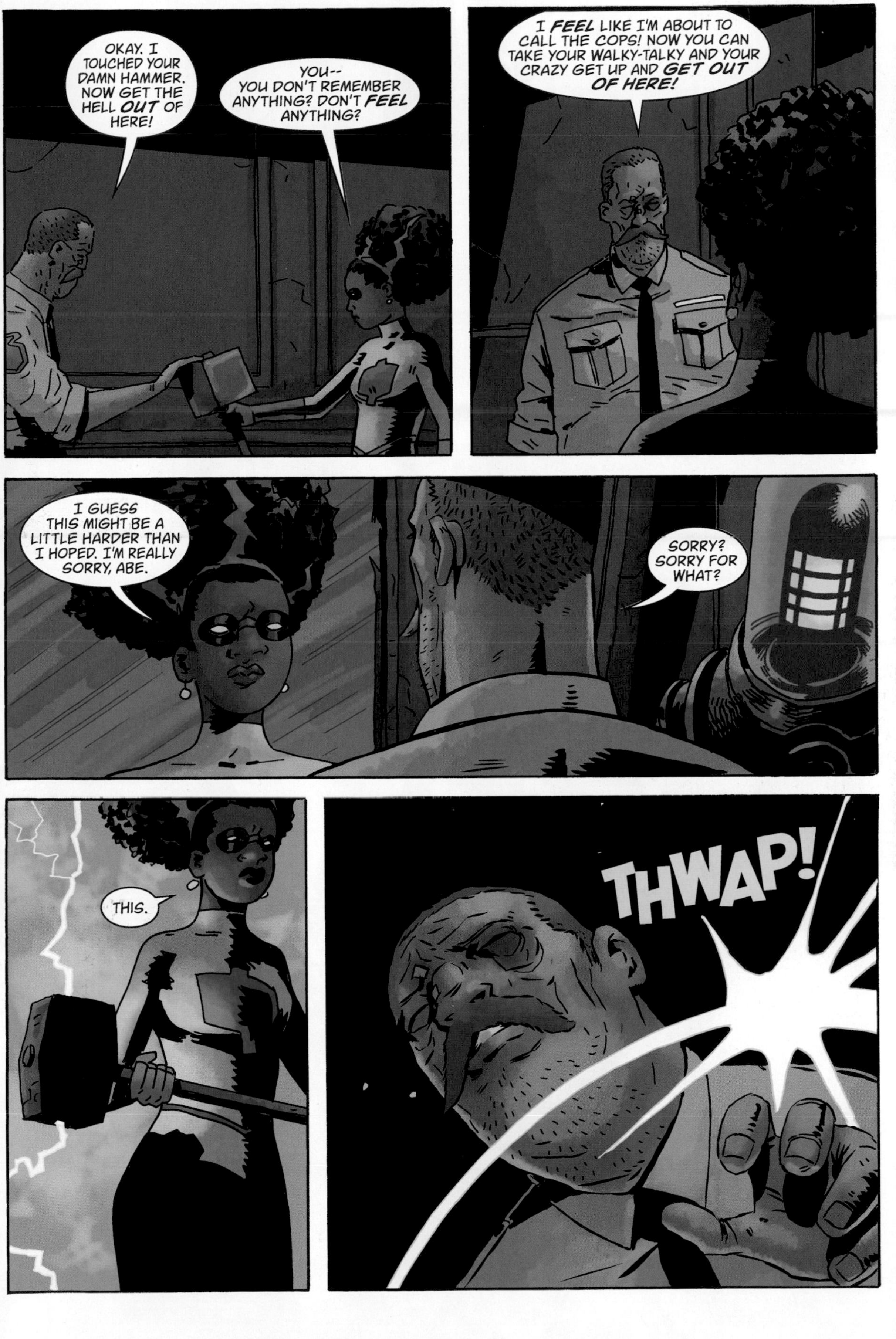
OKAY. I TOUCHED YOUR DAMN HAMMER. NOW GET THE HELL OUT OF HERE!
YOU-- YOU DON'T REMEMBER ANYTHING? DON'T FEEL ANYTHING?
I FEEL LIKE I'M ABOUT TO CALL THE COPS! NOW YOU CAN TAKE YOUR WALKY-TALKY AND YOUR CRAZY GET UP AND GET OUT OF HERE!
I GUESS THIS MIGHT BE A LITTLE HARDER THAN I HOPED. I'M REALLY SORRY, ABE.
SORRY? SORRY FOR WHAT?
THIS.
THWAP!

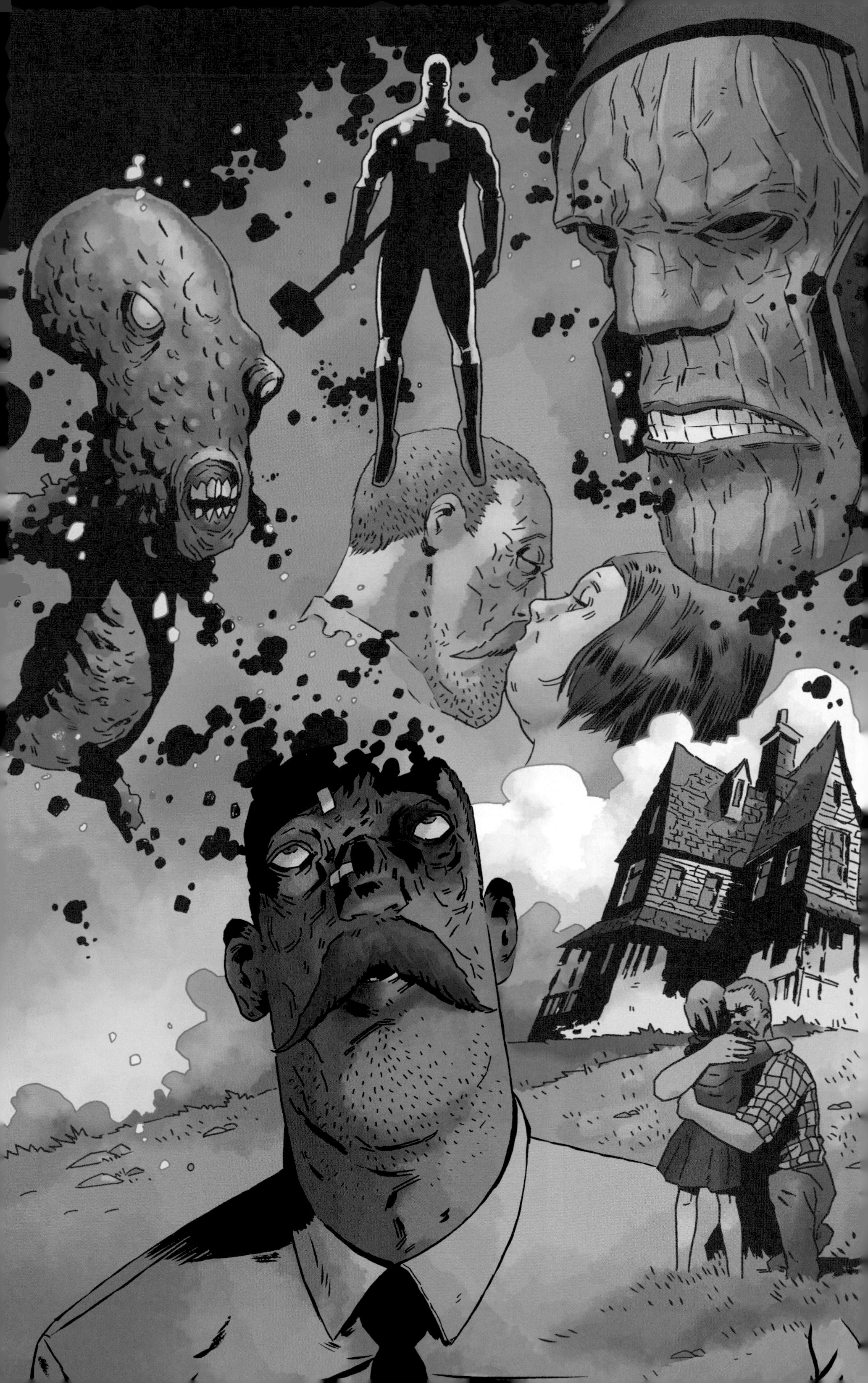

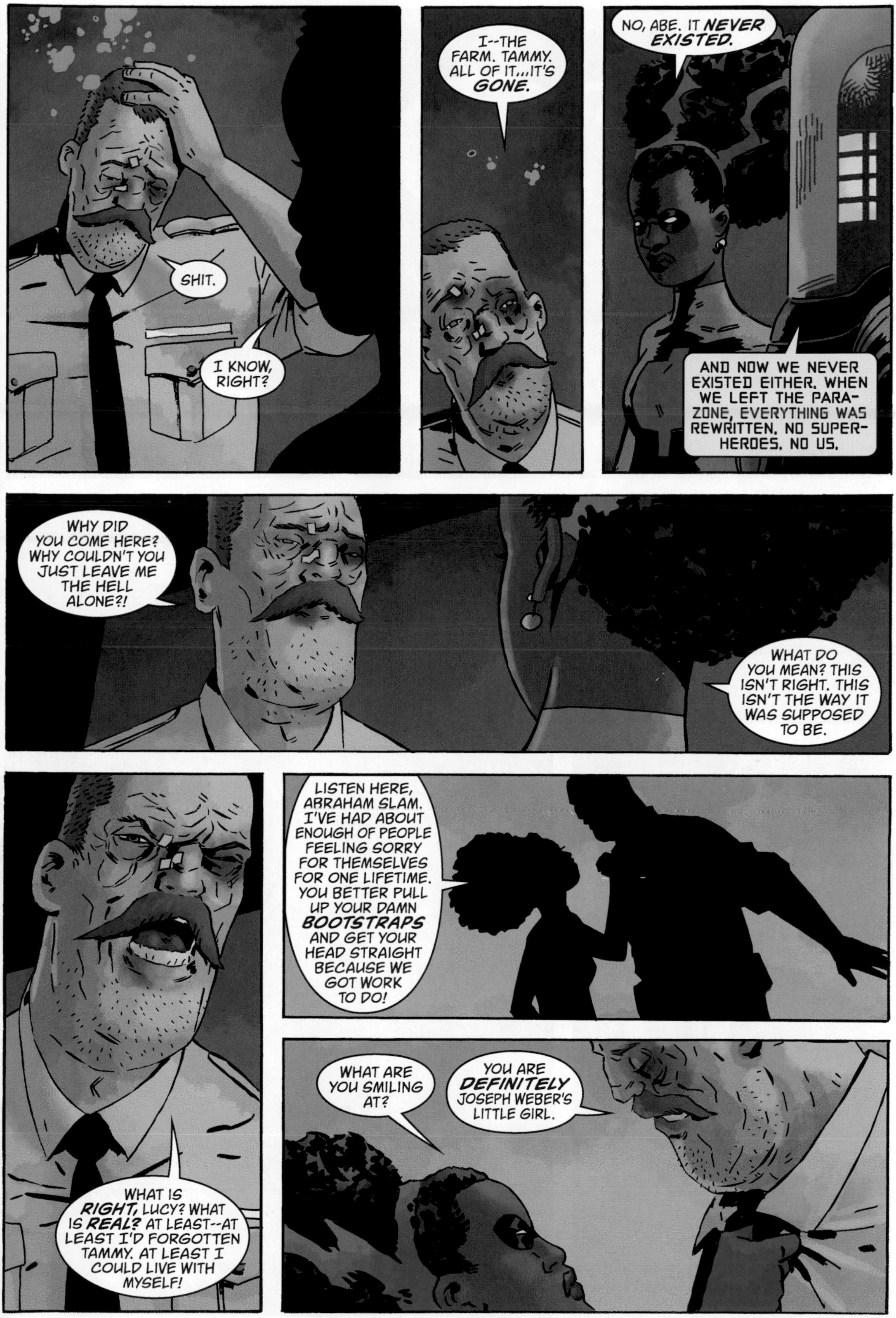
SHIT.
I KNOW, RIGHT?
I--THE FARM. TAMMY. ALL OF IT...IT'S GONE.
NO, ABE. IT NEVER EXISTED.
AND NOW WE NEVER EXISTED EITHER. WHEN WE LEFT THE PARA-ZONE, EVERYTHING WAS REWRITTEN. NO SUPER-HEROES. NO US.
WHY DID YOU COME HERE? WHY COULDN'T YOU JUST LEAVE ME THE HELL ALONE?!
WHAT DO YOU MEAN? THIS ISN'T RIGHT. THIS ISN'T THE WAY IT WAS SUPPOSED TO BE.
WHAT IS RIGHT, LUCY? WHAT IS REAL? AT LEAST--AT LEAST I'D FORGOTTEN TAMMY. AT LEAST I COULD LIVE WITH MYSELF!
LISTEN HERE, ABRAHAM SLAM. I'VE HAD ABOUT ENOUGH OF PEOPLE FEELING SORRY FOR THEMSELVES FOR ONE LIFETIME. YOU BETTER PULL UP YOUR DAMN BOOTSTRAPS AND GET YOUR HEAD STRAIGHT BECAUSE WE GOT WORK TO DO!
WHAT ARE YOU SMILING AT?
YOU ARE DEFINITELY JOSEPH WEBER'S LITTLE GIRL.

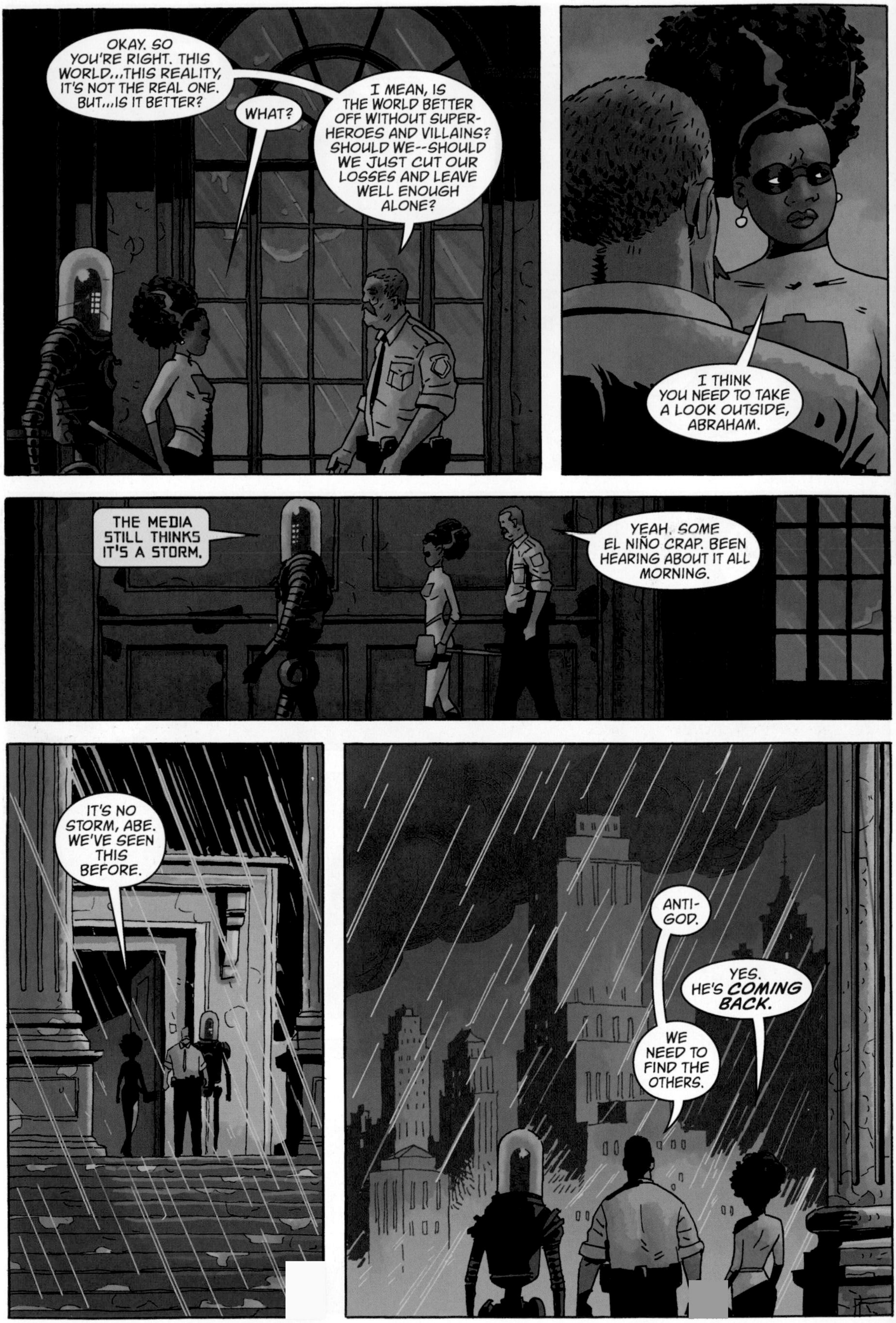
OKAY. SO YOU'RE RIGHT. THIS WORLD...THIS REALITY, IT'S NOT THE REAL ONE. BUT...IS IT BETTER?
WHAT?
I MEAN, IS THE WORLD BETTER OFF WITHOUT SUPER-HEROES AND VILLAINS? SHOULD WE--SHOULD WE JUST CUT OUR LOSSES AND LEAVE WELL ENOUGH ALONE?
I THINK YOU NEED TO TAKE A LOOK OUTSIDE, ABRAHAM.
THE MEDIA STILL THINKS IT'S A STORM.
YEAH. SOME EL NIÑO CRAP. BEEN HEARING ABOUT IT ALL MORNING.
IT'S NO STORM, ABE. WE'VE SEEN THIS BEFORE.
ANTI-GOD.
YES. HE'S *COMING BACK.*
WE NEED TO FIND THE OTHERS.

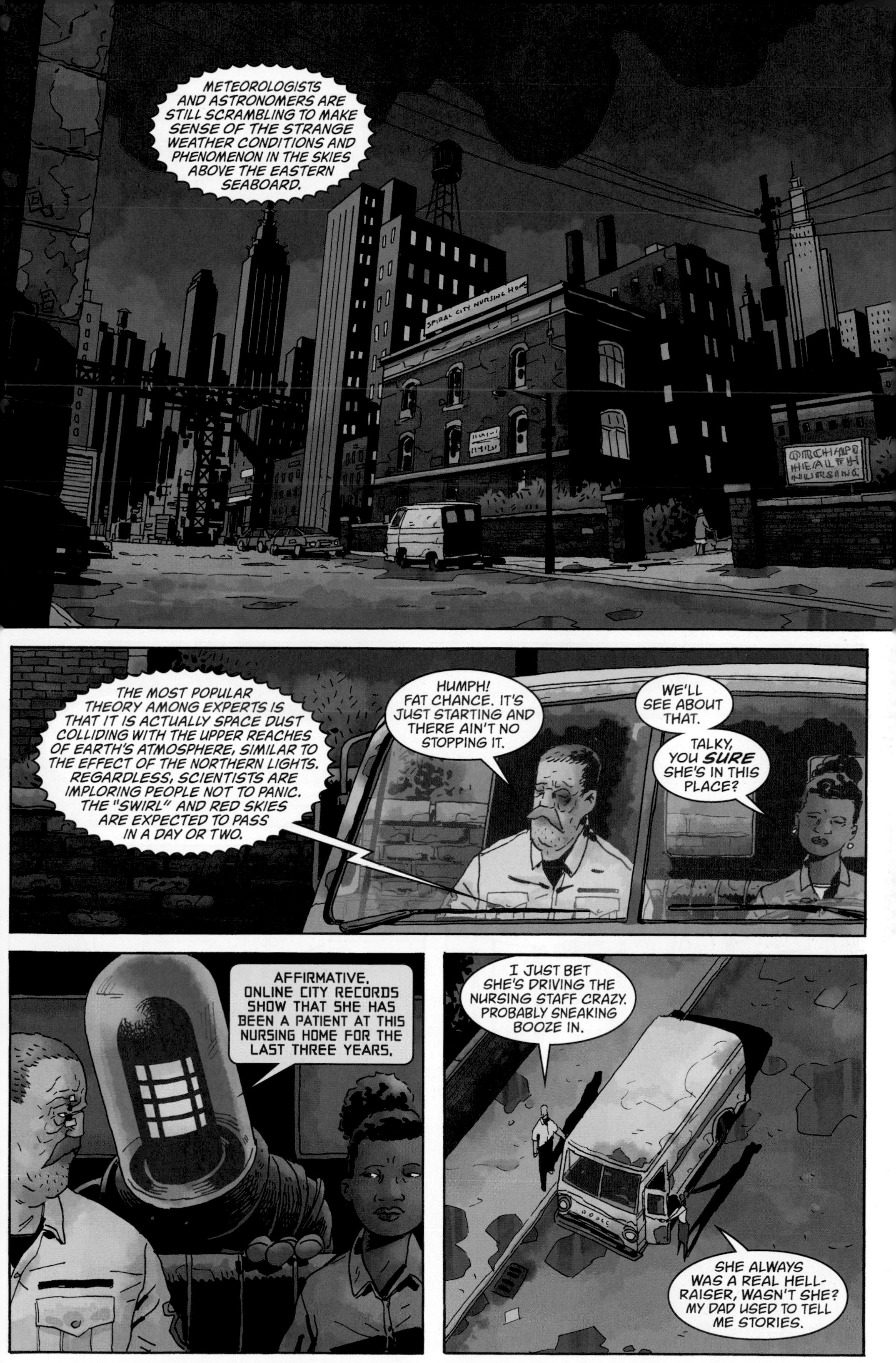
METEOROLOGISTS AND ASTRONOMERS ARE STILL SCRAMBLING TO MAKE SENSE OF THE STRANGE WEATHER CONDITIONS AND PHENOMENON IN THE SKIES ABOVE THE EASTERN SEABOARD.
SPIRAL CITY NURSING HOME
ORCHARD HEALTH NURSING
THE MOST POPULAR THEORY AMONG EXPERTS IS THAT IT IS ACTUALLY SPACE DUST COLLIDING WITH THE UPPER REACHES OF EARTH'S ATMOSPHERE, SIMILAR TO THE EFFECT OF THE NORTHERN LIGHTS. REGARDLESS, SCIENTISTS ARE IMPLORING PEOPLE NOT TO PANIC. THE "SWIRL" AND RED SKIES ARE EXPECTED TO PASS IN A DAY OR TWO.
HUMPH! FAT CHANCE. IT'S JUST STARTING AND THERE AIN'T NO STOPPING IT.
WE'LL SEE ABOUT THAT.
TALKY, YOU **SURE** SHE'S IN THIS PLACE?
AFFIRMATIVE. ONLINE CITY RECORDS SHOW THAT SHE HAS BEEN A PATIENT AT THIS NURSING HOME FOR THE LAST THREE YEARS.
I JUST BET SHE'S DRIVING THE NURSING STAFF CRAZY. PROBABLY SNEAKING BOOZE IN.
SHE ALWAYS WAS A REAL HELL-RAISER, WASN'T SHE? MY DAD USED TO TELL ME STORIES.

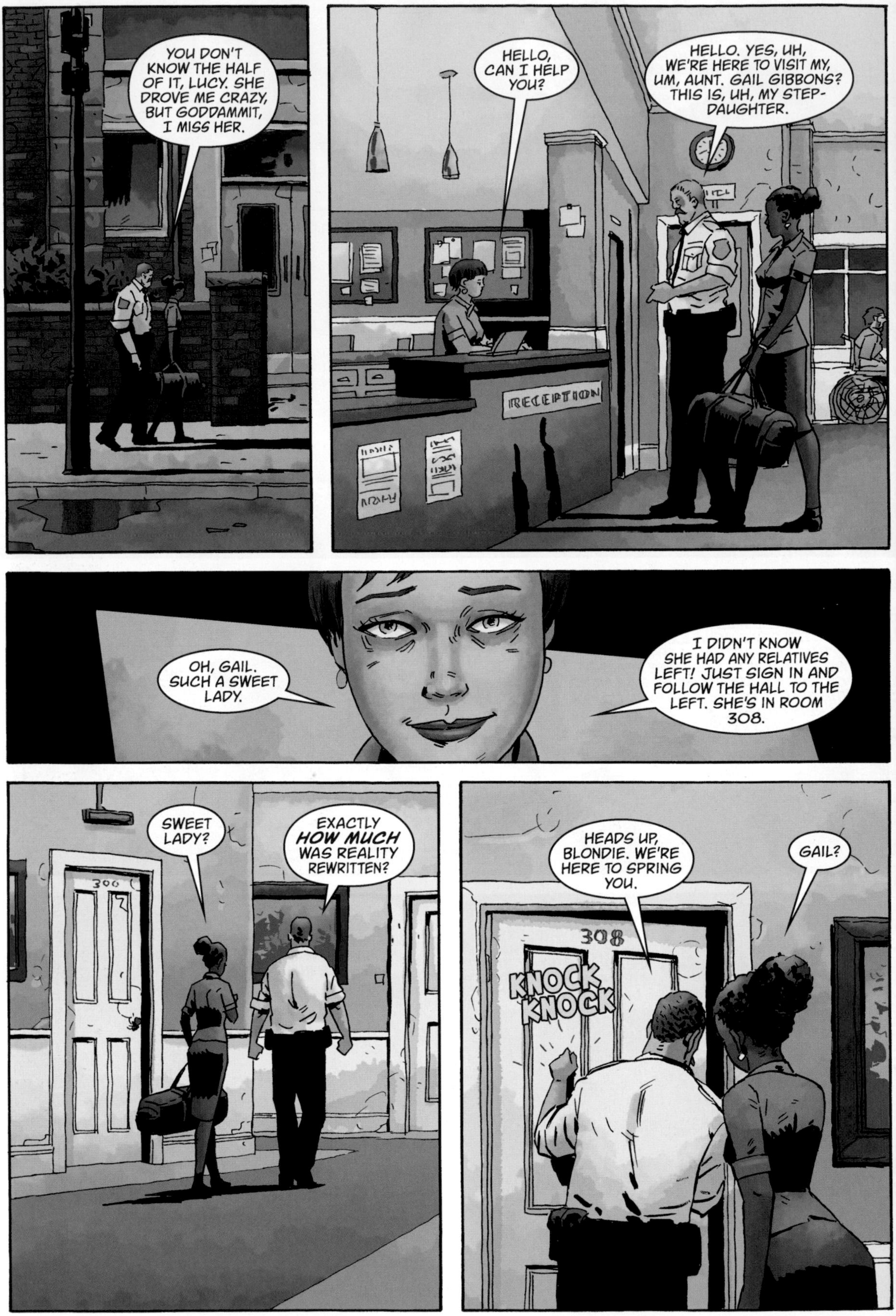
YOU DON'T KNOW THE HALF OF IT, LUCY. SHE DROVE ME CRAZY, BUT GODDAMMIT, I MISS HER.
HELLO, CAN I HELP YOU?
HELLO. YES, UH, WE'RE HERE TO VISIT MY, UM, AUNT. GAIL GIBBONS? THIS IS, UH, MY STEP-DAUGHTER.
RECEPTION
OH, GAIL. SUCH A SWEET LADY.
I DIDN'T KNOW SHE HAD ANY RELATIVES LEFT! JUST SIGN IN AND FOLLOW THE HALL TO THE LEFT. SHE'S IN ROOM 308.
SWEET LADY?
EXACTLY HOW MUCH WAS REALITY REWRITTEN?
308
KNOCK KNOCK
HEADS UP, BLONDIE. WE'RE HERE TO SPRING YOU.
GAIL?

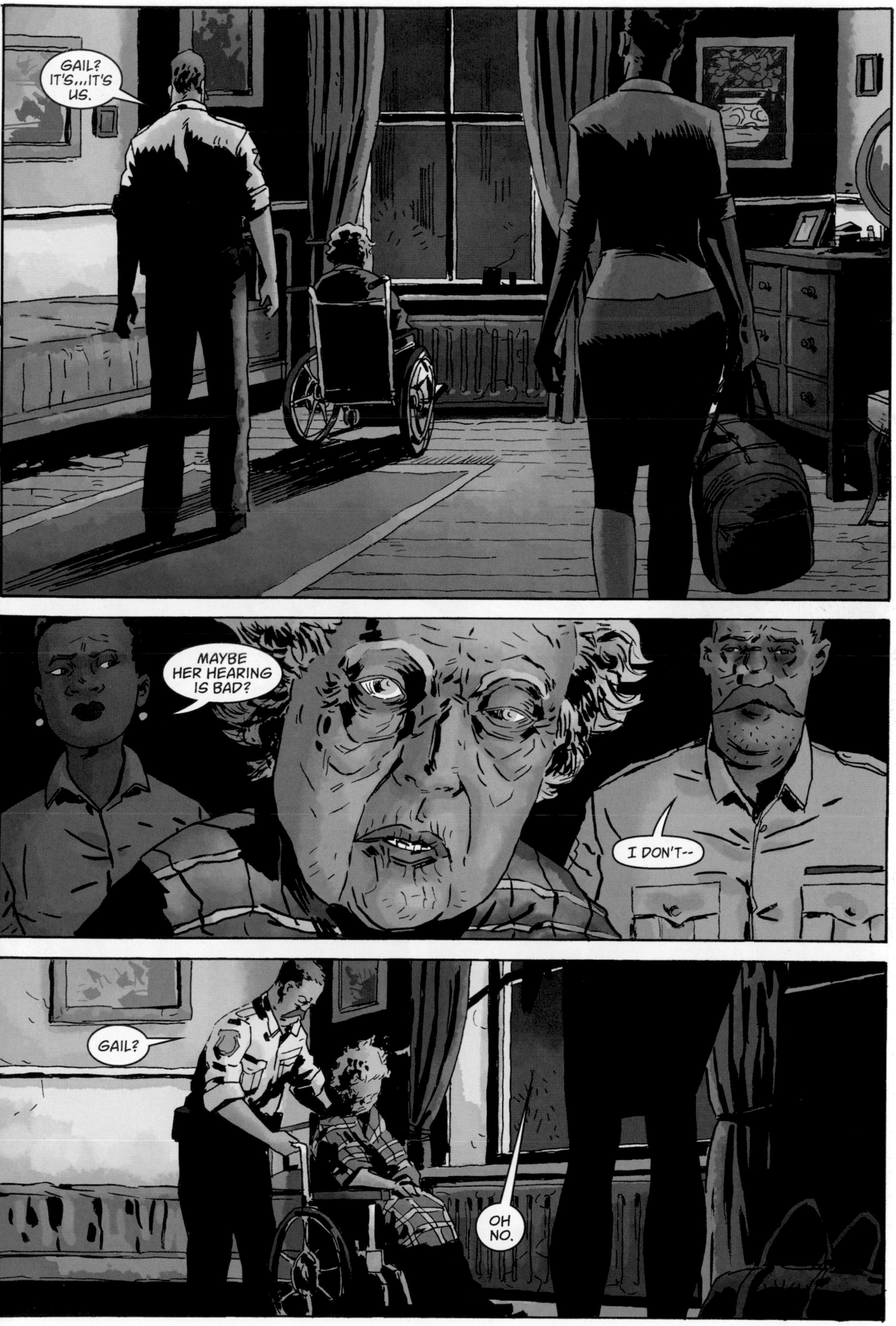
GAIL? IT'S...IT'S US.
MAYBE HER HEARING IS BAD?
I DON'T--
GAIL?
OH NO.

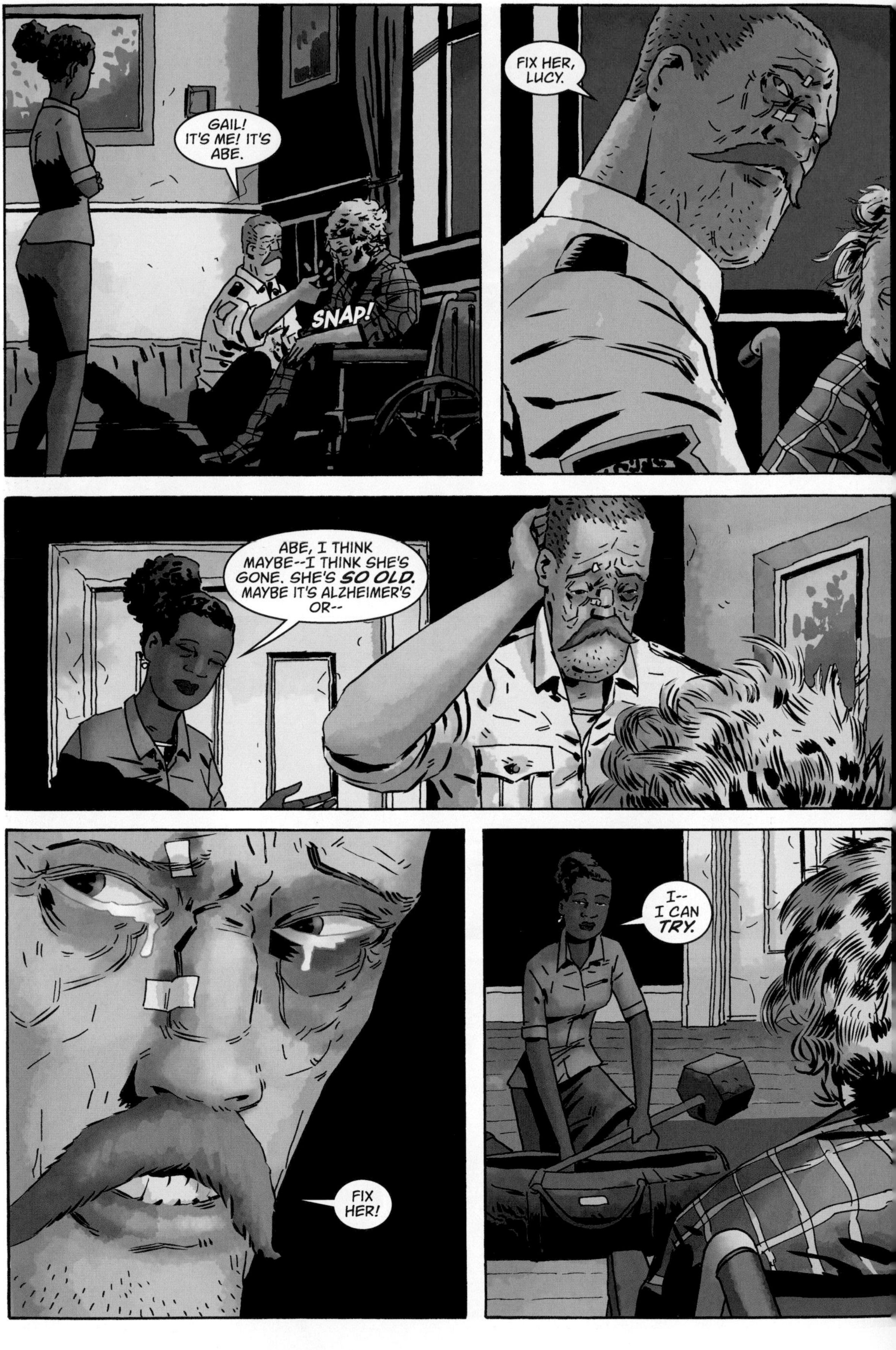
GAIL! IT'S ME! IT'S ABE.
SNAP!
FIX HER, LUCY.
ABE, I THINK MAYBE--I THINK SHE'S GONE. SHE'S SO OLD. MAYBE IT'S ALZHEIMER'S OR--
FIX HER!
I-- I CAN TRY.

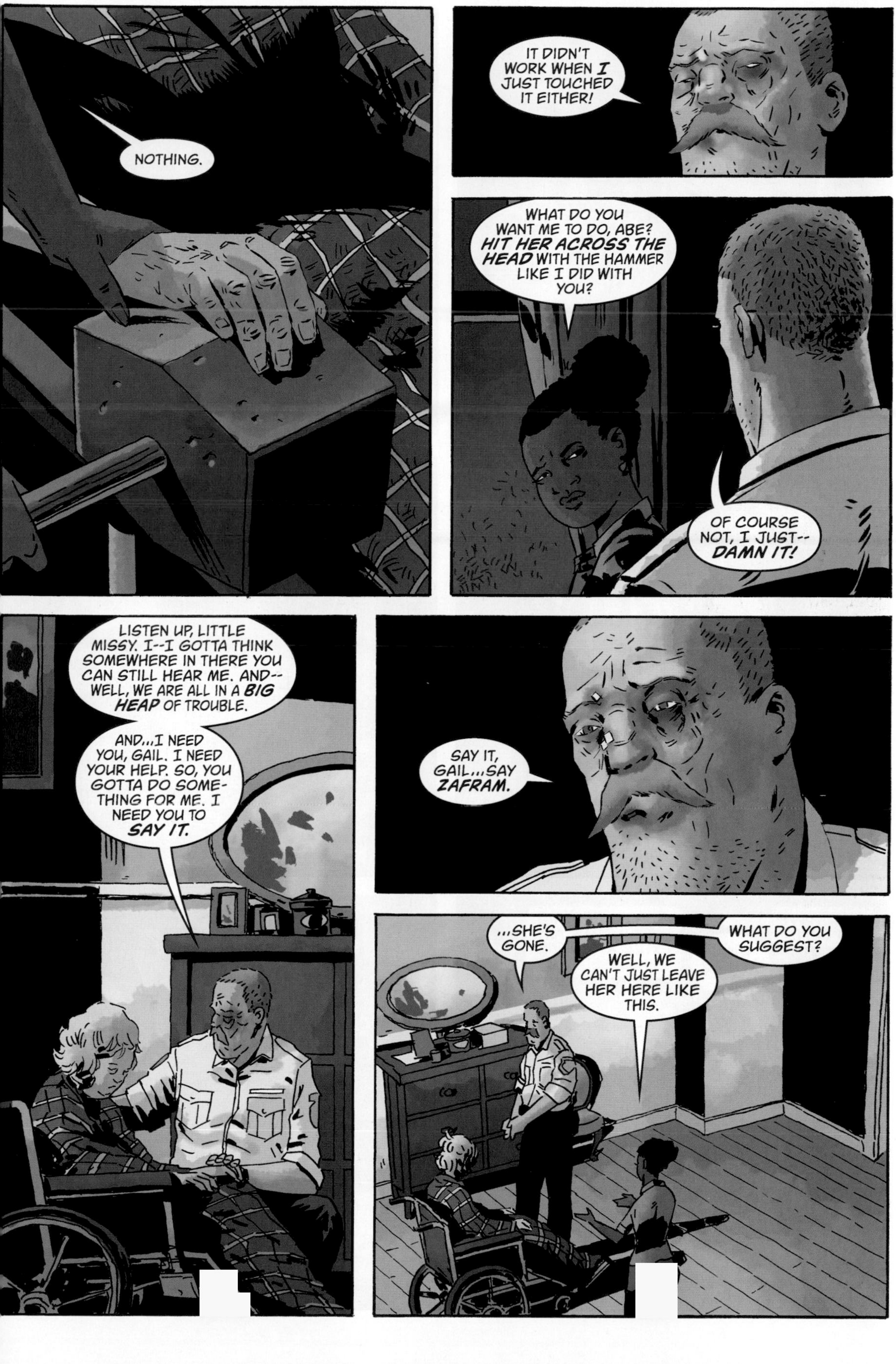
NOTHING.
IT DIDN'T WORK WHEN I JUST TOUCHED IT EITHER!
WHAT DO YOU WANT ME TO DO, ABE? HIT HER ACROSS THE HEAD WITH THE HAMMER LIKE I DID WITH YOU?
OF COURSE NOT, I JUST-- DAMN IT!
LISTEN UP, LITTLE MISSY. I--I GOTTA THINK SOMEWHERE IN THERE YOU CAN STILL HEAR ME. AND-- WELL, WE ARE ALL IN A BIG HEAP OF TROUBLE.
AND...I NEED YOU, GAIL. I NEED YOUR HELP. SO, YOU GOTTA DO SOMETHING FOR ME. I NEED YOU TO SAY IT.
SAY IT, GAIL...SAY ZAFRAM.
...SHE'S GONE.
WHAT DO YOU SUGGEST?
WELL, WE CAN'T JUST LEAVE HER HERE LIKE THIS.

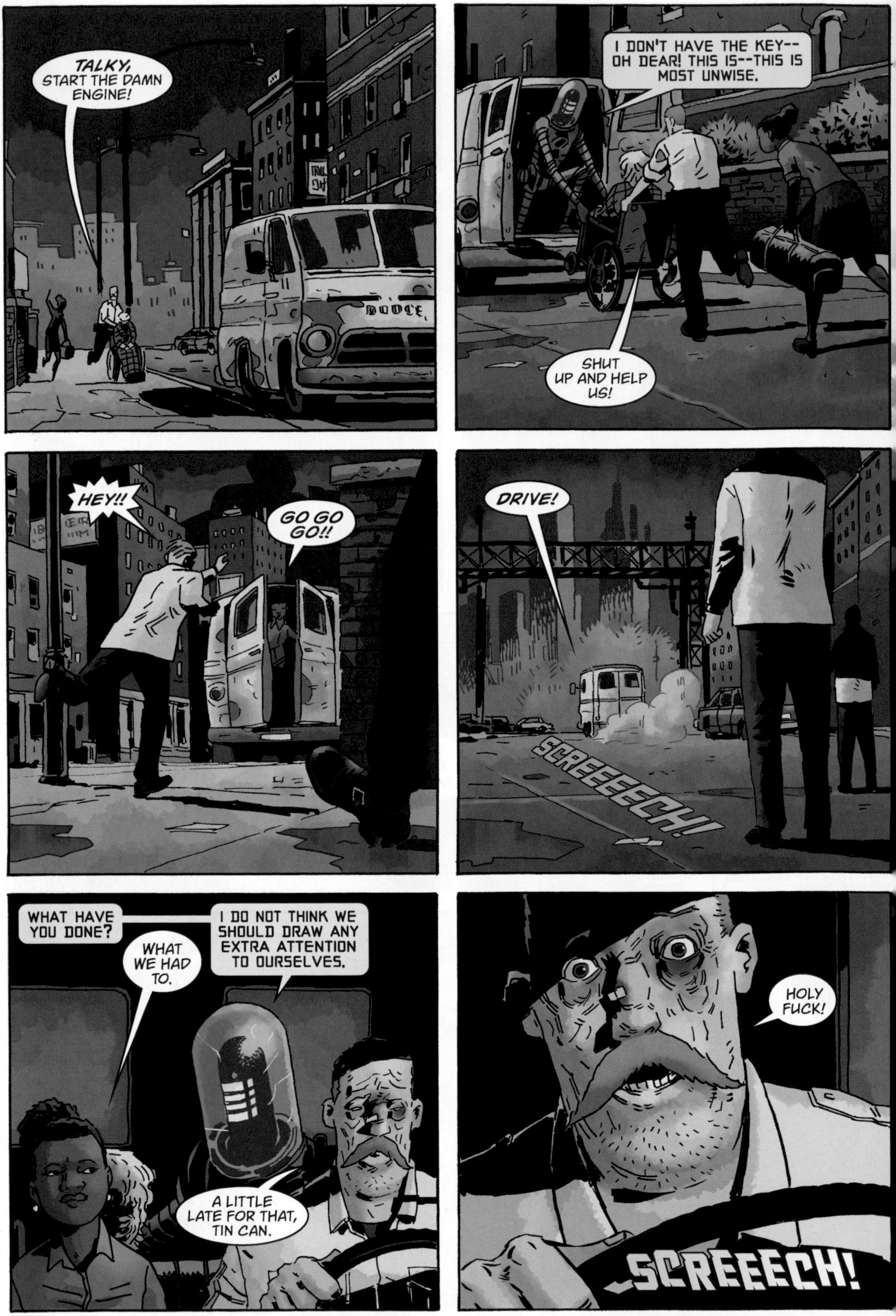
TALKY, START THE DAMN ENGINE!
DODGE
I DON'T HAVE THE KEY-- OH DEAR! THIS IS--THIS IS MOST UNWISE.
SHUT UP AND HELP US!
HEY!!
GO GO GO!!
DRIVE!
SCREEEECH!
WHAT HAVE YOU DONE?
WHAT WE HAD TO.
I DO NOT THINK WE SHOULD DRAW ANY EXTRA ATTENTION TO OURSELVES.
A LITTLE LATE FOR THAT, TIN CAN.
HOLY FUCK!
SCREEECH!

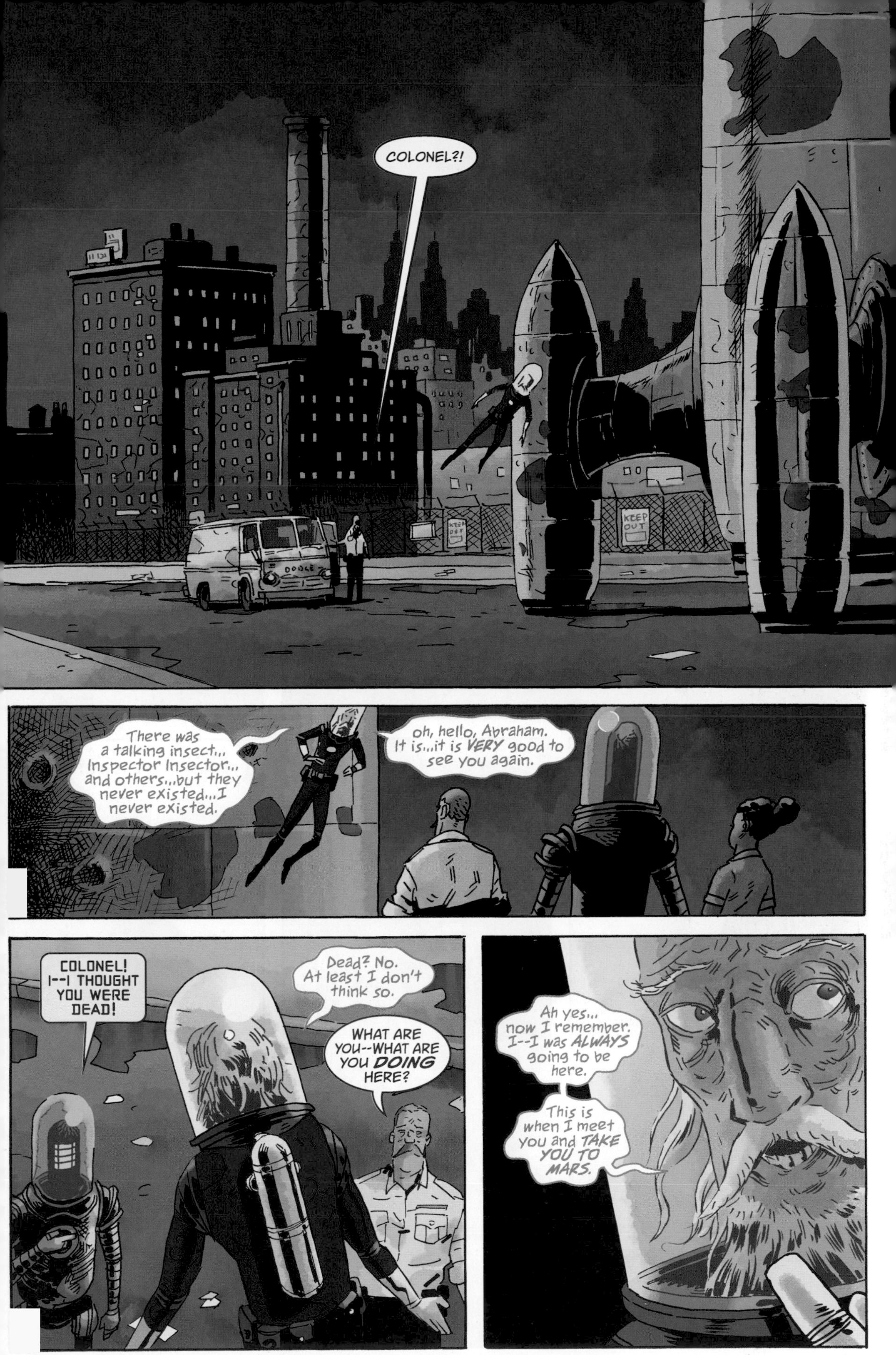

COLONEL?!
KEEP OUT
KEEP OUT
There was a talking insect... Inspector Insector... and others...but they never existed...I never existed.
oh, hello, Abraham. It is...it is VERY good to see you again.
COLONEL! I--I THOUGHT YOU WERE DEAD!
Dead? No. At least I don't think so.
WHAT ARE YOU--WHAT ARE YOU DOING HERE?
Ah yes... now I remember. I--I was ALWAYS going to be here.
This is when I meet you and TAKE YOU TO MARS.

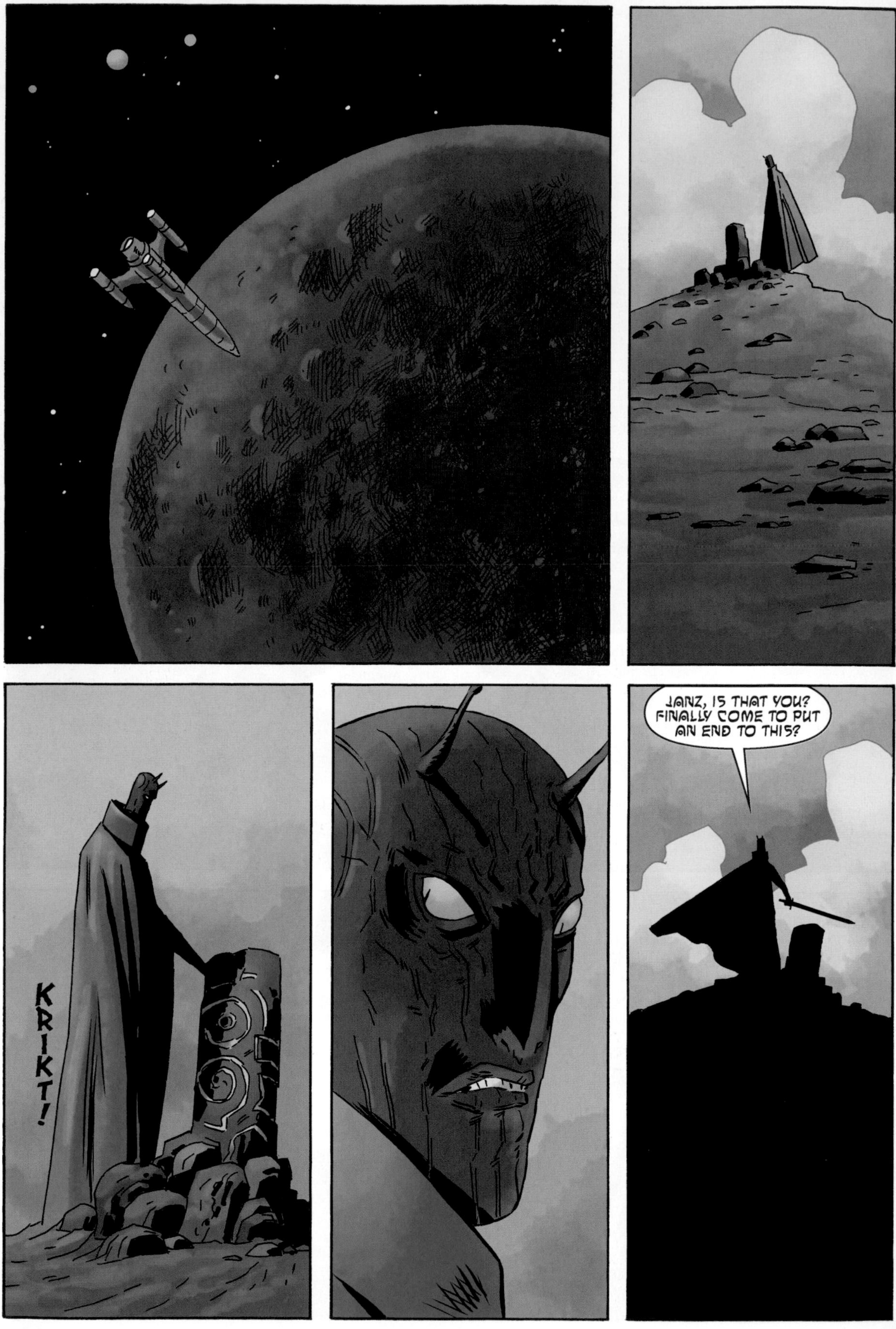
KRIKT!
JANZ, IS THAT YOU? FINALLY COME TO PUT AN END TO THIS?

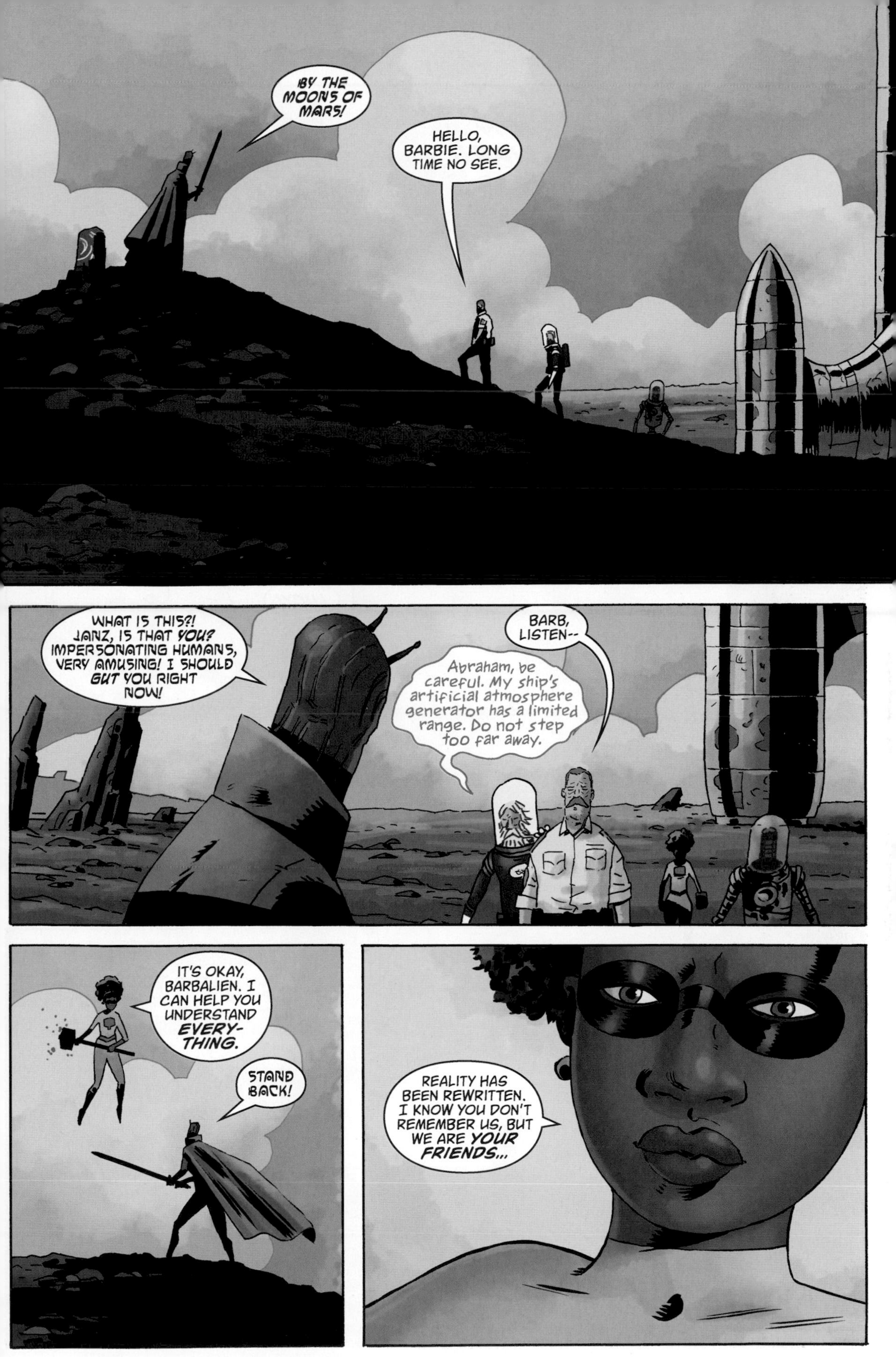
BY THE MOONS OF MARS!
HELLO, BARBIE. LONG TIME NO SEE.
WHAT IS THIS?! JANZ, IS THAT YOU? IMPERSONATING HUMANS, VERY AMUSING! I SHOULD GUT YOU RIGHT NOW!
BARB, LISTEN--
Abraham, be careful. My ship's artificial atmosphere generator has a limited range. Do not step too far away.
IT'S OKAY, BARBALIEN. I CAN HELP YOU UNDERSTAND EVERYTHING.
STAND BACK!
REALITY HAS BEEN REWRITTEN. I KNOW YOU DON'T REMEMBER US, BUT WE ARE YOUR FRIENDS...

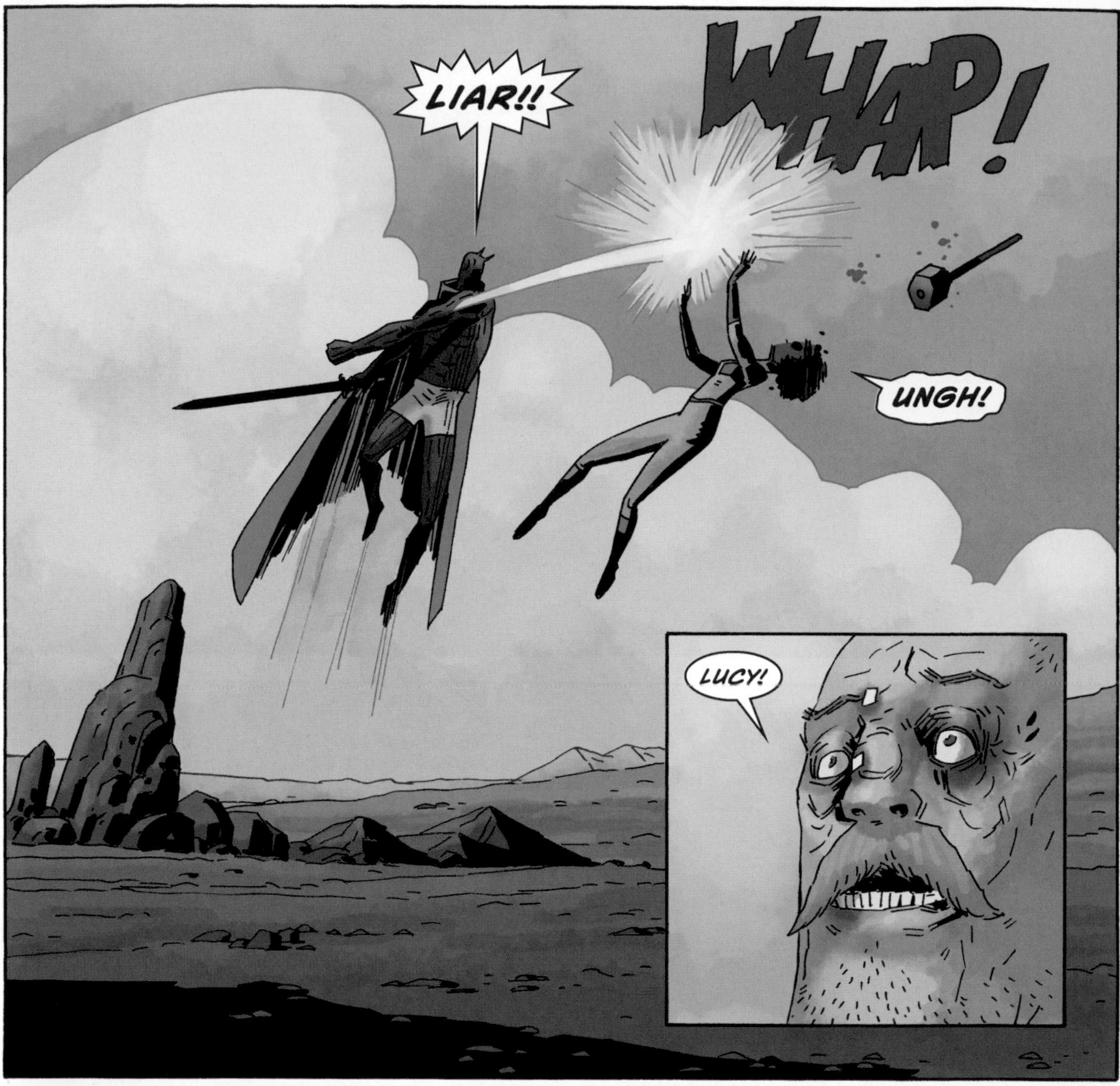
LIAR!!
WHAP!
UNGH!
LUCY!
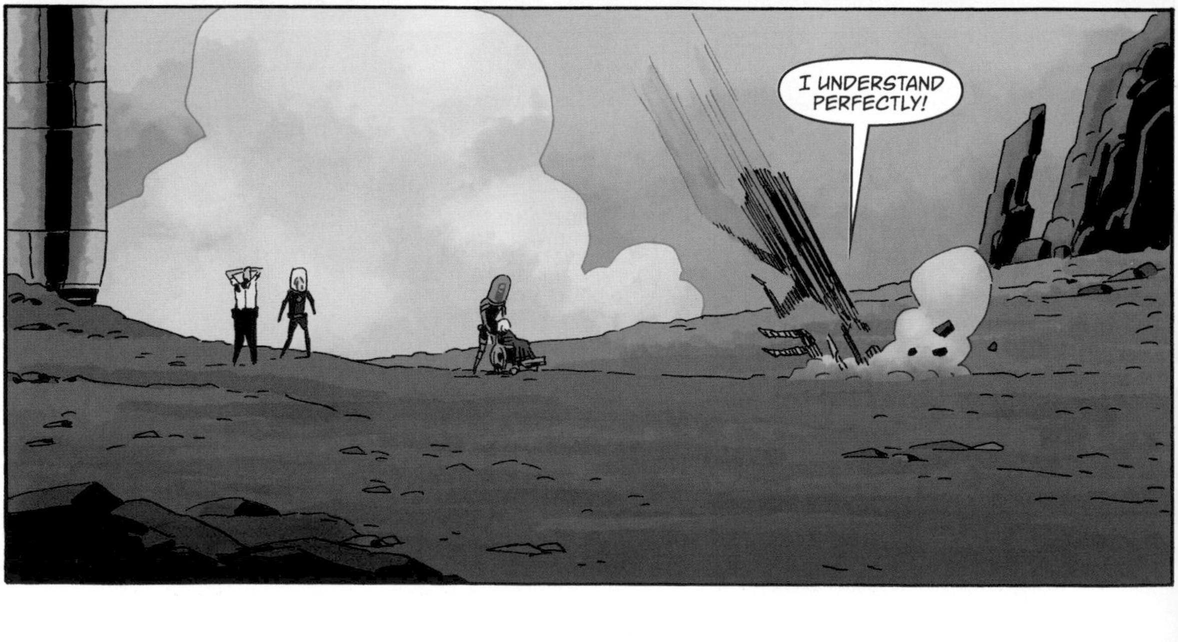
I UNDERSTAND PERFECTLY!

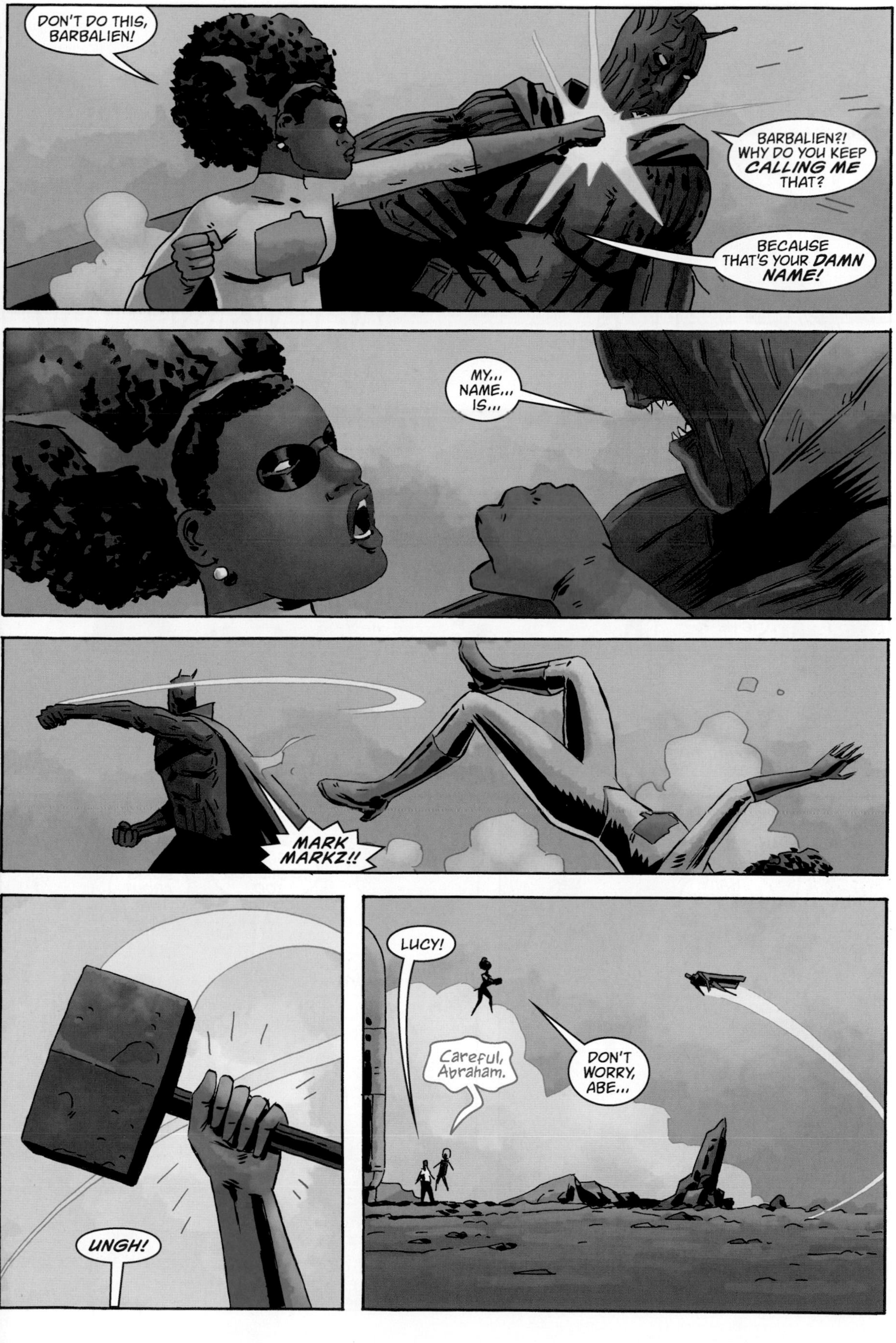
DON'T DO THIS, BARBALIEN!
BARBALIEN?! WHY DO YOU KEEP CALLING ME THAT?
BECAUSE THAT'S YOUR DAMN NAME!
MY... NAME... IS...
MARK MARKZ!!
UNGH!
LUCY!
Careful, Abraham.
DON'T WORRY, ABE...

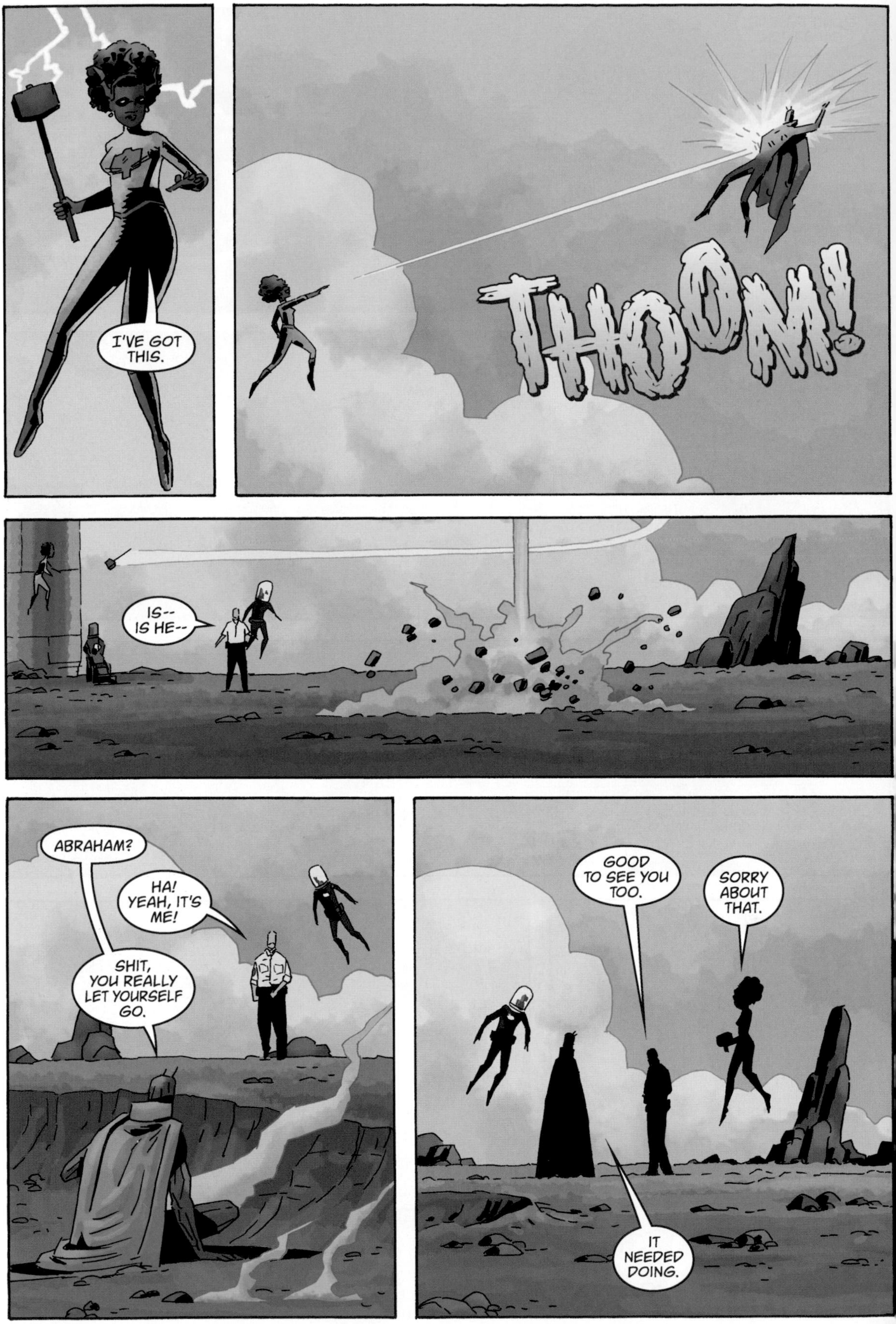

I'VE GOT THIS.
THOOM!
IS-- IS HE--
ABRAHAM?
HA! YEAH, IT'S ME!
SHIT, YOU REALLY LET YOURSELF GO.
GOOD TO SEE YOU TOO.
SORRY ABOUT THAT.
IT NEEDED DOING.

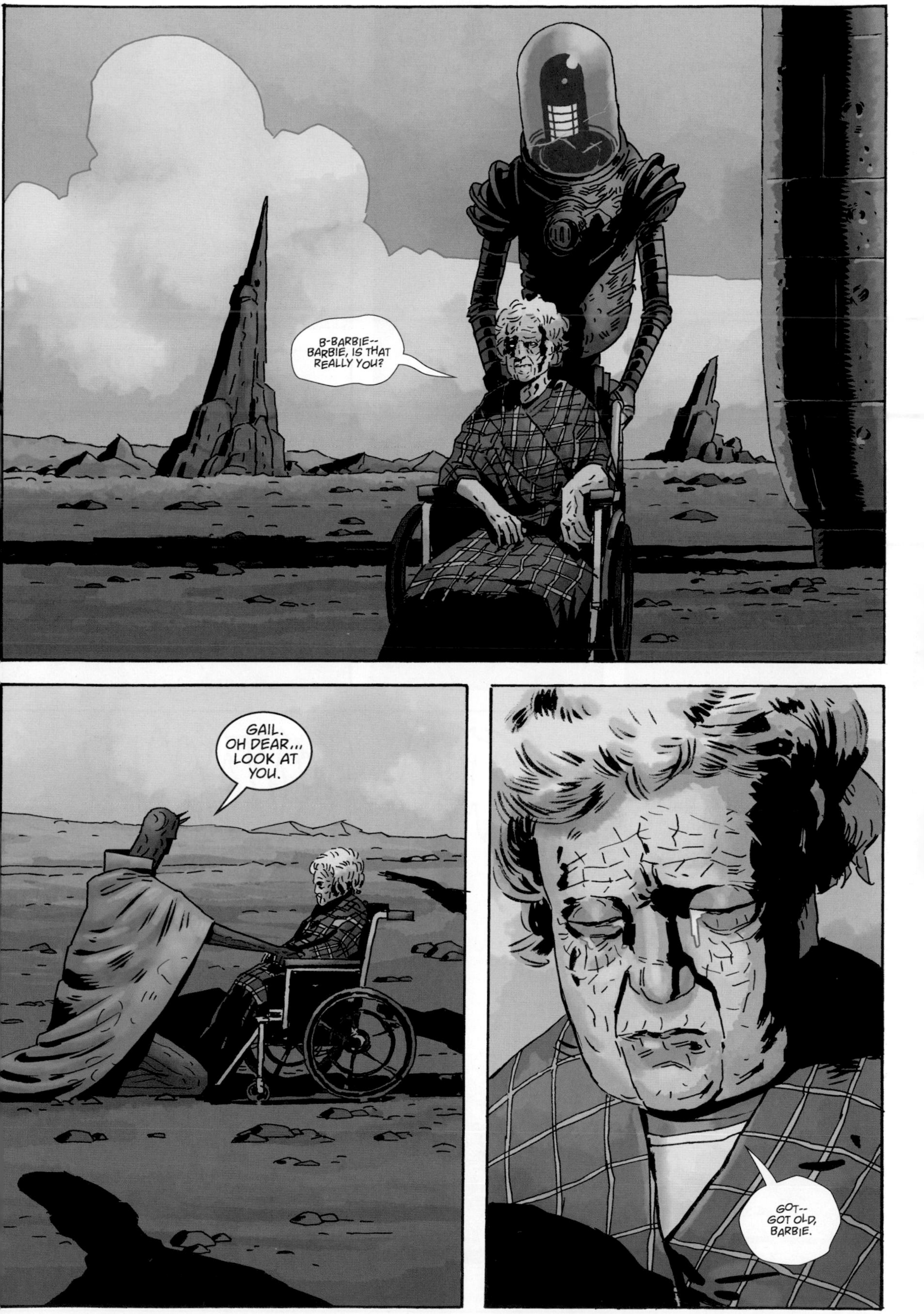
B-BARBIE-- BARBIE, IS THAT REALLY YOU?
GAIL. OH DEAR... LOOK AT YOU.
GOT-- GOT OLD, BARBIE.

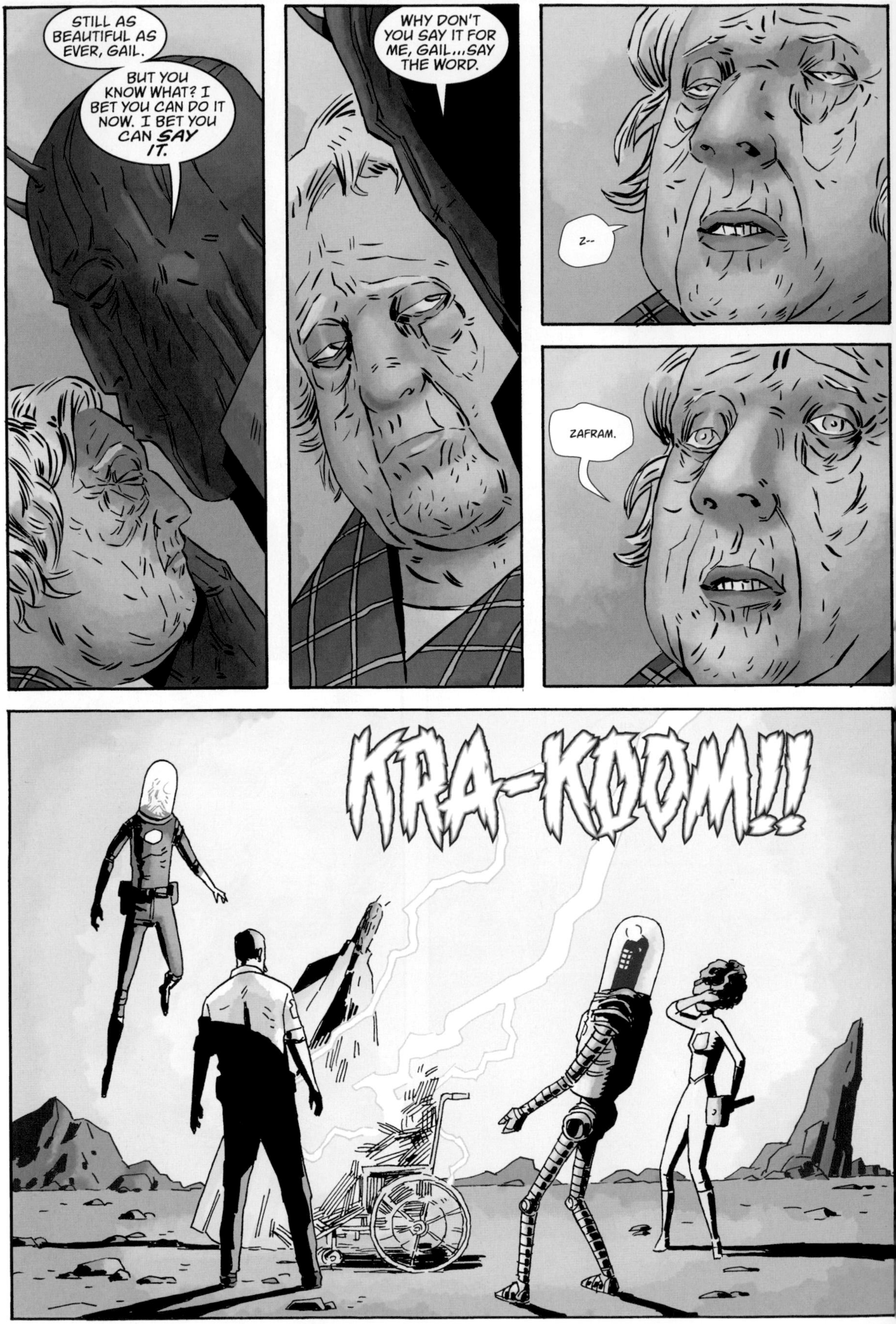
STILL AS BEAUTIFUL AS EVER, GAIL.
BUT YOU KNOW WHAT? I BET YOU CAN DO IT NOW. I BET YOU CAN SAY IT.
WHY DON'T YOU SAY IT FOR ME, GAIL...SAY THE WORD.
Z--
ZAFRAM.
KRA-KOOM!!

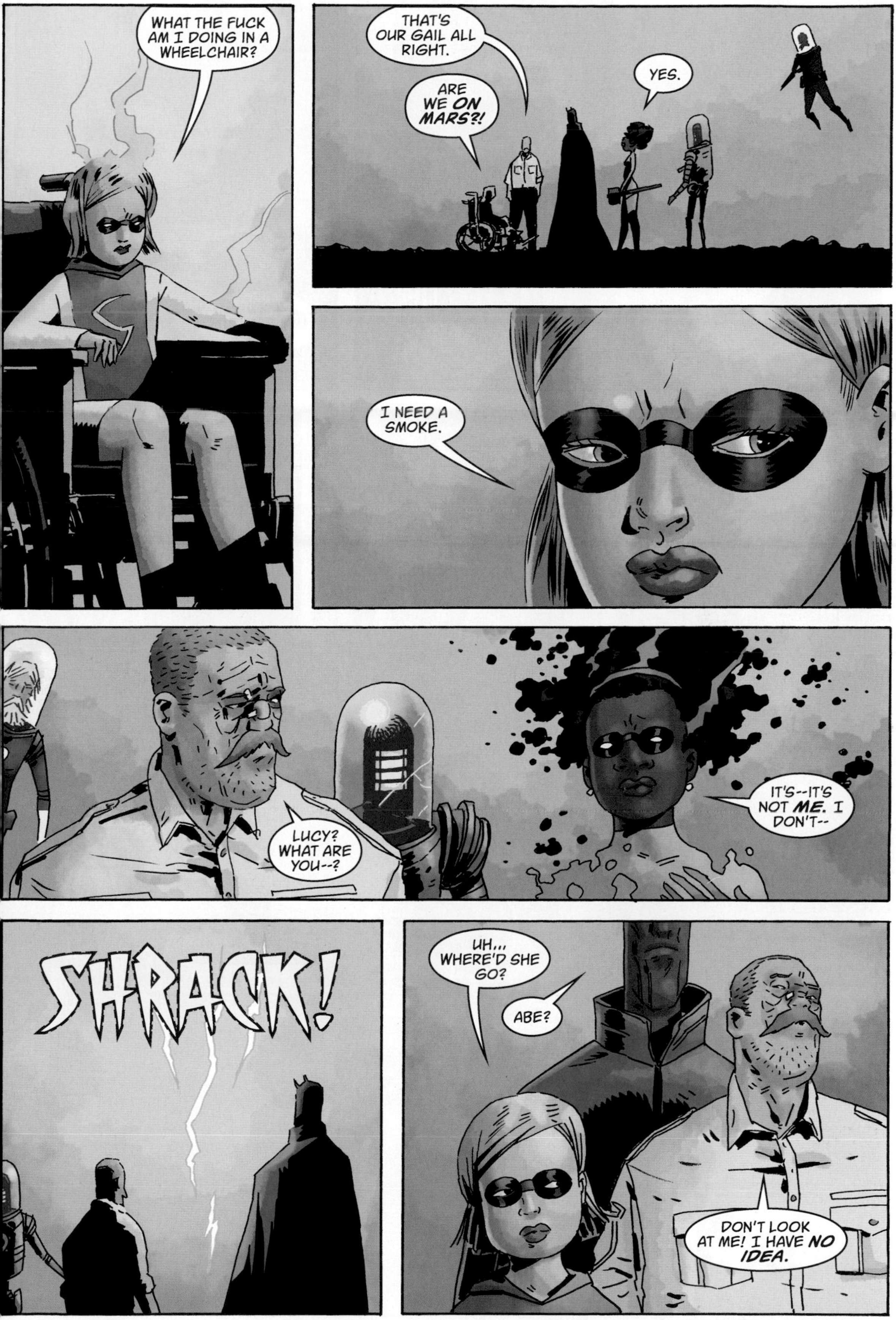
WHAT THE FUCK AM I DOING IN A WHEELCHAIR?
THAT'S OUR GAIL ALL RIGHT.
ARE WE ON MARS?!
YES.
I NEED A SMOKE.
LUCY? WHAT ARE YOU--?
IT'S--IT'S NOT ME. I DON'T--
SHRACK!
UH... WHERE'D SHE GO?
ABE?
DON'T LOOK AT ME! I HAVE NO IDEA.

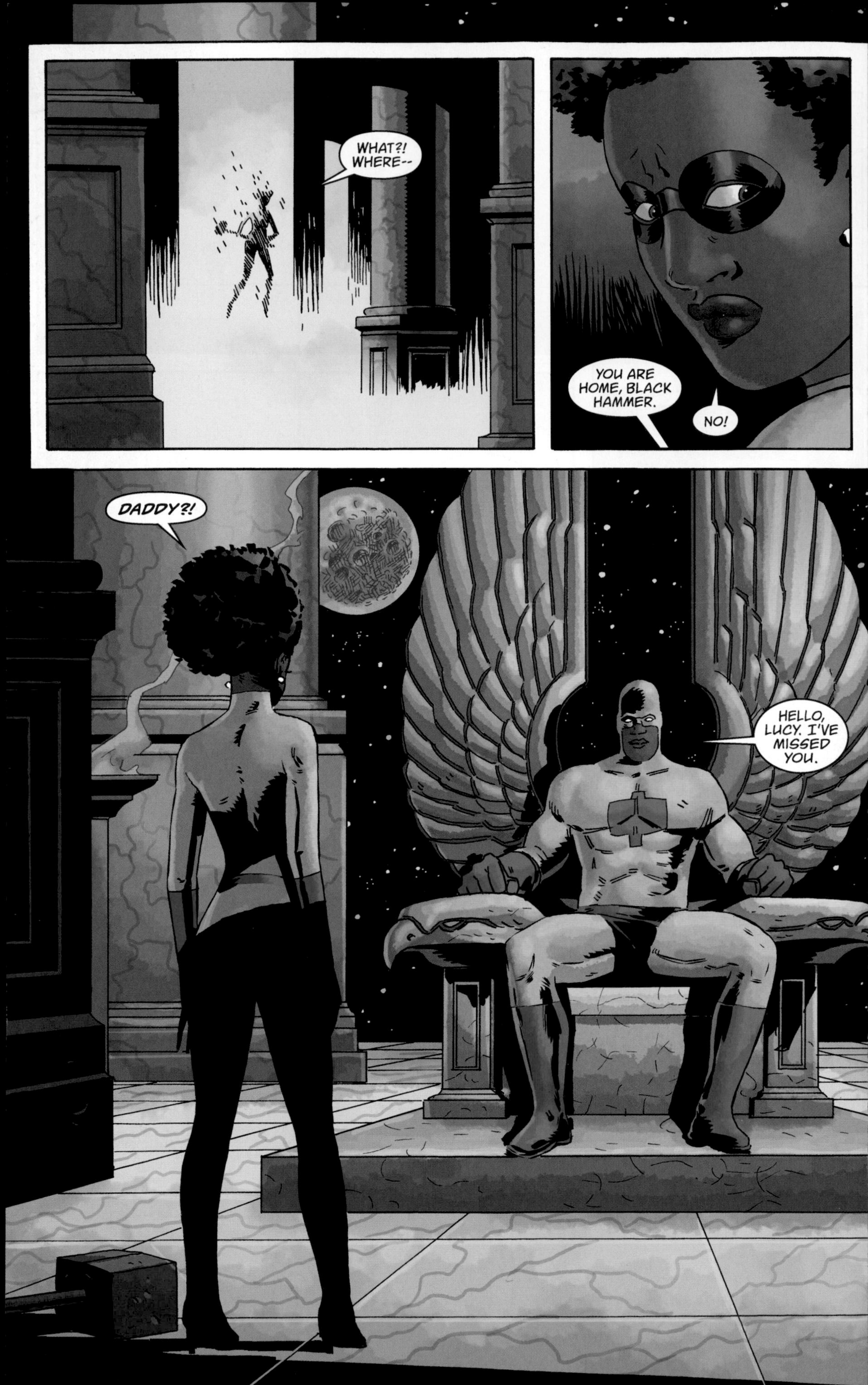
WHAT?! WHERE--
YOU ARE HOME, BLACK HAMMER.
NO!
DADDY?!
HELLO, LUCY. I'VE MISSED YOU.

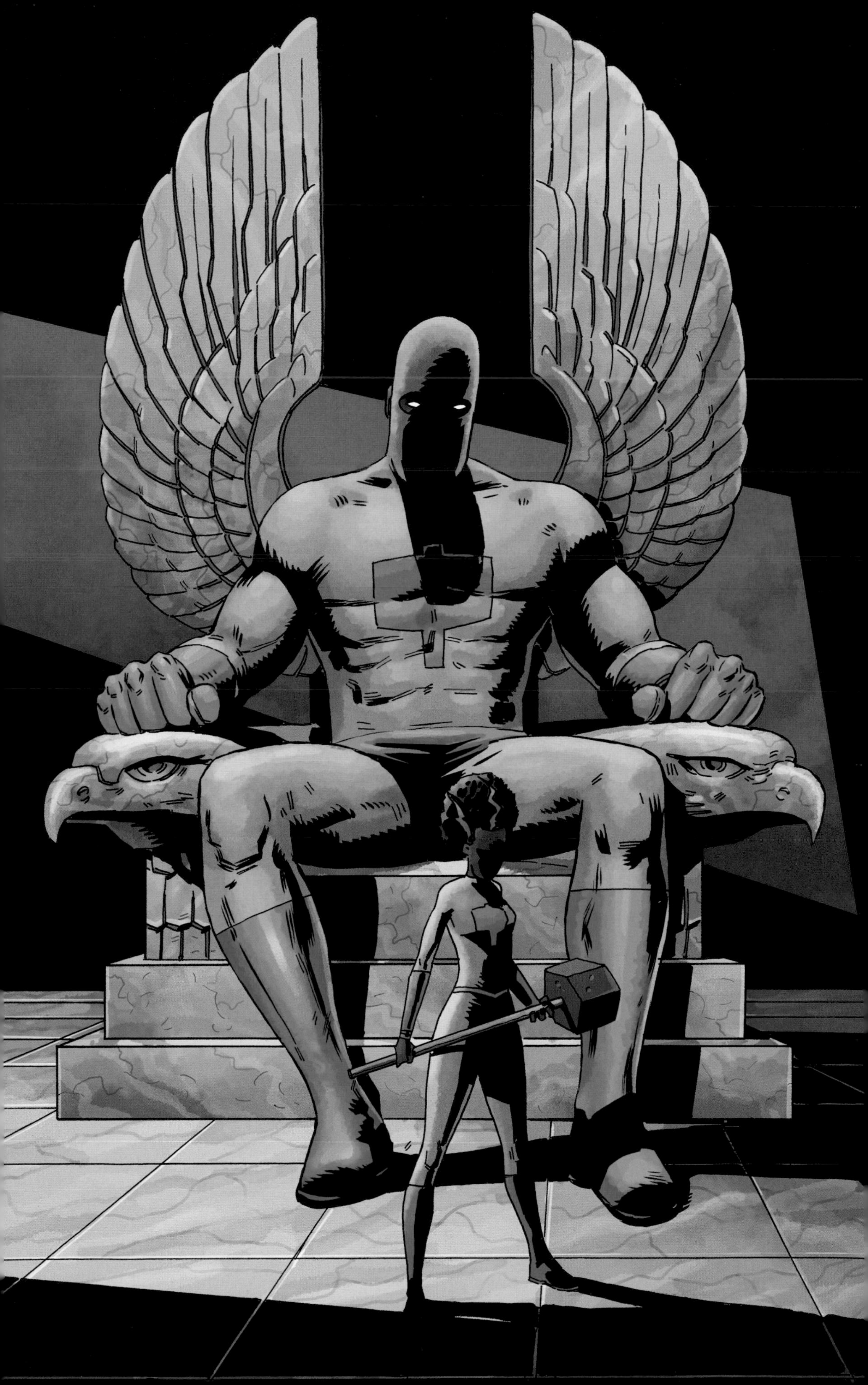

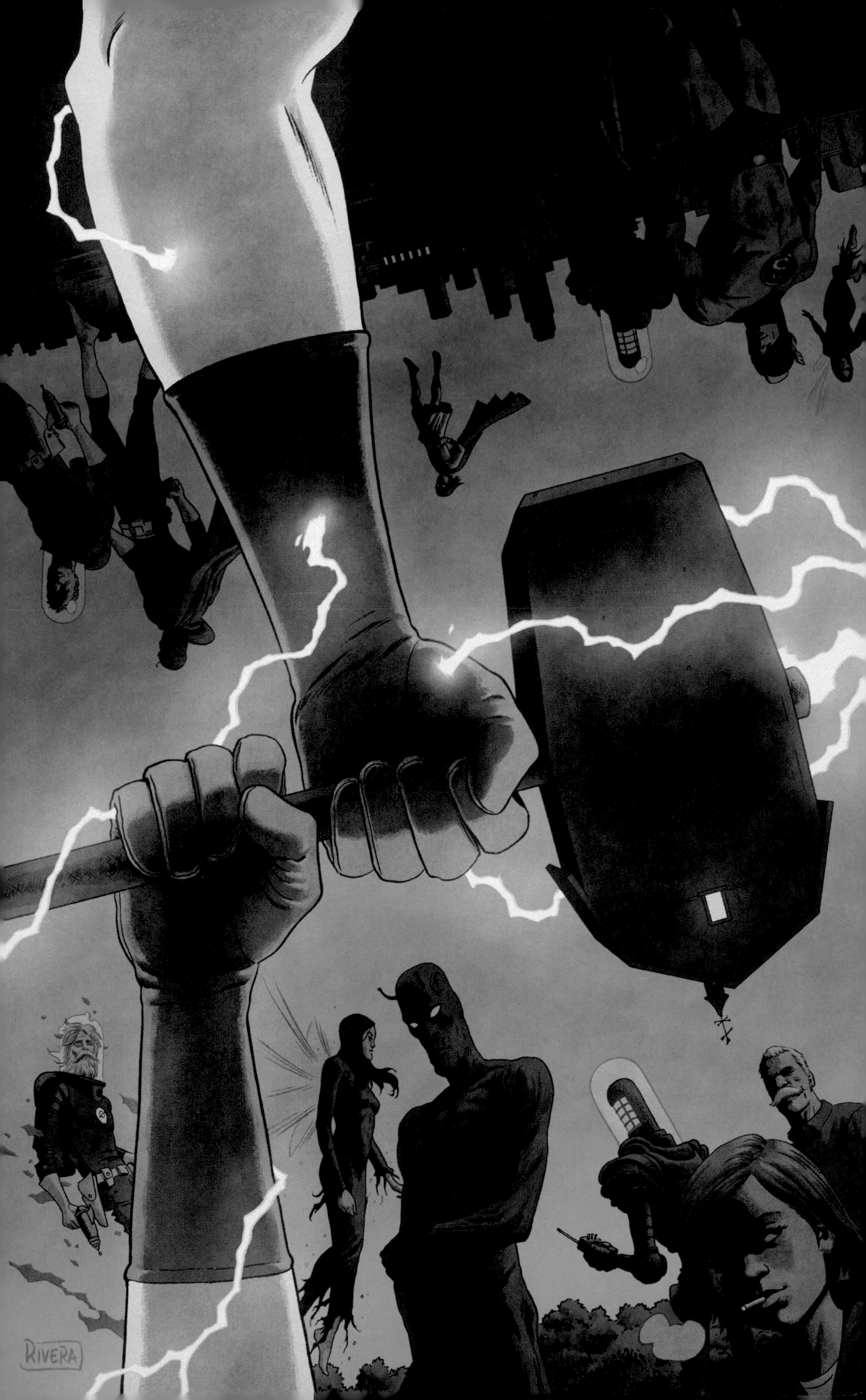
RIVERA

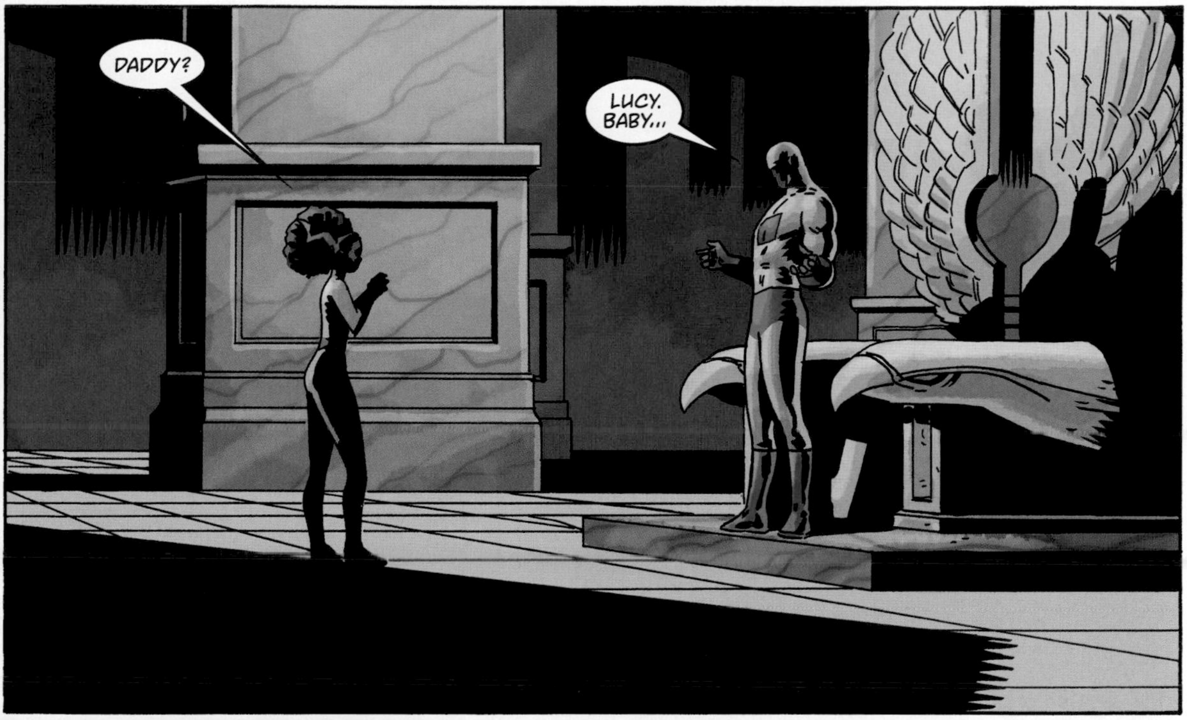
DADDY?
LUCY. BABY...

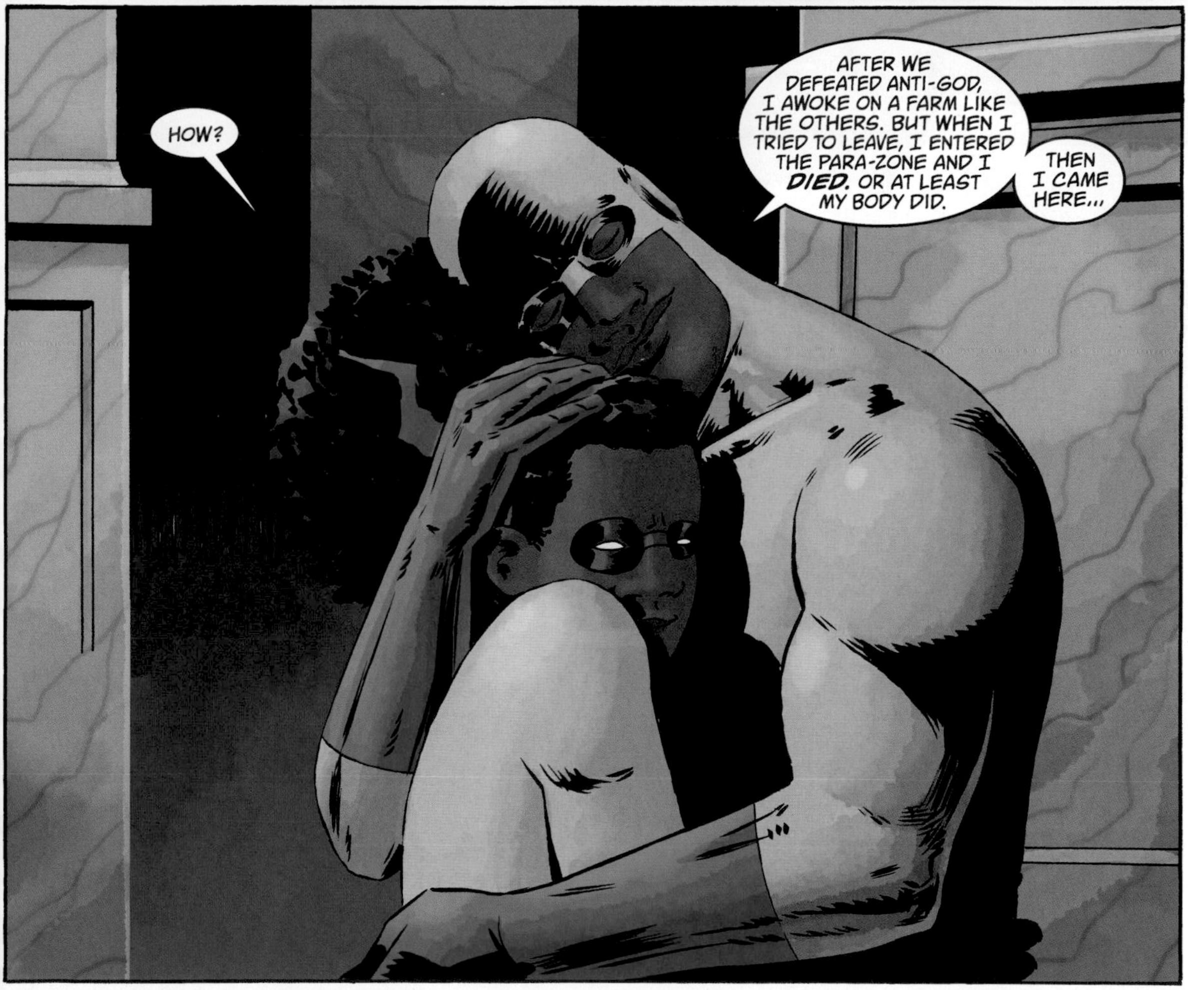
HOW?
AFTER WE DEFEATED ANTI-GOD, I AWOKE ON A FARM LIKE THE OTHERS. BUT WHEN I TRIED TO LEAVE, I ENTERED THE PARA-ZONE AND I **DIED.** OR AT LEAST MY BODY DID.
THEN I CAME HERE...

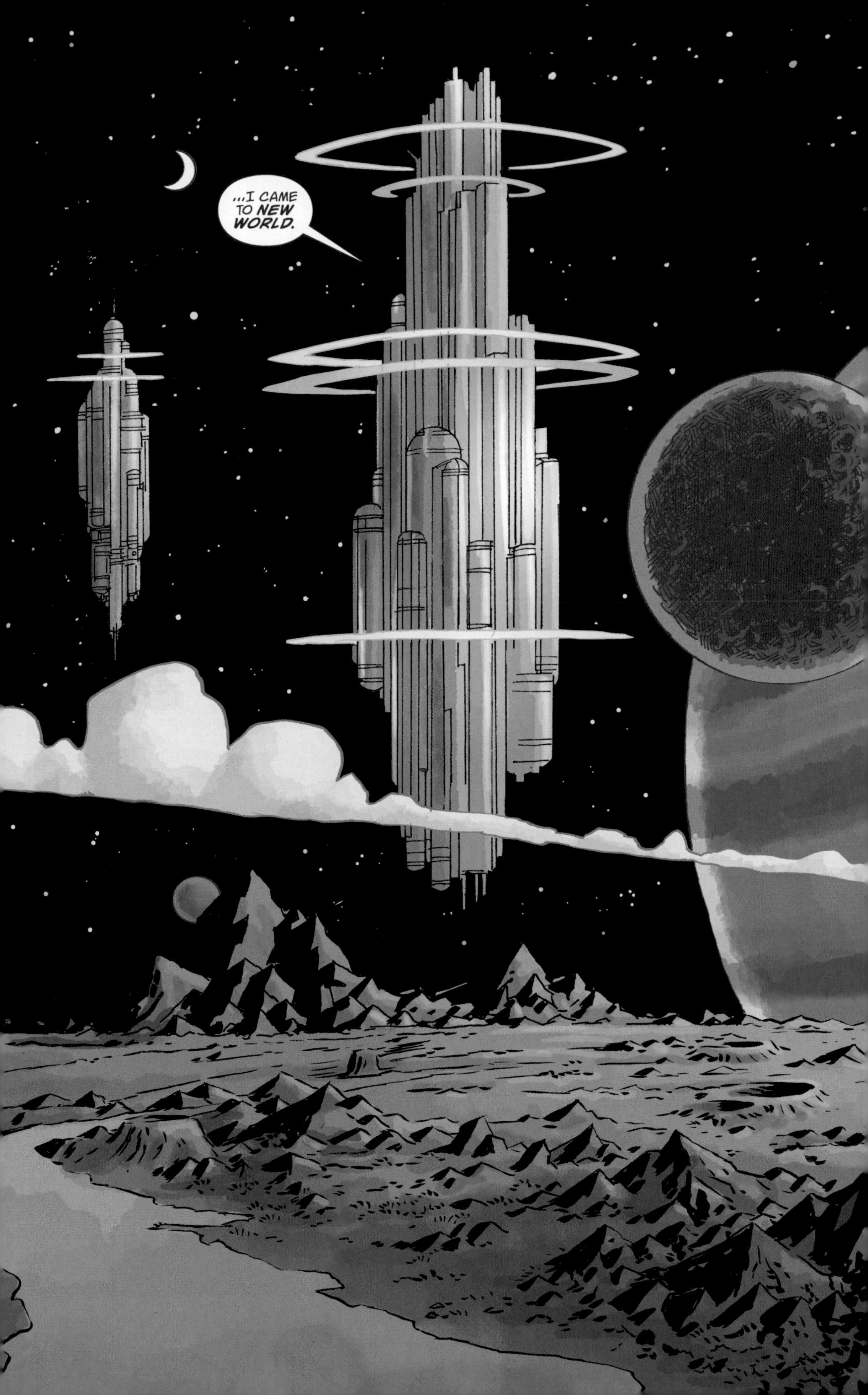
...I CAME TO NEW WORLD.

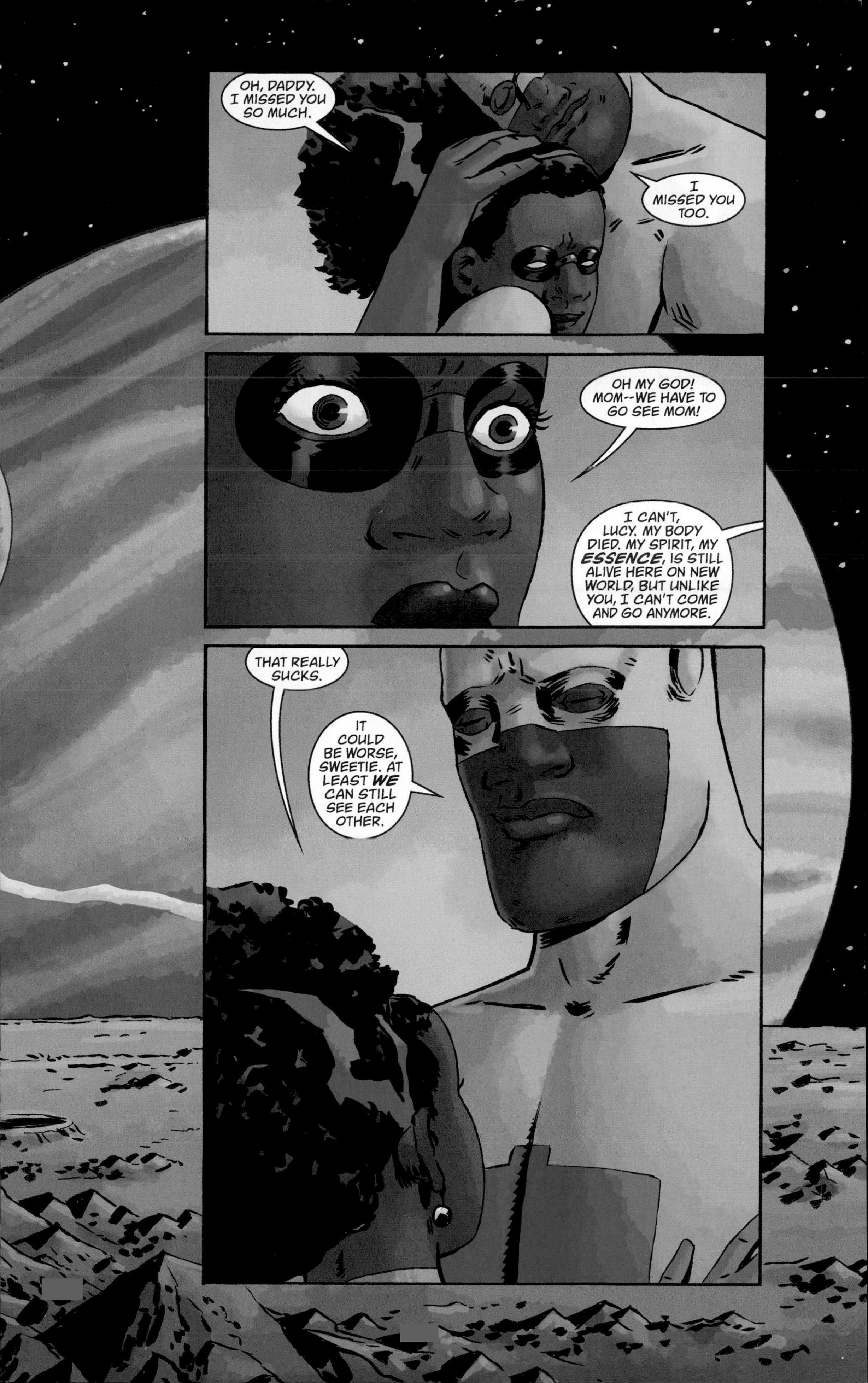
OH, DADDY. I MISSED YOU SO MUCH.
I MISSED YOU TOO.
OH MY GOD! MOM--WE HAVE TO GO SEE MOM!
I CAN'T, LUCY. MY BODY DIED. MY SPIRIT, MY ESSENCE, IS STILL ALIVE HERE ON NEW WORLD, BUT UNLIKE YOU, I CAN'T COME AND GO ANYMORE.
THAT REALLY SUCKS.
IT COULD BE WORSE, SWEETIE. AT LEAST WE CAN STILL SEE EACH OTHER.

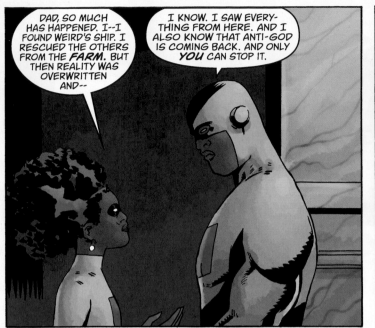

DAD, SO MUCH HAS HAPPENED. I--I FOUND WEIRD'S SHIP. I RESCUED THE OTHERS FROM THE *FARM*. BUT THEN REALITY WAS OVERWRITTEN AND--

I KNOW. I SAW EVERY-THING FROM HERE. AND I ALSO KNOW THAT ANTI-GOD IS COMING BACK. AND ONLY *YOU* CAN STOP IT.

ME?

YES, LUCY WEBER. THE BALANCE HAS BEEN UPSET. ANTI-GOD IS RETURNING. AND THE ONLY WAY TO STOP HIM IS IF YOUR *FRIENDS DIE.*

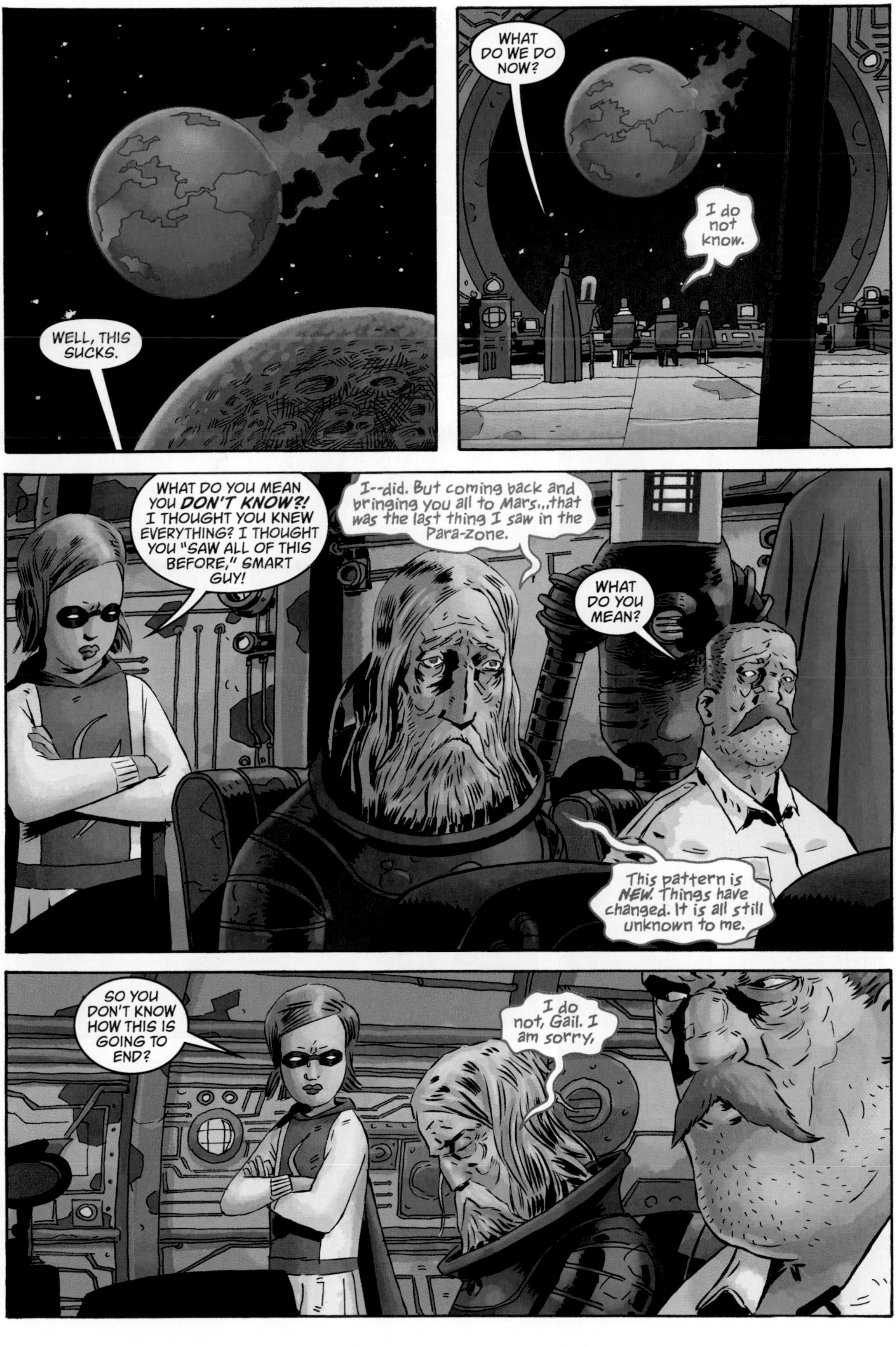

WELL, THIS SUCKS.
WHAT DO WE DO NOW?
I do not know.
WHAT DO YOU MEAN YOU DON'T KNOW?! I THOUGHT YOU KNEW EVERYTHING? I THOUGHT YOU "SAW ALL OF THIS BEFORE," SMART GUY!
I--did. But coming back and bringing you all to Mars...that was the last thing I saw in the Para-zone.
WHAT DO YOU MEAN?
This pattern is NEW. Things have changed. It is all still unknown to me.
SO YOU DON'T KNOW HOW THIS IS GOING TO END?
I do not, Gail. I am sorry.

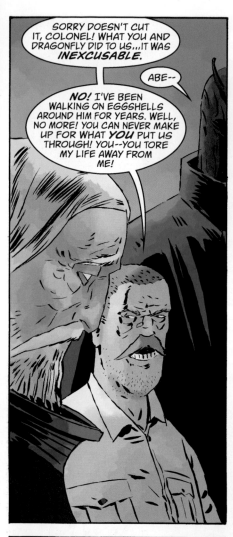

SORRY DOESN'T CUT IT, COLONEL! WHAT YOU AND DRAGONFLY DID TO US...IT WAS *INEXCUSABLE*.

ABE--

NO! I'VE BEEN WALKING ON EGGSHELLS AROUND HIM FOR YEARS. WELL, NO MORE! YOU CAN NEVER MAKE UP FOR WHAT *YOU* PUT US THROUGH! YOU--YOU TORE MY LIFE AWAY FROM ME!

What we did, we did to save the universe. And it was never your life, Abraham. Simply an illusion Dragonfly projected so that you could know peace.

WHAT DOES IT MATTER? WHAT DOES *ANY* OF IT MATTER? THE FARM FELT REAL. MY LIFE ON MARS-- EVERYTHING I LOST THERE-- FELT REAL. BUT IT WAS ALL A LIE.

THE FARM WAS A LIE AND THIS LIFE IS NO BETTER. I MEAN-- I CAN'T EVEN LOOK FOR SHERLOCK. EVEN IF I FOUND HIM, WOULD HE EVEN *REMEMBER ME?*

IT ALL SUCKS. I JUST WANT TO *FIND DRAGONFLY* AND STOP *ALL OF THIS.*

FIND HER? OH, NO, BARBIE, I'M NOT JUST GOING TO *FIND* HER...I'M GOING TO *KILL HER.*

THIS IS ALL **MY FAULT.**

THERE WAS NEVER ANY SECRET YOU DIDN'T TRY TO UNCOVER. NO STORY YOU'D LEAVE **UNTOLD.** YOU CAN'T HELP WHO YOU ARE, LUCY. YOU NEVER COULD.

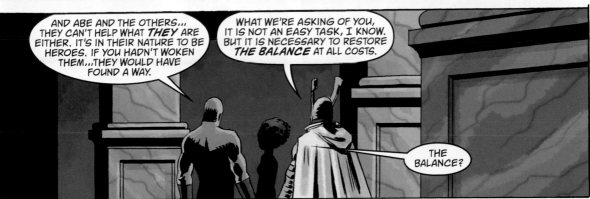

AND ABE AND THE OTHERS... THEY CAN'T HELP WHAT **THEY** ARE EITHER. IT'S IN THEIR NATURE TO BE HEROES. IF YOU HADN'T WOKEN THEM...THEY WOULD HAVE FOUND A WAY.

WHAT WE'RE ASKING OF YOU, IT IS NOT AN EASY TASK, I KNOW. BUT IT IS NECESSARY TO RESTORE **THE BALANCE** AT ALL COSTS.

THE BALANCE?

THE SOURCE OF OUR POWER, AND THE ENERGY THAT FLOWS THROUGH EVERYTHING IN THE **UNIVERSE,** LUCY.

THERE HAVE ALWAYS BEEN FORCES OF GOOD AND EVIL IN THE UNIVERSE. THAT BALANCE WAS UPENDED ONCE BEFORE.

THE FIRST TIME ANTI-GOD CAME.

YES.

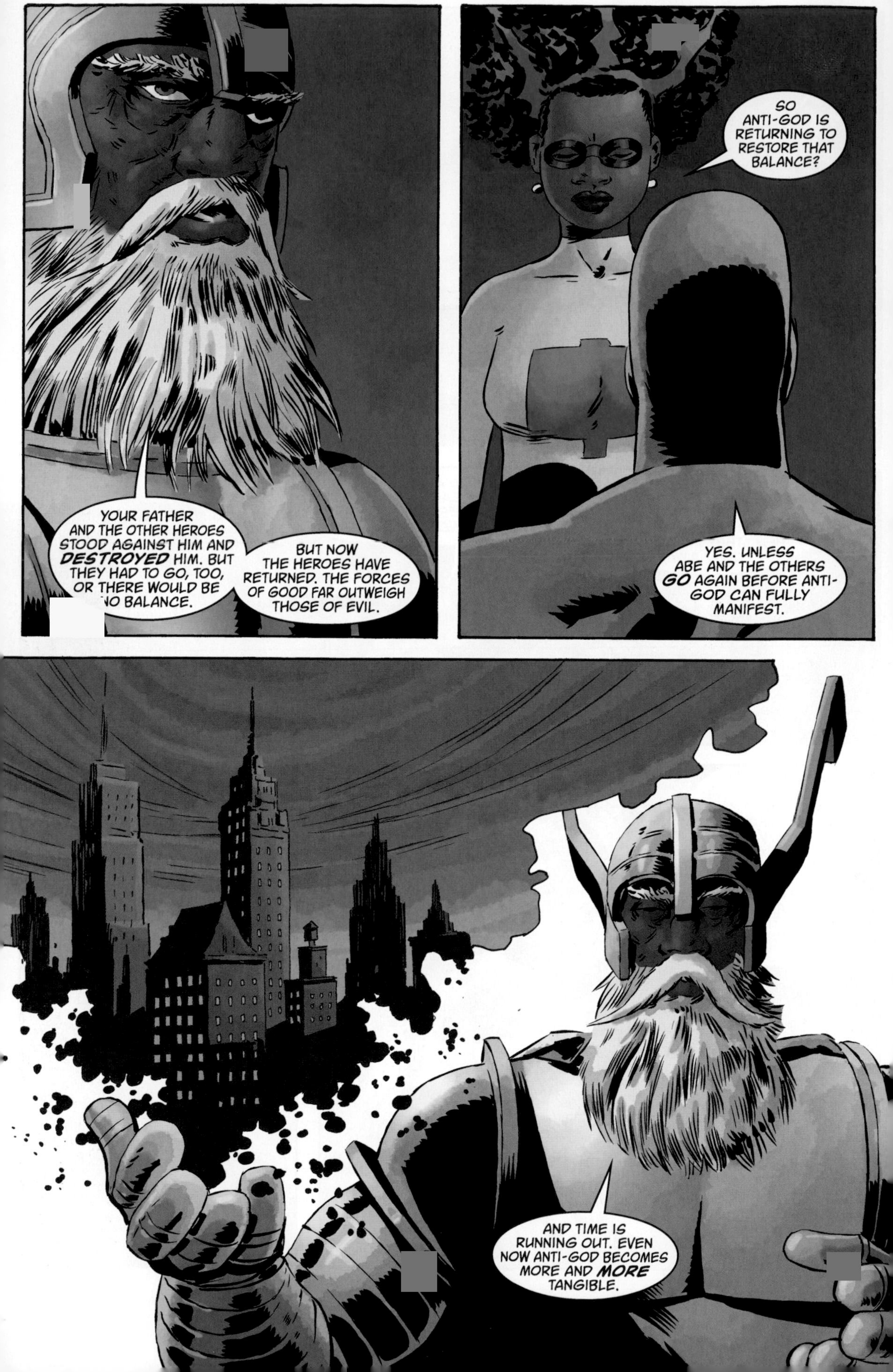
YOUR FATHER AND THE OTHER HEROES STOOD AGAINST HIM AND DESTROYED HIM. BUT THEY HAD TO GO, TOO, OR THERE WOULD BE NO BALANCE.
BUT NOW THE HEROES HAVE RETURNED. THE FORCES OF GOOD FAR OUTWEIGH THOSE OF EVIL.
SO ANTI-GOD IS RETURNING TO RESTORE THAT BALANCE?
YES. UNLESS ABE AND THE OTHERS GO AGAIN BEFORE ANTI-GOD CAN FULLY MANIFEST.
AND TIME IS RUNNING OUT. EVEN NOW ANTI-GOD BECOMES MORE AND MORE TANGIBLE.

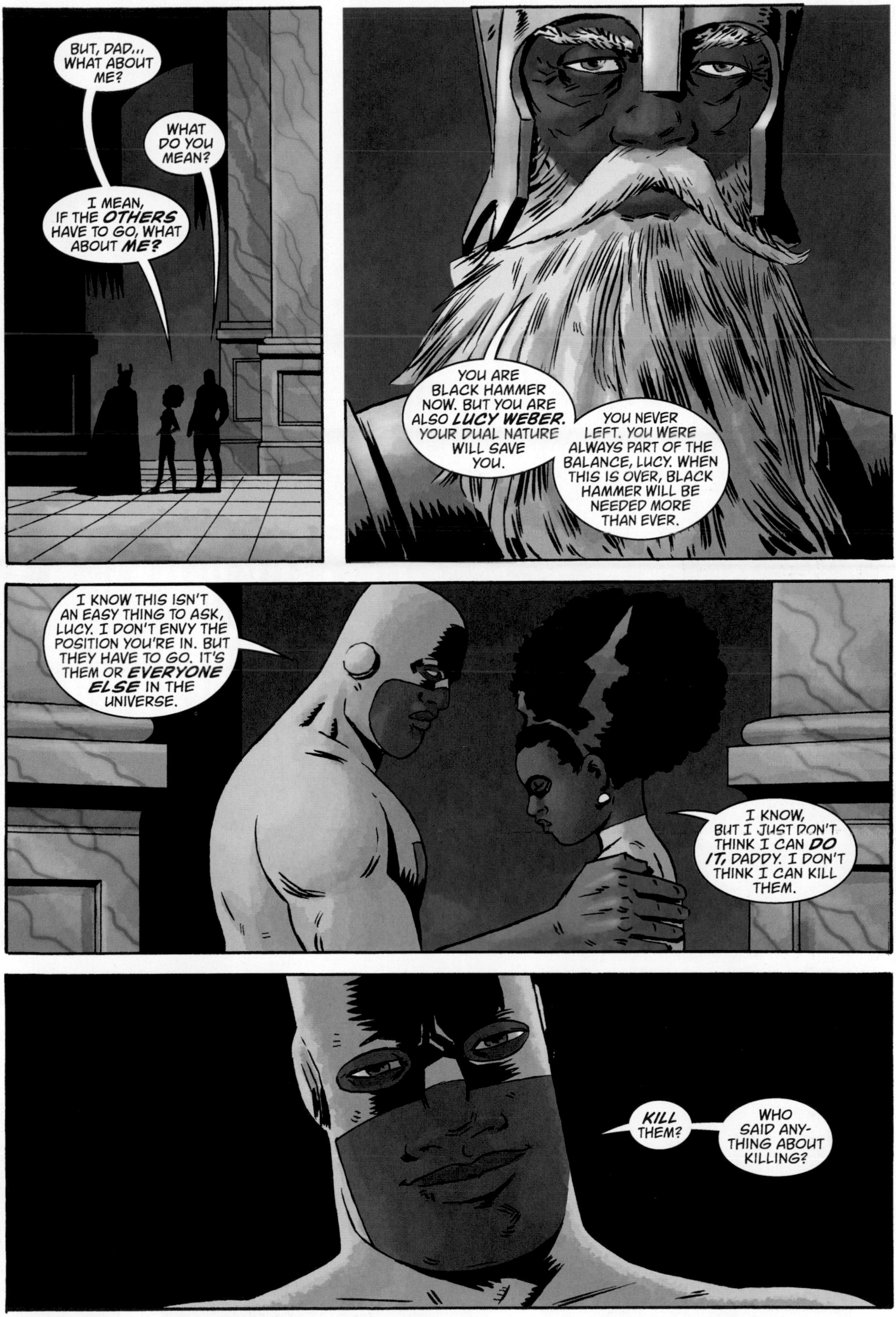
BUT, DAD... WHAT ABOUT ME?
WHAT DO YOU MEAN?
I MEAN, IF THE OTHERS HAVE TO GO, WHAT ABOUT ME?
YOU ARE BLACK HAMMER NOW. BUT YOU ARE ALSO LUCY WEBER. YOUR DUAL NATURE WILL SAVE YOU.
YOU NEVER LEFT. YOU WERE ALWAYS PART OF THE BALANCE, LUCY. WHEN THIS IS OVER, BLACK HAMMER WILL BE NEEDED MORE THAN EVER.
I KNOW THIS ISN'T AN EASY THING TO ASK, LUCY. I DON'T ENVY THE POSITION YOU'RE IN. BUT THEY HAVE TO GO. IT'S THEM OR EVERYONE ELSE IN THE UNIVERSE.
I KNOW, BUT I JUST DON'T THINK I CAN DO IT, DADDY. I DON'T THINK I CAN KILL THEM.
KILL THEM?
WHO SAID ANYTHING ABOUT KILLING?

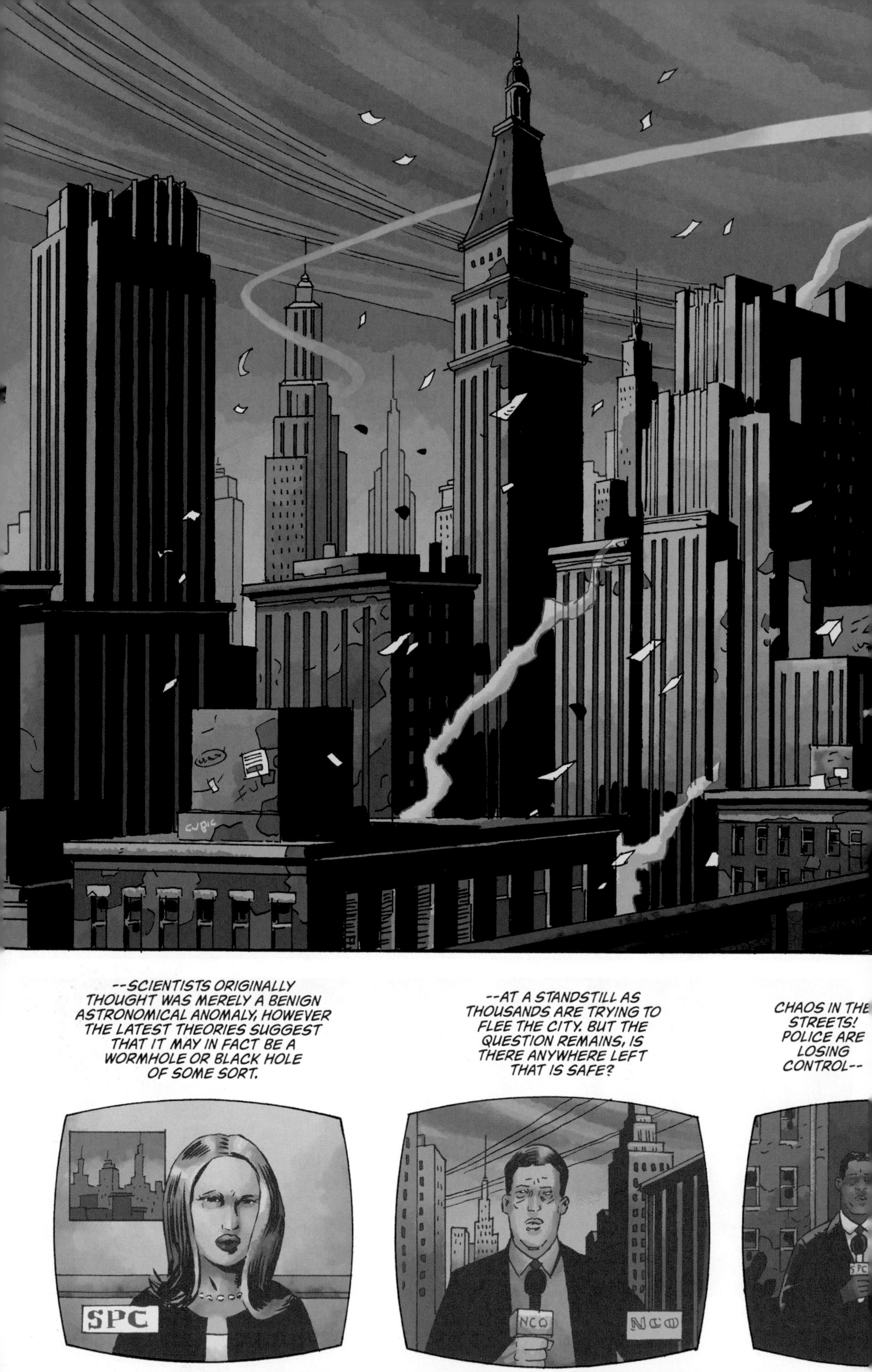
--SCIENTISTS ORIGINALLY THOUGHT WAS MERELY A BENIGN ASTRONOMICAL ANOMALY, HOWEVER THE LATEST THEORIES SUGGEST THAT IT MAY IN FACT BE A WORMHOLE OR BLACK HOLE OF SOME SORT.
SPC
--AT A STANDSTILL AS THOUSANDS ARE TRYING TO FLEE THE CITY. BUT THE QUESTION REMAINS, IS THERE ANYWHERE LEFT THAT IS SAFE?
NCO
NCO
CHAOS IN THE STREETS! POLICE ARE LOSING CONTROL--
SPC

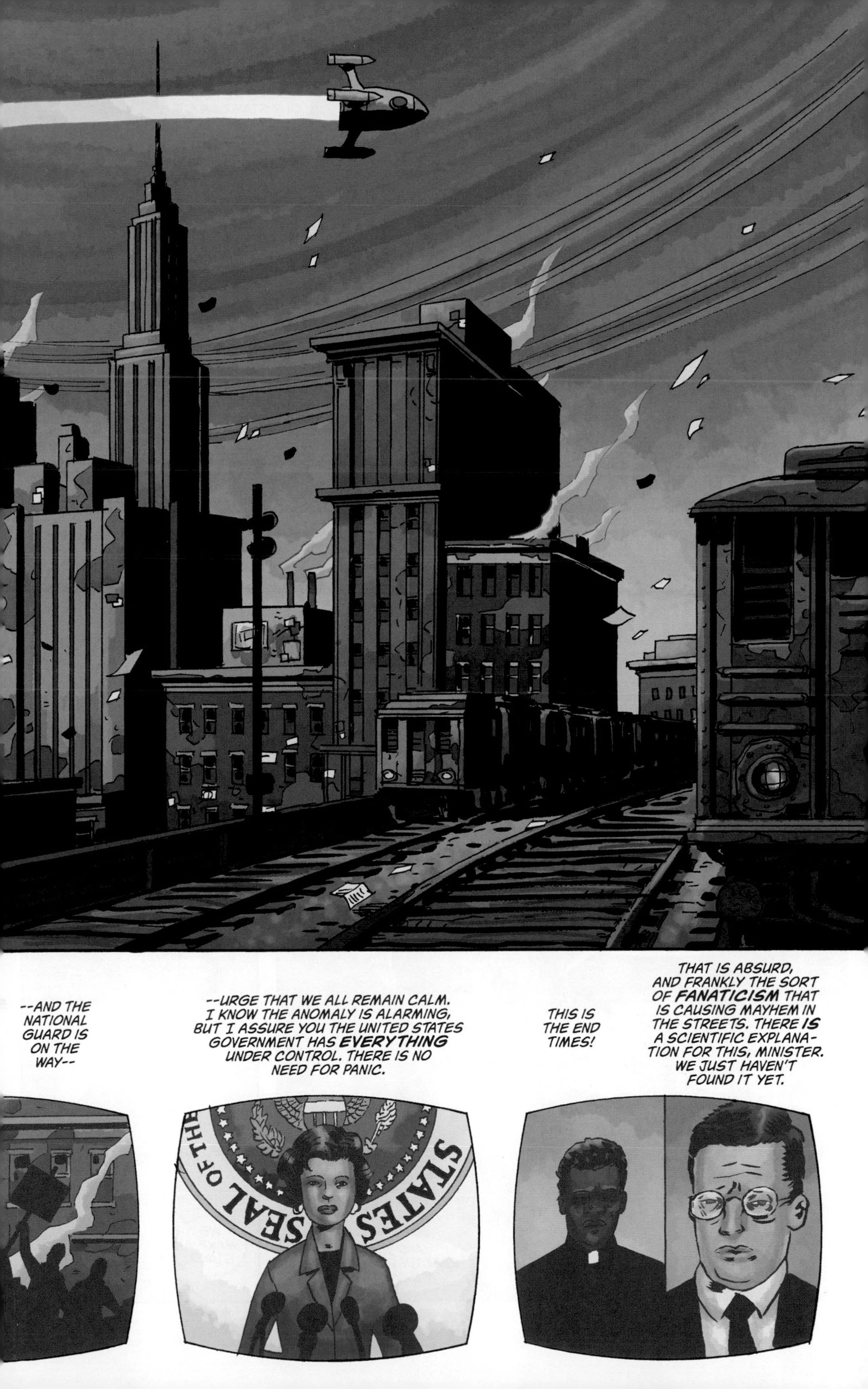
--AND THE NATIONAL GUARD IS ON THE WAY--
--URGE THAT WE ALL REMAIN CALM. I KNOW THE ANOMALY IS ALARMING, BUT I ASSURE YOU THE UNITED STATES GOVERNMENT HAS EVERYTHING UNDER CONTROL. THERE IS NO NEED FOR PANIC.
SEAL OF THE ... STATES
THIS IS THE END TIMES!
THAT IS ABSURD, AND FRANKLY THE SORT OF FANATICISM THAT IS CAUSING MAYHEM IN THE STREETS. THERE IS A SCIENTIFIC EXPLANATION FOR THIS, MINISTER. WE JUST HAVEN'T FOUND IT YET.

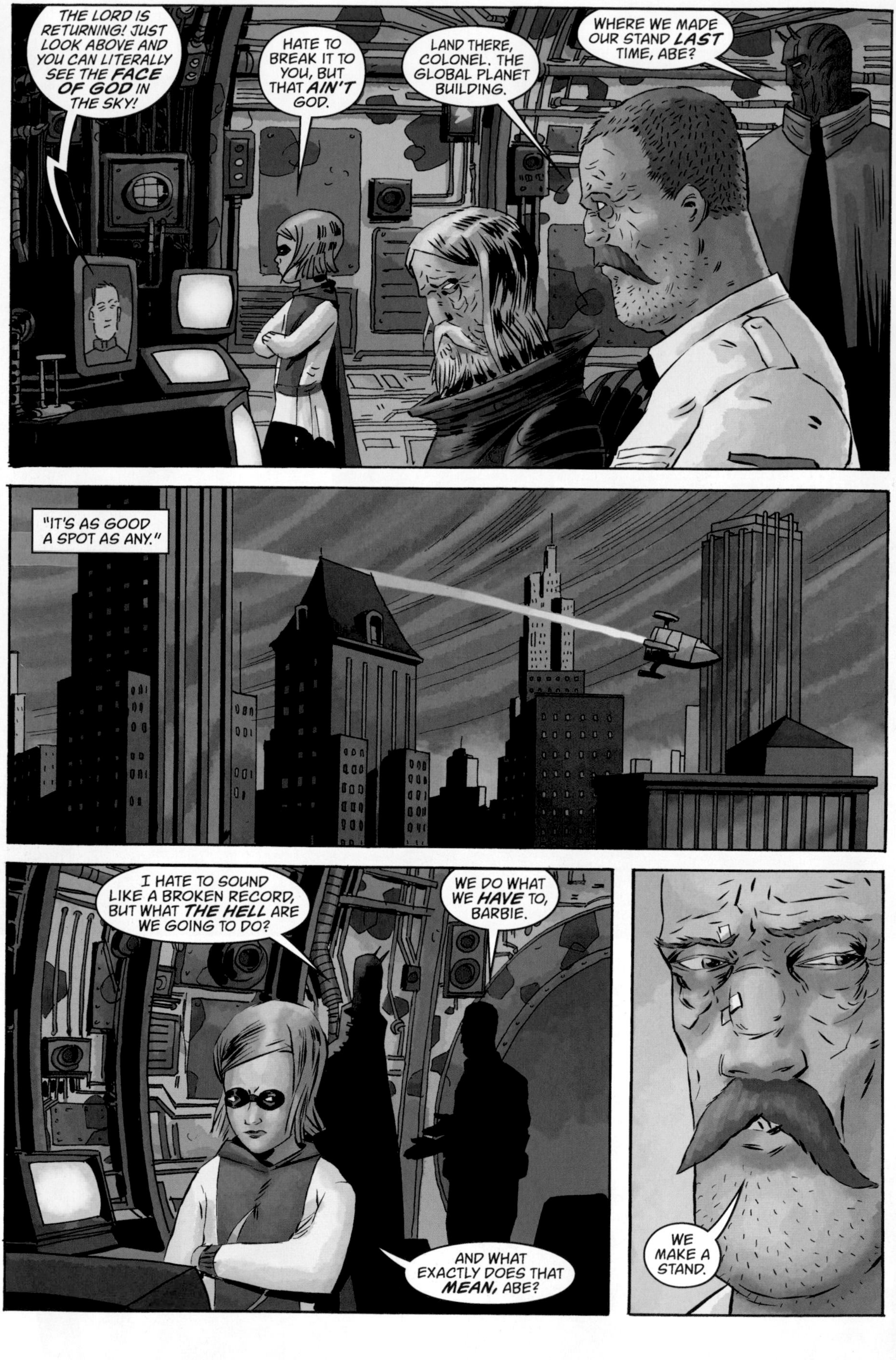

THE LORD IS RETURNING! JUST LOOK ABOVE AND YOU CAN LITERALLY SEE THE FACE OF GOD IN THE SKY!
HATE TO BREAK IT TO YOU, BUT THAT AIN'T GOD.
LAND THERE, COLONEL. THE GLOBAL PLANET BUILDING.
WHERE WE MADE OUR STAND LAST TIME, ABE?
"IT'S AS GOOD A SPOT AS ANY."
I HATE TO SOUND LIKE A BROKEN RECORD, BUT WHAT THE HELL ARE WE GOING TO DO?
WE DO WHAT WE HAVE TO, BARBIE.
AND WHAT EXACTLY DOES THAT MEAN, ABE?
WE MAKE A STAND.

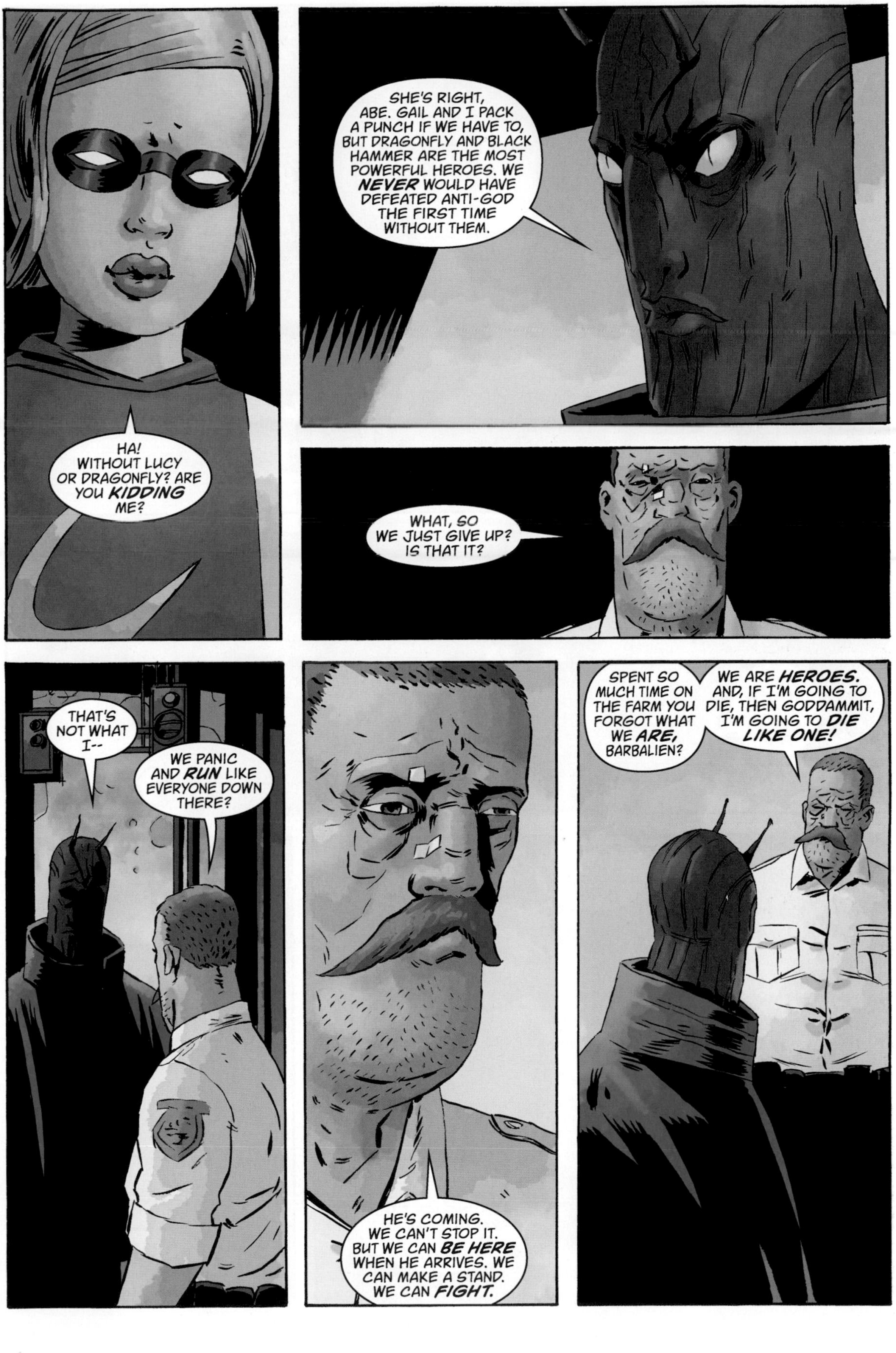
SHE'S RIGHT, ABE. GAIL AND I PACK A PUNCH IF WE HAVE TO, BUT DRAGONFLY AND BLACK HAMMER ARE THE MOST POWERFUL HEROES. WE NEVER WOULD HAVE DEFEATED ANTI-GOD THE FIRST TIME WITHOUT THEM.
HA! WITHOUT LUCY OR DRAGONFLY? ARE YOU KIDDING ME?
WHAT, SO WE JUST GIVE UP? IS THAT IT?
THAT'S NOT WHAT I--
WE PANIC AND RUN LIKE EVERYONE DOWN THERE?
HE'S COMING. WE CAN'T STOP IT. BUT WE CAN BE HERE WHEN HE ARRIVES. WE CAN MAKE A STAND. WE CAN FIGHT.
SPENT SO MUCH TIME ON THE FARM YOU FORGOT WHAT WE ARE, BARBALIEN?
WE ARE HEROES. AND, IF I'M GOING TO DIE, THEN GODDAMMIT, I'M GOING TO DIE LIKE ONE!

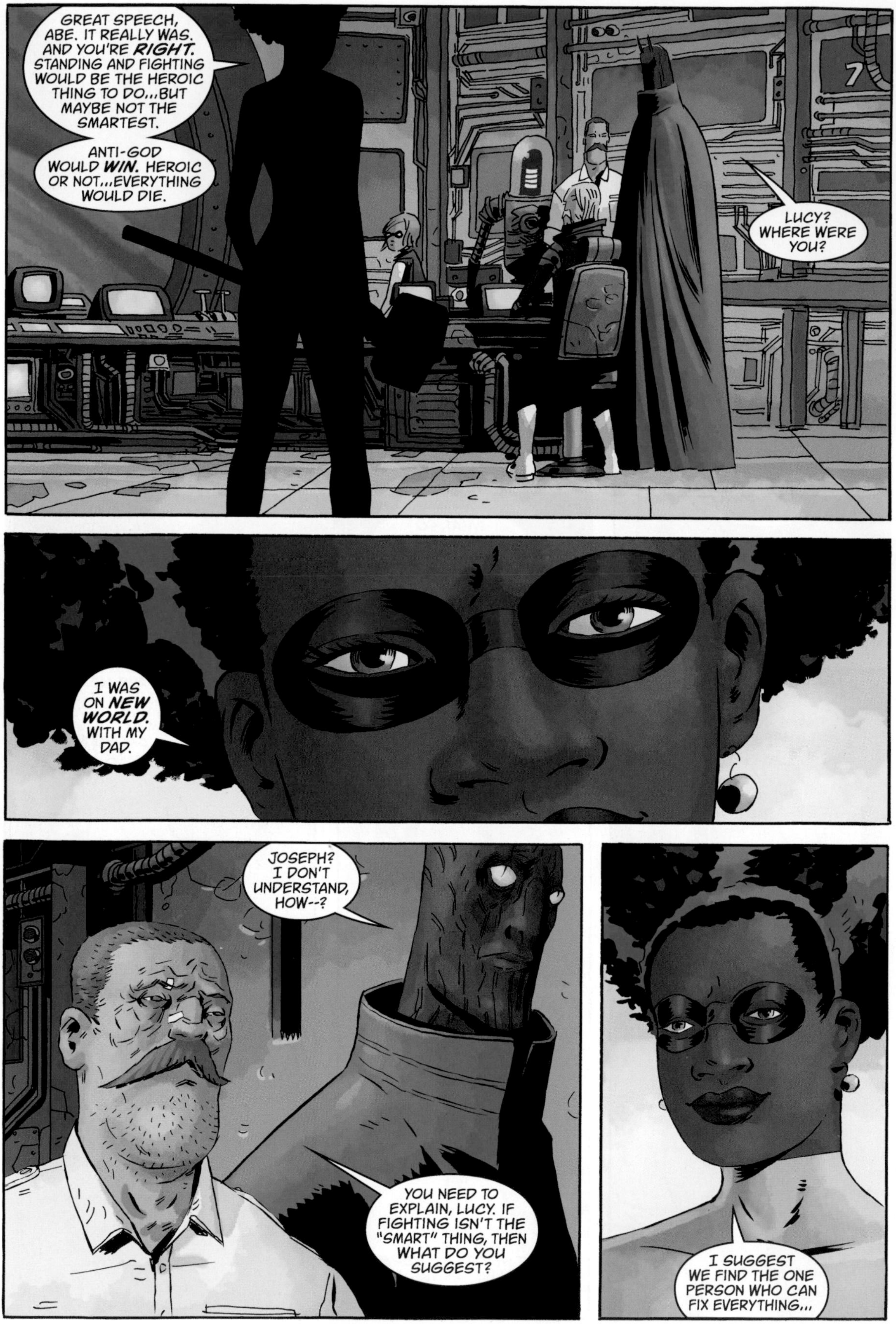
GREAT SPEECH, ABE. IT REALLY WAS. AND YOU'RE RIGHT. STANDING AND FIGHTING WOULD BE THE HEROIC THING TO DO...BUT MAYBE NOT THE SMARTEST.
ANTI-GOD WOULD WIN. HEROIC OR NOT...EVERYTHING WOULD DIE.
LUCY? WHERE WERE YOU?
I WAS ON NEW WORLD. WITH MY DAD.
JOSEPH? I DON'T UNDERSTAND, HOW--?
YOU NEED TO EXPLAIN, LUCY. IF FIGHTING ISN'T THE "SMART" THING, THEN WHAT DO YOU SUGGEST?
I SUGGEST WE FIND THE ONE PERSON WHO CAN FIX EVERYTHING...

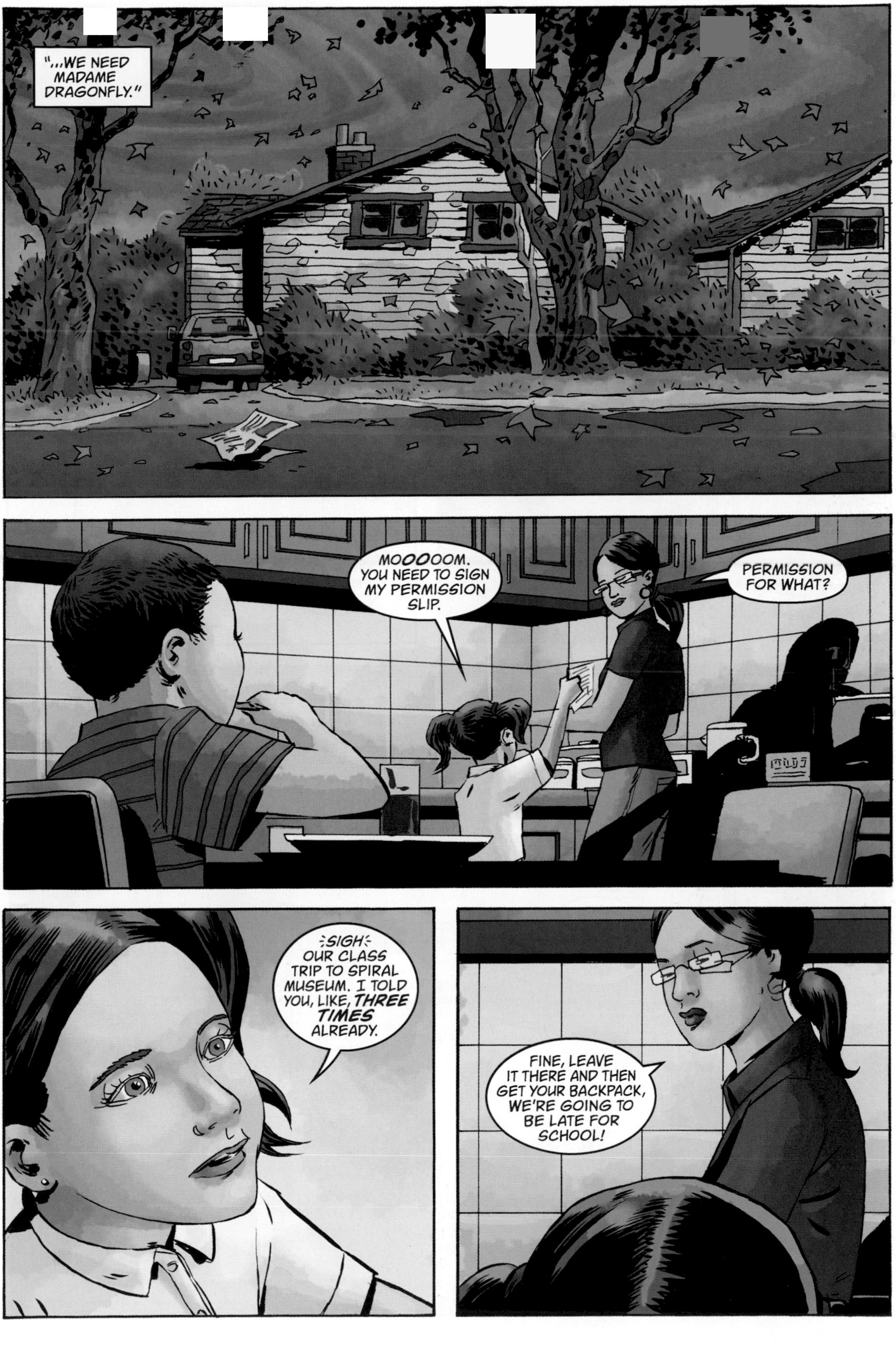
"...WE NEED MADAME DRAGONFLY."
MOOOOOM. YOU NEED TO SIGN MY PERMISSION SLIP.
PERMISSION FOR WHAT?
SIGH OUR CLASS TRIP TO SPIRAL MUSEUM. I TOLD YOU, LIKE, THREE TIMES ALREADY.
FINE, LEAVE IT THERE AND THEN GET YOUR BACKPACK, WE'RE GOING TO BE LATE FOR SCHOOL!

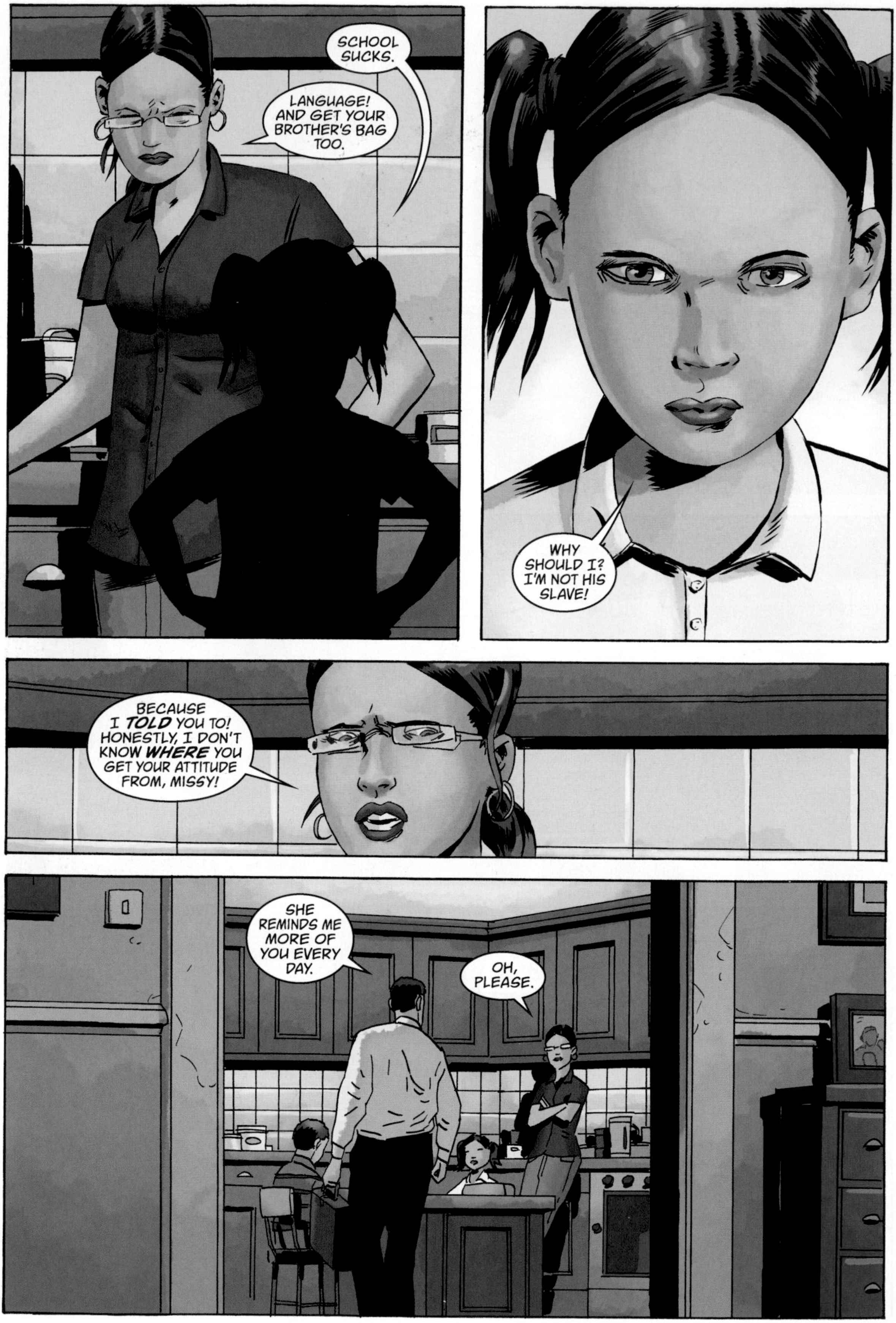
SCHOOL SUCKS.
LANGUAGE! AND GET YOUR BROTHER'S BAG TOO.
WHY SHOULD I? I'M NOT HIS SLAVE!
BECAUSE I TOLD YOU TO! HONESTLY, I DON'T KNOW WHERE YOU GET YOUR ATTITUDE FROM, MISSY!
SHE REMINDS ME MORE OF YOU EVERY DAY.
OH, PLEASE.

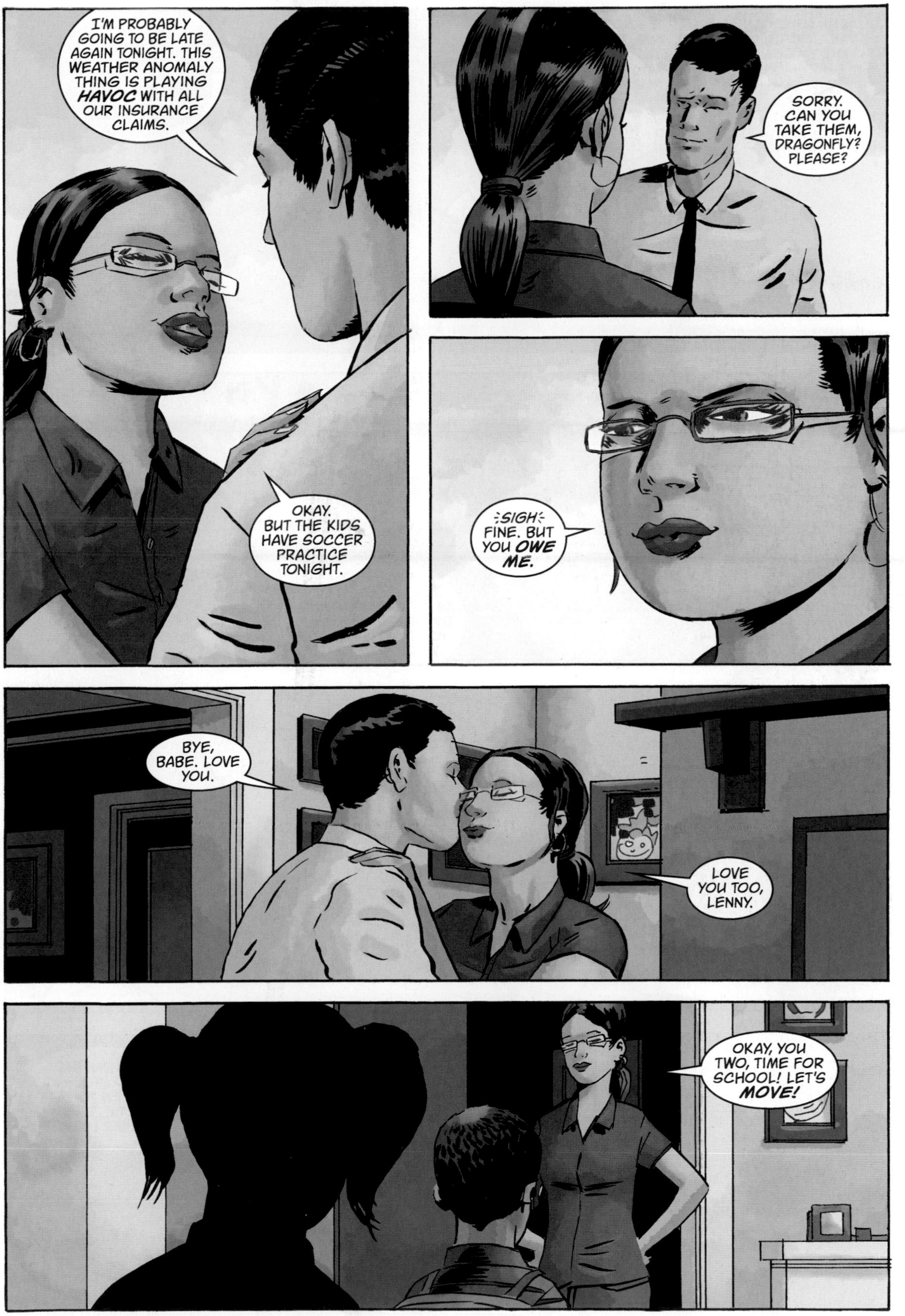
I'M PROBABLY GOING TO BE LATE AGAIN TONIGHT. THIS WEATHER ANOMALY THING IS PLAYING HAVOC WITH ALL OUR INSURANCE CLAIMS.
OKAY. BUT THE KIDS HAVE SOCCER PRACTICE TONIGHT.
SORRY. CAN YOU TAKE THEM, DRAGONFLY? PLEASE?
SIGH FINE. BUT YOU OWE ME.
BYE, BABE. LOVE YOU.
LOVE YOU TOO, LENNY.
OKAY, YOU TWO, TIME FOR SCHOOL! LET'S MOVE!

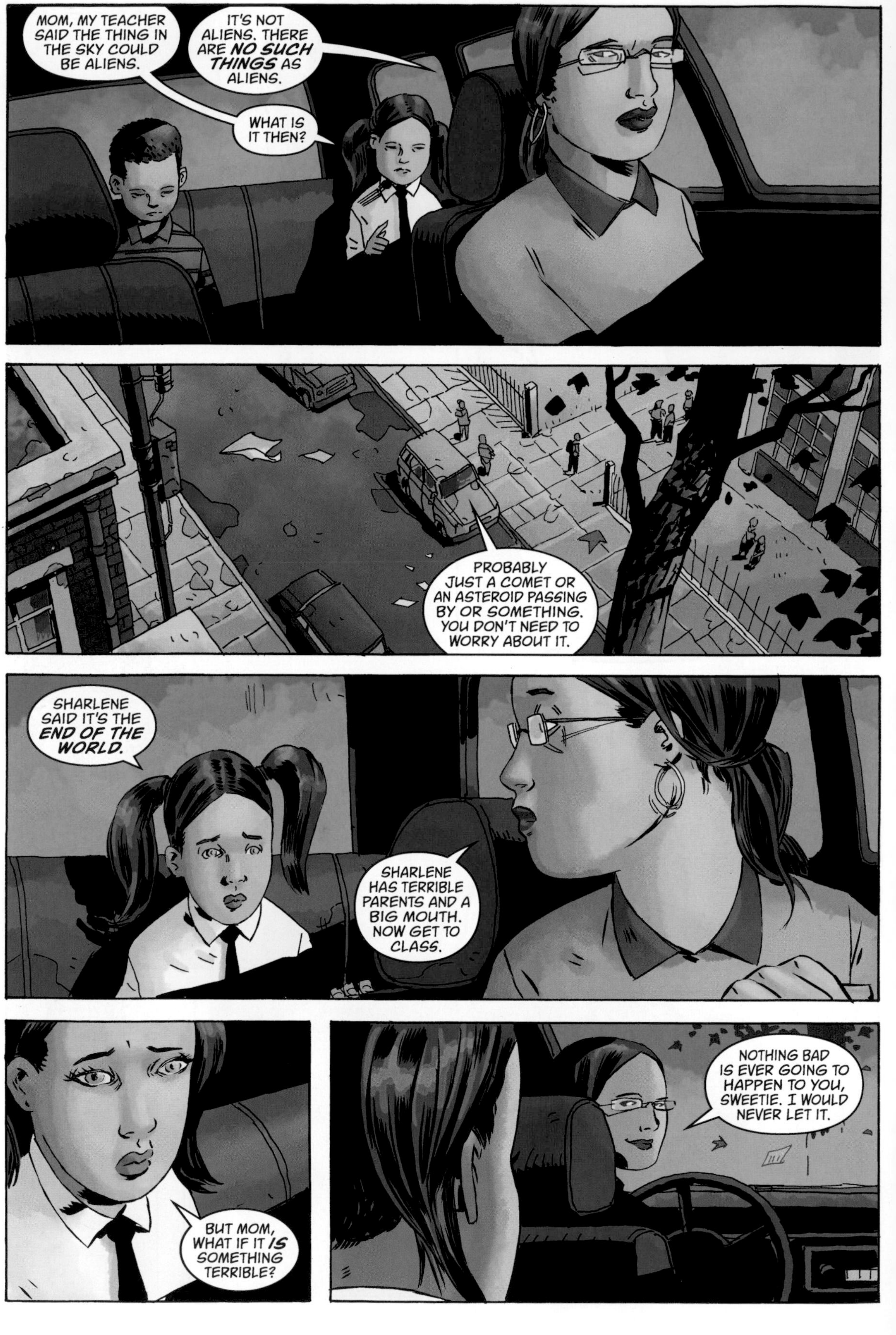

MOM, MY TEACHER SAID THE THING IN THE SKY COULD BE ALIENS.
IT'S NOT ALIENS. THERE ARE NO SUCH THINGS AS ALIENS.
WHAT IS IT THEN?
PROBABLY JUST A COMET OR AN ASTEROID PASSING BY OR SOMETHING. YOU DON'T NEED TO WORRY ABOUT IT.
SHARLENE SAID IT'S THE END OF THE WORLD.
SHARLENE HAS TERRIBLE PARENTS AND A BIG MOUTH. NOW GET TO CLASS.
BUT MOM, WHAT IF IT IS SOMETHING TERRIBLE?
NOTHING BAD IS EVER GOING TO HAPPEN TO YOU, SWEETIE. I WOULD NEVER LET IT.

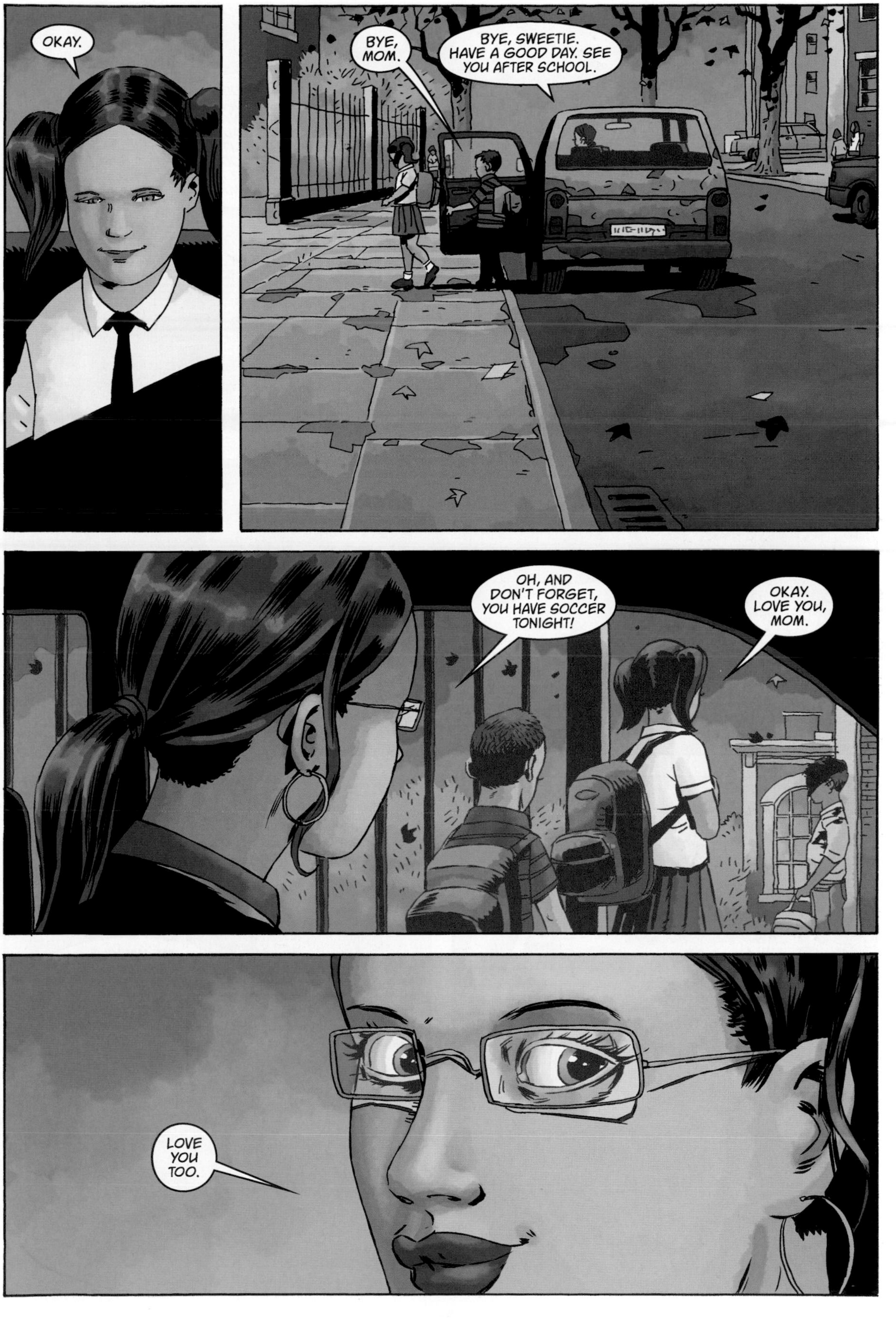
OKAY.
BYE, MOM.
BYE, SWEETIE. HAVE A GOOD DAY. SEE YOU AFTER SCHOOL.
OH, AND DON'T FORGET, YOU HAVE SOCCER TONIGHT!
OKAY. LOVE YOU, MOM.
LOVE YOU TOO.

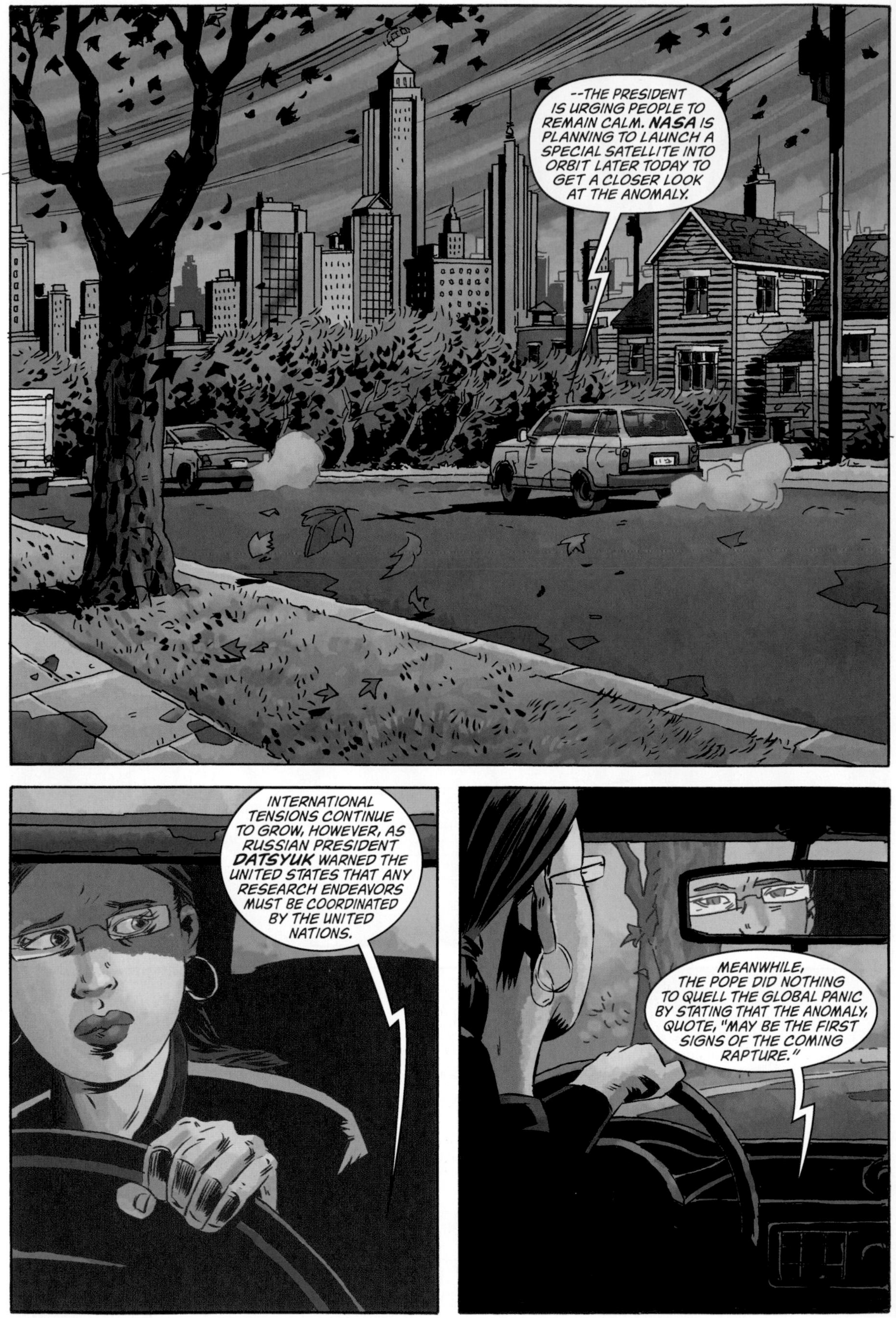
--THE PRESIDENT IS URGING PEOPLE TO REMAIN CALM. NASA IS PLANNING TO LAUNCH A SPECIAL SATELLITE INTO ORBIT LATER TODAY TO GET A CLOSER LOOK AT THE ANOMALY.
INTERNATIONAL TENSIONS CONTINUE TO GROW, HOWEVER, AS RUSSIAN PRESIDENT DATSYUK WARNED THE UNITED STATES THAT ANY RESEARCH ENDEAVORS MUST BE COORDINATED BY THE UNITED NATIONS.
MEANWHILE, THE POPE DID NOTHING TO QUELL THE GLOBAL PANIC BY STATING THAT THE ANOMALY, QUOTE, "MAY BE THE FIRST SIGNS OF THE COMING RAPTURE."

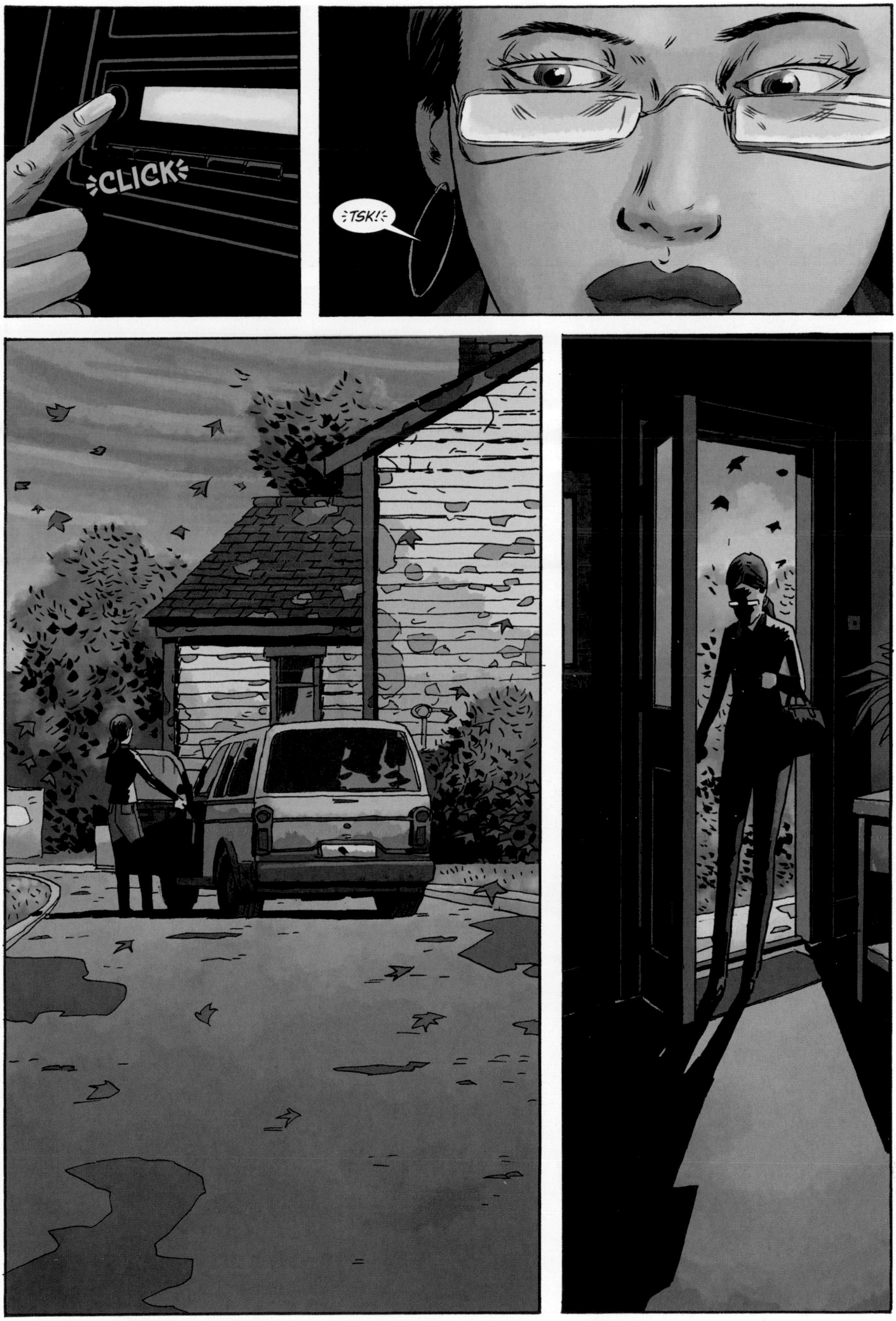
CLICK
TSK!

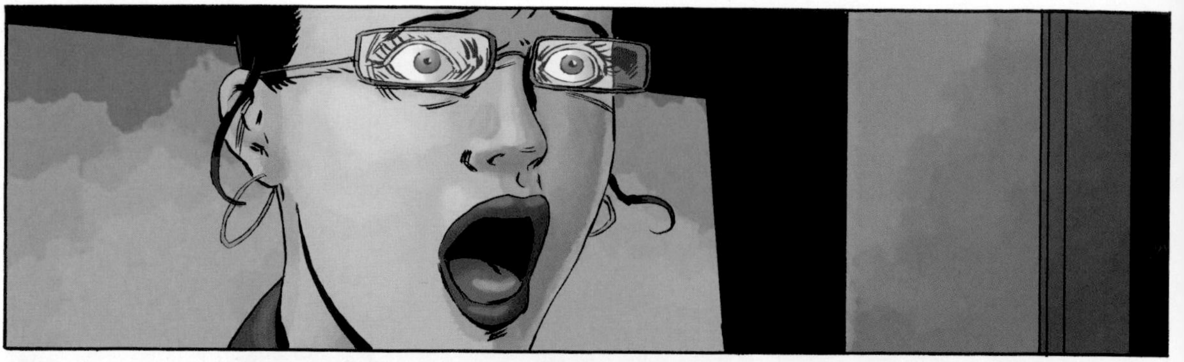

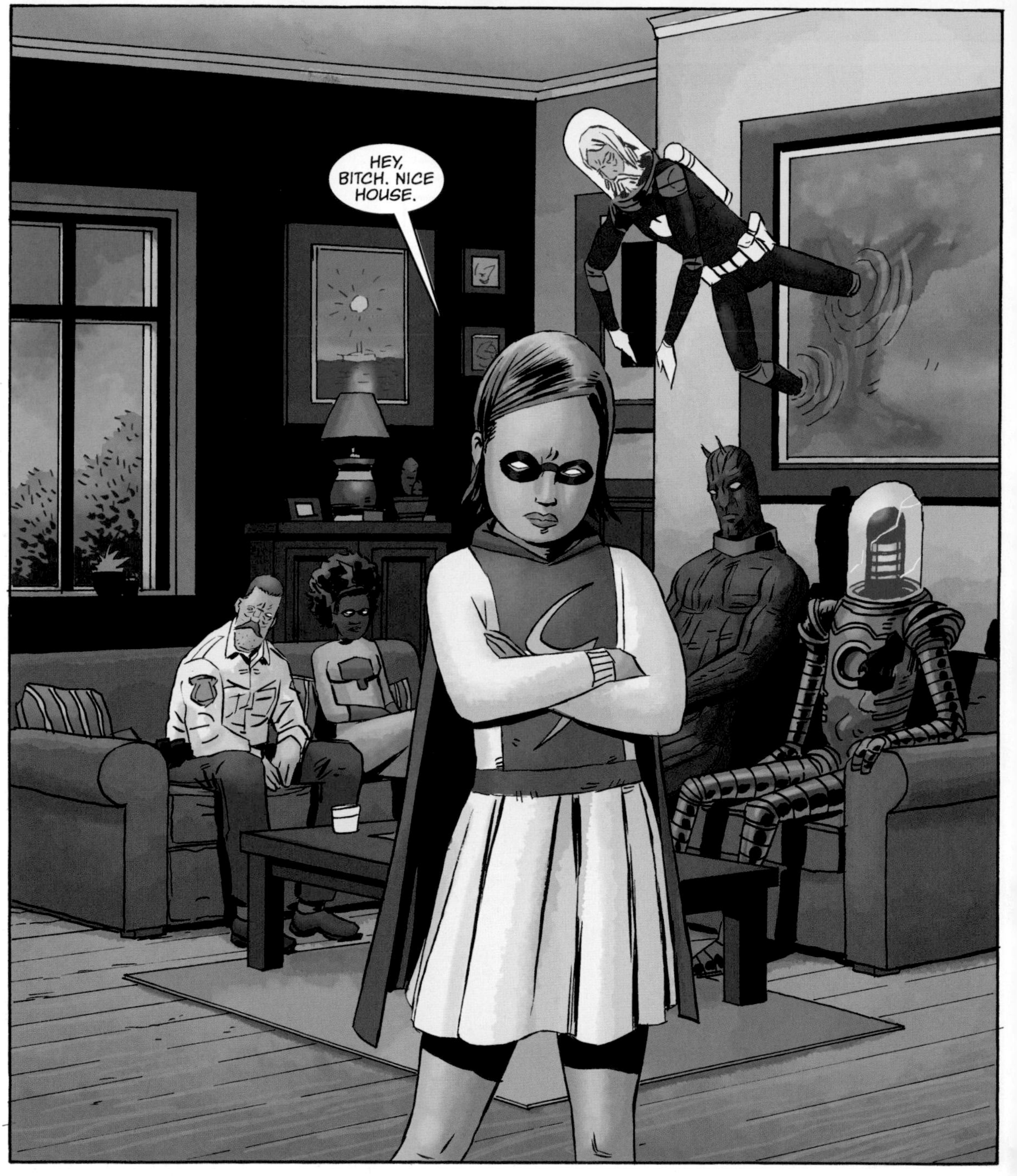
HEY, BITCH. NICE HOUSE.

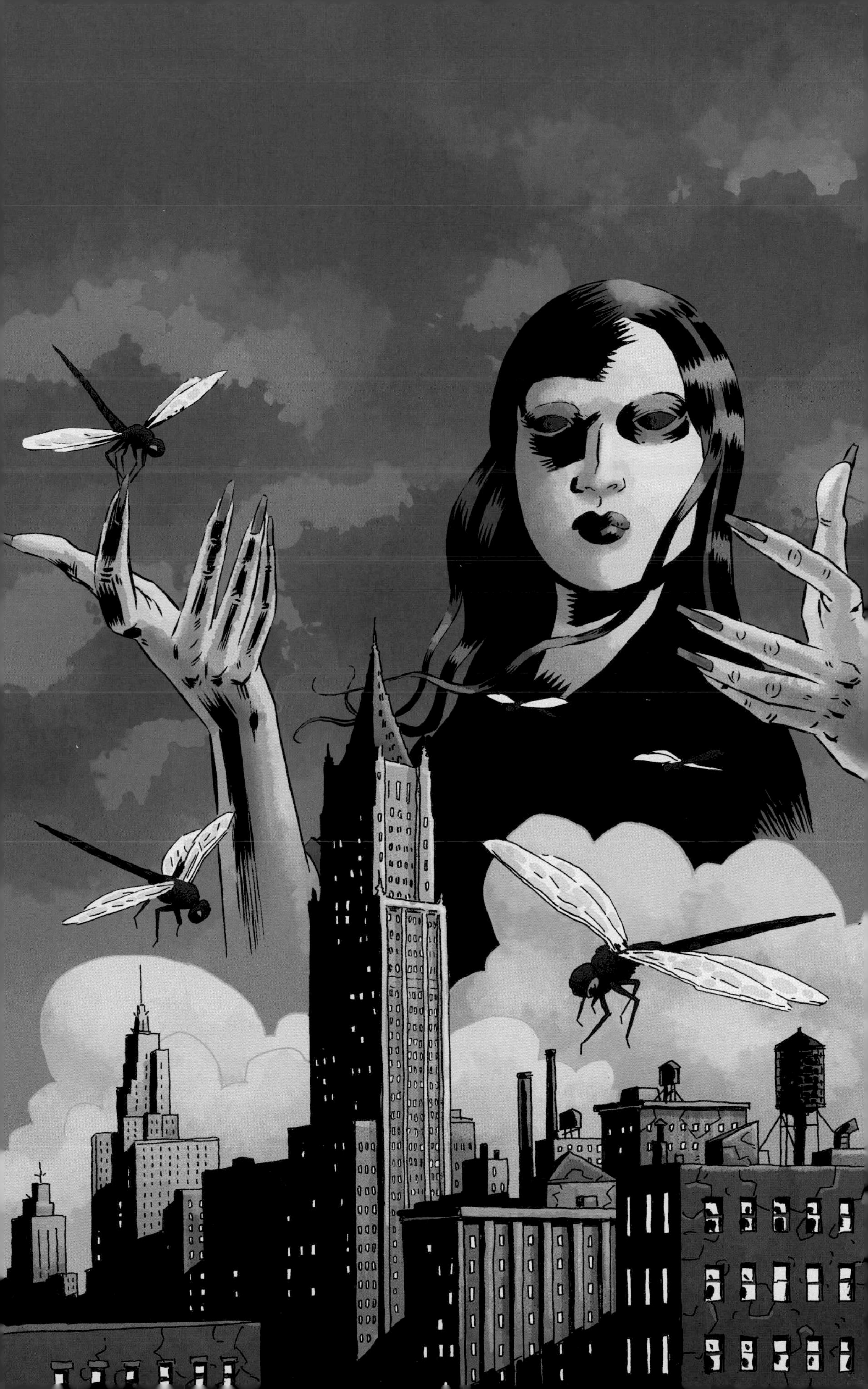

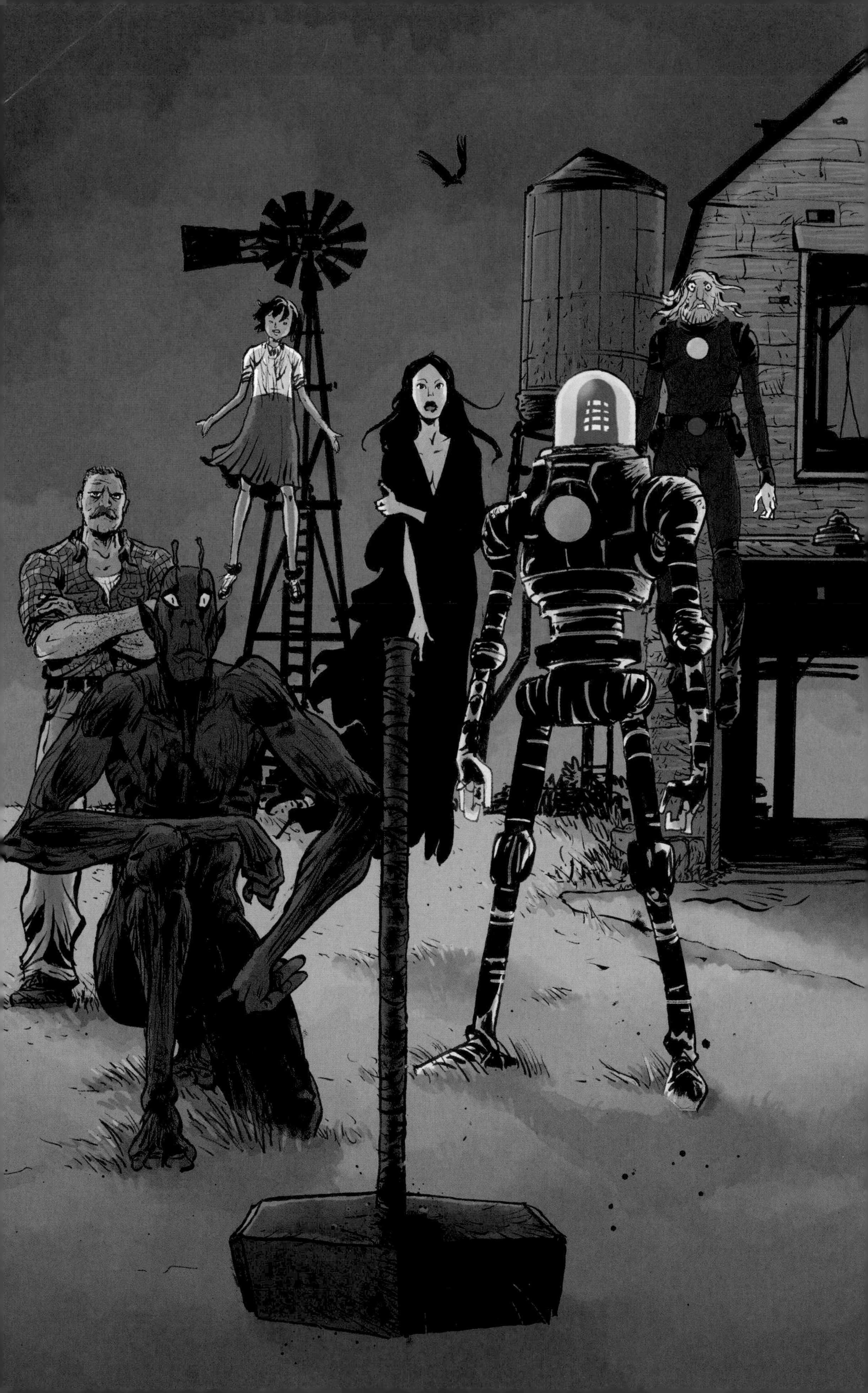

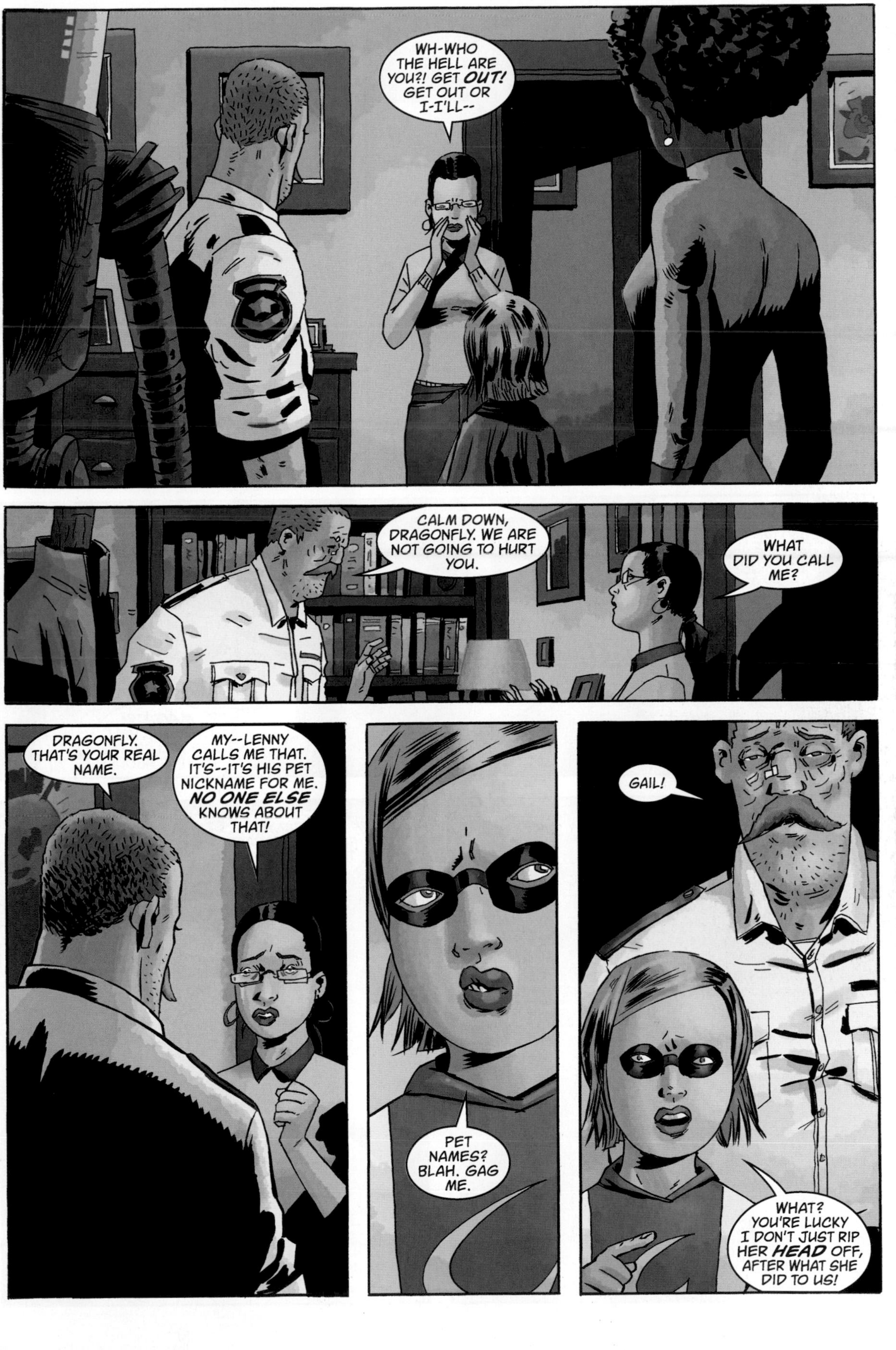
WH-WHO THE HELL ARE YOU?! GET OUT! GET OUT OR I-I'LL--
CALM DOWN, DRAGONFLY. WE ARE NOT GOING TO HURT YOU.
WHAT DID YOU CALL ME?
DRAGONFLY. THAT'S YOUR REAL NAME.
MY--LENNY CALLS ME THAT. IT'S--IT'S HIS PET NICKNAME FOR ME. NO ONE ELSE KNOWS ABOUT THAT!
PET NAMES? BLAH. GAG ME.
GAIL!
WHAT? YOU'RE LUCKY I DON'T JUST RIP HER HEAD OFF, AFTER WHAT SHE DID TO US!

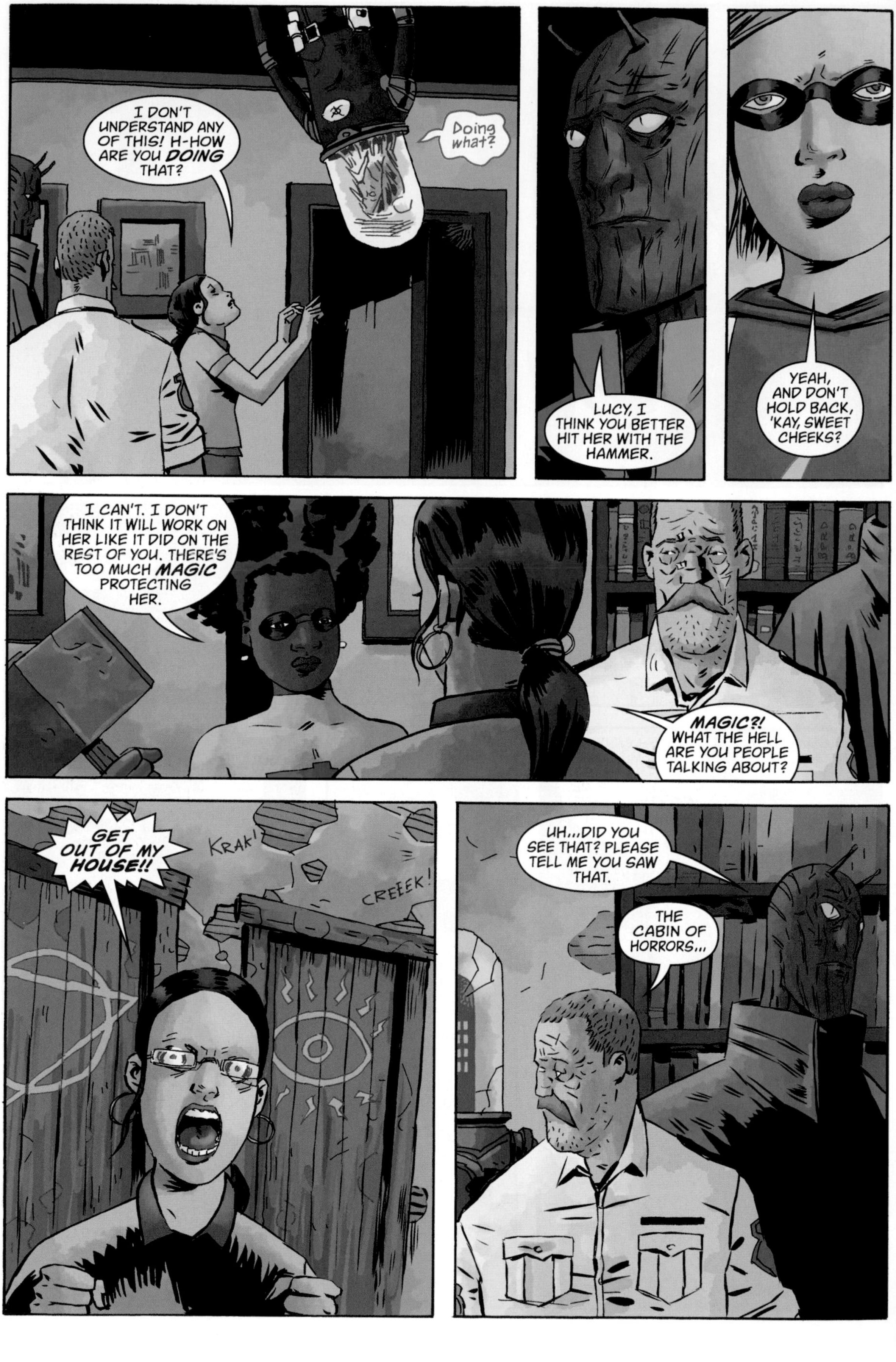
I DON'T UNDERSTAND ANY OF THIS! H-HOW ARE YOU **DOING** THAT?
Doing what?
LUCY, I THINK YOU BETTER HIT HER WITH THE HAMMER.
YEAH, AND DON'T HOLD BACK, 'KAY, SWEET CHEEKS?
I CAN'T. I DON'T THINK IT WILL WORK ON HER LIKE IT DID ON THE REST OF YOU. THERE'S TOO MUCH **MAGIC** PROTECTING HER.
MAGIC?! WHAT THE HELL ARE YOU PEOPLE TALKING ABOUT?
GET OUT OF MY HOUSE!!
KRAK!
CREEEK!
UH...DID YOU SEE THAT? PLEASE TELL ME YOU SAW THAT.
THE CABIN OF HORRORS...

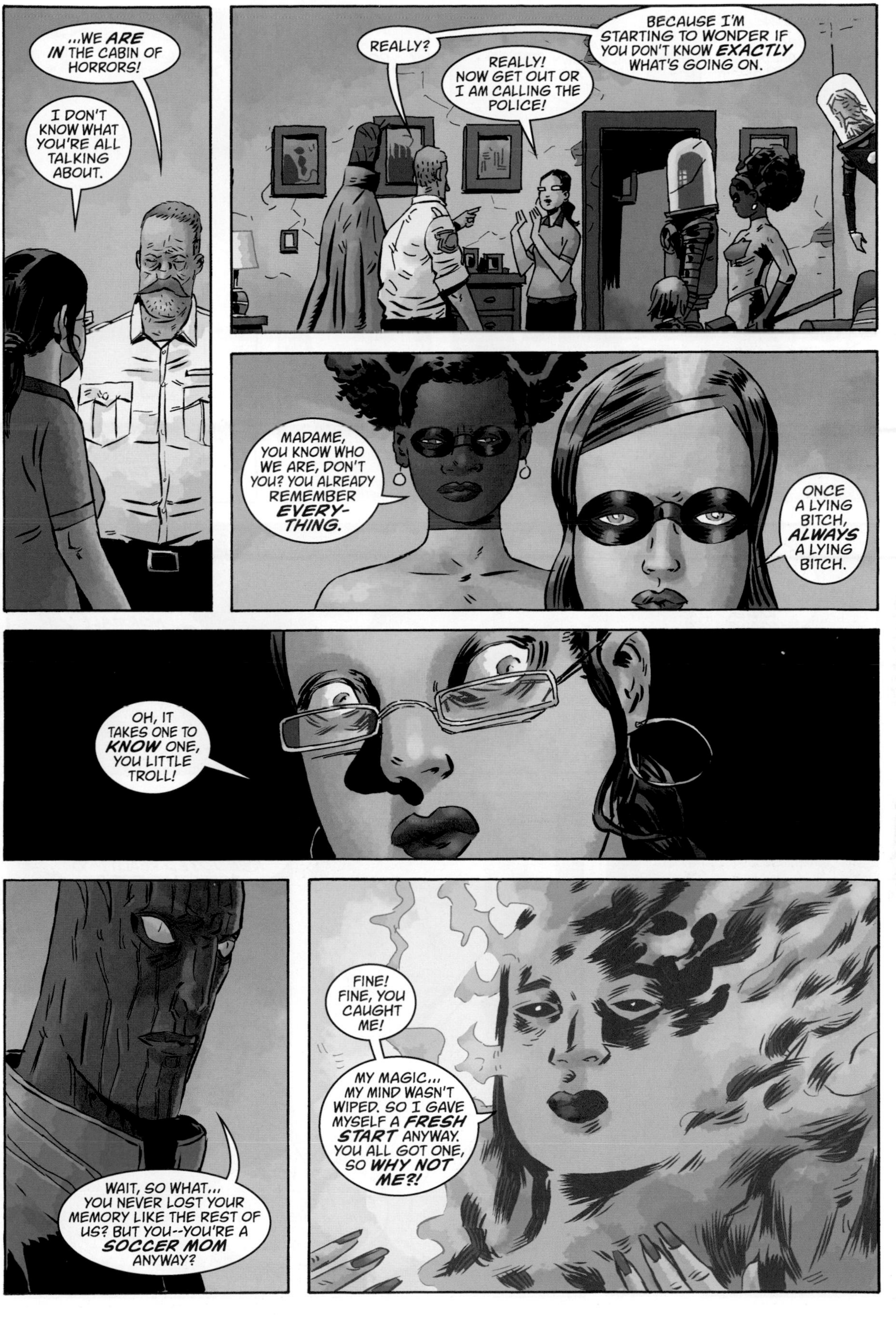
...WE ARE IN THE CABIN OF HORRORS!
I DON'T KNOW WHAT YOU'RE ALL TALKING ABOUT.
REALLY?
BECAUSE I'M STARTING TO WONDER IF YOU DON'T KNOW EXACTLY WHAT'S GOING ON.
REALLY! NOW GET OUT OR I AM CALLING THE POLICE!
MADAME, YOU KNOW WHO WE ARE, DON'T YOU? YOU ALREADY REMEMBER EVERYTHING.
ONCE A LYING BITCH, ALWAYS A LYING BITCH.
OH, IT TAKES ONE TO KNOW ONE, YOU LITTLE TROLL!
WAIT, SO WHAT... YOU NEVER LOST YOUR MEMORY LIKE THE REST OF US? BUT YOU--YOU'RE A SOCCER MOM ANYWAY?
FINE! FINE, YOU CAUGHT ME!
MY MAGIC... MY MIND WASN'T WIPED. SO I GAVE MYSELF A FRESH START ANYWAY. YOU ALL GOT ONE, SO WHY NOT ME?!

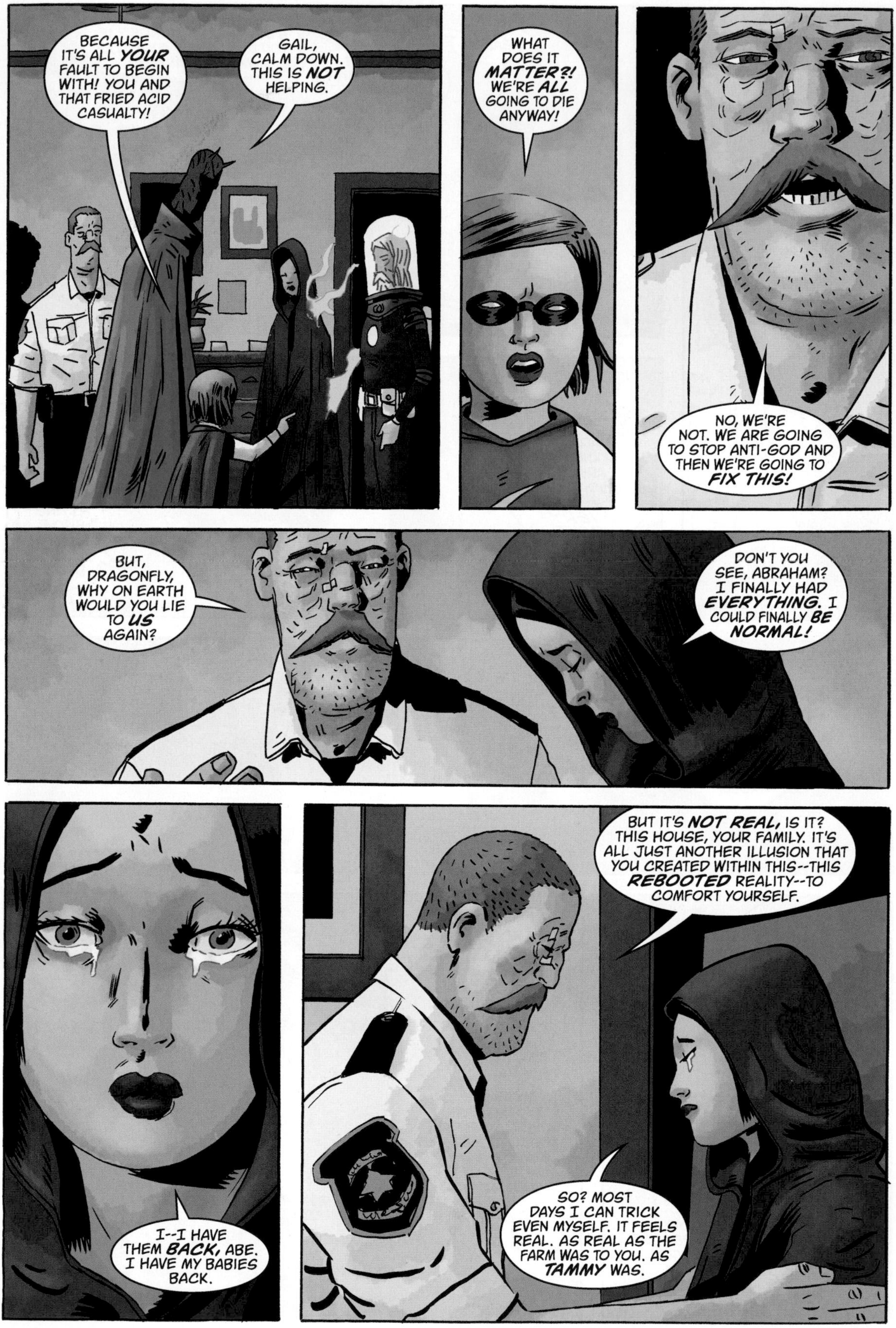
BECAUSE IT'S ALL YOUR FAULT TO BEGIN WITH! YOU AND THAT FRIED ACID CASUALTY!
GAIL, CALM DOWN. THIS IS NOT HELPING.
WHAT DOES IT MATTER?! WE'RE ALL GOING TO DIE ANYWAY!
NO, WE'RE NOT. WE ARE GOING TO STOP ANTI-GOD AND THEN WE'RE GOING TO FIX THIS!
BUT, DRAGONFLY, WHY ON EARTH WOULD YOU LIE TO US AGAIN?
DON'T YOU SEE, ABRAHAM? I FINALLY HAD EVERYTHING. I COULD FINALLY BE NORMAL!
I--I HAVE THEM BACK, ABE. I HAVE MY BABIES BACK.
BUT IT'S NOT REAL, IS IT? THIS HOUSE, YOUR FAMILY. IT'S ALL JUST ANOTHER ILLUSION THAT YOU CREATED WITHIN THIS--THIS REBOOTED REALITY--TO COMFORT YOURSELF.
SO? MOST DAYS I CAN TRICK EVEN MYSELF. IT FEELS REAL. AS REAL AS THE FARM WAS TO YOU. AS TAMMY WAS.

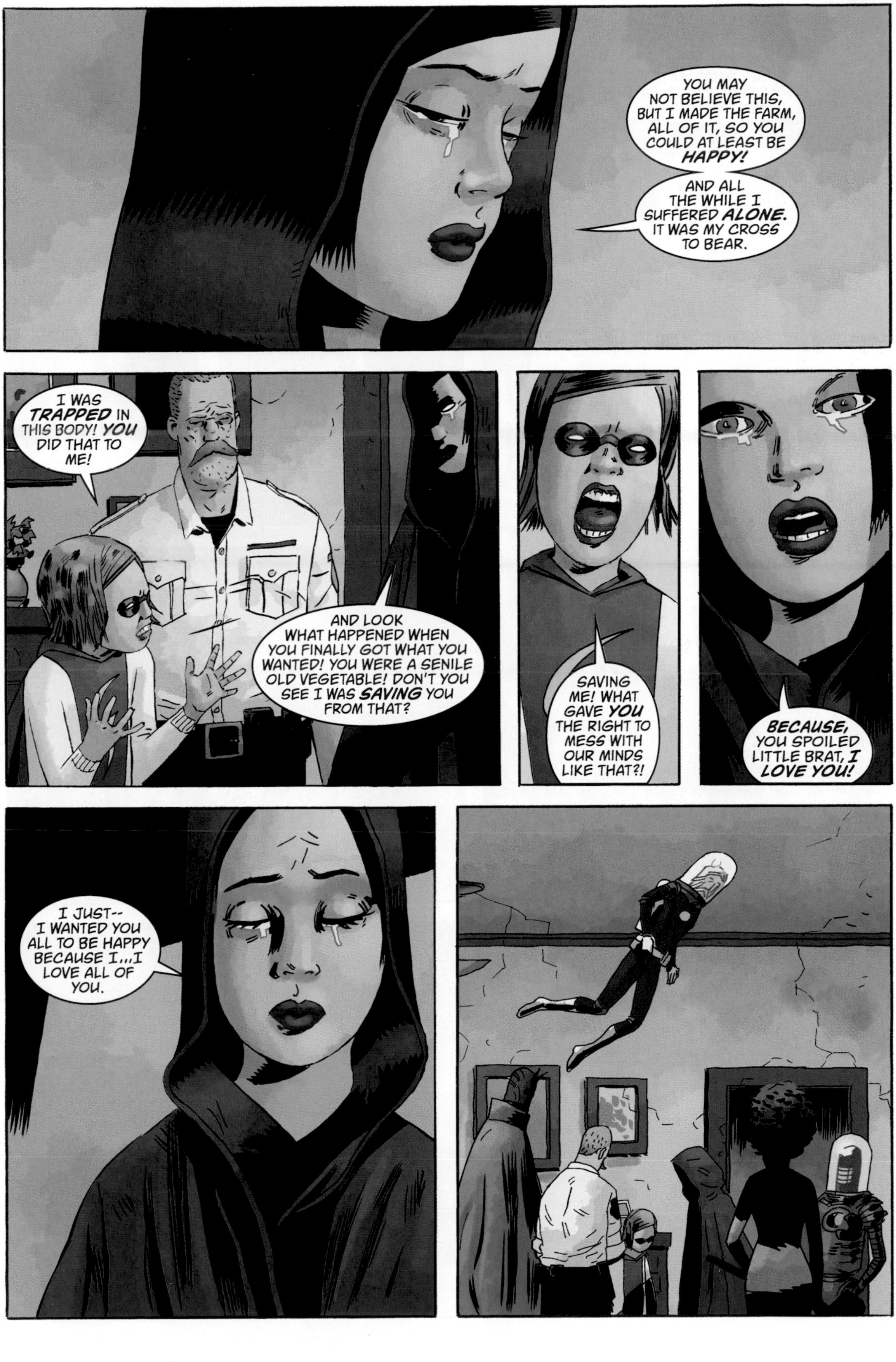
YOU MAY NOT BELIEVE THIS, BUT I MADE THE FARM, ALL OF IT, SO YOU COULD AT LEAST BE HAPPY!
AND ALL THE WHILE I SUFFERED ALONE. IT WAS MY CROSS TO BEAR.
I WAS TRAPPED IN THIS BODY! YOU DID THAT TO ME!
AND LOOK WHAT HAPPENED WHEN YOU FINALLY GOT WHAT YOU WANTED! YOU WERE A SENILE OLD VEGETABLE! DON'T YOU SEE I WAS SAVING YOU FROM THAT?
SAVING ME! WHAT GAVE YOU THE RIGHT TO MESS WITH OUR MINDS LIKE THAT?!
BECAUSE, YOU SPOILED LITTLE BRAT, I LOVE YOU!
I JUST-- I WANTED YOU ALL TO BE HAPPY BECAUSE I...I LOVE ALL OF YOU.

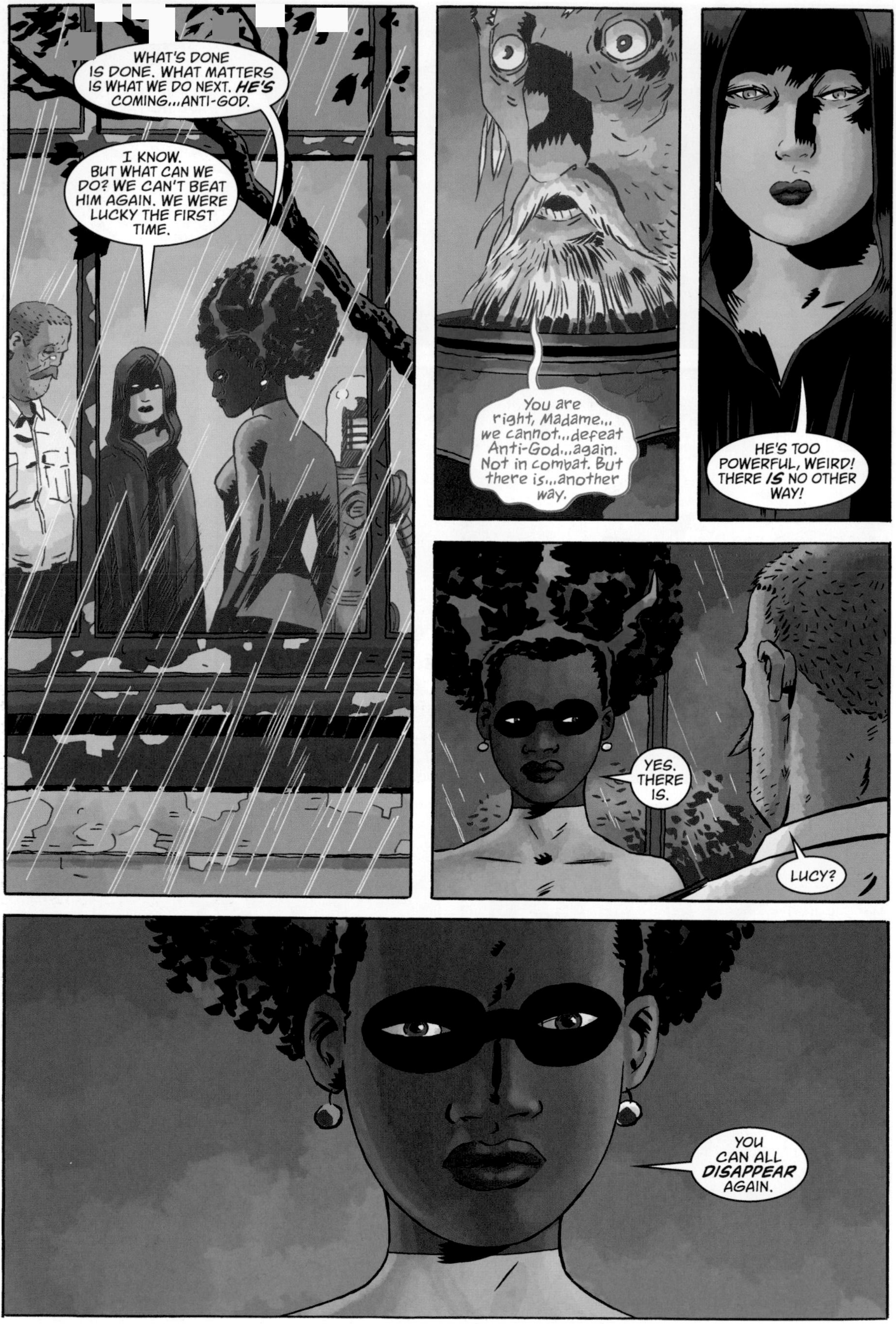
WHAT'S DONE IS DONE. WHAT MATTERS IS WHAT WE DO NEXT. HE'S COMING...ANTI-GOD.
I KNOW. BUT WHAT CAN WE DO? WE CAN'T BEAT HIM AGAIN. WE WERE LUCKY THE FIRST TIME.
You are right, Madame... we cannot...defeat Anti-God...again. Not in combat. But there is...another way.
HE'S TOO POWERFUL, WEIRD! THERE IS NO OTHER WAY!
YES. THERE IS.
LUCY?
YOU CAN ALL DISAPPEAR AGAIN.

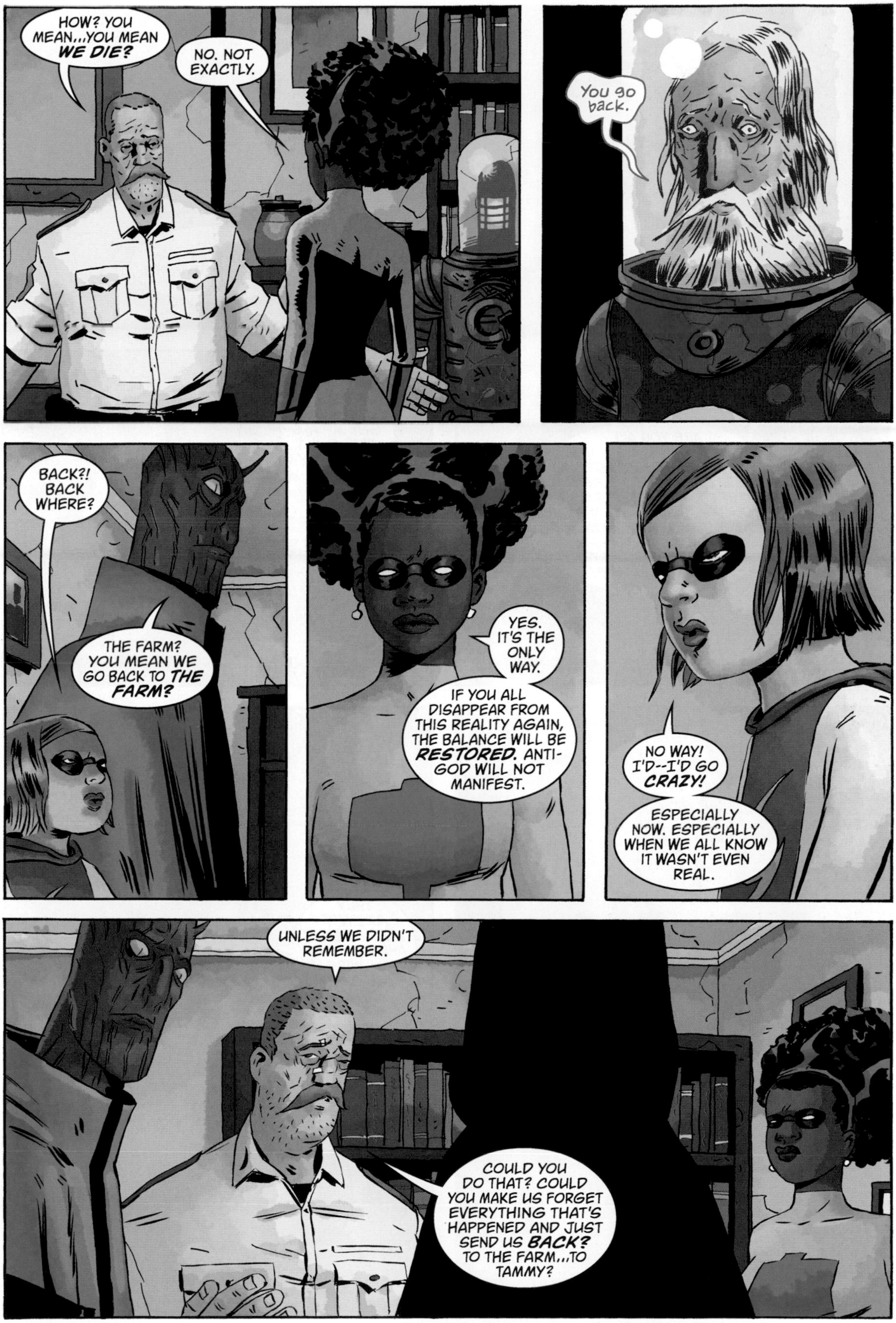
HOW? YOU MEAN...YOU MEAN WE DIE?
NO. NOT EXACTLY.
You go back.
BACK?! BACK WHERE?
THE FARM? YOU MEAN WE GO BACK TO THE FARM?
YES. IT'S THE ONLY WAY.
IF YOU ALL DISAPPEAR FROM THIS REALITY AGAIN, THE BALANCE WILL BE RESTORED. ANTI-GOD WILL NOT MANIFEST.
NO WAY! I'D--I'D GO CRAZY!
ESPECIALLY NOW. ESPECIALLY WHEN WE ALL KNOW IT WASN'T EVEN REAL.
UNLESS WE DIDN'T REMEMBER.
COULD YOU DO THAT? COULD YOU MAKE US FORGET EVERYTHING THAT'S HAPPENED AND JUST SEND US BACK? TO THE FARM...TO TAMMY?

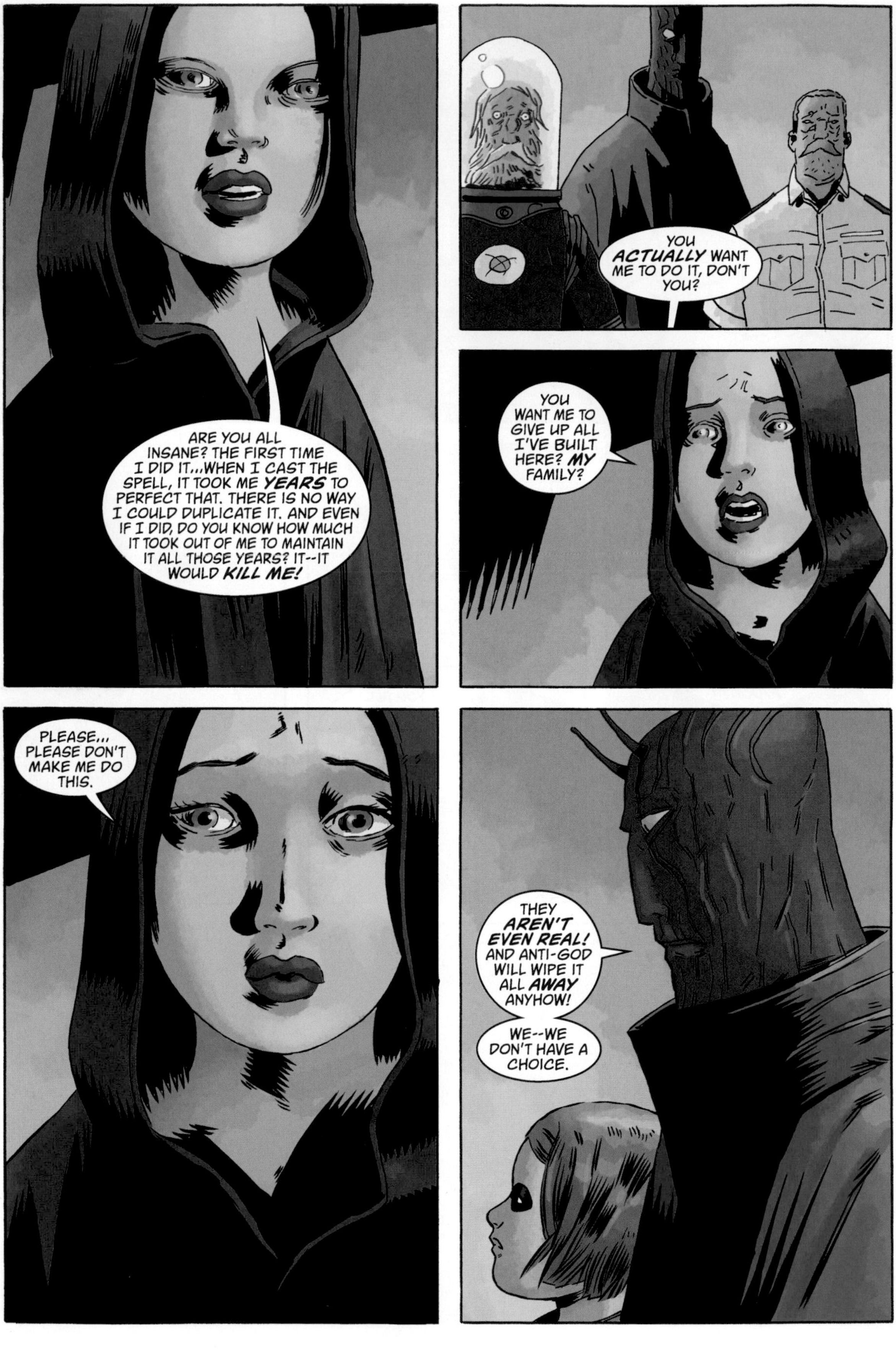
ARE YOU ALL INSANE? THE FIRST TIME I DID IT...WHEN I CAST THE SPELL, IT TOOK ME YEARS TO PERFECT THAT. THERE IS NO WAY I COULD DUPLICATE IT. AND EVEN IF I DID, DO YOU KNOW HOW MUCH IT TOOK OUT OF ME TO MAINTAIN IT ALL THOSE YEARS? IT--IT WOULD KILL ME!
YOU ACTUALLY WANT ME TO DO IT, DON'T YOU?
YOU WANT ME TO GIVE UP ALL I'VE BUILT HERE? MY FAMILY?
PLEASE... PLEASE DON'T MAKE ME DO THIS.
THEY AREN'T EVEN REAL! AND ANTI-GOD WILL WIPE IT ALL AWAY ANYHOW!
WE--WE DON'T HAVE A CHOICE.

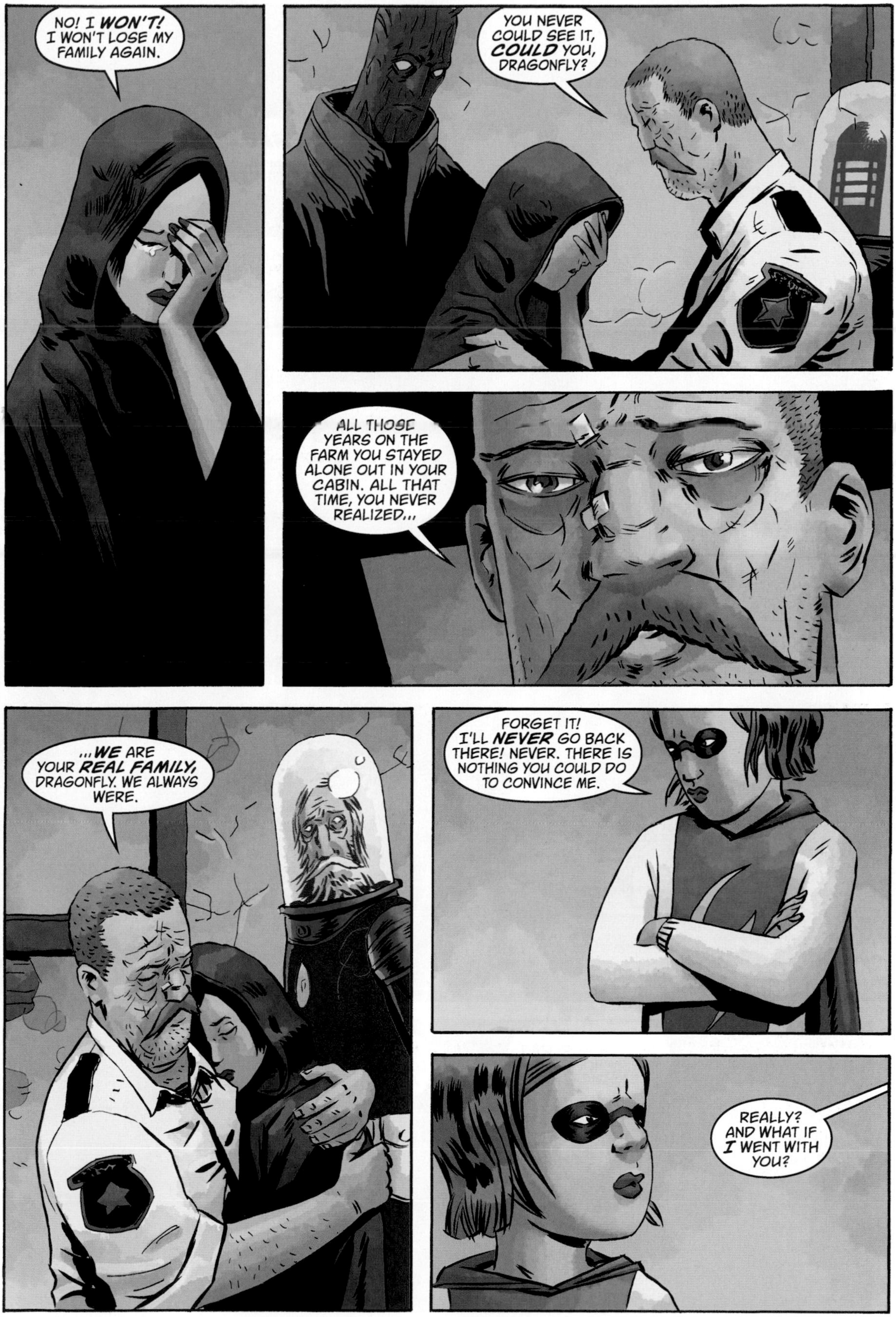
NO! I *WON'T!* I WON'T LOSE MY FAMILY AGAIN.
YOU NEVER COULD SEE IT, *COULD* YOU, DRAGONFLY?
ALL THOSE YEARS ON THE FARM YOU STAYED ALONE OUT IN YOUR CABIN. ALL THAT TIME, YOU NEVER REALIZED...
...*WE* ARE YOUR *REAL FAMILY,* DRAGONFLY. WE ALWAYS WERE.
FORGET IT! I'LL *NEVER* GO BACK THERE! NEVER. THERE IS NOTHING YOU COULD DO TO CONVINCE ME.
REALLY? AND WHAT IF *I* WENT WITH YOU?

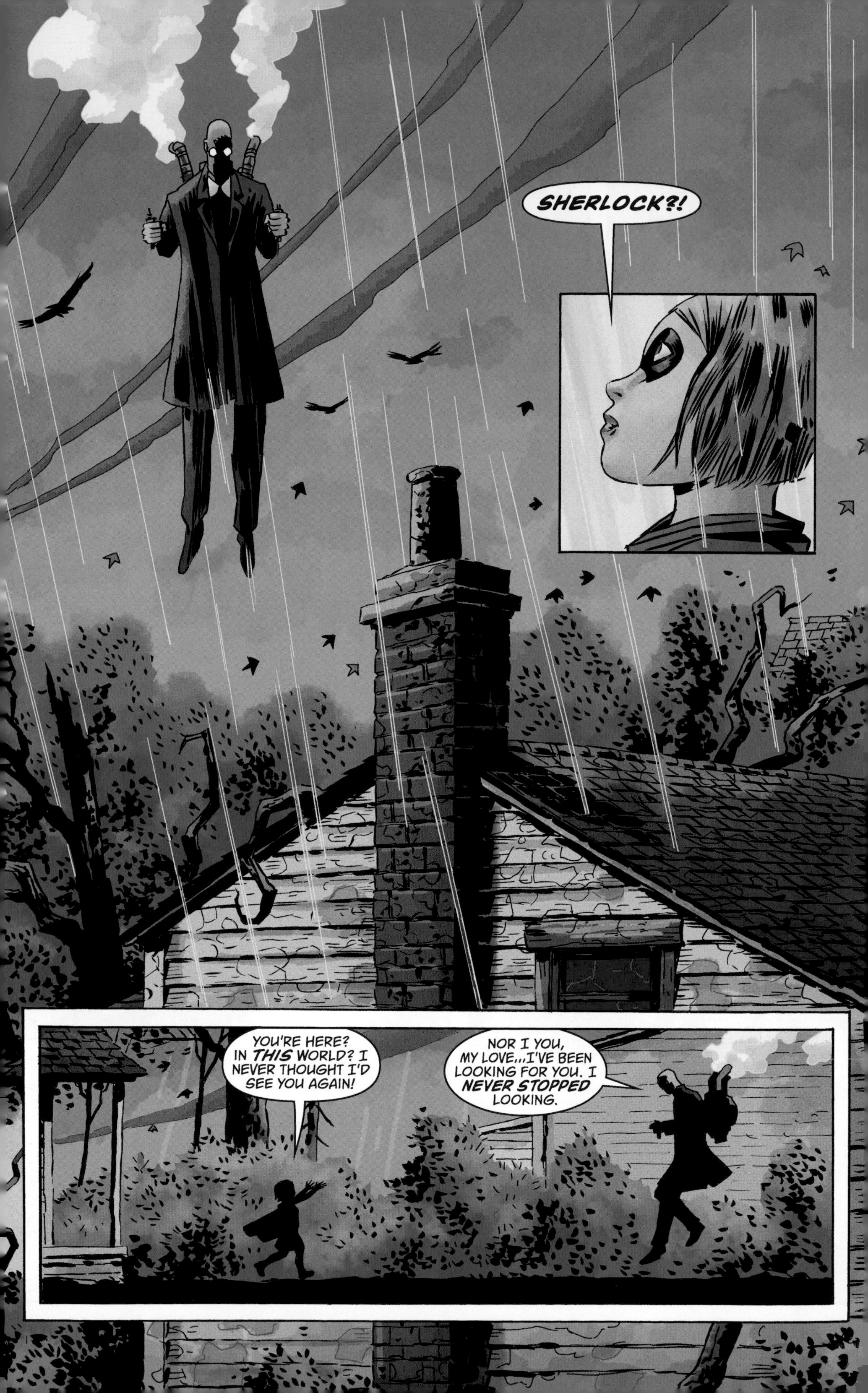
SHERLOCK?!
YOU'RE HERE? IN THIS WORLD? I NEVER THOUGHT I'D SEE YOU AGAIN!
NOR I YOU, MY LOVE... I'VE BEEN LOOKING FOR YOU. I NEVER STOPPED LOOKING.

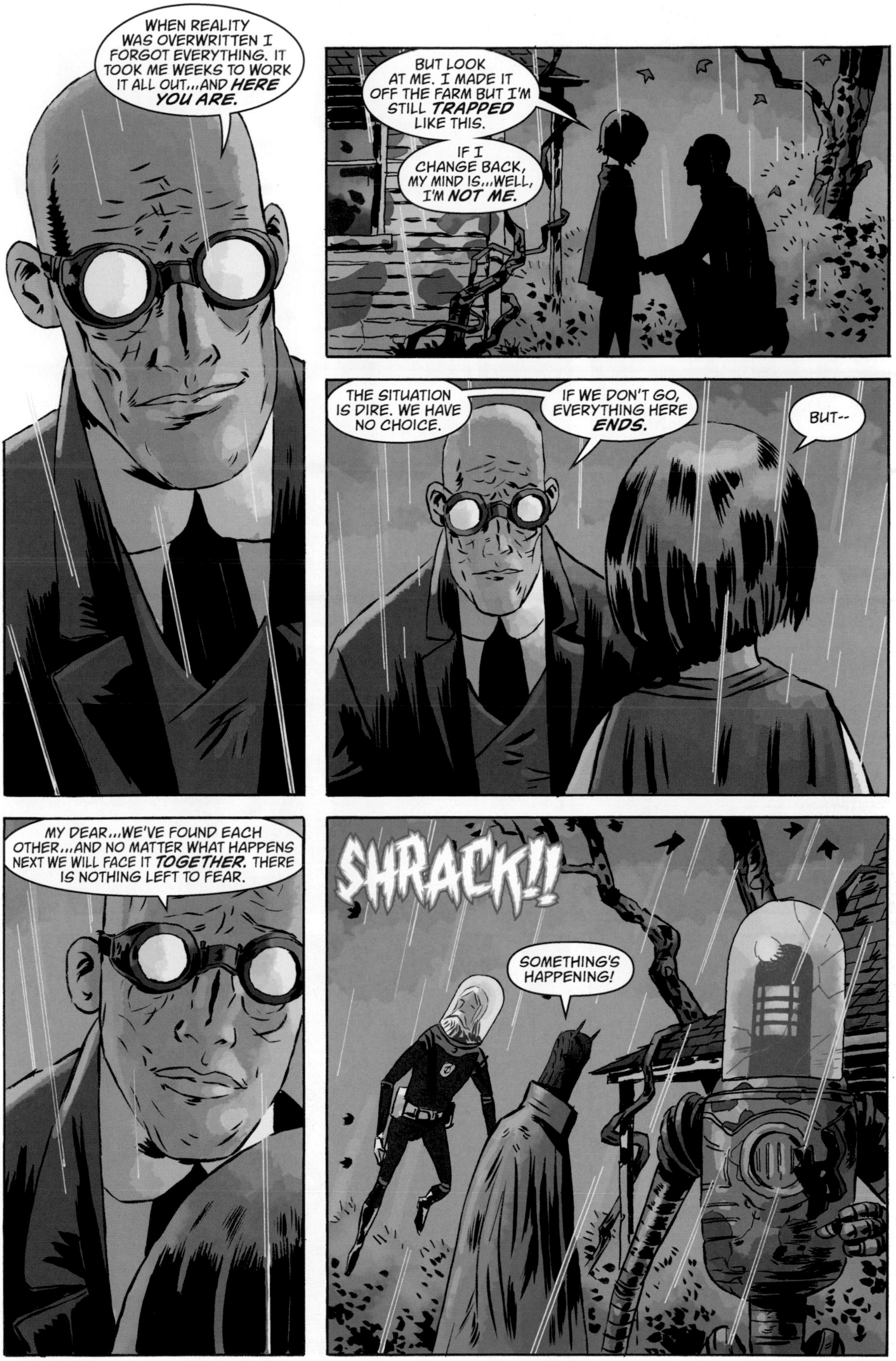
WHEN REALITY WAS OVERWRITTEN I FORGOT EVERYTHING. IT TOOK ME WEEKS TO WORK IT ALL OUT...AND **HERE YOU ARE.**
BUT LOOK AT ME. I MADE IT OFF THE FARM BUT I'M STILL **TRAPPED** LIKE THIS.
IF I CHANGE BACK, MY MIND IS...WELL, I'M **NOT ME.**
THE SITUATION IS DIRE. WE HAVE NO CHOICE.
IF WE DON'T GO, EVERYTHING HERE **ENDS.**
BUT--
MY DEAR...WE'VE FOUND EACH OTHER...AND NO MATTER WHAT HAPPENS NEXT WE WILL FACE IT **TOGETHER.** THERE IS NOTHING LEFT TO FEAR.
SHRACK!!
SOMETHING'S HAPPENING!

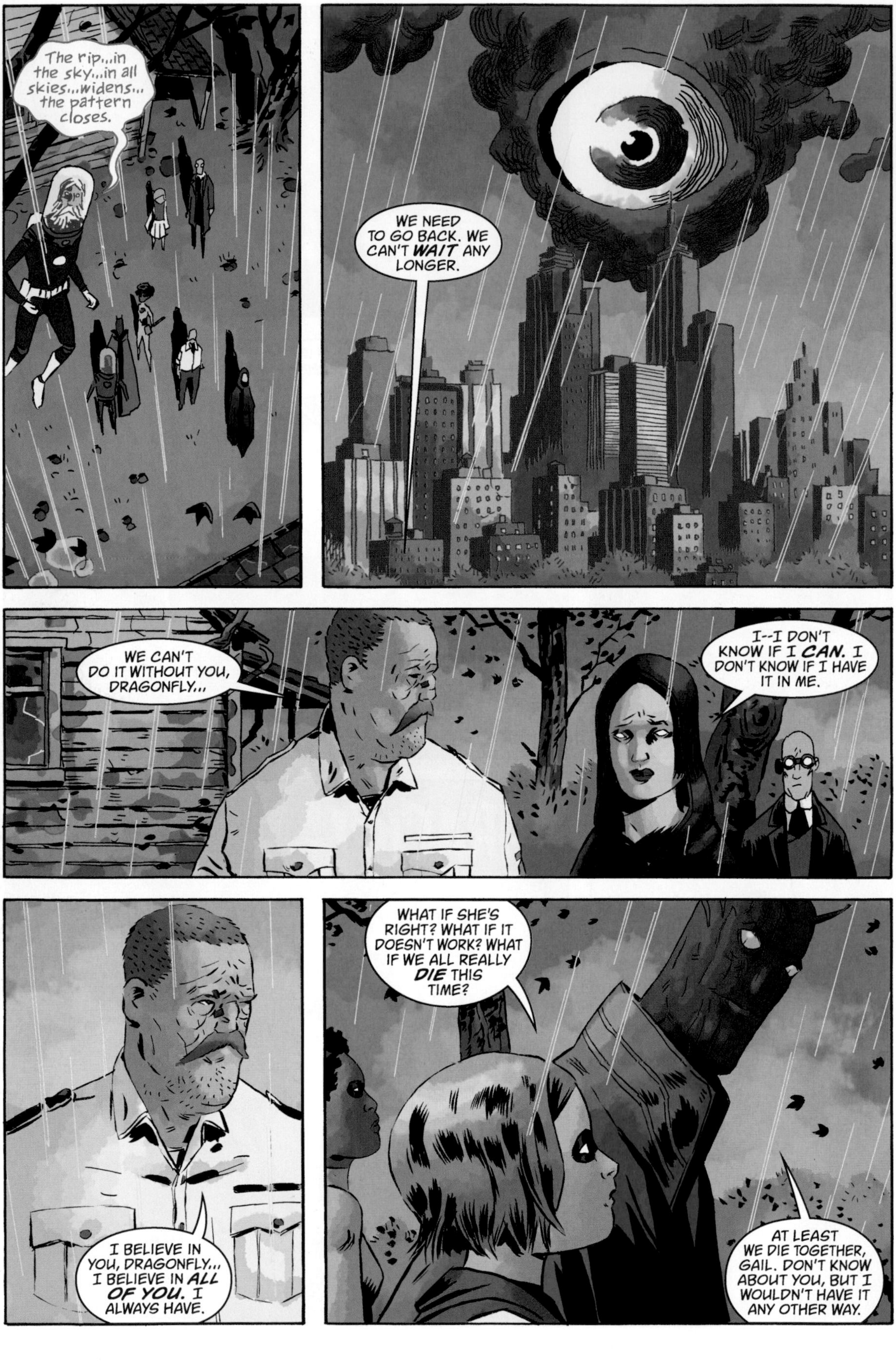

The rip...in the sky...in all skies...widens... the pattern closes.
WE NEED TO GO BACK. WE CAN'T WAIT ANY LONGER.
WE CAN'T DO IT WITHOUT YOU, DRAGONFLY...
I--I DON'T KNOW IF I CAN. I DON'T KNOW IF I HAVE IT IN ME.
I BELIEVE IN YOU, DRAGONFLY... I BELIEVE IN ALL OF YOU. I ALWAYS HAVE.
WHAT IF SHE'S RIGHT? WHAT IF IT DOESN'T WORK? WHAT IF WE ALL REALLY DIE THIS TIME?
AT LEAST WE DIE TOGETHER, GAIL. DON'T KNOW ABOUT YOU, BUT I WOULDN'T HAVE IT ANY OTHER WAY.

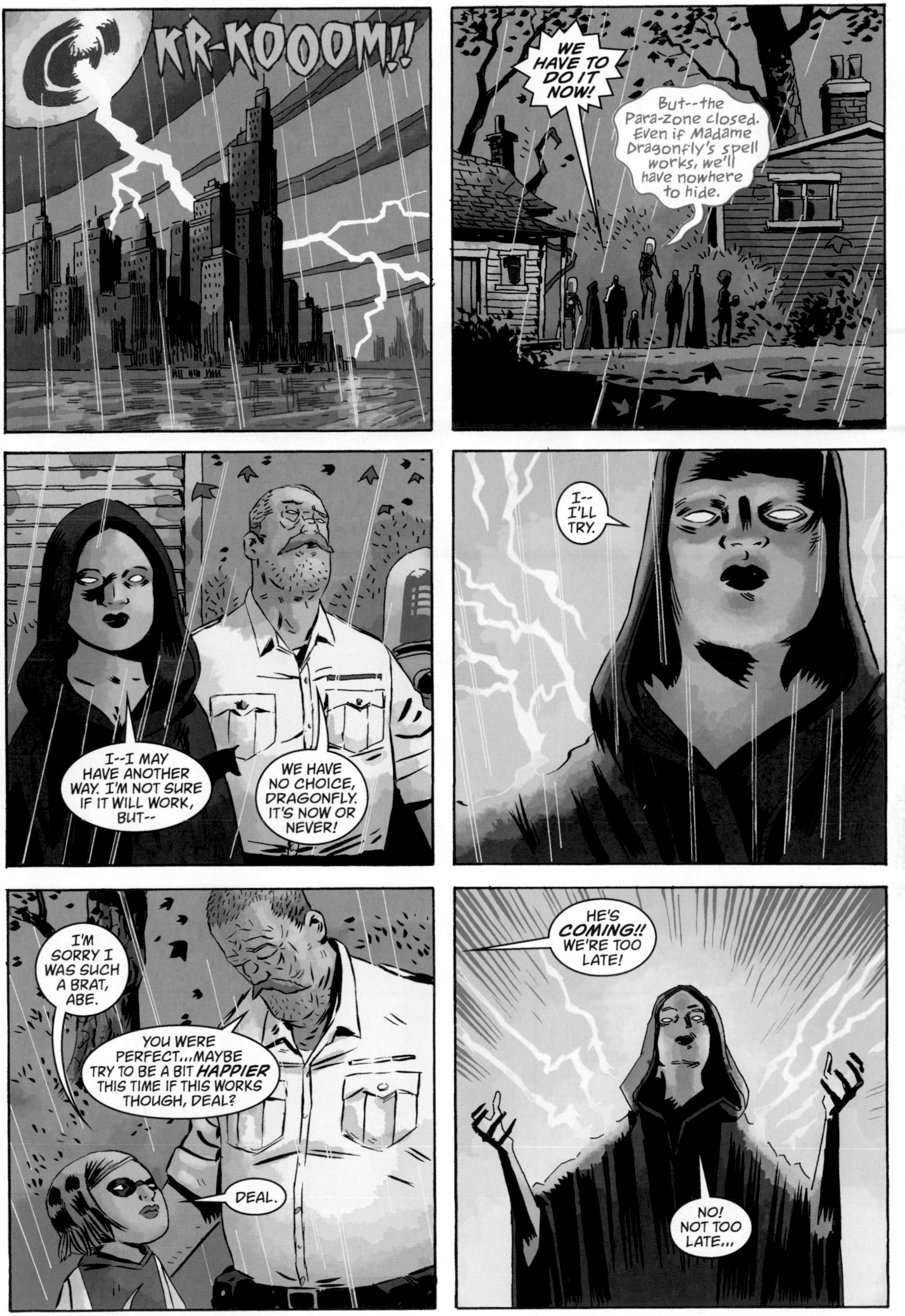
KR-KOOOM!!
WE HAVE TO DO IT NOW!
But--the Para-zone closed. Even if Madame Dragonfly's spell works, we'll have nowhere to hide.
I--I MAY HAVE ANOTHER WAY. I'M NOT SURE IF IT WILL WORK, BUT--
WE HAVE NO CHOICE, DRAGONFLY. IT'S NOW OR NEVER!
I-- I'LL TRY.
I'M SORRY I WAS SUCH A BRAT, ABE.
YOU WERE PERFECT...MAYBE TRY TO BE A BIT HAPPIER THIS TIME IF THIS WORKS THOUGH, DEAL?
DEAL.
HE'S COMING!! WE'RE TOO LATE!
NO! NOT TOO LATE...

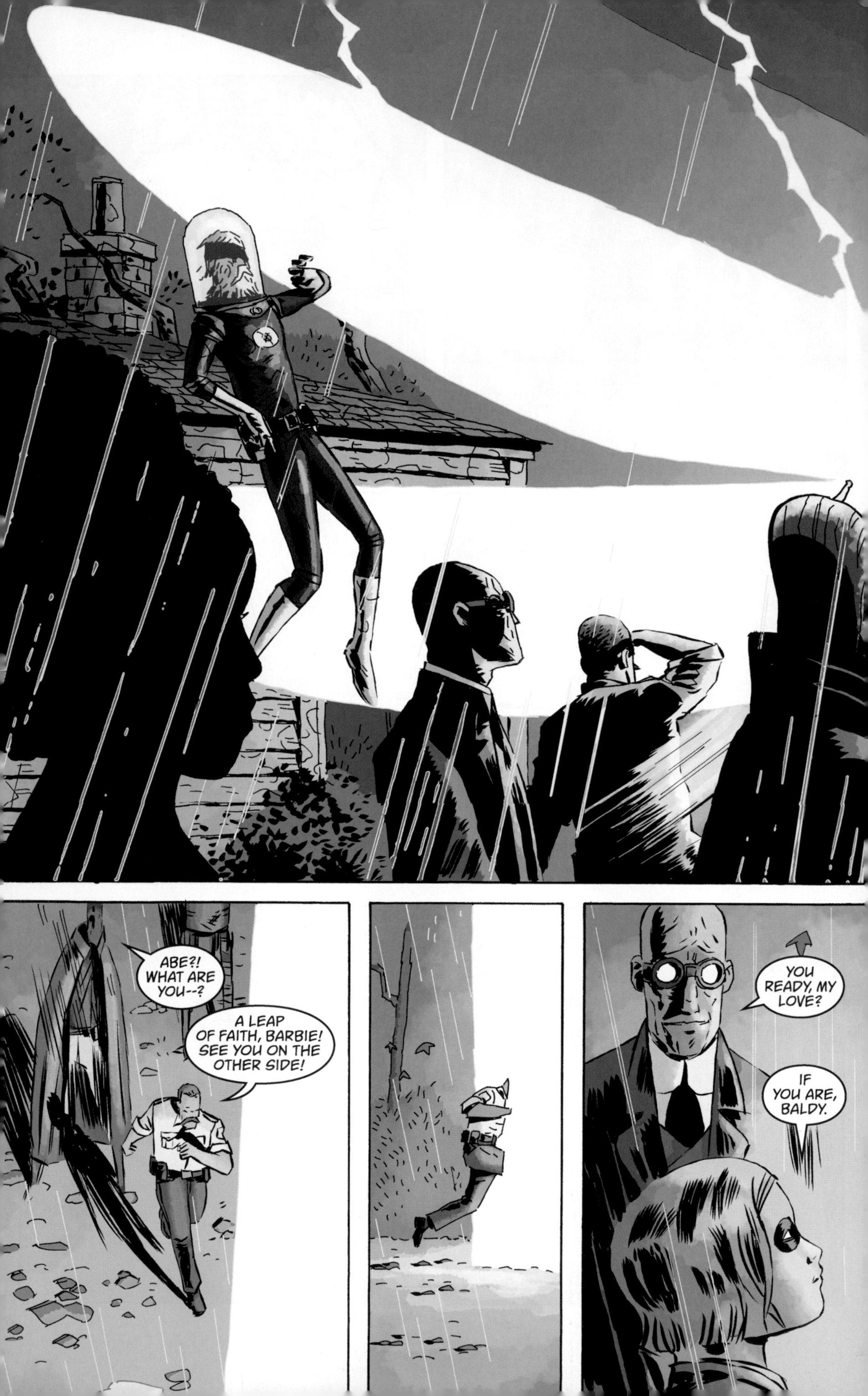
ABE?! WHAT ARE YOU--?
A LEAP OF FAITH, BARBIE! SEE YOU ON THE OTHER SIDE!
YOU READY, MY LOVE?
IF YOU ARE, BALDY.

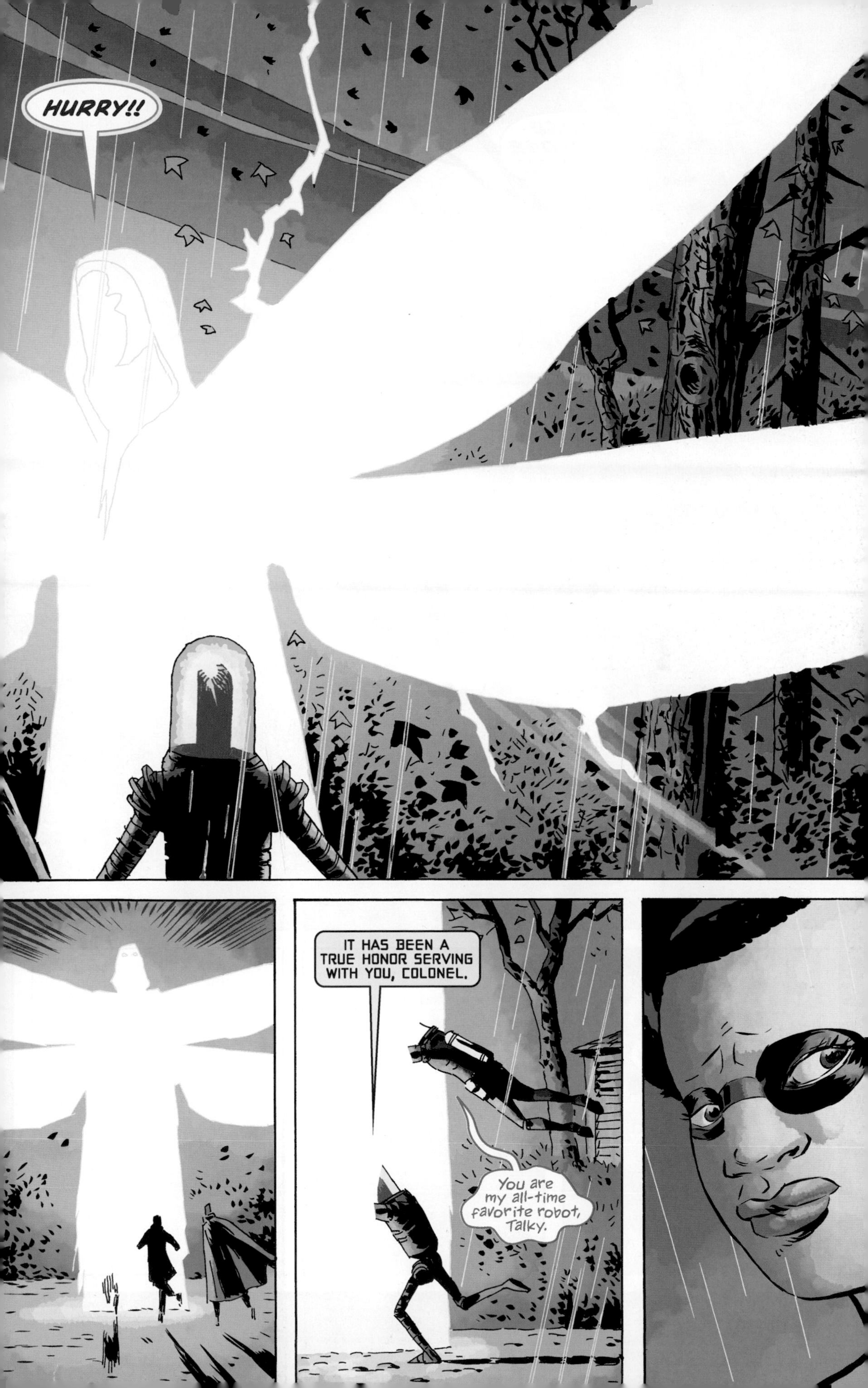

HURRY!!
IT HAS BEEN A TRUE HONOR SERVING WITH YOU, COLONEL.
You are my all-time favorite robot, Talky.

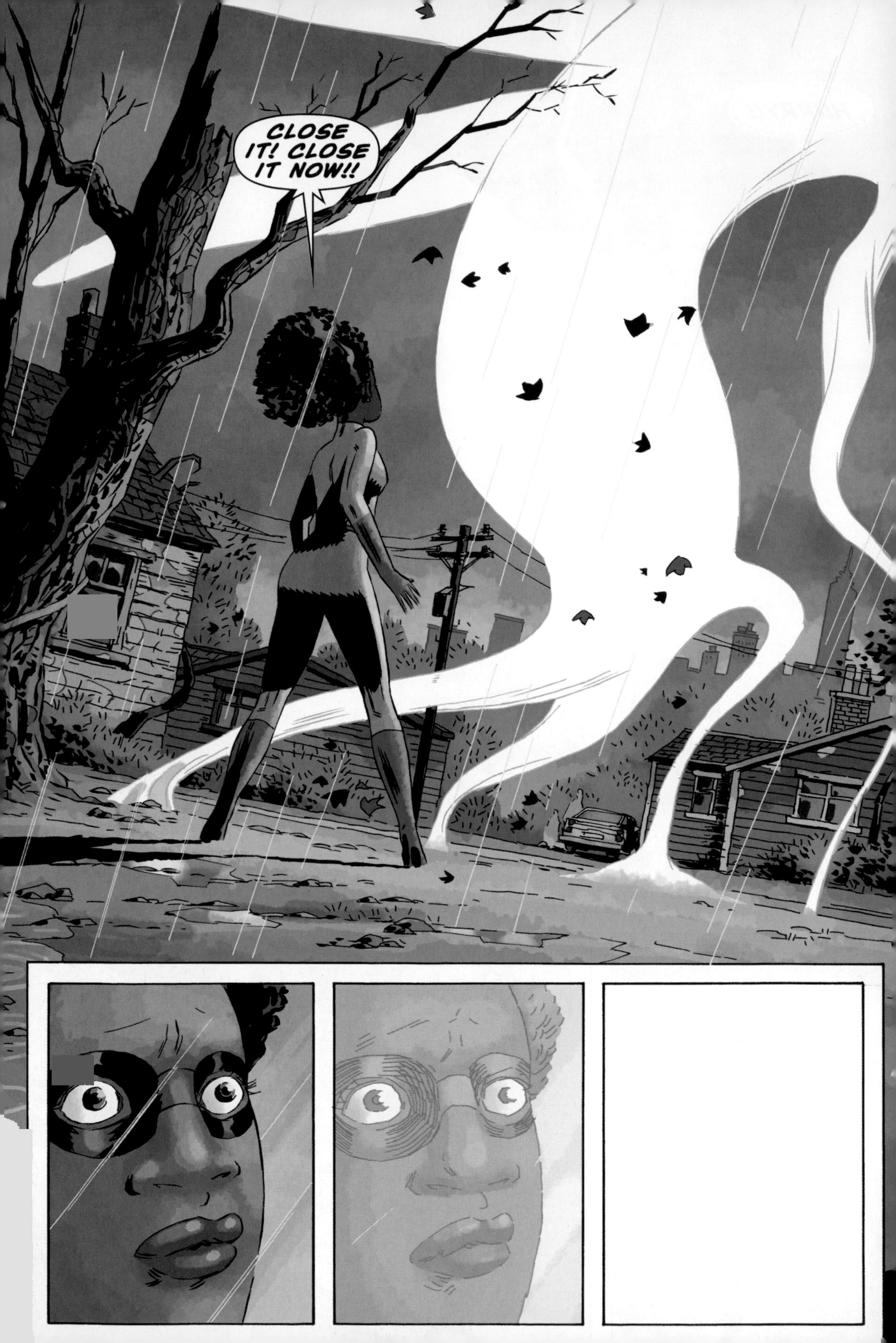
CLOSE IT! CLOSE IT NOW!!

SPIRAL
CITY
BONE CHINA

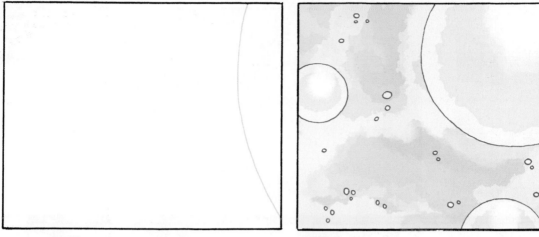

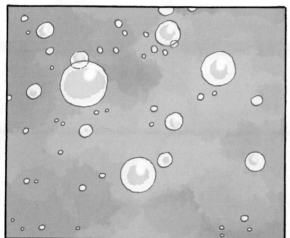

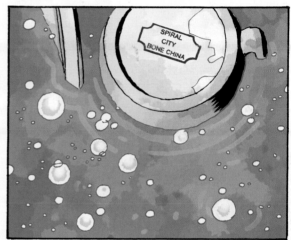

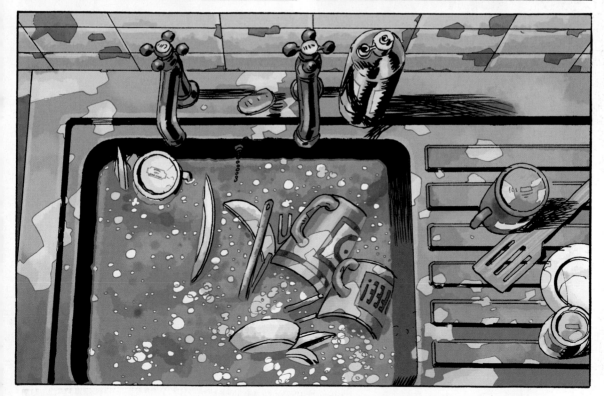

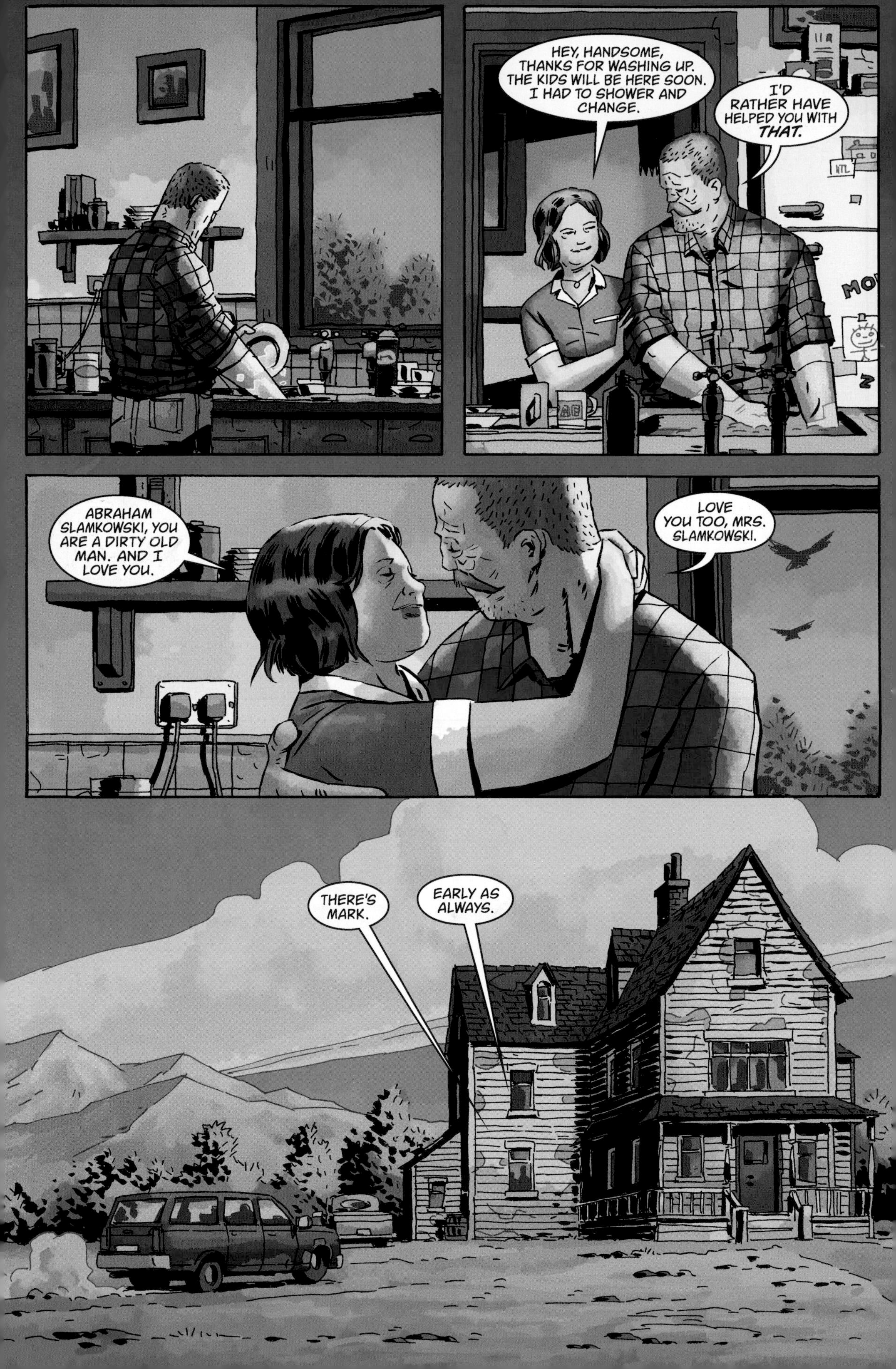
HEY, HANDSOME, THANKS FOR WASHING UP. THE KIDS WILL BE HERE SOON. I HAD TO SHOWER AND CHANGE.
I'D RATHER HAVE HELPED YOU WITH *THAT.*
ABRAHAM SLAMKOWSKI, YOU ARE A DIRTY OLD MAN. AND I LOVE YOU.
LOVE YOU TOO, MRS. SLAMKOWSKI.
THERE'S MARK.
EARLY AS ALWAYS.

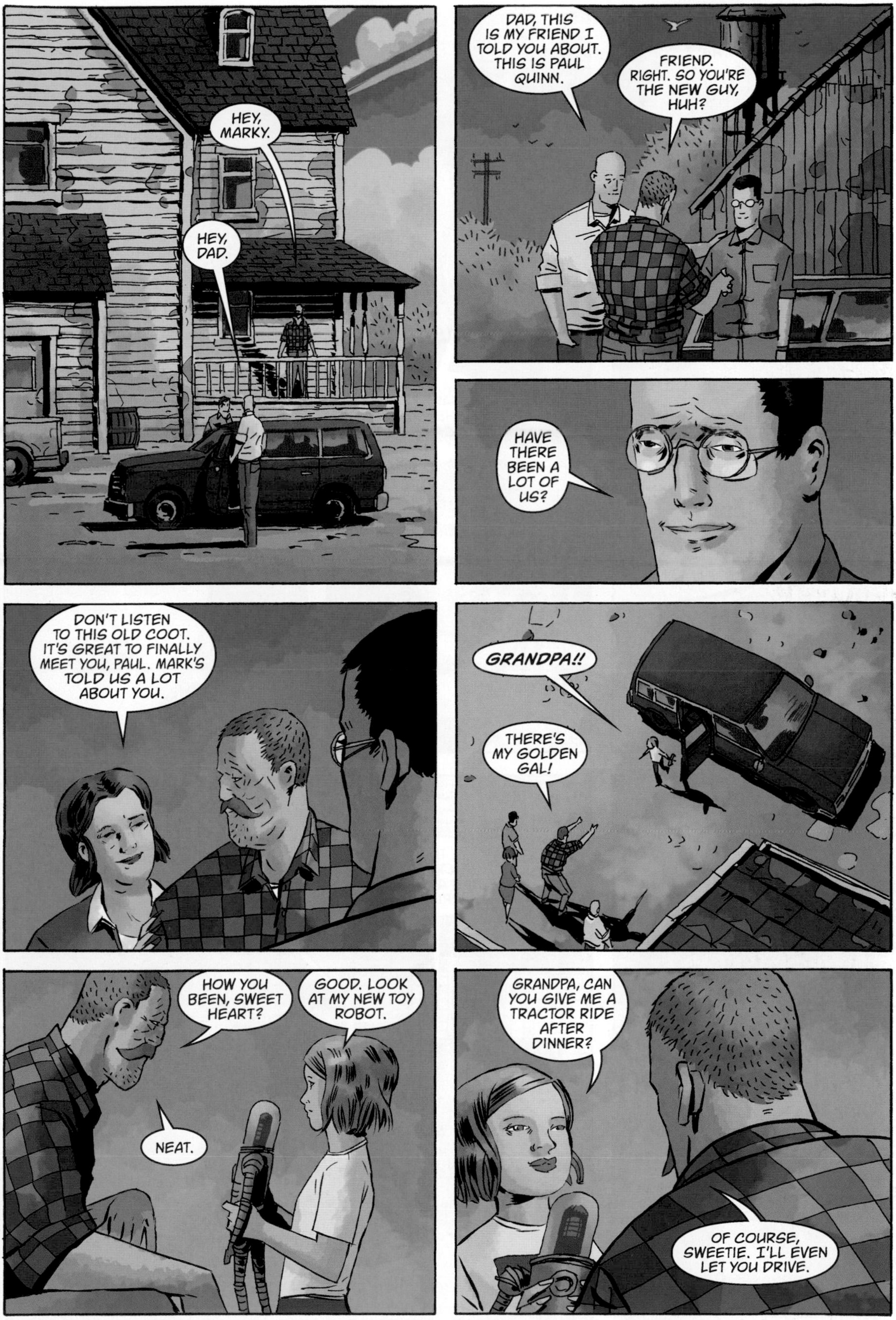
HEY, MARKY.
HEY, DAD.
DAD, THIS IS MY FRIEND I TOLD YOU ABOUT. THIS IS PAUL QUINN.
FRIEND. RIGHT. SO YOU'RE THE NEW GUY, HUH?
HAVE THERE BEEN A LOT OF US?
DON'T LISTEN TO THIS OLD COOT. IT'S GREAT TO FINALLY MEET YOU, PAUL. MARK'S TOLD US A LOT ABOUT YOU.
GRANDPA!!
THERE'S MY GOLDEN GAL!
HOW YOU BEEN, SWEET HEART?
GOOD. LOOK AT MY NEW TOY ROBOT.
NEAT.
GRANDPA, CAN YOU GIVE ME A TRACTOR RIDE AFTER DINNER?
OF COURSE, SWEETIE. I'LL EVEN LET YOU DRIVE.

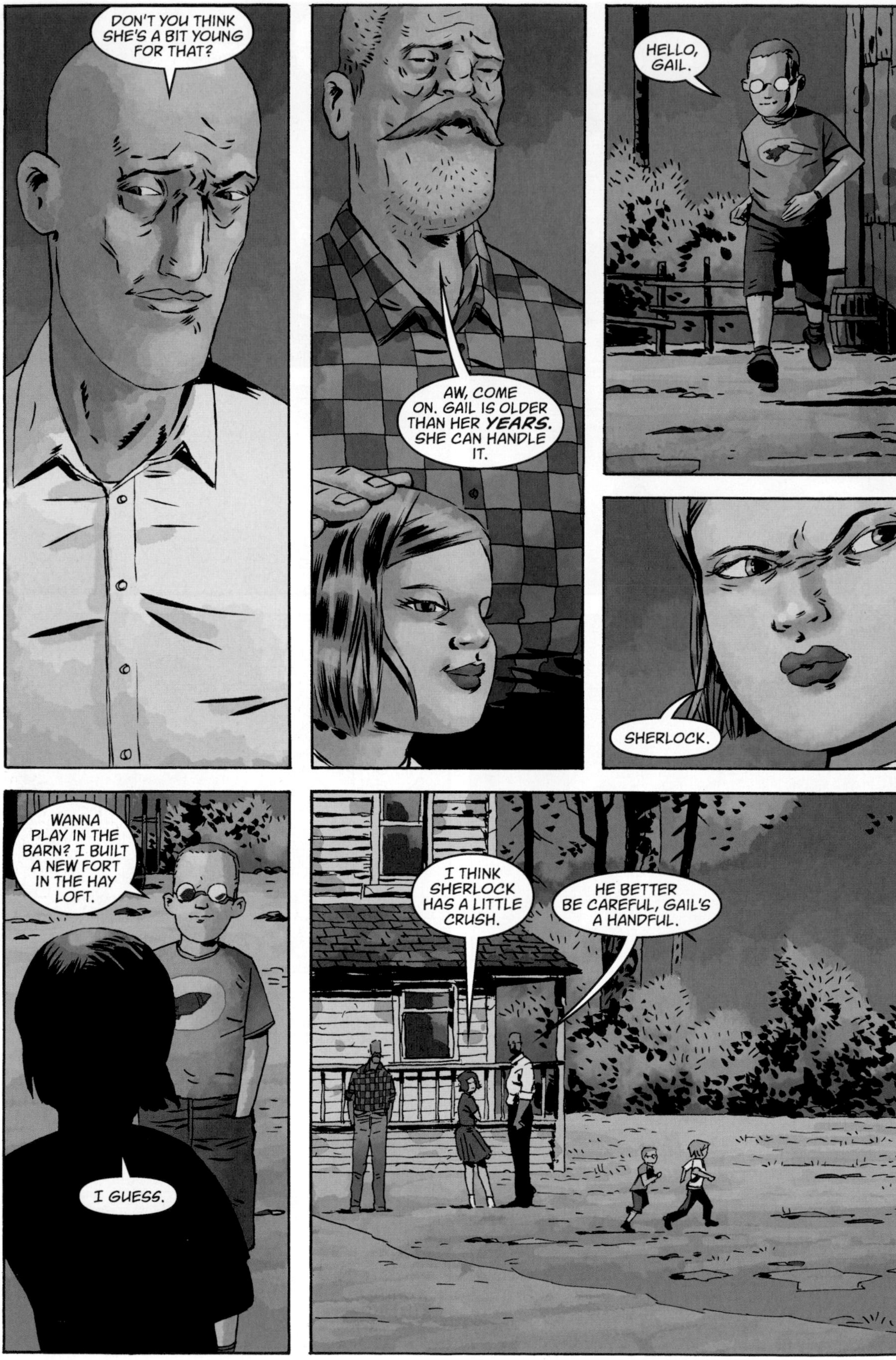
DON'T YOU THINK SHE'S A BIT YOUNG FOR THAT?
AW, COME ON. GAIL IS OLDER THAN HER *YEARS.* SHE CAN HANDLE IT.
HELLO, GAIL.
SHERLOCK.
WANNA PLAY IN THE BARN? I BUILT A NEW FORT IN THE HAY LOFT.
I GUESS.
I THINK SHERLOCK HAS A LITTLE CRUSH.
HE BETTER BE CAREFUL, GAIL'S A HANDFUL.

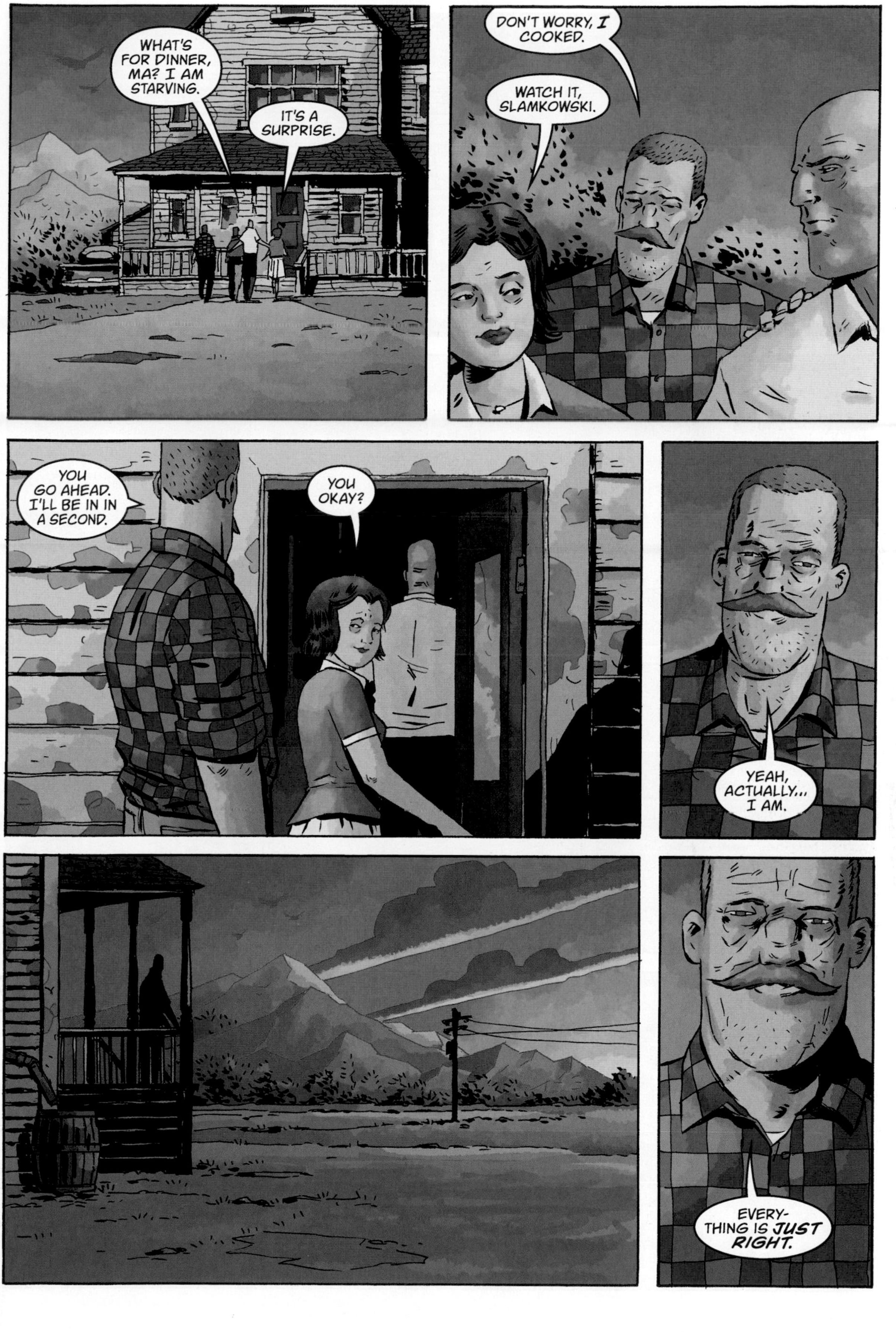
WHAT'S FOR DINNER, MA? I AM STARVING.
IT'S A SURPRISE.
DON'T WORRY, I COOKED.
WATCH IT, SLAMKOWSKI.
YOU GO AHEAD. I'LL BE IN IN A SECOND.
YOU OKAY?
YEAH, ACTUALLY... I AM.
EVERY-THING IS JUST RIGHT.

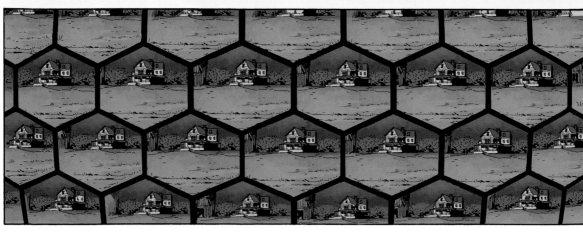

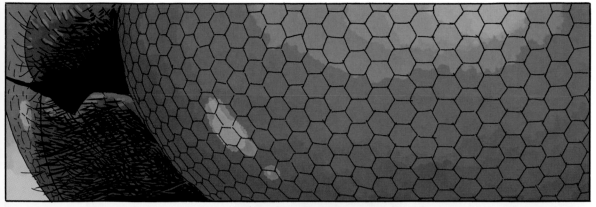

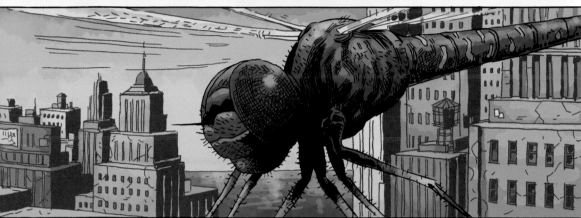

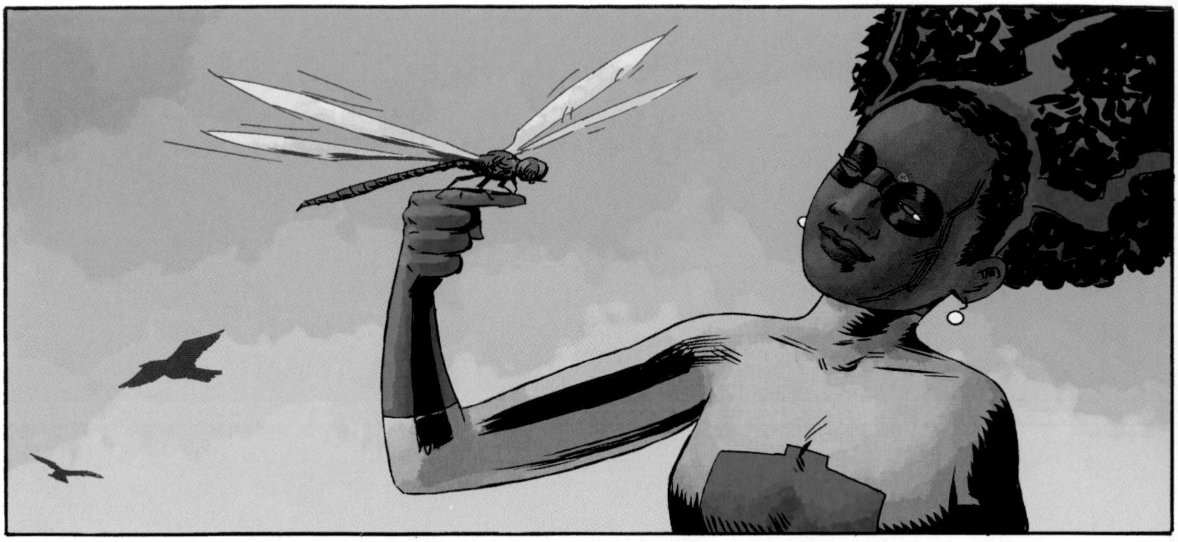

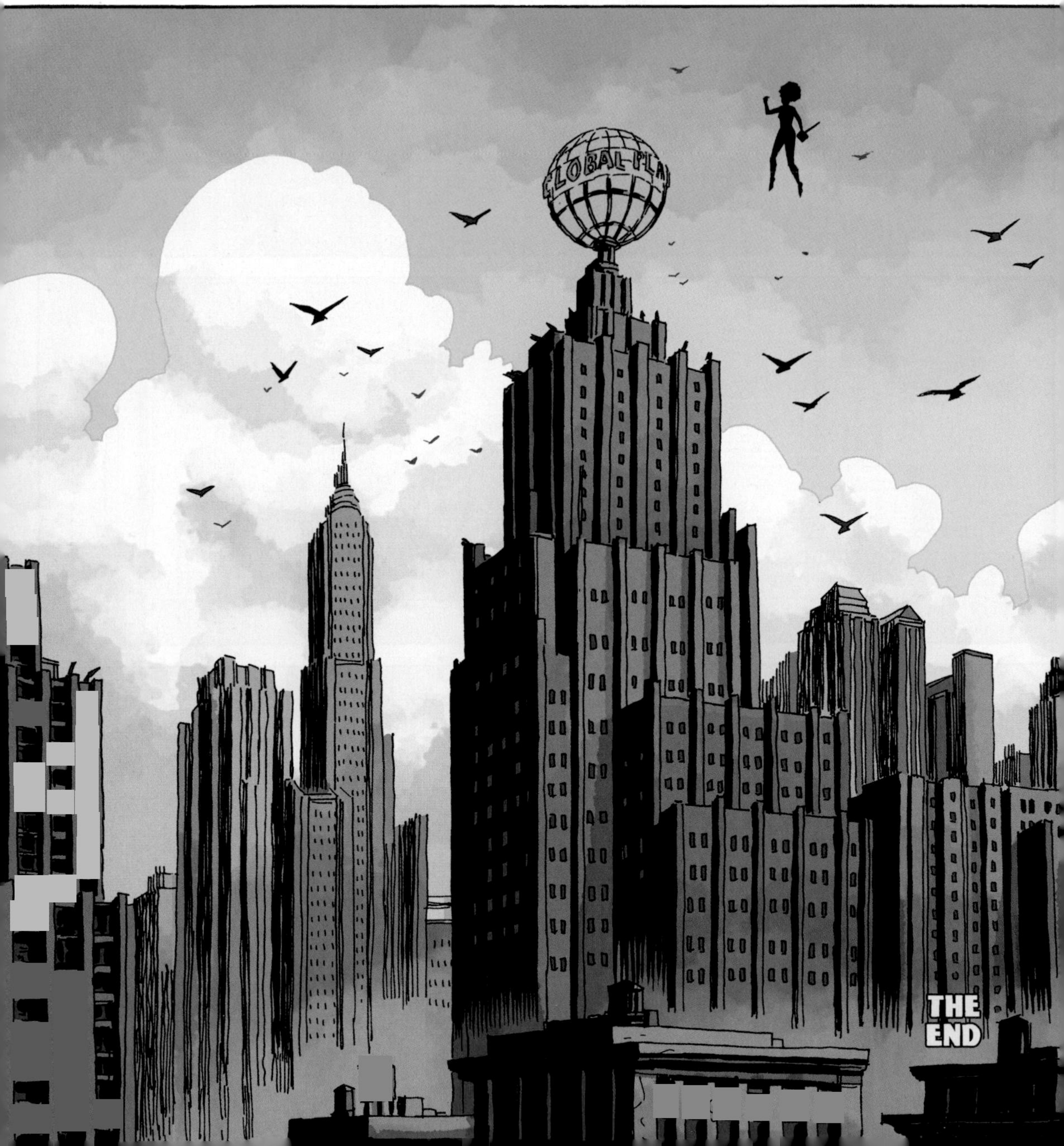
THE
END

BLACK HAMMER™
SKETCHBOOK
NOTES BY DEAN ORMSTON

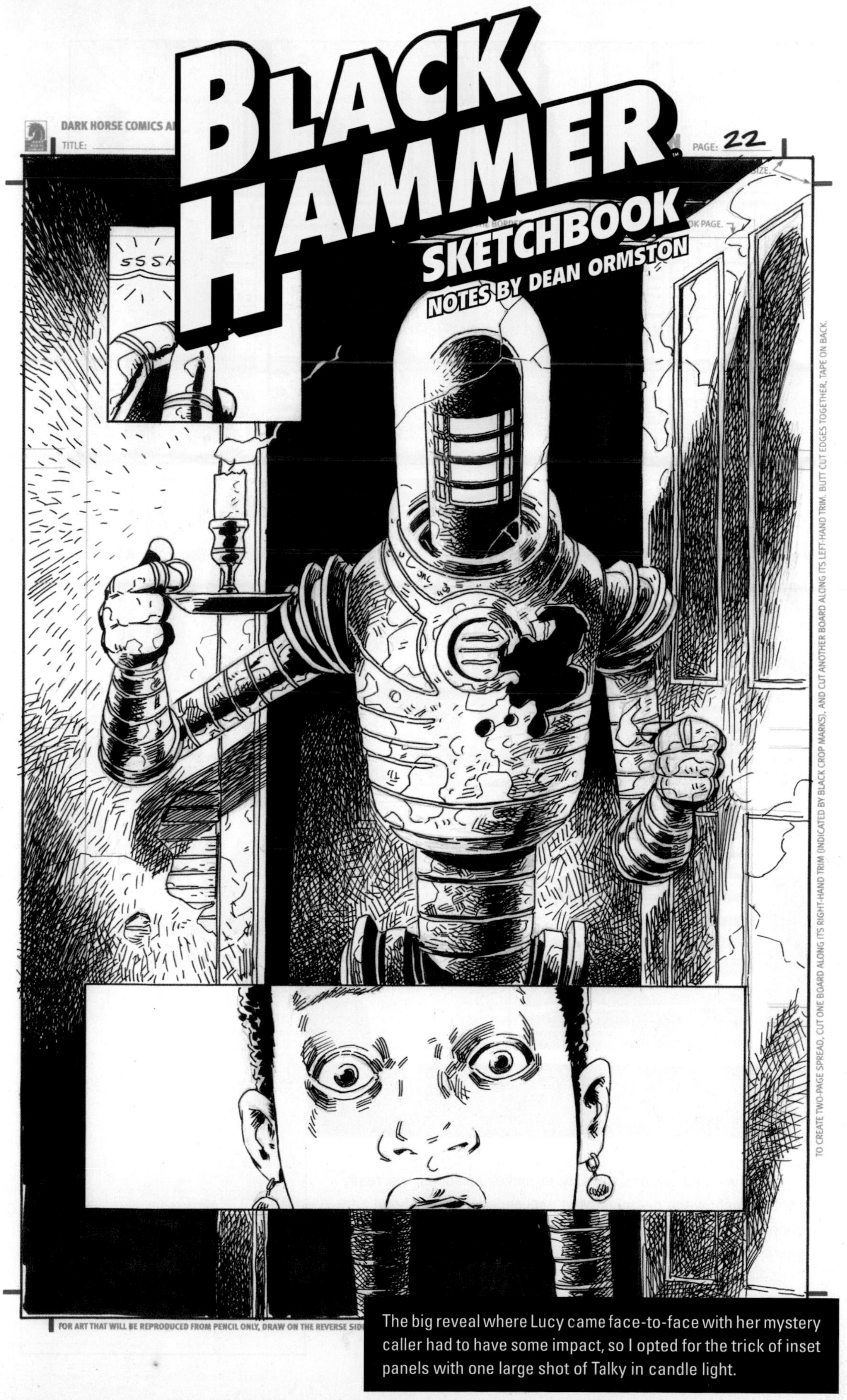

PAGE: 22
SSSK
TO CREATE TWO-PAGE SPREAD, CUT ONE BOARD ALONG ITS RIGHT-HAND TRIM (INDICATED BY BLACK CROP MARKS), AND CUT ANOTHER BOARD ALONG ITS LEFT-HAND TRIM. BUTT CUT EDGES TOGETHER, TAPE ON BACK.

The big reveal where Lucy came face-to-face with her mystery caller had to have some impact, so I opted for the trick of inset panels with one large shot of Talky in candle light.

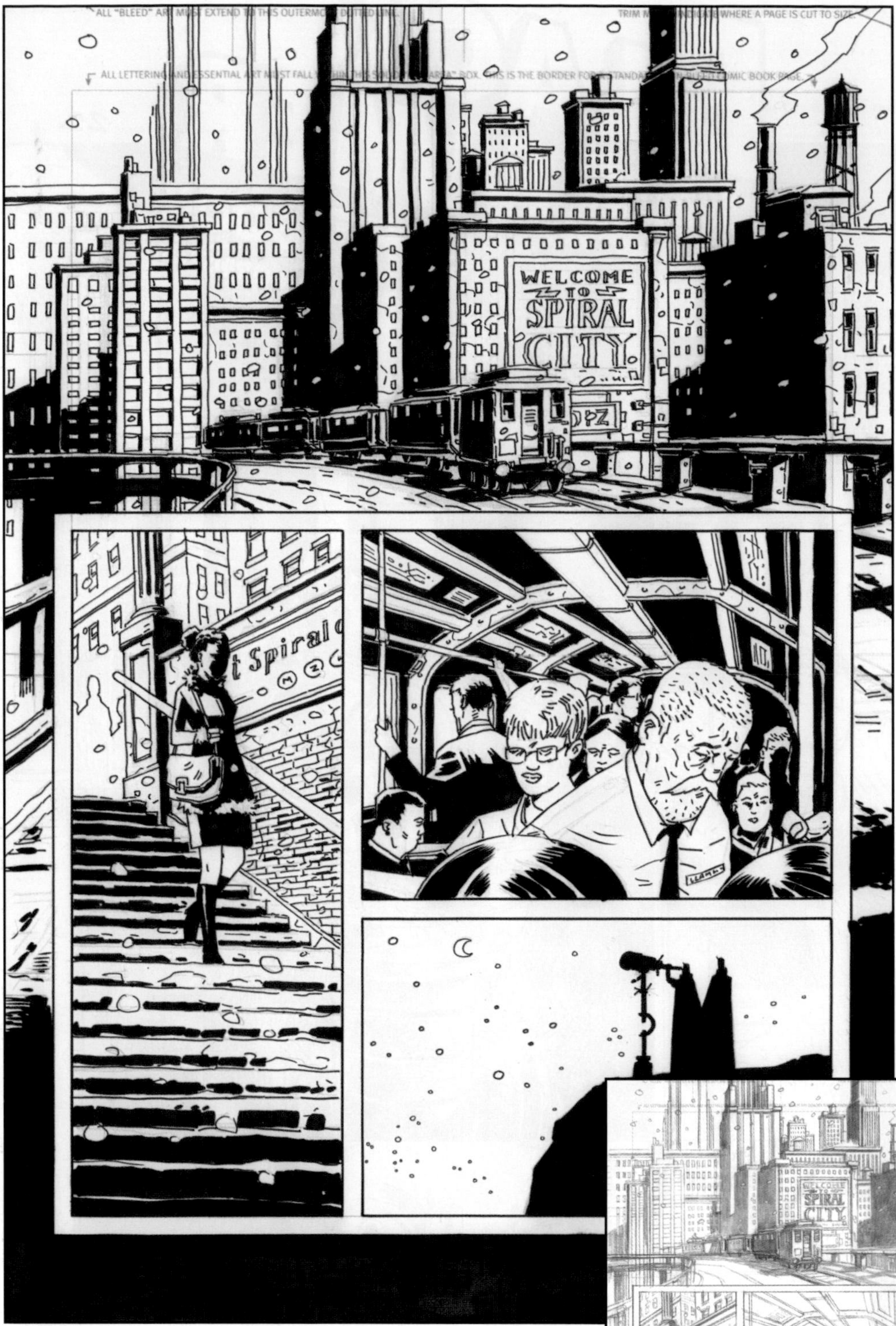
WELCOME
TO
SPIRAL
CITY
t Spiral

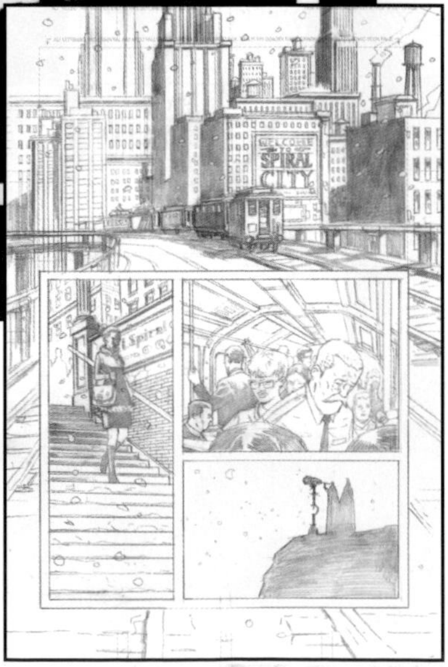

Although we had seen Spiral City in earlier episodes, we really wanted to show the decay of what was once a place of hope and wonder. Now it's oppressive and mundane—yet another place where Lucy and Abe seem to be trapped.

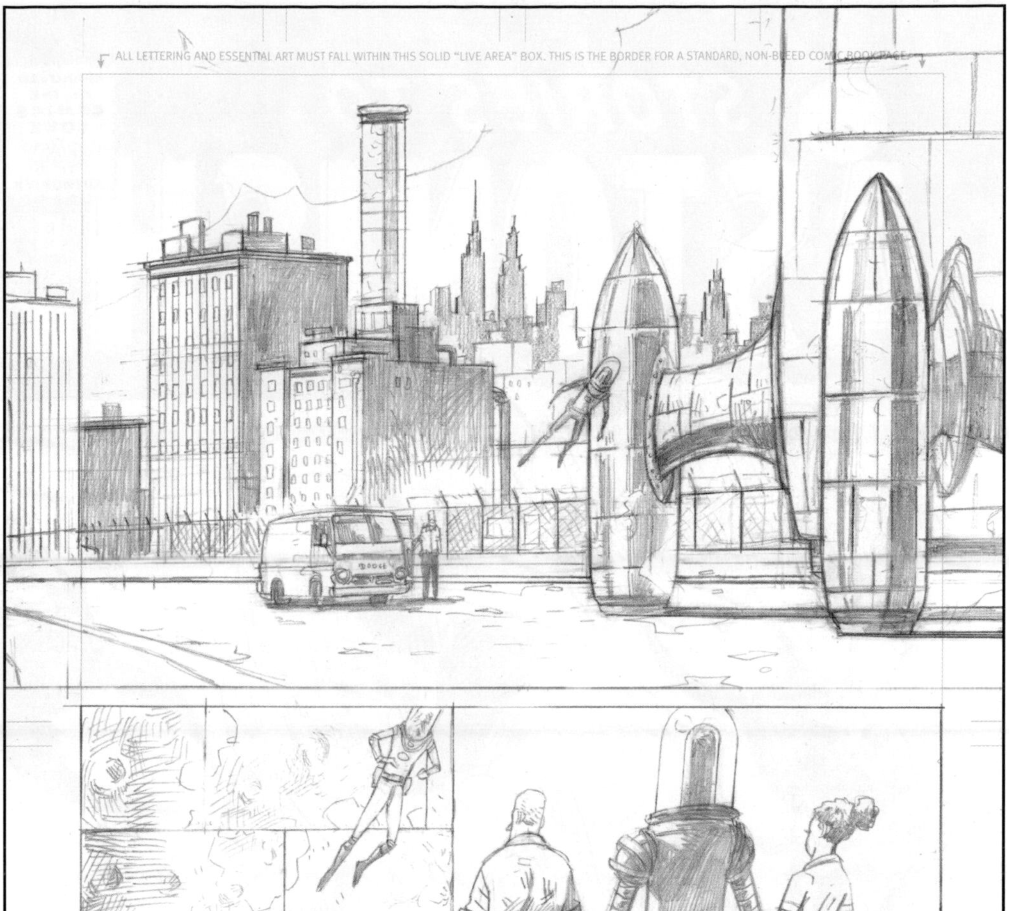
ALL LETTERING AND ESSENTIAL ART MUST FALL WITHIN THIS SOLID "LIVE AREA" BOX. THIS IS THE BORDER FOR A STANDARD, NON-BLEED COMIC BOOK PAGE.

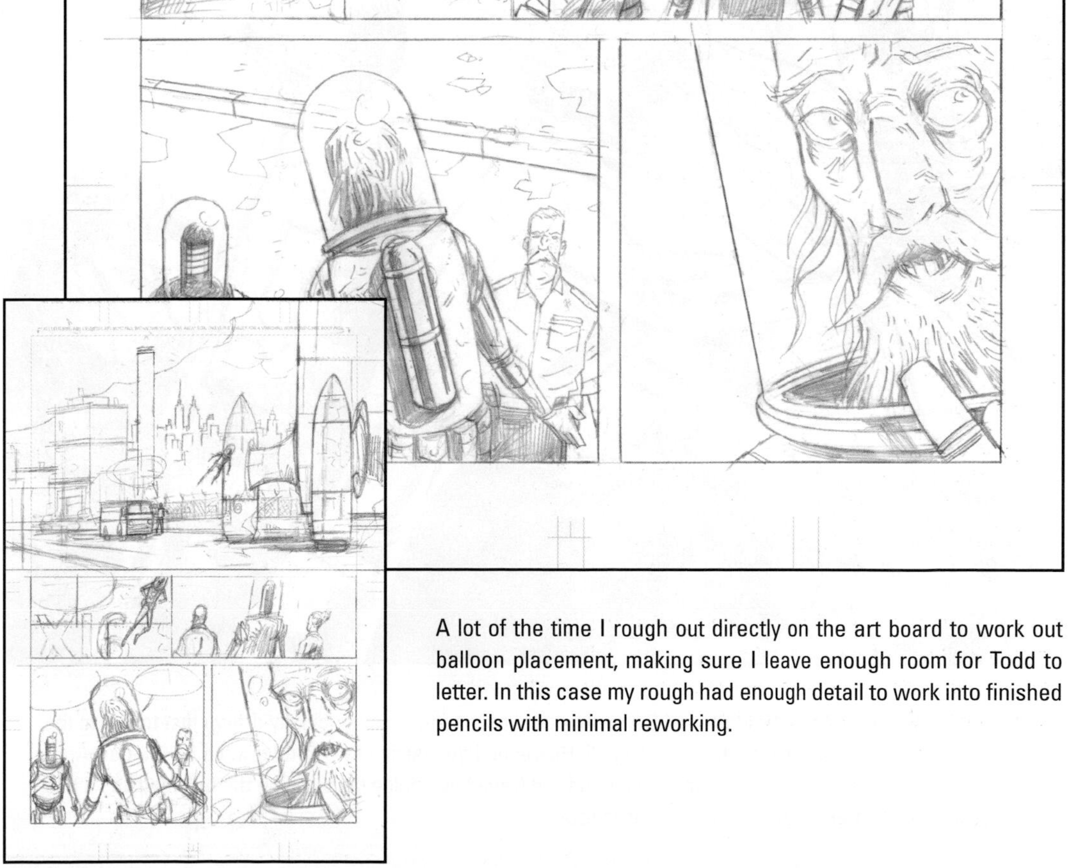

A lot of the time I rough out directly on the art board to work out balloon placement, making sure I leave enough room for Todd to letter. In this case my rough had enough detail to work into finished pencils with minimal reworking.

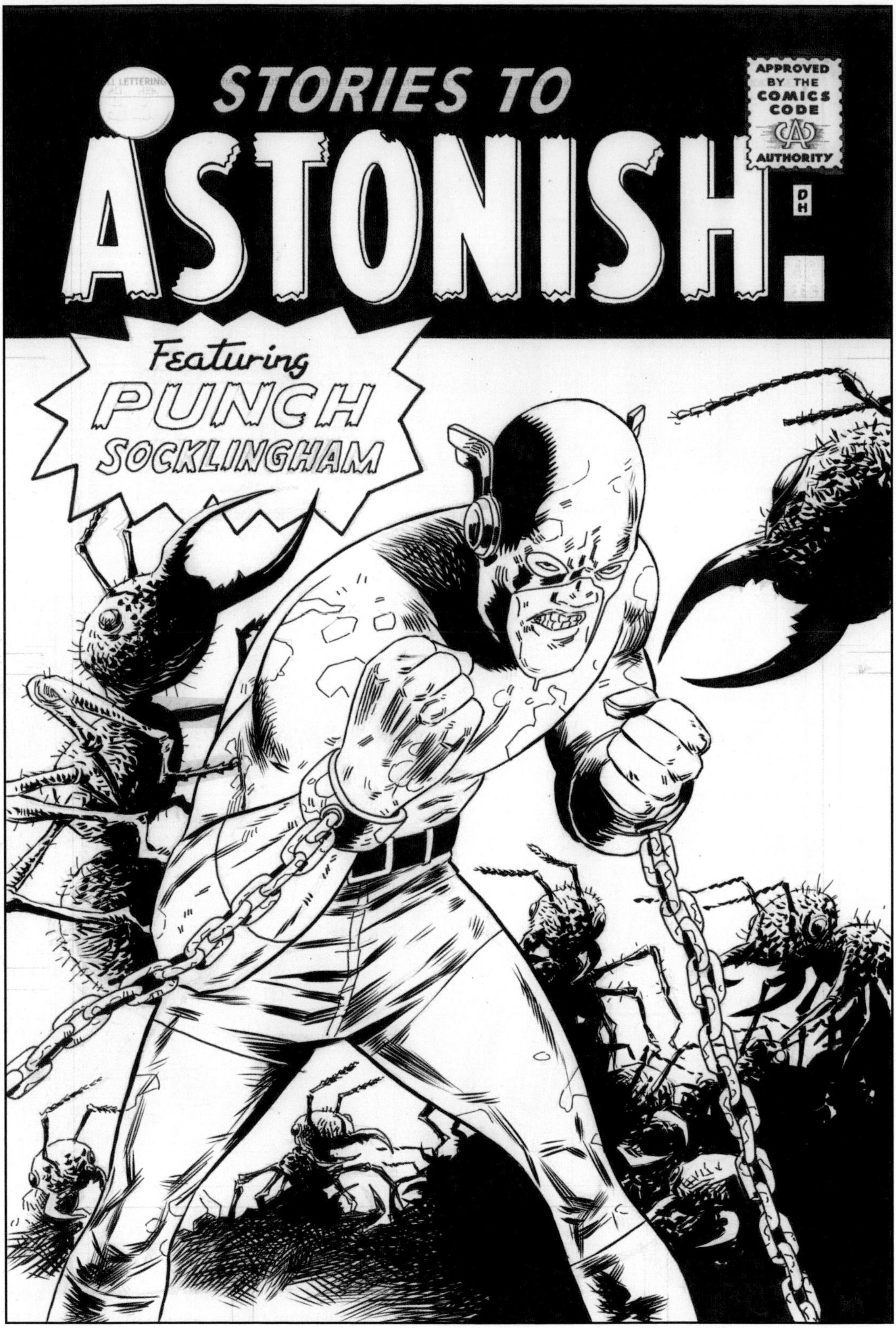
STORIES TO
ASTONISH
APPROVED BY THE COMICS CODE AUTHORITY
DH
Featuring
PUNCH
SOCKLINGHAM

I have a real affection for Golden- and Silver-Age comics, and this was originally drawn just to use in the panel where Abe holds it in his hand on page 6. However, I got carried away and drew a full Golden-Age-size piece. I loved the retro feel so much I persuaded Daniel to indulge me by using the full image as a title page to issue 8, making the issue 23 pages in total.

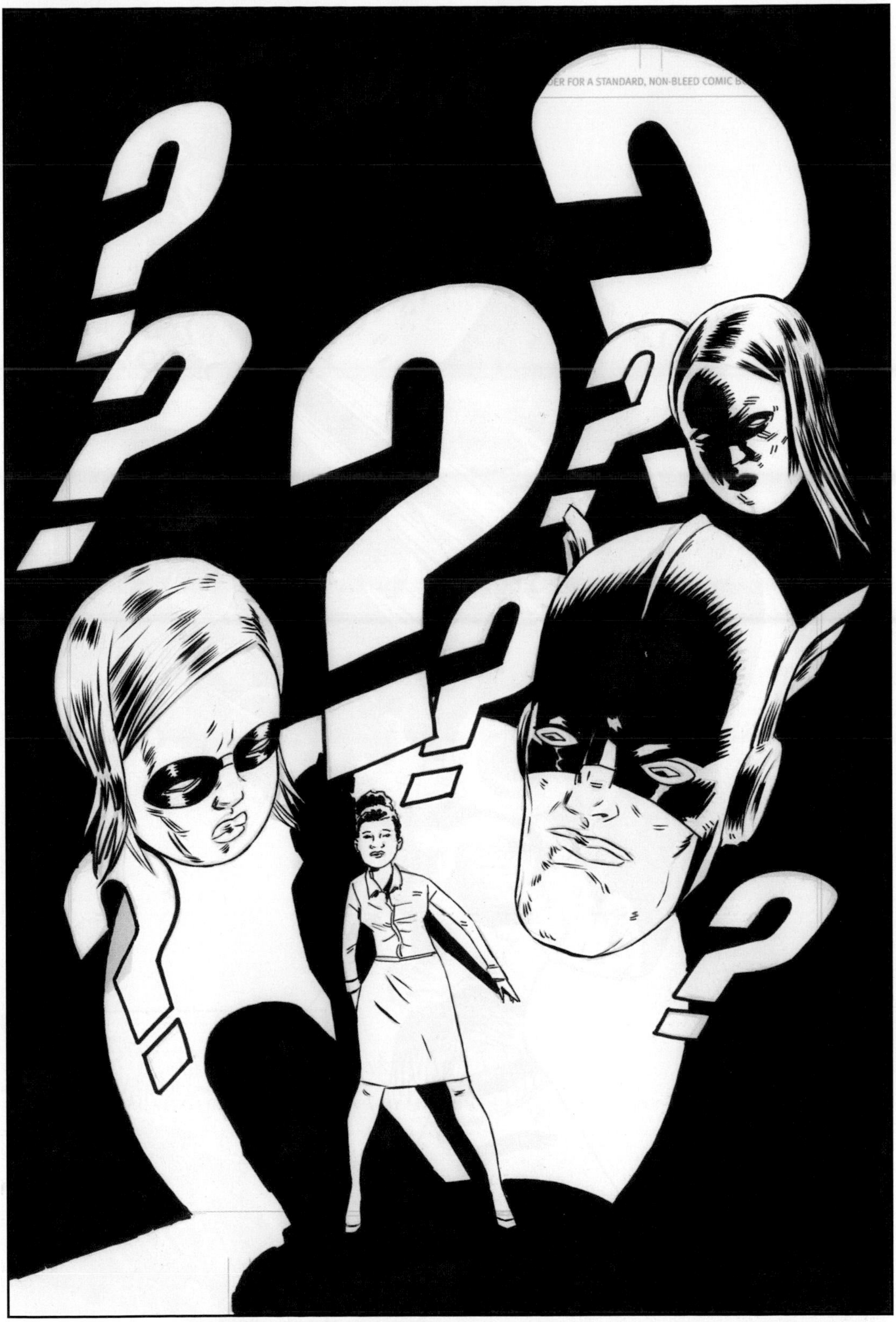

I had finished the cover to issue 8 but felt that Lucy lacked dynamism and decided to redraw her with more drama and a little bit more exaggerated. I still like the retro feel of both versions.

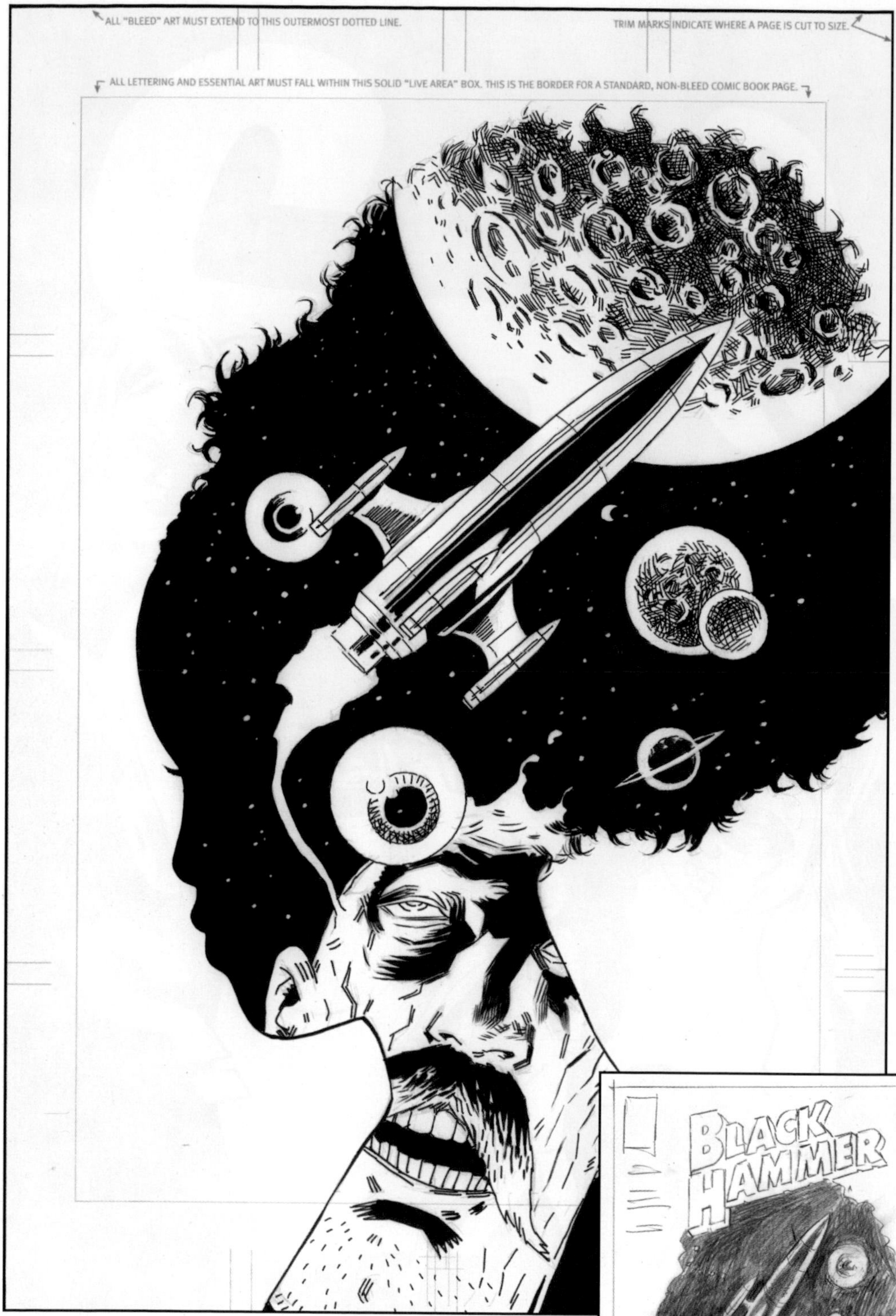
ALL "BLEED" ART MUST EXTEND TO THIS OUTERMOST DOTTED LINE.
TRIM MARKS INDICATE WHERE A PAGE IS CUT TO SIZE.
ALL LETTERING AND ESSENTIAL ART MUST FALL WITHIN THIS SOLID "LIVE AREA" BOX. THIS IS THE BORDER FOR A STANDARD, NON-BLEED COMIC BOOK PAGE.

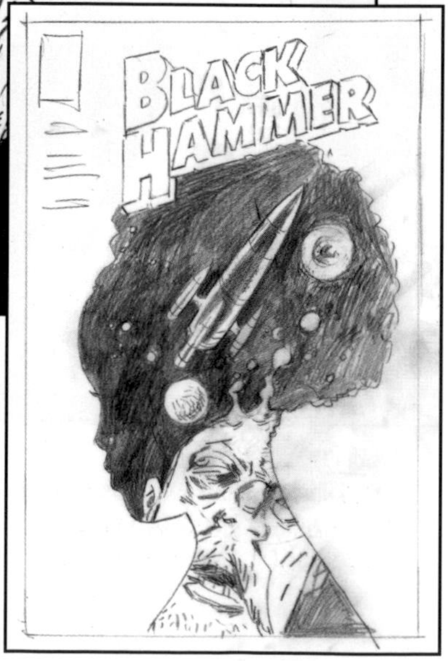
BLACK HAMMER

Sometimes a small rough sketch works out so well it barely needs any alterations and this is one example. This idea of images set within a profile in silhouette has been used many times before and I couldn't resist adding to the list.

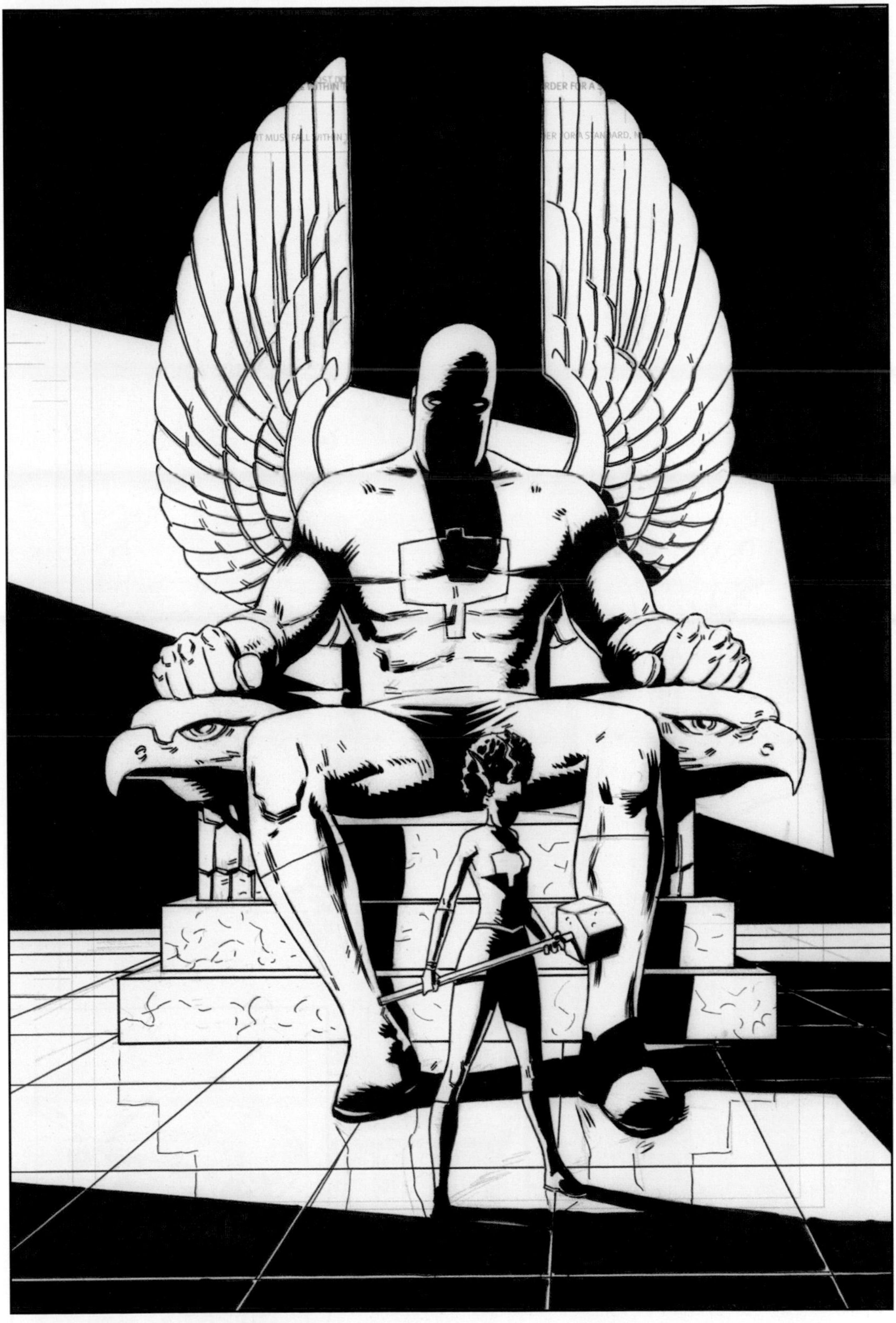

I don't consider myself any kind of superhero artist, so having the daunting task of trying to create an archetypal genre image of the two Black Hammers on a cover filled me with dread. However, drawn and rendered in my own lumpen way, this didn't turn out too bad.

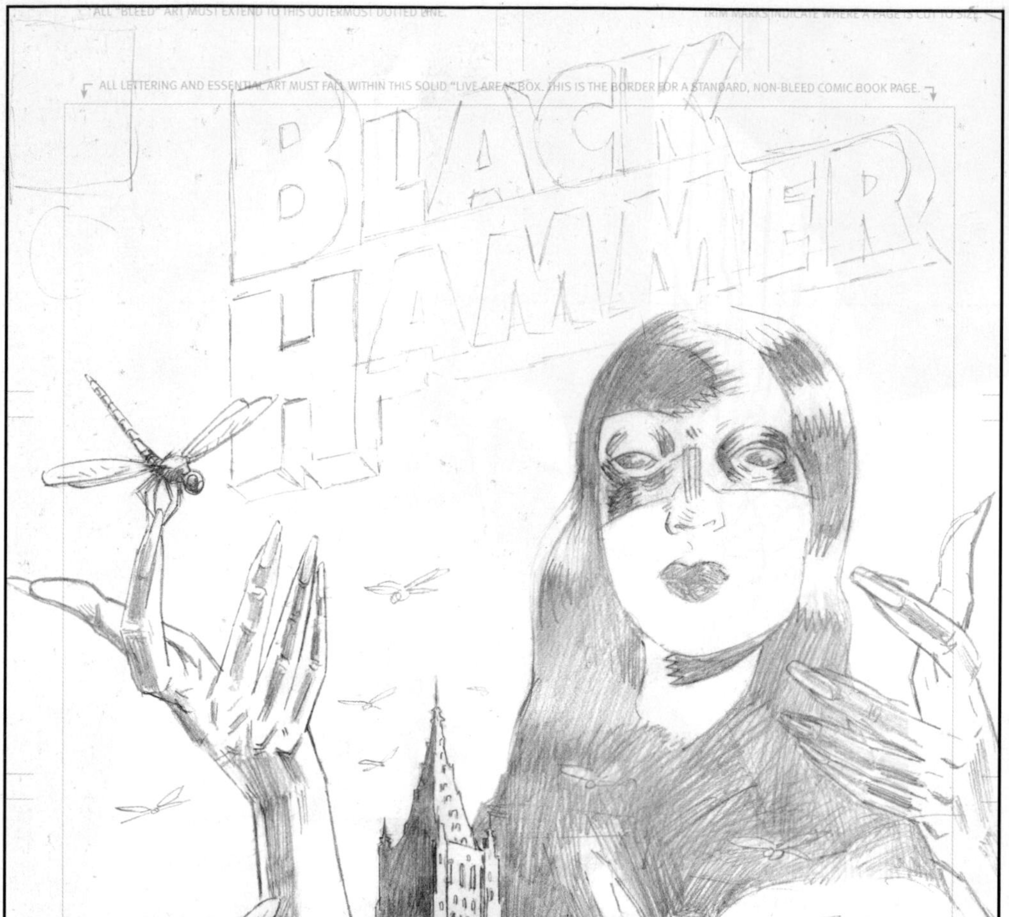
ALL LETTERING AND ESSENTIAL ART MUST FALL WITHIN THIS SOLID "LIVE AREA" BOX. THIS IS THE BORDER FOR A STANDARD, NON-BLEED COMIC BOOK PAGE.
BLACK HAMMER

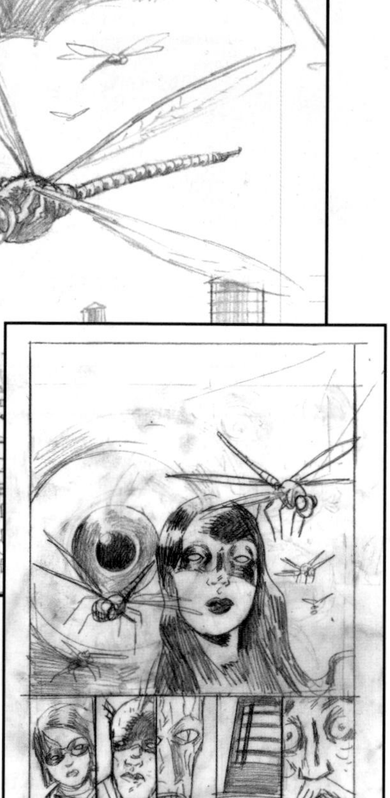

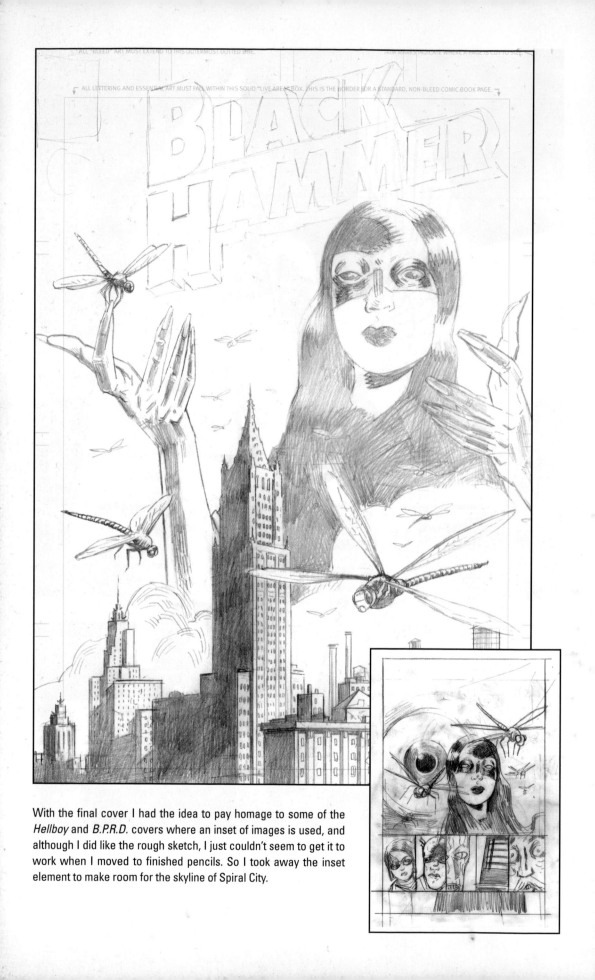

With the final cover I had the idea to pay homage to some of the *Hellboy* and *B.P.R.D.* covers where an inset of images is used, and although I did like the rough sketch, I just couldn't seem to get it to work when I moved to finished pencils. So I took away the inset element to make room for the skyline of Spiral City.

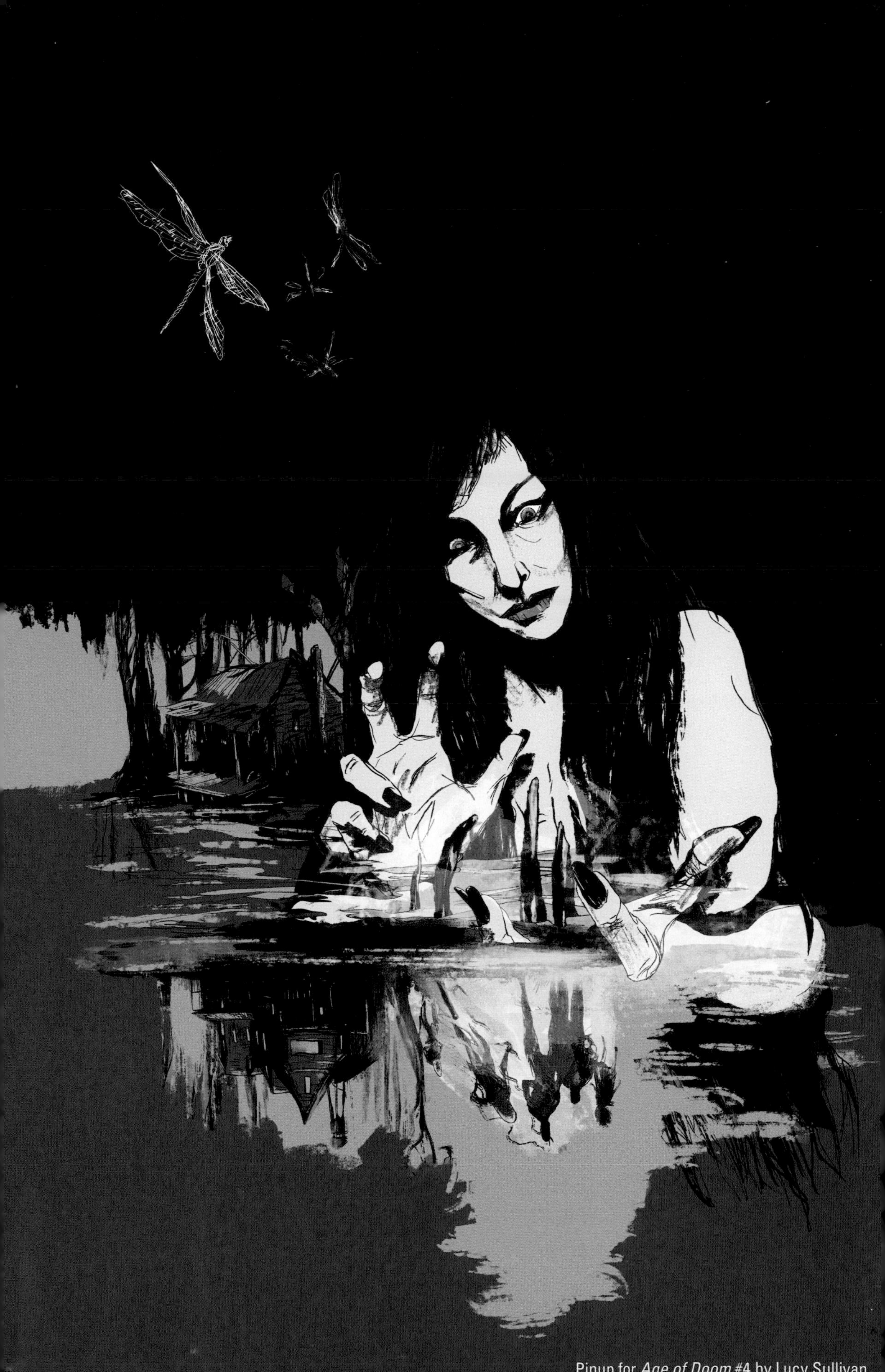

Pinup for *Age of Doom* #4 by Lucy Sullivan

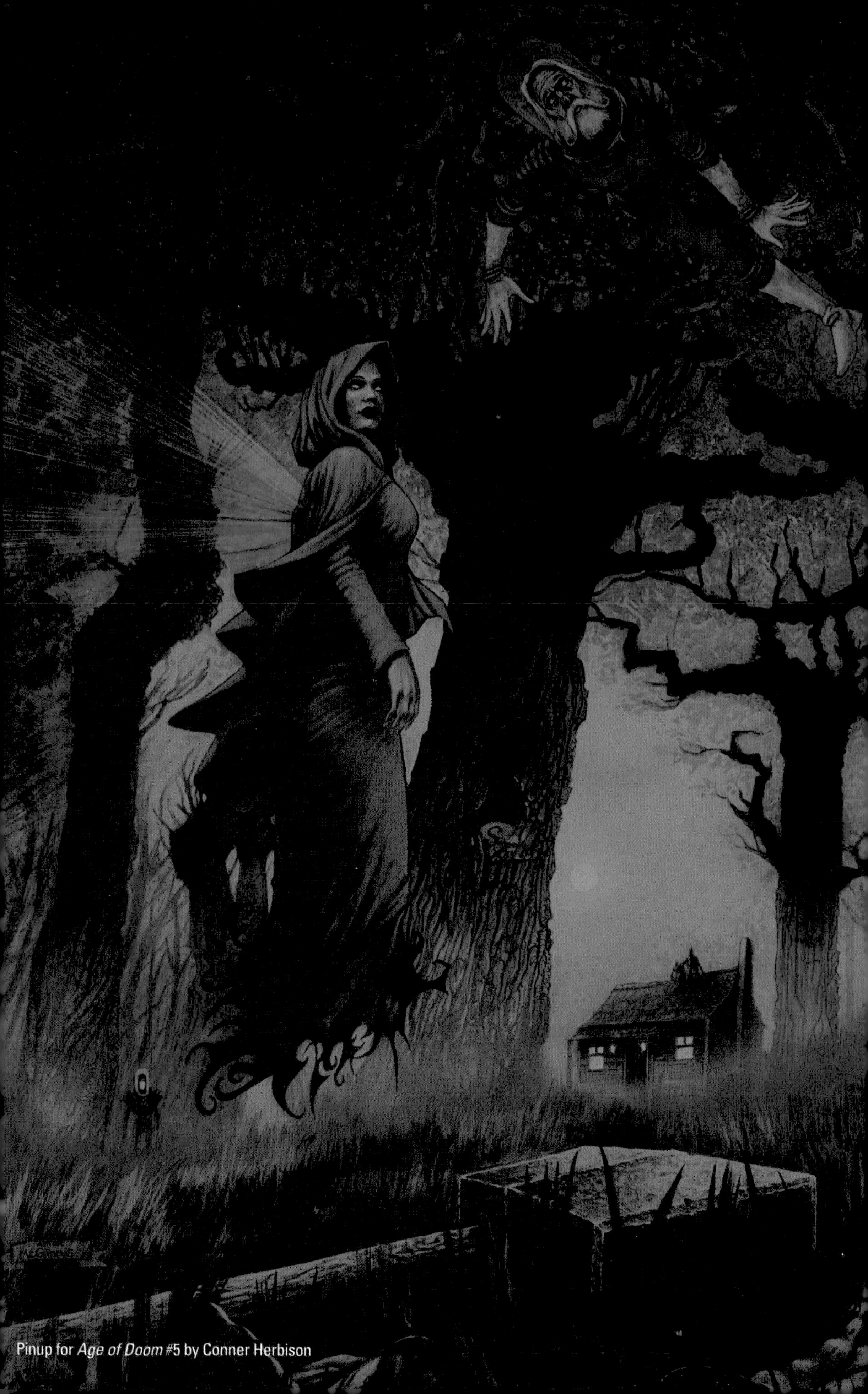

Pinup for *Age of Doom* #5 by Conner Herbison

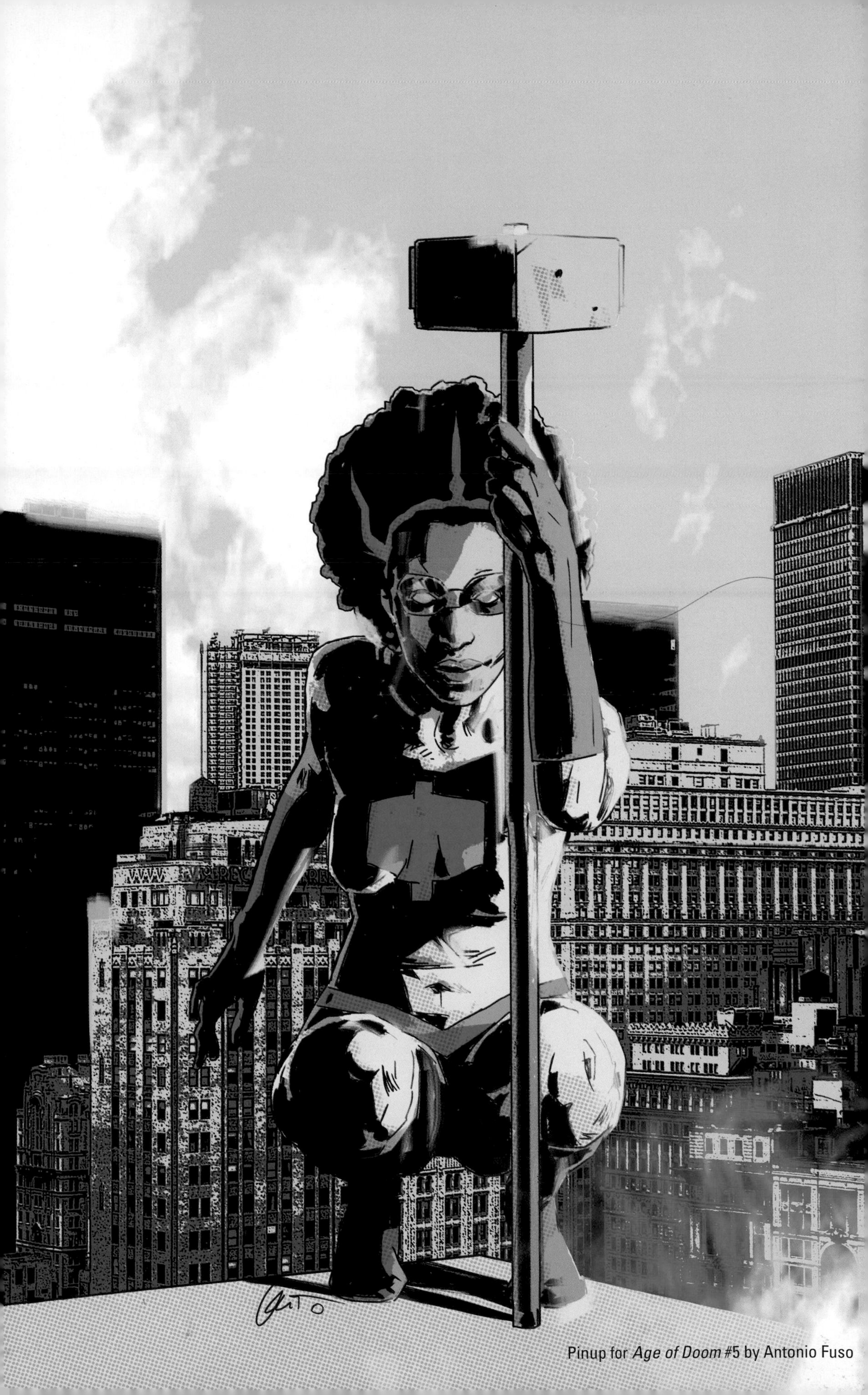

Pinup for *Age of Doom* #5 by Antonio Fuso

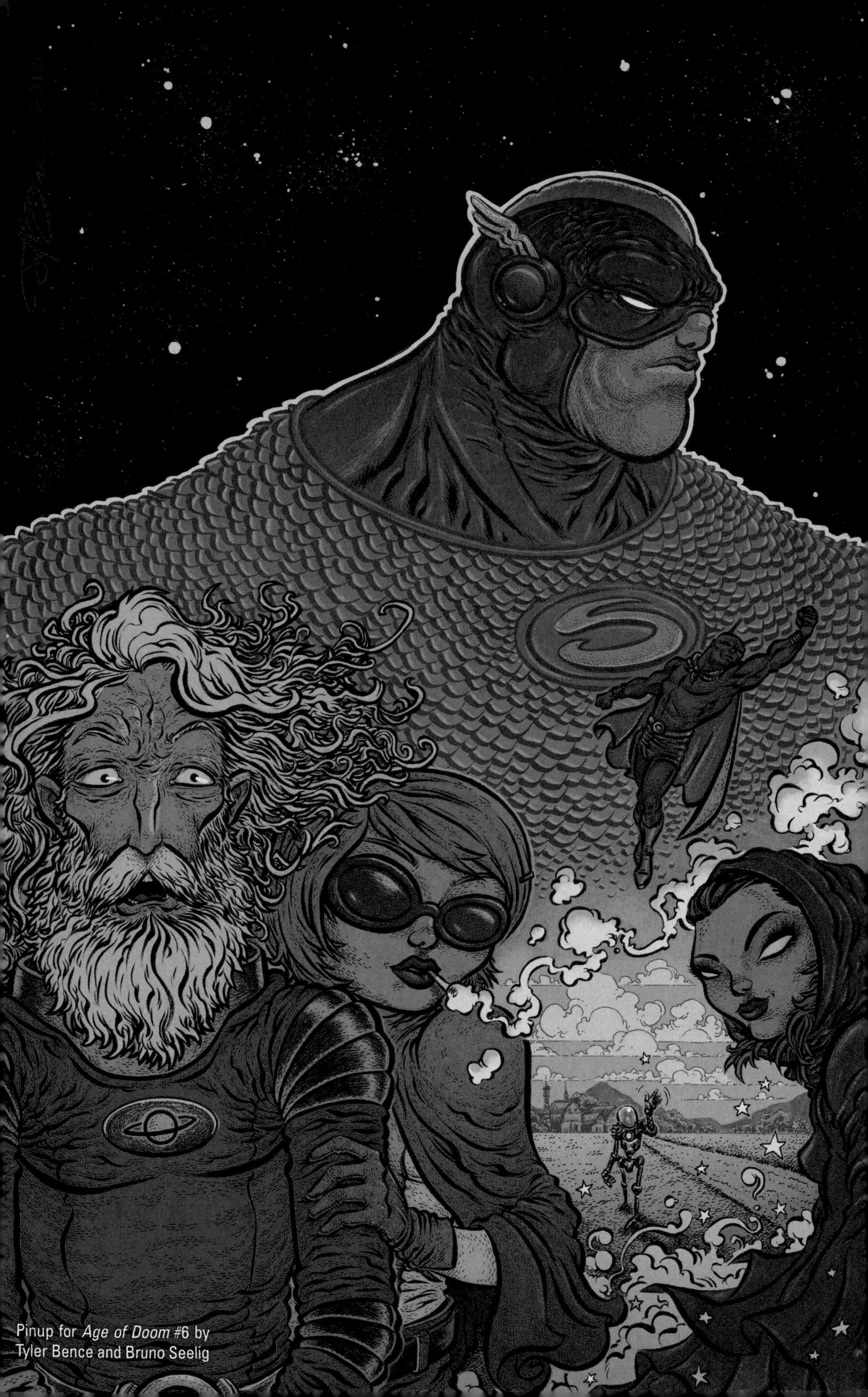

Pinup for *Age of Doom* #6 by
Tyler Bence and Bruno Seelig

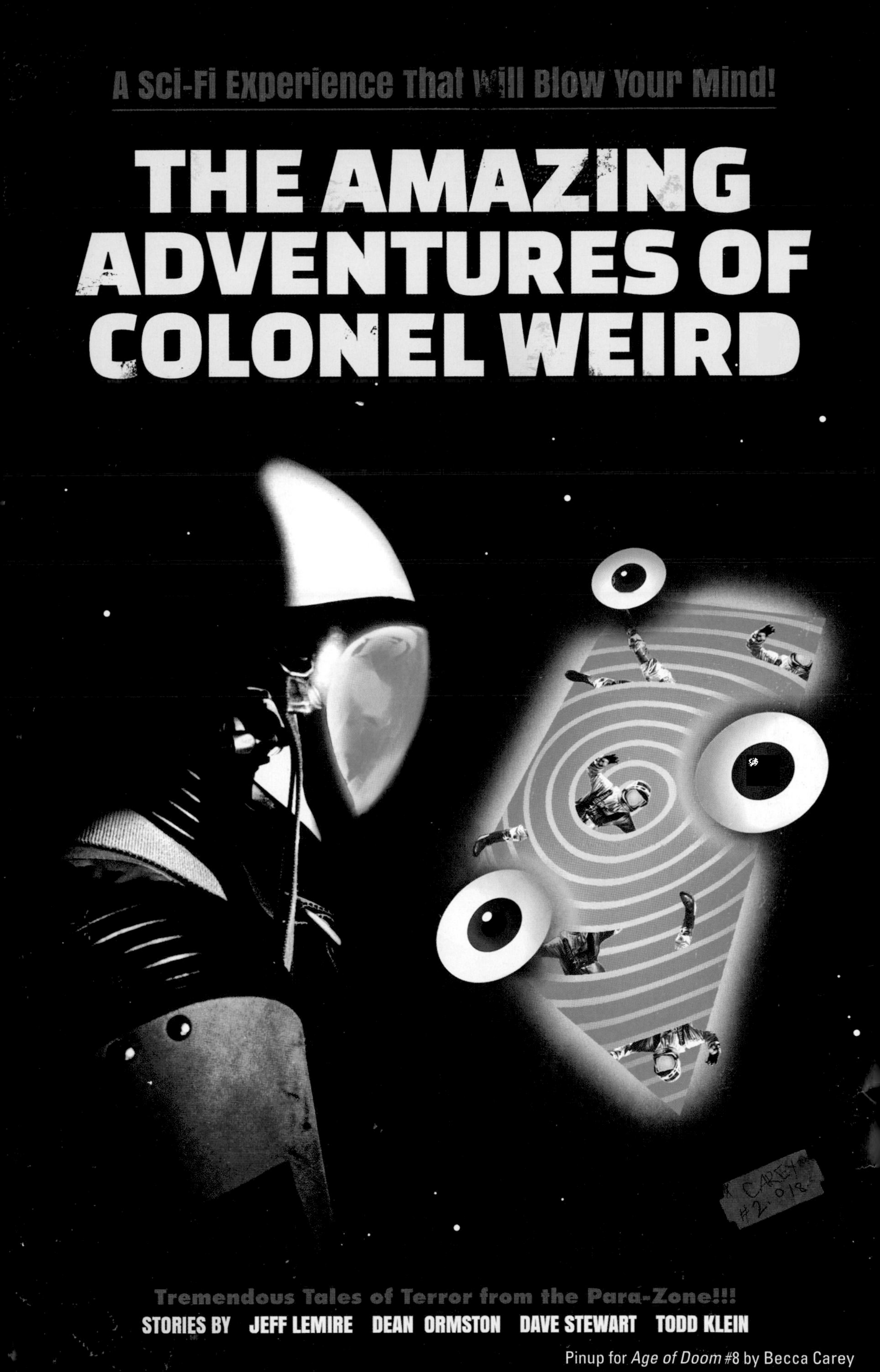
A Sci-Fi Experience That Will Blow Your Mind!
THE AMAZING ADVENTURES OF COLONEL WEIRD
Tremendous Tales of Terror from the Para-Zone!!!
STORIES BY JEFF LEMIRE DEAN ORMSTON DAVE STEWART TODD KLEIN

Pinup for *Age of Doom* #8 by Becca Carey

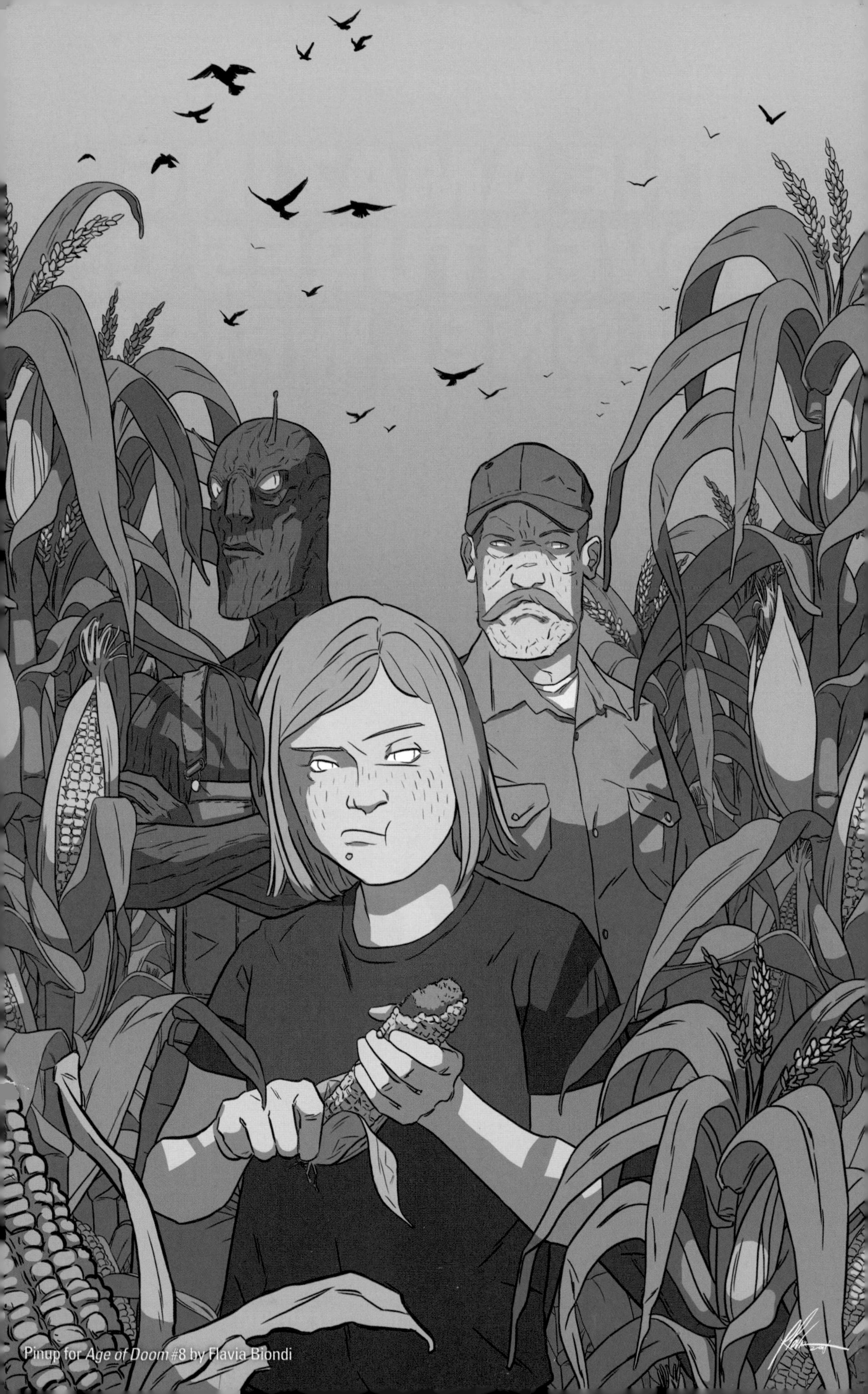

Pinup for *Age of Doom* #8 by Flavia Biondi

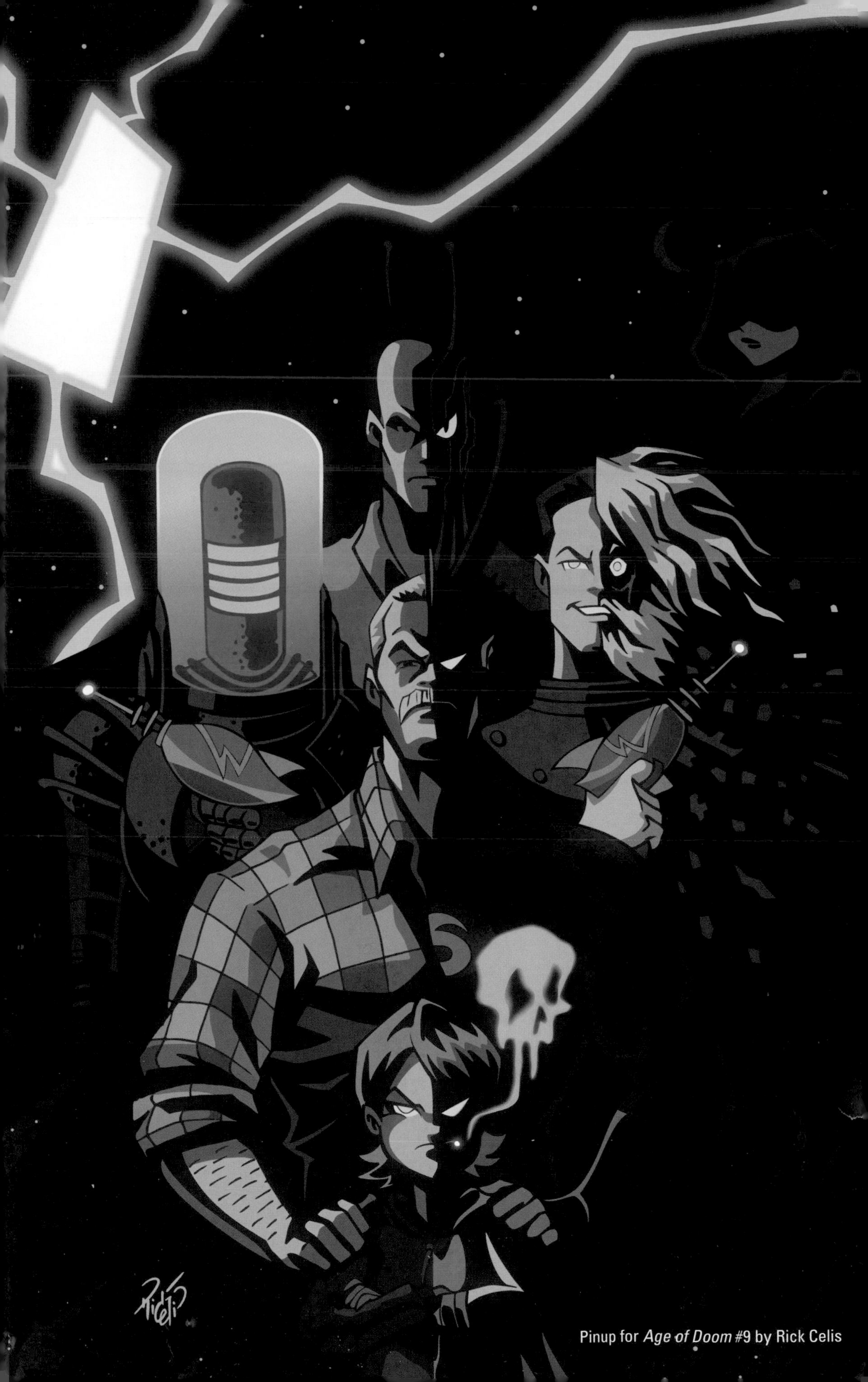

Pinup for *Age of Doom* #9 by Rick Celis

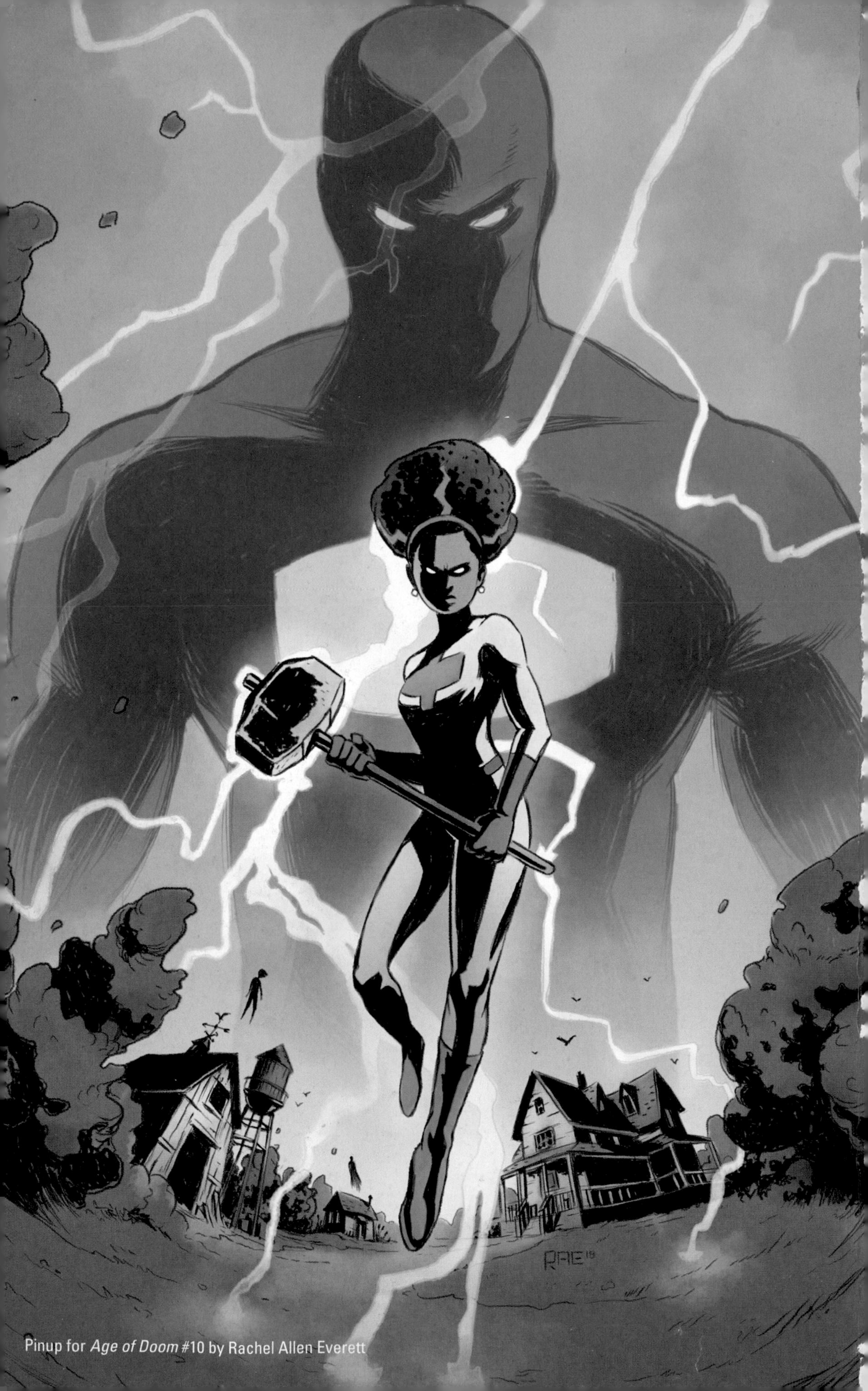

Pinup for *Age of Doom* #10 by Rachel Allen Everett